roles which the modern novelist shuns. He was not only storyteller but also a dispenser of information and ideas, moral guide, intellectual stimulant—a teacher in the widest sense. Each novelist fulfilled the dual role of artist and educator according to his unique sensibility, drawing upon popular tastes and interests, but also modifying and enriching them.

To explore the complex purposes which these novels originally served, as Mr. Colby so effectively does, is both to gain insight into the Victorian mentality and to recognize the real achievement of each writer, for the difference between— for example—*Mansfield Park* and popular treatises of the period on "female education" is a significant index of Jane Austen's genius. As Mr. Colby remarks of the great nineteenth-century novelists: "we can better take their measure by seeing their novels against the literary landscape that once surrounded them, rather than as isolated peaks." Following this thesis, he has produced stimulating literary criticism and a valuable addition to the history of ideas.

ROBERT A. COLBY, Associate Professor of Library Science at Queens College, is co-author with Vineta Colby of *The Equivocal Virtue: Mrs. Oliphant and the Victorian Literary Market Place.*

Fiction With a Purpose

MAJOR AND MINOR
NINETEENTH-CENTURY
NOVELS

Fiction With a Purpose

MAJOR AND MINOR NINETEENTH-CENTURY NOVELS

Robert A. Colby

Indiana University Press

BLOOMINGTON & LONDON

Library of Congress catalog card number: 67-13019

Manufactured in the United States of America

by American Book-Stratford Press, Inc.

CONTENTS

ACKNOWLEDGMENTS

THIS BOOK has been so long in the making, and the research involved so far flung, that it is impossible to give due credit to the many heads and hands that cooperated in its various stages of progress. I feel especially indebted to the staffs of the British Museum, Dr. Williams' Library in London, the Bodleian Library of Oxford University, the Cambridge University Library, the Fitzwilliam Museum of Cambridge University, and the Library of the University of Edinburgh for opening up their rich resources to me. At the Foundling Hospital in London I was pleased to find a letter bearing on Dickens' interest in that institution. In America, Dr. John Gordan, Chief of the Berg Collection, New York Public Library; Mr. Herbert Cahoon, Curator of Autograph Manuscripts, Morgan Library, New York City; Mr. Melvin Edelstein, Director of Special Collections, and Professor Joel W. Egerer, Curator of the Fales Collection, New York University; Miss Marjorie G. Wynne, Beinecke Research Librarian, Yale University; and Dr. Louis B. Wright, Director of the Folger Library, Washington, D.C. were most generous in allowing me access to letters, manuscripts, and other rare materials in their care.

Among those who have aided me in special ways, I wish to express my appreciation to Dr. James Clarkson Corson, Librarian of the University of Edinburgh, for sharing with me some of his vast erudition on Sir Walter Scott; to Professor Sara Keith, of Gustavus Adolphus College, for making available to me the lists she has compiled, based on the catalogues of Mudie's Select Library; and to Hon. David John Smith, Chairman of W. H. Smith and Son, Ltd., for allowing me to duplicate the one remaining catalogue of books circulated by their firm in the last century—covering the year 1876.

I would like to indicate here my deep gratitude to Professor Bradford A. Booth of the University of California at Los Angeles, and to the late Professor Myron F. Brightfield of the University of California at Berkeley, whose encouragement of my study in an early version sustained me through the ardors of revision.

Most of the research embodied in this book was accomplished on a sabbatical leave which was granted to me by Queens College of the City University of New York. My colleague Mr. Kenneth Freyer, General Reference Librarian, Paul Klapper Library, Queens College, was most helpful in securing books on interlibrary loan. Dr. Sidney Axelrad, Dean of Graduate Studies at Queens College, kindly furnished typing service for me from his office. Much of the typing of the manuscript was done by Mrs. Florence G. Waldhetter. I also want to thank Mrs. Eva U. Schlochauer for typing assistance.

To Mr. Bernard B. Perry, Director of the Indiana University Press, to Miss Miriam S. Farley, Managing Editor, and to her assistants I feel grateful for their efficient handling of the many details attendant upon transforming a rough manuscript into a published book.

Finally, to my wife Vineta Colby, who has been with this book from inception to final polishing, I owe not merely thanks, but a tribute. For her infinite patience and insight, for her help all along the way in shaping my ideas, she really deserves to be designated a collaborator.

R.A.C.

Fiction With a Purpose

MAJOR AND MINOR
NINETEENTH-CENTURY
NOVELS

CHAPTER I

INTRODUCTION

WE ARE very much in need of a history of nineteenth-century fiction. This is not it. But if such a history is ever to be written, we need to know far more about what our great-grandparents read and to read their books, as far as possible, through their eyes. A first step is to accommodate our vision to a generation for whom James meant G. P. R. James, Lawrence meant George Alfred Lawrence, and whose leading novelist from Dublin was Charles Lever. Some of them could remember when Hannah More was as popular as Scott and more popular than Jane Austen. In their early youth, the most widely read author in England was Theodore Hook. They grew up during the years when a struggling young journalist-hack named Thackeray envied Mrs. Gore her success, and Currer Bell eagerly sought the judgment and approval of Harriet Martineau. Within their life span, a certain "Miss Evans," author of novels of country life, was cited by a Parisian review as a new rival of Miss Mulock; Annie Thomas and Edmund Yates were singled out as the most representative of English novelists by another French journal; a prominent weekly praised Mrs. Oliphant as one of the dozen or so Victorian writers destined to survive into the next age; Bulwer shared a triple crown with Thackeray and Dickens; Rhoda

3

Broughton reigned as queen both of the circulating library and of Oxford society; and Charlotte Yonge's heroes were emulated by university students.

As this brief retrospect suggests, our ancestors read, revered, and supported many more novelists than we have admitted into our classrooms, bookstores, and private libraries. Owing to inadequate records, not even scholars of the period know how many novels were published in England during the years marked off by *Castle Rackrent* at one end and *Lord Jim* at the other. An educated guess places the number at about 40,000—and this is probably an underestimate. Mackenzie Bell, in his anthology, *Representative Novelists of the Nineteenth Century,* considered some 130 worthy of commemoration by quotation, with an additional 900 meriting honorable mention in an appendix. Some of his judgments sound quaint to twentieth-century ears. "A writer of unquestionable genius" is Gerald Griffin, whose *The Collegians* extended its life mainly through a play by Dion Boucicault. The Trollope lauded by Bell is neither Anthony nor Frances, but Thomas Adolphus, who shows "more evidence of thought on the deeper problems of life, and a keener sense of humour" than either his mother or his brother. Mortimer Collins is hailed among the noteworthy disciples of Thackeray, and Frederick William Robinson is saluted as the inheritor of Dickens' mantle.

Examples of the vagaries of fame and reputation could be multiplied. Yesterday's "living library" is today's archive, literary memory being notoriously short and capricious, and the bookshelves of the general reader in constant process of weeding. We may be sure, therefore, that our Everymans and World Classics are but a fraction of our grandparents' Family Library and Household Editions. Dusting off the spines of Bentley's Standard Novels, to name but one once eminent series, reveals some familiar names—Miss Edgeworth, Miss Austen, Madame de Staël —with some forgotten ones—Mrs. Brunton, the Misses Lee, Mrs. Inchbald, Mrs. Gore; still great names like Manzoni, Schiller,

Irving, and Cooper, along with minor but enduring ones like Beckford, the Banims, Galt, Marryat, and Bulwer; and ephemeral ones like Thomas Hope, Horace Smith, Theodore Hook, William Maxwell, and Frederick Chamier. If some of the standard fiction of Bentley's readers seems substandard today, it shows that the taste of our forefathers ranged both wide and deep, taking in a spectrum of geniuses, talents, and hacks.

Probably most of the books now lost to sight deserved their fate, but their disappearance somehow diminishes, in a subtle way, those which have survived. The first readers of our nineteenth-century classics not only read them differently, but saw them differently. To them, these books were not literature but "current reading" arrayed side by side with many a now forgotten title on the shelves of the guinea-a-year circulating library in half-calf; gold-lettered, ribbed-grain cloths of claret, blue, magenta, green, or olive drab; pictorial boards; or strewn about the stalls of the railroad stations in soiled wrappers. The books in Mudie's Select Library were books for their times. Our select library of great novels contains books for all times. We tend nowadays to look at them out of time altogether. Such a myopic view needs to be corrected if ever we are to achieve proper perspective over this great age of fiction.

The sheer expanse of the fiction of the past century makes any student of the period pale in dismay. Obviously no individual can hope to know more than a portion of it, and it has seemed best to those who have ventured into the territory to chart out segments for concentrated exploration. Apart from the numerous critical studies of the major luminaries, recent years have seen historical studies focused on themes, such as the Woman Question (Patricia Thomson's *The Victorian Heroine*), Public Schools (John R. Reed's *Old School Ties*), and Religion (Margaret Maison's *The Victorian Vision*); character types (Edgar Rosenberg's *From Shylock to Svengali*); genres, such as the Irish Novel (Thomas J. Flanagan's *The Irish Novelists, 1800–1850*), the University Novel (Mortimer R. Proctor's *The English Uni-*

versity Novel), "Gallows Fiction" (Joseph Keith Hollingsworth's *The Newgate Novel, 1830–47*) ; and popular formats, such as the magazine serial (Margaret Dalziel's *Popular Fiction a Hundred Years Ago*, Robert Mayo's *The English Novel in the Magazines, 1740–1815*), or penny-issue tales (Louis James' *Fiction for the Working-Class Reader*). Here and there studies have emerged of significant minor novelists (Wayne Burns' *Charles Reade: A Study in Victorian Authorship*; George J. Worth's *James Hannay: His Life and Works*; W. J. Keith's *Richard Jefferies*). Probably the most brilliant book in the field to appear in our time, Kathleen Tillotson's *Novels of the Eighteen Forties*, has demonstrated the rewards of an intensive investigation of a decade.

As my particular interest is in the relationship of authors to their original literary environment, this study shifts attention to great novels themselves as repositories of literary history. I have selected for examination seven important novels—two pre-Victorian, five mid-Victorian—spread out in time from 1814 to 1872. These novels—*Waverley, Mansfield Park, Oliver Twist, Pendennis, Villette, The Mill on the Floss,* and *Middlemarch*—although not equally great, are all by major authors, were among the most popular novels of their respective decades, and have stood the test of time. They therefore lend themselves to scrutiny under the dual aspect of temporality and eternity. From the historical standpoint, this is primarily a study of some literary tastes and trends from the "teens" of the nineteenth century (in Thackeray's phrase) to its late middle age. Our great nineteenth-century novelists, considered as representative writers of their times, fall into place not as originators, but as developers, taking over established genres and moulding them to their own unique sensibilities. Concurrently, from the more purely critical standpoint, we can better take their measure by seeing their novels against the literary landscape that once surrounded them, rather than as isolated peaks.

Various conditions of literary life in the nineteenth century invite this approach. This was the period before the splintering of the audience for the novel, described by Q. D. Leavis in her *Fiction and the Reading Public.* "Classics" and "commercials" reached the same body of readers virtually throughout the century. From at least the 1830's on, serious literature and entertainment alike were transmitted through conspicuous, widely accessible media like the magazine and newspaper. With the advent of Mudie in the 1840's, books—the "Select" along with the less so—were delivered to readers' doors in vans; and shortly afterward, thanks to the enterprise of W. H. Smith, they became available at railway stations. Authors' pictures were pasted in omnibuses and on the walls of depots, and a best seller was a national event. Books and writers were well known; the public was relatively homogeneous; and the literary profession was closely interconnected.

During these times when writers were in close touch not only with their public, but with each other, it was impossible for them to work in isolation, as they are likely to do today. The abundance of literary discussion—often backbiting—in novels of the last century, early and late, offers ample evidence of this awareness of fellow writers. Hannah More, "Monk" Lewis, and Madame de Genlis are speared by Mrs. Sarah Green's poison pen in *Romance Readers and Romance Writers,* as are Scott, Galt, and Hogg in her later *Scotch Novel Writing.* Jane Austen loses out to Mary Shelley in the unconsidered judgment of one novel-reading miss in Thomas Henry Lister's *Granby.* Better known is the altercation between Miss Deborah and Captain Brown over *Pickwick Papers* in Mrs. Gaskell's *Cranford.* Thackeray is caricatured in both Lever's *Roland Cashel* and Disraeli's *Endymion.* Miss Thorne of *Barchester Towers* allows no writer later than Fielding into her library, but Bishop Proudie reads a number of *Little Dorrit* in a moment of leisure. Charlotte Yonge's name comes up in two novels otherwise worlds apart—Miss Braddon's *Aurora Floyd* and Mrs. Oliphant's *Phoebe, Junior.* Two of the ladies in Mrs. Oliphant's *The Ladies Lin-*

dores argue the merits of *Middlemarch*. The heroine's sister in Mrs. Humphry Ward's *Robert Elsmere* is reading *Villette*.

The novel served writers generally as a literary forum. Critics and novel readers may now ignore the lesser contemporaries of Scott, Jane Austen, the Brontës, Dickens, Thackeray, and George Eliot, but we may be sure that these novelists themselves did not. At the beginning of *Waverley*, Scott teases his readers about the romances and gossip chronicles that were then the reading of the hour. In *Northanger Abbey*, Catherine Morland is "in training for a heroine" of the kind of story Jane Austen is trying not to write. In "London Recreations" (one of the *Sketches by Boz*), Dickens refers to "tradesmen and clerks with fashionable novel-reading families and circulating-library-subscribing daughters," anticipating Kate Nickleby's susceptible patron Mrs. Wititterly. Thackeray's first novel, *Catherine*, is a farrago of the popular pap of the 1830's—not only the Newgate Novel, but also the sabre-rattling fiction of Maxwell and Gleig, the historical panache of Bulwer, the fashionable novels of Lady Charlotte Bury and Lady Morgan, as well as the edifying tales of Maria Edgeworth and her successors in the juvenile line. Like that other secluded minister's daughter, Jane Austen, Charlotte Brontë was an avid reader of romances as well as of sermons. Unlike Miss Austen, she was also a writer of romances in her youth, but in *The Professor*, her first novel intended for publication, she assures her readers that she has left all that behind, and proves it by deliberately giving them a drab hero and a colorless story. Presumably George Eliot, like Rebecca Linnet in "Janet's Repentance," knew the fiction in "Mr. Procter's circulating library" (or the equivalent in her native Coventry) and had been well steeped, before she herself undertook fiction, in those "light vehicles of weighty morals" which she attributes to the evangelical authoress Eliza Pratt in that same story.

Any appraisal of the major novelists of the nineteenth century is incomplete if it fails to take into account their apprenticeship to fiction as readers, critics, even satirists, of their contemporaries.

Jane Austen's first writings were parodies of some of her justly neglected predecessors. Sir Walter Scott, like George Eliot later in the century, reviewed novels for critical quarterlies before taking up fiction himself. Thackeray and Dickens both started their careers as contributors to popular magazines and miscellanies, and Thackeray had some reputation as a parodist before his success with *Vanity Fair*. Both Dickens and Thackeray became editors, accepting and rejecting manuscripts and blue-penciling many besides their own. Satire of outmoded vogues lurks between the lines of Charlotte Brontë's novels. She also knew what her fellow writers were doing, thanks in part to her publisher George Smith, who lightened the gloom around Haworth Parsonage with his boxes of books, and occasionally an author sent her a manuscript for judgment (notably Thackeray with *Henry Esmond*). The main effect of George Eliot's reviewing of numerous "Silly Novels of Lady Novelists" for the *Westminster Review* was to make her determined to do better. She had the additional good fortune of the encouragement and companionship of George Henry Lewes, a student of human nature as well as of literature, a failed novelist, whose learning she could turn to artistic use as he was never able to do.

All of these writers were well in command of their literary milieus, and their novels are interesting, therefore, not only for themselves, but for their implicit commentary on contemporaneous fiction. To look at some of the masterpieces along with some of their forgotten competitors, as I propose to do in the chapters to follow, gives one a clearer sense of what their authors were inveighing against. However, it is all too easy by overstressing their iconoclasm to give the misleading impression that the great novelists were out of tune with their times. Close study of major novelists in relation to minor ones reveals affinities at least as important as divergences. A balanced view of the era sees greater and lesser writers alike as conditioned in the same literary environment and sharing a common fund of ideas on human nature and the function of literature. The literary charlatan who

exploited fiction drew the scorn of those, including our novelists, who were trying to raise the stature of fiction from the "light
literature" category, to which it was all too frequently consigned
in the reviews, to a place alongside the best that was known and
thought in the world. In retrospect the nineteenth century is seen
as the epoch of the novel's struggle for prestige, in which
novelists from Scott to Eliot are joined in tacit compact. In this
great aim the major novelists and some of their inferior rivals
meet on common ground.

One persistent objection the novel had to meet was the religious one that it made men too worldly, but in due time both
Church and Chapel consecrated it. Early in the century religious
educators like Mrs. Barbauld and Hannah More appropriated
fiction to their purposes in something like the way in which early
Christianity adapted pagan ceremonies. Thereby they established
a climate for the novel as a moral force. Charlotte Elizabeth
Tonna, editor of *The Christian Lady's Magazine,* turned reluctantly to the novel to spread her gospel. Their better successors,
like Charlotte Yonge and Elizabeth Missing Sewell, moved readily into fiction from Sunday School teaching. Dinah Mulock, one
of the most popular of mid-Victorian novelists, thought of herself
as a lay minister—one of her books, in fact, was called *Sermons
Outside of Church*—with a wider congregation and a greater
command over them. "The essayist may write for his hundreds;
the preacher preach to his thousands; but the novelist counts his
audience by millions," she wrote in a critical article. "His power
is three-fold—over heart, reason and fancy. The orator we hear
eagerly, but as his voice fades from us its lessons depart: the moral
philosopher we read and digest, by degrees, in a serious, ponder-
ous way; but the really good writer of fiction takes us by storm."
Her conception of fiction was shared by the clergyman's wife
Elizabeth Gaskell, the clergyman's daughter Charlotte Brontë,
and the piously reared George Eliot. Trollope, who would suffer
no atheists as contributors to *The Fortnightly Review,* obviously
assumed a clerical as well as a lay audience in *Barchester Towers,*

even presuming at one point to advise clergymen on improving their sermons. Even Thackeray confided to a fellow writer that "our profession seems to me to be as serious as the Parson's own." Many a novelist of the time could have justified his calling in words echoing George Herbert's "The Church Porch":

> A *tale* may find him, who a sermon flies,
> And turn delight into a sacrifice.

The novel met with equally strong objection on the utilitarian ground that it was impractical and visionary. Bentham stipulated when he founded *The Westminster Review* that one half be devoted to important subjects like politics and morals, "the other half to literary insignificancies." Charlotte Brontë, in *Shirley*, strikes out at the "many Hiram Yorkes in the world," her version of the Benthamite: "Even when utilitarians sit in judgment on him [the writer] and pronounce him and his art useless, he hears the sentence with such a hard derision, such a broad, deep, comprehensive and merciless contempt of the unhappy Pharisees who pronounce it, that he is rather to be chidden than condoled with." Nevertheless, she searched the files of Leeds newspapers to get her economic history straight before she set pen to paper. Novelists, both before and after Bentham, sought with various degrees of success to demonstrate the utility of the novel and its relation to reality. The most outlandish tales were represented as "Founded upon Fact." Novels were frequently camouflaged as "annals," "chronicles," "diaries," or "memoirs." Novelists went to ludicrous lengths to establish manuscript "sources" in the manner of Scott's Captain Clutterbuck.

This frequent disguise, however thin, of fiction as nonfiction has a tradition extending back at least as far as Defoe, but the nineteenth century gave the convention a new impetus. The century began with a revolt against imagination in fiction, which left the "fine frenzy" suspect to the next generations. Many of the early novels of the age, including those which first made Scott and Jane Austen famous, were written in reaction to such effusions as the tale of terror, the prose medieval romance, and the Oriental fable. To be sure, romance and realism continued in coexistence, as in the popular anthology, Limbird's *British Novelists* (1824), which featured Mrs. Radcliffe, Dr. Hawkesworth's *Almoran and Hamet,* and *The Arabian Nights Entertainments* in Galland's version, along with Smollett, Mackenzie, and Dr. John Moore. But Limbird's collection also betrays a prejudice of his time against "feigned history." "The incident which gave rise to this history is founded upon truth," states the preface to one of the novels, Madame Cottin's *Elizabeth; or, The Exiles of Siberia,* a tale of filial devotion read subsequently by many Victorian children. "No imagination however fertile," continues the translator, "could produce actions so heroic, or sentiments so noble and elevated. The heart alone could inspire them."

This conviction is reiterated in the Victorian period by George Henry Lewes, who may be taken as representative of the educated attitude toward the novel. He insisted that "incidents however wonderful, adventures however perilous, are almost as naught when compared with the deep and lasting interest excited by anything like a correct representation of life." He accounted for the success of *Jane Eyre* and *Mary Barton* in particular by their having given "imaginative expression to actual experience—they have not invented but reproduced." In his opinion, the way to reach the public is through "the transcript of some actual incident, character or emotion." This antipathy toward "invention" is betrayed by numerous titles: "Truth through Fiction," "Romances of Real Life," "Truth Answers Best," "Novels of Nature," "Life and Its Realities," "A Tale of Life Real and Earnest," "A Heart History," "A Chapter from Life's History," "The Experience of Life," recur with variations. Significantly, Dickens' first book was entitled *Sketches by Boz Illustrative of Every-Day Life and Every-Day People;* Thackeray's first tales were "Sketches," "Papers," "Diaries," and "Memoirs"; Charlotte Brontë's first published novel was subtitled "An Autobiography" (the author calling herself an "editor"); and George Eliot made her debut in fiction with a series of "Scenes."

The illusion of "the Actual" (one of Wilkie Collins' favorite terms) sought by writers throughout the nineteenth century was aided by contemporaneity. The ephemeral format of much of Victorian fiction—weekly or monthly paper-wrapped shilling parts, bound up with advertisements for food, clothing, furnishings, and patent medicines—caught readers up in the flux of day-by-day experience and domestic life. On a somewhat higher level, connections with topics of the day often linked up literature with life and blurred the line between the newspaper and the novel. Thackeray mentions a recent address by Harriet Beecher Stowe in one number of *The Newcomes,* although the novel takes place during the reigns of the last of the Georges. Even the stately three- (or four-) decker managed to keep in touch with popular issues. Dickens' prefaces to successive editions of *Oliver Twist* refer to current developments in civic reform and sanitation, though he does not update the story itself, just as in his introduction to the 1863 edition of *Martin Chuzzlewit* he mentions improvements in hospital administration since the days of Sairy Gamp and Betsy Prig. *Jane Eyre* almost coincided in time with the establishment of the Governesses' Benevolent Institution and Queens College, as twenty-five years later *Middlemarch* appeared in the wake of the excitement over the founding of Girton College for Women. *Daniel Deronda* undoubtedly owed some of its initial interest to its publication in the same year that Disraeli became Lord Beaconsfield. *Pendennis, Shirley, Barchester Towers, The Bachelor of the Albany* (by Marmion Savage) , *Zoe: A History of Two Lives* (by Geraldine Jewsbury) , and *The Perpetual Curate* (by Mrs. Oliphant) are all touched in one way or another by the Oxford Movement, despite their various time settings. *Henry Esmond,* which takes place during the reign of Queen Anne, and *Villette,* presumably recalling the days of George IV, both allude to the Papal Aggression of 1850. Historical novels, no matter how remote their period, were frequently tracts for the times, sometimes to the point of blatant anachronism.

Subject matter and form of publication alike riveted the novel, as it came of age, more and more to the everyday world. Further influence in this direction came from the distributor's end. George Henry Lewes contrasted the truth of representation of *Jane Eyre* and *Mary Barton* with "the vague, false, conventional notions current in circulating libraries." Indeed, the proprietor of the circulating library was the favorite villain of critics of the novel. In novels themselves the salvation of many a hero and heroine consisted of a kind of purification rite, ridding them of the contamination of his wares. However, the more influential circulation librarians did all they could to erase their noxious image. William Henry Smith set up his chain of railroad libraries to eliminate the alleged trash from the stalls at the stations, and is said to have stocked fiction only under pressure. The most successful of all, Charles Edward Mudie, circumspectly advertised: "principal Recent Works in History, Biography, Religion, Philosophy, Travel and Adventure, and the Higher Class of Fiction." The hierarchy itself tells a tale. Mudie's relegation of his staple of commerce to the end of his list betrays perhaps a certain condescension (he was a clergyman), but more significantly it associates the "Higher Class of Fiction" with the world of prose, fact, and ideas.

With the enlargement of the audience for the novel, the more conscientious writers, critics, and disseminators of fiction endeavored, as all this evidence indicates, to relate it at once to the practical and serious interests of readers. The chapters that follow try to trace two concomitant developments that enhanced the prestige of the novel: its growth as an instrument of learning and the extension of the role of the author.

The modern drama, it is well known, was cradled in the church. Not so well recognized, perhaps, is how much the nineteenth-century novel owes its origins to the school. Early in the century, as we shall see, the novel was cross-bred with the treatise on education, and it retained this heritage throughout the Victorian age in its recurrent preoccupation with mental and moral cultivation. Among the story books recalled by Thackeray from his childhood reading—which included Maria Edgeworth's *Parents' Assistant* and the *Evenings at Home* of Dr. Aikin and Mrs. Barbauld—was a spelling book illustrated with an allegory of Education leading Youth up to the Temple of Industry, where two schoolmasters stand waiting with crowns of laurel. His own illustrations, such as the drawing in *Pendennis* labeled "Youth between Pleasure and Duty" (showing his hero flanked on one side by a wastrel youth, on the other by a schoolmaster) carry over this type of pictorial fable. George Eliot mocked the edifying authors of her youth through the bluestocking Eliza Pratt, author of "Letters to a Young Man on His Entrance into Life" and "De Courcy, or the Rash Promise, a Tale for Youth." Yet in her first long novel Arthur Donnithorne reads, without taking to heart, Dr. John Moore's *Zeluco: Various Views of Human Nature,* a late eighteenth-century didactic tale also addressed to the young man making his entrance into life, and in *The Mill on the Floss* young Maggie Tulliver discovers Dr. Gregory's once famous vade mecum for girls, *Letters to His Daughter,* along with Thomas à Kempis.

George Eliot and Thackeray are two outstanding examples of the conditioning of Victorian novelists by pre-Victorian childhoods and point up two prevailing motifs that dominate much of the fiction of both generations. The title "Entrance into Life," inherited from *Evelina* and echoed in the perennial *Fatherless Fanny* and numerous successors, announces a theme implicit in Victorian novels concerned with the proper guidance of youth. Once the entrance is made—with various degrees of difficulty, according to circumstances—life itself is conceived as a series of steps toward gaining the sanctuary of wisdom. In view of the didactic origins of nineteenth-century fiction, the pervasiveness of the school as a setting and of teachers among the cast of characters comes as no surprise. Furthermore, our heroes and heroines never really close the classroom door behind them. The tendency of novelists to look upon life as an extension of the academy is exposed most baldly in titles like *Life's Lessons, Lessons and Trials of Life, Two Generations; or, Birth, Parentage and Education, Chance and Choice; or, The Education of Circumstances, The Discipline of Life,* and *Harry Beaufoy; or, The Pupil of Nature.*

All of the novels reconsidered on the following pages are informed by this scheme. They begin with children or young people undergoing some kind of formal education—lax and permissive with Edward Waverley and Arthur Pendennis, more systematic, if somewhat patronizing, with Fanny Price, rough-handed with Oliver Twist, practical with Lucy Snowe, who is preparing herself to teach, fitful and perfunctory with Maggie Tulliver (whose brother Tom gets preferential treatment), superficial with the sheltered Dorothea Brooke—and continuing their education in the graduate school of experience. This pattern, while not universal, is frequent enough in Georgian, early and mid-Victorian novels to be encountered with variations in such diverse classics as *Emma, The Abbot, Jane Eyre, Shirley, Wuthering Heights, Vanity Fair, Henry Esmond, The Newcomes, The Adventures of Philip, Hard Times, David Copperfield, Great Expectations, Westward Ho!, The Cloister and the Hearth, North and South, Wives and Daughters, The Ordeal of Richard Feverel,* and *The Adventures of Harry Richmond.* It can be traced through the century at least as far as Henry James' Hyacinth Robinson. These heroes and heroines may win their badges and prizes in school, but life grants them their diplomas. Charlotte Brontë's valedictory on Caroline Helstone, emerging from her course of instruction with Madame Moore, expresses the sentiments of many an author: "At eighteen, the school of Experience is to be entered, and her humbling, crushing, grinding, but yet purifying and invigorating lessons are yet to be learnt."

The academic atmosphere, the didactic framework, the adolescent hero and heroine, the ethical plot, are all characteristics inherited by Victorian novelists from their predecessors, who emerged amidst a rage for systems of youth education. As the century moved on, novelists became equally absorbed with adult education, the growth of the novel coinciding with such projects as the Society for the Diffusion of Useful Knowledge, the Mechanics Institutes, the People's Instruction Societies, the Cabinet Library of "Dionysius Diddler" (as Charles Yellowplush calls him), and Charles Knight's *Penny Cyclopedia* and *Papers for the People*—all of which endeavored to extend literacy and stimulate the appetites of the cultural new masses for capsule learning. The first novel of Charles Kingsley, *Alton Locke,* has a self-improver for its hero. Disraeli, who started his career as a society novelist, soon recognized the usefulness of the novel as a vehicle for propagandizing his political theories, and Bulwer, another intellectual dandy who thought of himself as a philosopher in fiction, seized upon the circulating library to disseminate his misty ideas on history, government, morals, and theosophy. The novel became variously platform, podium, and pulpit as politicians, schoolmasters, and clergymen of all persuasions gravitated to it. Leading theologians of the age like Newman, Wiseman, and Maurice wrote novels, as did statesmen like the Marquis of Normanby and Lord Lytton, civil servants like Marmion Savage and Sir Arthur Helps, historians like James Anthony Froude and John Mason Neale, lawyers like Samuel Warren, physicians like David Macbeth Moir, adventurers like Laurence Oliphant and George Augustus Sala, and naturalists like Richard Jefferies. Even that vehement opponent of the novel, Thomas Carlyle, tried it.

No wonder that Dinah Mulock could declare at mid-century: "The amount of new thoughts scattered broadcast over society within one month of the appearance of a really popular novel, the innumerable discussions it creates, and the general influence which it exercises in the public mind form one of the most remarkable facts of the day." A writer for the *Spectator,* while a little uneasy about the situation, verified Miss Mulock's observation in a subleader of 1869 entitled "The Empire of Novels," in which he spoke of "that predominant system of conveying all instruction, from the deepest difficulties of religious inquiry to the elementary facts of physical geography, through the medium of stories, which has given the Novel for a moment such a preposterous place in the literature of Great Britain." Trollope, apparently aware of this development, opens *Orley Farm* by warning away readers who might be led to expect from his title "new precepts . . . in the pleasing guise of a novel, as to cream-cheeses, pigs with small bones, wheat sown in drills, or artificial manure." Undoubtedly, too much fiction of the time was sermon, polemics, or lecture parceled out in dialogue, but novelists in general filled a widely felt need. Even at their least inspired they served as intermediaries between scholars and intellectuals and the public, predigesting and filtering down ideas. At their best they crystalized the thought of their times, notably George Eliot, who served her apprenticeship under Lewes, one of the most skilled popularizers of philosophy and science that the Victorian Age knew. In referring to herself in late career as an "aesthetic teacher," she was simply articulating what writers and readers had long accepted as the function of the man (or woman) of letters in society.

During the age we are considering, the author was looked to increasingly as a dispenser of information and ideas, but he became much more. In the long run, wrote David Masson in reviewing *Pendennis* and *David Copperfield*, "it is . . . by that unity of view and aim which pervades it, and which is the result of all the author's natural convictions and endowments, all his experience of life, and all his intellectual conclusions on questions great and little—it is by this that the worth of a work of fiction, and its title to an honourable place in literature, ought ultimately to be tried." With the growth of the novel as a medium of education—or, in Trollope's suggestive phrase, "rational amusement"—evolved the function of the novelist as a guide to life. For Miss Mulock, to turn to her once more, the novelist was far from "a mere story-teller or romancist." "Fiction forsooth! It is the core of all the truths of this world; for it is the truth of life itself," she affirmed. "He who dares to reproduce it is a Prometheus who has stolen celestial fire: let him take care that he uses it for the benefit of his fellow mortals." These ringing words might have been written by George Eliot. They unite the author of *John Halifax, Gentleman* with her greater contemporary in an inspired sense of literary vocation and indicate the heights to which "the low-heeled buskin of modern fiction" (in Trollope's words) aspired.

The novelist's responsibility toward his readers as mental stimulant (sometimes goad), aide, and confidant was recognized from the beginning of the century. Sir Walter Scott speaks of himself as a "moralist," recreating history not merely to entertain and thrill his readers but to demonstrate man's past errors. Jane Austen clearly regarded herself as a youth's companion and advisor on conduct and manners. The introduction of monthly part publication enabled the author to speak with more familiarity and pertinency. Dickens, as reporter turned novelist, exposes hidden shame and tries to shock his more affluent readers out of their smugness. Thackeray enters his readers' homes, bringing them cultural "news," advising the young on love and their parents on education and marriage prospects. Charlotte Brontë and George Eliot enter not only their readers' homes but their minds and consciences. Miss Brontë, through Lucy Snowe, ministers to the soul in anguish. George Eliot, from a more detached viewpoint, becomes a guide to the perplexed in matters of faith and morality. The "obtrusive" narrator, so much deplored in our times, was natural to an age when the didactic purpose of the novel was taken for granted and the novelist was widely regarded as a friend to man. Fiction writers were child psychologists, marriage counselors, vocational advisors, and lay analysts before these professions were even identified.

The intimate relation between author and reader, surely one of the most remarkable features of the literary life of the past century, was made possible by the integration of the public itself. Many illustrations emphasize this homogeneity. The comic-grotesque wrapper designed by Cruikshank for *Sketches by Boz* takes the form of a tableau of society, with lovers, merrymakers, criminals, politicians, fat old dowagers, and stately aristocrats intermingled. The famous *Punch* cartoon that decorates the original monthly parts of *Vanity Fair*—the clown-moralist "holding forth" from a barrel top—parodies the popular image of the novelist on his rostrum practicing the "oratory of literature," as Bulwer called it in *England and the English*. One notices, on close inspection, a shovel hat among the dunce caps in the audience, a boy playing soldier, and a woman with an infant in her arms among the assembled listeners. "Young and old, grave and gay, learned or imaginative, who of us is safe from his [the novelist's] influence?" asks Miss Mulock. "We have become a novel-reading public . . . from the Prime Minister down to the last-appointed scullery maid," observed Trollope.

The "manager" of *Vanity Fair* seems to have assumed that he was being read by everybody, to judge by his frequent shift of address: in one chapter he speaks to the "ladies"; in another it is "dear sir"; later he replies to "some unknown correspondent with a pretty little handwriting and a pink seal to her note"; he alternately begs the indulgence of the "good-natured reader" and apologizes to his "intelligent readers." One of Lucy Snowe's apologies in *Villette* is all-embracing: "Religious reader, you will preach to me a long sermon about what I have just written; and so will you, moralist, and you, stern sage; you, stoic, will frown; you, cynic, sneer; you, epicure, laugh. Well, each and all, take it your own way. I accept the sermon, frown, sneer, and laugh." Trollope, a real chameleon of a narrator, directs his remarks variously to naive and sophisticated, clergymen, statesmen, aspiring writers (with whom he discusses his craftsmanship), critics, as well as just plain readers. He assumed a faithful as well as a wide

readership when he refused to recapitulate the story of *The
Warden* in *Barchester Towers*. The Victorian author cultivated
his "kind audience of unknown friends" (as Mrs. Oliphant
called them in her dedication to *A Beleaguered City*) as both
disciples and fans.

A wide, varied, and responsive audience, it appears, was assumed among Victorian novelists. This public is represented on
the simple domestic level by the pervasive custom of family
reading recalled by Amy Cruse in *The Victorians and Their
Reading*. The title of Dickens' famous journal reminds us that
the novel too in its heyday was a household word, a fact easy to
overlook in our day, when reading is pretty much the diversion
of silence and solitude. Many a Victorian's memory of novels was
based on *hearing* rather than *reading* them; indeed, the custom
of family reading extended back to the beginning of the century.
The Austens and the Brontës certainly read other writings
besides their own around the sewing table, and they were only
the most famous of such households. The headpiece to *The
Mysteries of Udolpho* in Limbird's edition of 1824 depicts a
family—two elders, a husband and a wife, three children, one
playing with a cat—gathered around in a circle, being read to by
the young wife. The generations are joined by a similar engraving on the title page of Charlotte Yonge's *The Daisy Chain* in
the 1850's, also showing grandparents, parents, and tots collected
by a chimney corner. Publishers took the hearthside story hour
for granted, as Geraldine Jewsbury was well aware in advising
Bentley in the late 1860's to reject a manuscript sent to her for
judgment called "The Latest Chronicle of Marriage," on the
ground that it was "impossible for family reading." The popularity and persistence of the tradition is registered in such widely
known series as Murray's Family Library, Simms and M'In-
tyre's Parlour Library, Burns' Fireside Library, Clarke's Home
Library, and Ward, Lock and Tyler's Country House Library.

"The republic of the fireside," as George Meredith disparag-
ingly referred to it, has survived in reputation as a tyranny, but

on the whole it freed writers' creative minds more than it inhibited them. The custom of family reading, for one thing, enabled, even obliged, the writer to address himself to all ages. The necessity for providing "parts" for all yielded one of the richest blessings of Victorian fiction—its multiplicity and variety of characters, ranging through all the life cycle. Knowing that he was going to be read aloud tested the writer's sensitivity to colloquial speech and brought out his dramatic gifts. The consciousness of young ears in the audience, however it may have limited his subject matter and language, certainly did not force the author to simplify or condescend. Many a writer adopted an attitude toward children like that of Sir Walter Scott, dedicating his *Tales of a Grandfather* to his grandson Hugh in the hope that "You may make a great exertion, and get at the meaning, just as you might contrive to reach something placed upon a high shelf, by standing on your tiptoes, instead of waiting till you grow a little taller." Hugh's sons and grandsons too were expected to stretch their toes and brains. Mrs. Sarah Ellis, author of *Daughters of England,* argued that young minds, being especially lively and alert, were ripe for challenge. Mrs. Oliphant, the most prolific novelist of the Victorian age, far from advocating a special "teen-age" literature, held that "if the boys and girls are not equal to entering upon their national inheritance of English literature by the time they have seen out their first dozen years in the world, it is the more shame for them; and we shall not mend the matter by writing down to the capacity which should be rising to the height of *Ivanhoe.*" The family moreover assured the novelist a receptive and cohesive audience and kept the novel itself close to domestic life, to ordinary people and their problems. "We are a fireside-loving nation," observed Anne Marsh-Caldwell in the preface to *Emilia Wyndham,* and one, she added, more disposed toward oral narration than toward the theatre: ". . . the perfect illusion, the feeling of absolute reality, of sympathy—as with beings who, like ourselves, have actually enjoyed and suffered—is, I believe, more intense when the novel, from the voice of a really good reader, gives life and interest to the winter fireside."

The Victorian novelist conceived his public as the family circle extended out into the great human family. The novel was "Designed for the Entertainment and Instruction of all classes of readers," as the prospectus of *Household Words* reads, bringing together not only all ages, but all stations and professions. The writer, according to Mrs. Oliphant in her *Literary History of England,* speaks to the "public ear," "the general heart," and "popular sympathy." She took for granted the existence of such intangibles, as apparently did many of her contemporaries with the all-encompassing titles they gave their works. Panoramic titles abound, on the order of Thackeray's *Vanity Fair: Pen and Pencil Sketches of English Society.* Among numerous others are: *Bathurst: Church, State and Country as They Were; The Cost of a Coronet: A Romance of Modern Life; Milton Davenant, A Tale of the Times We Live In,* and Trollope's better known *The Way We Live Now.* Modal titles too are frequent, such as *Edward and Mary Bennett; or, Marriage as It Should Be; Aunt Agnes; or, The Why and Wherefore of Life; Ellen Walsingham; or, Growth in Grace,* and characters are often presented as concrete universals: *John Halifax, Gentleman; Gresham; or, Youth and Manhood; Lucretia; or, The Heroine of the Nineteenth Century; Adventures of a Gentleman in Search of the Church of England;* and *Adventures of an Attorney in Search of a Practice; or, A Delineation of Professional Life.*

The omnipresent author, the family group, the generalized address, the universal reference—all confirm the extent to which literature in the last century was a collective experience, a reciprocal relation of author, characters, and readers united in empathy. Readers themselves were bound by that subtle tie of shared assumptions, shared feelings, and shared responses, summed up by Louis Cazamian as "l'état général de la sensibilité." The novelist's function was to give voice to the tacit

ideals and aspirations of this corporate audience. His tripartite
role of instructor, guide, and inspirer thus evolved spontaneously.
Our age shuns didacticism in art. The nineteenth-century
novelist believed that art was didactic precisely because life,
which it imitated, was didactic. Thackeray, enjoying a book of
adventures during his Irish travels, asserted that if it has a moral
it is "that dubious one which the poet admits may be elicited
from a rose, and which every man may select according to his
own mind." Charlotte Brontë, at the end of *Shirley*, wishes God-
speed to "the judicious reader putting on his spectacles to look
for the moral." Her point was that if the reader read her right,
he did not have to *look* for the moral—it was implicit in the
book. Miss Brontë and Thackeray assumed, along with many
of their fellow novelists, that life amply and correctly represented yields its own "message." An articulate spokesman for
this view is Anne Marsh-Caldwell. "Human life—the grand
model, the vast treasury from which all fictions must be drawn—
produces no such obvious arrangements of circumstances to prove
a principle—or exemplify a maxim," she declared in the preface
to *Emilia Wyndham*. "But is human life, on that account, a
picture without a moral? Far otherwise to those who read it
aright—it is one vast school of moral instruction. To teach men
to read it aright is the business of the novelist." The novelist thus
conceived operates upon the flux of experience as the historian
operates upon the past, abstracting the logic of events from what
seems mere random sequence. His object, according to Mrs.
Marsh-Caldwell, is "to bring actions and their consequences,
passions, principles and their results, into that sort of connexion,
which though it certainly and inevitably takes place in actual
life, escapes the careless, or, perhaps, undiscerning eye of the
reader of the vast volume amid the multiplicity of circumstances
in which it is involved."

Drawing upon life's "vast school of moral instruction," novelists created their characters to demonstrate life's lessons. "I have
nothing else to premise, save that if my tale have little wit, it has

some warning," Charles Lever has his light-headed hero, Tom
Burke, write. If he gives his readers more of the first than of the
second, he knows what they expect. More positively, George Eliot
asserts in her essay "The Progress of Fiction as an Art": "He who
furnishes innocent amusement does something; he who draws a
faithful picture of life does more; but he who, whilst drawing the
picture chooses models who may elevate and improve . . . has
reached the highest excellence in his art, and deserves the thanks
of the world."

"Models" in the sense of ideal constructions aptly describes the
concept of the novel that evolved in our period. Life was envisaged as at once an academy and a proving ground for the
testing of character. The novel accordingly was a laboratory in
which one could observe how that "mysterious mixture" called
man "behaves under the varying experiments of Time," as
George Eliot writes in her "Prelude" to *Middlemarch*. Furthermore he is observed under controlled conditions. Events are "set
up" to yield the maximum of instruction; heroes and heroines
are pupils, taken over by tutors and mentors, surrogates of the
author as guide to experience; characters are patterns or ex-
emplars—good and bad. Titles like *Aids to Development, The
Discipline of Life,* and *The Progress of Character* indicate the
prevailing view that the principal end of life was ethical, the
formation of character; and readers and writers become joint
witnesses of and participants in this process. One source of the
greatness of the writers to be considered in this study is that
through their novels they gave life to ideals of character and
conduct current in their times and brought them to fruition. My
treatments of individual novels, therefore, are focused on representative types of heroes and heroines. *Waverley* will be read in
relation to the converted romantic, a recurrent character of early
nineteenth-century fiction; *Mansfield Park* in relation to treatises
on Female Education and "search for a spouse" novels; *Oliver
Twist* will be seen against the background of the orphan and
foundling literature of the 1830's; *Pendennis* will be reexamined

as a fashionable novel different in degree but not in kind from those which Thackeray scoffs at on its pages; similarly, *Villette* will be considered afresh along with more typical governess and religious novels of its decade; *The Mill on the Floss* with family fiction; and *Middlemarch* with some other novels of female emancipation and community life.

My choice of novels perhaps requires some explanation. Others might have been selected, but these, in my judgment, are at once significant in their respective authors' development and symptomatic of important literary vogues. The two pre-Victorian novels —*Waverley* and *Mansfield Park*—established modes of fiction carried on by their successors, and emphasize the continuity between the Age of George and the Age of Victoria. *Oliver Twist,* read by Queen Victoria in serial form shortly before her coronation, appropriately introduces the era. The others enable us to follow various phases of the course of Victorian fiction. Two novels of George Eliot are treated, an early one and a late one, because she brought the novel to its intellectual fulfilment, the aspect of its history on which I concentrate in this particular study. *Middlemarch* seemed the appropriate novel with which to conclude in the light of Henry James' famous judgment that it "sets a limit . . . to the development of the old-fashioned novel." It is generally regarded as the apex of the Victorian novel, and a number of trends that I trace culminate here—the relation of the novel to theories of education and psychology, the tendency toward fuller factual documentation, and its extension into new areas of thought.

The chapters themselves are organized about the stages of the novel from inception to completion, treating along the way the various circumstances—cultural, literary, and psychological—that brought it into being. Generally speaking, each novel is related to its times, to contemporaneous popular fiction and ideas, and to the author's intentions, as well as to his other work. Contemporaneous reviews and extant lists of circulating libraries suggested titles to me. I have tried to read as much as I could of popular literature, particularly books we can be sure our authors themselves knew. Of great help in providing necessary historical background have been scholarly editions of letters, one of the great contributions of recent years to our knowledge of this era. If I seem to neglect some recent criticism of these novelists, it is not for lack of respect. The present purpose is to discover how the first readers of these novels reacted to them, not how we react to them. Inevitably, obscure and forgotten names will turn up with some frequency. In justification I can invoke the authority of Robert Louis Stevenson, who assures us that "the most imbecile production of any literary age gives us sometimes the very clue to comprehension we have sought long and vainly in contemporary masterpieces." Whatever the eventual value of this investigation, the stirring up of the dust of the past has its own pleasures and occasional rewards, for the unread is not necessarily unreadable.

CHAPTER II

Waverley

Edward Waverley and the
Fair Romance Reader

And to go from one important subject to another I must account
for my own laziness which I do by referring you to a small
anonymous sort of a novel in 3 volumes which you will receive by
the Mail of this day. It was a very old attempt of mine to embody
some traits of those characters and manners peculiar to Scotland
the last remnants of which vanishd during my own youth so that
few or no traces now remain. I had written great part of the first
volume and sketchd other passages when I mislaid the manuscript
and only found it by the merest accident as I was rummaging the
drawers of an old cabinet and I took the fancy of finishing it which
I did so fast that the last two volumes were written in three weeks.
I had a great deal of fun in the accomplishment of this task though
I do not expect that it will be popular in the South as much of the
humour if there is any is local, and some of it even professional. . . .
I intend to maintain my incognito. Let me know your opinion
about it. I should be most happy if I could think it would amuse a
painful thought at this anxious moment.

—Sir Walter Scott, letter to John B. S. Morritt,
9th July, 1814[1]

The title of this work has not been chosen without the grave and solid deliberation, which matters of importance demand from the prudent. . . . Had I, for example, announced in my frontispiece, 'Waverley, a Tale of Other Days,' must not every novel reader have anticipated a castle scarce less than that of Udolpho, of which the eastern wing had long been uninhabited, and the keys either lost, or consigned to the care of some aged butler or housekeeper, whose trembling steps about the middle of the second volume, were doomed to guide the hero, or heroine, to the ruinous precincts? Would not the owl have shrieked and the cricket cried in my very title-page? . . . Again, had my title borne 'Waverley, a Romance from the German,' what head so obtuse as not to image forth a profligate abbot, an oppressive duke, a secret and mysterious association of Rosycrucians and Illuminati, with all their properties of black cowls, caverns, daggers, electrical machines, trapdoors, and dark-lanterns? Or if I had rather chosen to call my work a 'Sentimental Tale,' would it not have been a sufficient presage of a heroine with a profusion of auburn hair, and a harp, the soft solace of her solitary hours, which she fortunately finds always the means of transporting from castle to cottage. . . . Or again, if my *Waverley* had been entitled 'A Tale of the Times,' wouldst thou not, gentle reader, have demanded from me a dashing sketch of the fashionable world, a few anecdotes of private scandal thinly veiled, and if lusciously painted so much the better?

—From Chapter One of *Waverley; or, 'Tis Sixty Years Since*

The nineteenth-century novel was delayed in getting started. Had it not been for a lucky chance, the novel which struck its generation, according to one witness, "with an electric shock of delight" and dazzled its first readers, according to another, "like the sun bursting through clouds,"[2] might never have come to light. Scott had been discouraged by friends and even by his publisher Ballantyne from continuing with the writing of *Waverley* when it was in its fragmentary stage. The unfinished manuscript languished about five years in an old desk drawer, to be retrieved only when he was searching for some fishing tackle for a guest one day in 1814.[3] As a further irony, of all Scott's friends only Morritt, to whom he sent a complimentary copy along with the note quoted above, forecast its popularity. Morritt may have been aware, as was the reviewer of *Waverley* for the *Scots Magazine,* that among the new varieties of fiction being offered the public, "none are more pleasing than those which undertake to delineate the peculiarities of national manners."[4] The way had been prepared for Scott's "national novel" by Maria Edgeworth's *Castle Rackrent* and *The Absentee,* which Scott admired, followed by more flamboyant works like Lady Morgan's *The Wild Irish Girl,* Maturin's *The Wild Irish Boy* and *The Milesian Chief,* and Ann of Swansea's *Cambrian Pictures,* which catered to the public's newly aroused appetite for picturesque ethnography. Scott's own country too had been opened up to readers—the harshness of its rural life by Elizabeth Hamilton in *The Cottagers of Glenburnie,* its scenic grandeur by Peter Darling in *The Romance of the Highlands,* its legendary past by Jane Porter in *The Scottish Chiefs.* Certainly the times were ripe for an "attempt . . . to embody some traits and manners peculiar to Scotland," particularly from one who, unlike many of the then flourishing "mannerists," knew them at first hand. Yet Scott was remarkably casual about *Waverley,* considering the massive impact it was to make on novel readers. He entered his career of novelist rather halfheartedly, on the brink of middle age, preoccupied with other interests. Ironically, these very interests—law, antiquarian research, scholarly editing, collecting and composing ballads—proved but a preparation for the most phenomenally successful of his careers.

Waverley departed from most of the other "national" novels in its freedom from chauvinism and insularity. Much as Scott points up the oddities of the Highlanders, he emphasizes their kinship with the Sassenachs. He had good reason to extend hands across the Tweed at the time he began *Waverley*—1805—a year which happened to be an especially tense one for Anglo-Scotch relations. The impeachment proceedings against Henry Dundas, Lord Melville, the unofficial minister for Scotland, were then beginning. The trial, which took place in the following year, stirred up new bitterness between the two countries, an indica-

tion that the echoes of the '45 had not yet died down. Fortunately for the cause of national unity, Melville was acquitted;
Scott himself attended a dinner held in the minister's honor to
celebrate his vindication and composed a poem for the occasion
in which he proclaims not only Lord Melville's loyalty but that
of all Scotland. Looking back over the last century, he writes:

> They would turn us adrift; though rely, sir, upon it,
>   Our own faithful chronicles warrant us that,
> The free mountaineer, and his bonny blue bonnet
>   Have oft gone as far as the regular's hat.
> We laugh at their taunting,
>   For all we are wanting
> Is license our life, for our country to give.
>   Off with it merrily;
>   Horse, foot, and artillery,—
> Each loyal Volunteer, long may he live![5]

These "faithful chronicles" were turned to good use in *Waverley* and its successors, where the loyalty of the Scotch is tested in
civil conflict. The particular subject of Scott's first novel has been
traced to his friend and fellow ballad collector Robert Surtees,
who thought that the Jacobite rebellions of the previous century
would provide ideal material for a poem. "Whilst Scotland can
boast a minstrel," wrote Surtees, "why is posterity to trace those
interesting periods only in the cold pages of a professed historian?"[6] Surtees' suggestion fitted in with a plan Scott once had
of publishing a supplement to the *Border Minstrelsy* that would
incorporate songs and poems about the insurrections of 1715 and
1745, with the intention, as he wrote to a friend, of "bringing
down the Ballad history of Scotland to the middle of the
eighteenth century."[7]

Although this "ballad history" became instead the prose history *Waverley*, the poems put into the mouths of some of the
characters make it appear at times like a continuation of the
Border Minstrelsy. The period between the inception and publication of *Waverley* coincided with the composition of Scott's

most famous metrical romances. Indeed, the evocative atmosphere of the Highland episodes of the novel and its picturesque
descriptions indicate that Scott was making a gradual transition
from *The Lay of the Last Minstrel, Marmion,* and *The Lady of
the Lake.* Even as late as the publication of *Waverley* Scott was
not certain whether his direction lay with poetry or with fiction.
One of the reasons he gave for anonymity was that to have his
name on the title page of a novel "would just give me that sort of
ill name which precedes hanging—which would be in many
respects inconvenient if I thought of again trying a grande
opus."[8] He was undoubtedly gratified when a number of the
first reviewers of *Waverley* guessed at its authorship on the basis
of its kinship with his romances.[9] Since at first he had considered
the novel an inferior form and had turned to it with reluctance,
one of the most pleasing to him of all the encomia he had
received must have been that of a friend who remarked that
"there wants but verse to make all Waverley an enchanting
poem."[10]

Scott's condescension toward prose fiction, expressed both in
his letter to Morritt and in the teasing address to his readers in
the first chapter of *Waverley,* was echoed by reviewers. One,
responding to the rumor that Scott was the author of *Waverley,*
wondered why "a poet of established fame should dwindle into a
scribbler of novels."[11] Others praised the book for not being a
novel as they understood the term. "The object of the work
before us, was evidently to present a faithful and animated
picture of the manners and state of society in this northern part
of the island, in the earlier part of the last century," conjectured
one of the more influential journals. Another, although finding a
few errors, praised *Waverley* for its accurate descriptions and "its
generic representation of a class of gentry now extinct in Great
Britain." The anonymous author was congratulated for managing "to content himself, even in the marvellous parts of his story,
with copying from actual existences, rather than from the phan-
tasms of his own imagination." Imagination, one gathers, is all

well and good in its place—that is, in poetry—but the prose writer should confine himself to the real world. "It requires no ordinary talent, indeed, to choose such realities as may outshine the bright imaginations of the inventive . . . but when this is once accomplished, the result is sure to be something more firm, impressive and engaging than can ever be produced by mere fiction."[12]

"Mere fiction" is what Scott mocks in the introductory chapter of his novel, where he looks back on the principal types of escapist reading of the late eighteenth century that were still finding readers—Gothic romances, "monkish" tales of terror, sentimental-sublime travelogues, and scandal chronicles. His own novel attempts to counteract fancy with fact. The castles that Edward Waverley visits are not Otranto or Udolpho, but Holyrood House and Doune. "A Romance from the German" meant to Scott's first readers mainly "Monk" Lewis' renderings of the *schrecksromane* of Heinrich Zschokke and Veit Weber. The German writers Scott prefers are Goethe and Schiller. "The heroine with a profusion of auburn hair" could be, among others, Madame de Staël's Corinne or Lady Morgan's Wild Irish Girl Glorvina. Flora Mac-Ivor of *Waverley* may differ from her literary sisters only by her dark hair, but she does have the good sense to leave her harp behind when battles are raging.[13] For his capsule plot of "A Tale of the Times," supposedly "founded on fact" but really on gossip, Scott may well have been recalling Charles Johnstone's *Chrysal; or, The Adventures of a Guinea,* but his first readers could have supplied from their recent reading such titles as *The Mask of Fashion, The Barouche Driver and His Wife: A Tale for Haut Ton,* and *The Royal Sufferer; or, Intrigues at the Close of the Eighteenth Century.* For Scott the political intrigues of aristocrats, not their amorous ones, were the proper subject for literature.

Among more serious fiction writers of his time Scott mentions only Miss Edgeworth, to whom he acknowledges indebtedness at the end, and Mrs. Hamilton, whom he praises.[14]He does not

refer anywhere to pious novelists like Hannah More and Medora
Gordon Byron, although like them he professes to be a "moralist," the main purpose of his excursion into the past being "to
illustrate the moral lessons, which I would willingly consider as
the most important part of my plan" (CH. I). It might have been
these ladies, among others, whom Morritt had in mind when he
wrote Scott after reading the manuscript of *Waverley:* "Your
method of narrating is so different from the slipshod, sauntering
verbiage of common novels, and from the stiff, precise and prim
sententiousness of some of our female moralists, that I think it
can't fail to strike anybody who knows what style means."[15] One
reader, at least, found Scott's variety of "moral lessons" a refreshing change.

What Scott brought to novel readers that was new was not
manners or morals, but scholarship. "I beg pardon, once and for
all, of all those readers who take up novels merely for amusement, for plaguing them so long with old-fashioned politics, and
Whig and Tory, and Hanoverians and Jacobites," he apologizes.
"The truth is, I cannot promise them that this story shall be
intelligible, not to say probable without it" (CH. V). Probability
and causality, he implies, were hardly matters of importance to
most of his predecessors in the art of fiction. The elaborate detail
and painstaking documentation that cram the pages of *Waverley,*
intended to clarify "the motives on which its action proceeded,"
establish the author as a man of learning as well as a man of
letters. The minds of readers, accustomed perhaps to nothing
more demanding than *The Scottish Chiefs* and *The Romance of
the Highlands,* are stretched with minutiae about the ministry of
George I, the Tory nobility, the various localities of the Chevalier
Saint George's exiled court, Dyer's *Weekly Letter,* the Supreme
Court of Session of Scotland, the dissensions among English and
Scottish Jacobites, and the tactics of the Battle of Preston. If now
and then *Waverley* seems overloaded with erudition, one can
understand why the author flaunts it as a time when fiction
writers were denounced by the critics for their ignorance and

inanity. Where romance writers tended to be vague or inaccurate, Scott draws on his exact knowledge of genealogy, folklore, law, and topography to pin his events down to time and place. Not surprisingly, he refers to *Waverly* more frequently as "my history" than "my story," meaning history literally rather than in its eighteenth-century sense of autobiography or adventure.

Scott's passion for fact made him impatient with speculative inquiry, as well as with flights of fancy. His brief catalogue of contemporaneous fiction is significant, therefore, for another omission—the philosophical novel—but one gathers from other evidence that he was uneasy with it. He was very much in tune, certainly, with the more staid opinion of the time toward Godwin, whose *Caleb Williams* he found powerful, "although the story . . . be unpleasing, and the moral sufficiently mischievous."[16] A conservative, Scott believed strongly in tradition and, unlike Godwin, was satisfied with "Things as They Are"; a rationalist, he assumed that sensible men of all ages tended to think alike. His subject, he reminds his readers, is drawn from "the great book of Nature, the same through a thousand editions, whether of black-letter or wire-wove and hot pressed" (CH. I). He meant *human* nature. Believing in the instructive function of the novel but generally shunning polemics, he warned readers away from the libertarian thought of Robert Bage, along with Godwin's radicalism. While he felt compelled to admire Bage's ability at introspection and psychological analysis, he had no desire to emulate it. In fact, he deplored in Bage the lack of just those more practical and documentary skills he himself cultivated—narrative drive, the notation of national traits and professional habits, an eye for the typical, and an ear for colloquial speech.[17]

Scott's sense of values is close to that expressed in a popular cautionary tale of the period, Amelia Opie's *Adeline Mowbray*. Here the heroine's downfall is traced to her mother's disdain for essential subjects like "history, biography, poetry and discoveries in natural philosophy," while she "pored with still unsatisfied delight over abstruse systems of morals and metaphysics, or new theories in politics" (I, CH. I). Scott's danger zones, like Mrs. Opie's, are abstruse systems of morals, metaphysics, and politics. Unsettling ideas prove the undoing of Adeline Mowbray, and Scott did not want to bother his younger readers' minds with them either. His strictures against Godwin and Bage prepare us for the vein of anti-intellectualism that runs through *Waverley* concurrently with its anti-romanticism.

In his first novel, along with his commitment to documented fact, Scott set himself time limitations. "I would have my readers understand that they will meet in the following pages neither a romance of chivalry, nor a tale of modern manners," he declares in his opening chapter. He seems to expect his subtitle, " 'Tis Sixty Years Since" to disappoint readers fresh from his metrical romances, which dealt with "ancient manners," or those familiar with such prose tales as *The Borderers: An Historical Romance Illustrative of the Manners of the Fourteenth Century; Edwy and Elgiva: A Historical Romance of the Tenth Century; Black Knights: A Tale of the Eighth Century;* and *Anglo-Saxons: or, The Court of Ethelwulf.* Scott preferred to deal not with "antiquity," like these prose romances, but with living history. As for modern tales, their only virtue to him was novelty. He thought the novel of contemporary life, which at this time was the society novel, was inevitably transient in its interest. Late in life he described Thomas Henry Lister's *Granby* as "one of that very difficult class [of novels] which aspires to describe the actual current of society, whose colours are so evanescent that it is difficult to fix them on the canvas."[18] His desire to "fix" his colors makes Scott abjure both what is too old and too new. Both ancient and modern settings stress, in his opinion, the temporary and changing aspects of life; he is interested in the permanent and the changeless in human nature. By setting his first novel in "a period too recent to be romantic and too far gone by to be familiar," as the *Edinburgh Review* put it, Scott was trying to

give his readers the illusion of life actually being lived, but in a
time sufficiently distant to be invested with quaintness.

Scott rejected controversial subjects, mystery, horror, sentimentality, and contemporary society; but all people were poten-
tially princes to him. He refused to confine himself to the upper
classes, like the novelists of manners, or to the middle class, like
his greatest contemporary, Jane Austen,[19] making his province
"those passions common to men in all stages of society," as he
announces in his introduction. Later, in his General Preface to
the 1829 edition of the Waverley Novels, Scott reminded his public of the close and varied acquaintance he had enjoyed with his
country and people during his youth, "having travelled through
most parts of Scotland, both Highland and Lowland; having
been familiar with the elder, as well as the more modern race;
and having had from my infancy free and unrestrained communication with all ranks . . . from the Scottish peer to the
Scottish ploughman." In *Waverley* he does indeed involve "all
sorts and conditions of men"—peasantry, professionals, peerage
—in the action of the story, which in turn is widely distributed
around camp, country, and court.

Endeavoring also to bring several kinds of readers together,
Scott sets his novel in a not too distant past, which could be
recalled by the grandparents of his first readers, thereby appealing at once to the nostalgia of the older generation and the
historical curiosity of the younger. He addresses himself at one
time to "readers who take up novels merely for amusement," at
another to "the understanding critic." At the beginning of the
second volume (CH. XXIV in modern editions), he refers to the
tastes both of "scholars" and of "the vulgar." At the end of
Chapter V he addresses his "fair readers" with the customary
assumption that his audience is made up principally of immature
and impressionable young ladies, but at the same time he seems
to be bidding for male readers. By making his central character a
young man and involving him in battles and politics, Scott is not
only elevating the novel but "masculinizing" it as well. Thus he

reintroduces into English fiction the vigor and plenitude of the two masters he so much admired, the "powers of strong and national humor, and forcible yet natural exhibition of character" of the author of *Tom Jones,* the "life, action and bustle" of the author of *Humphry Clinker.* He revives the gusto of Fielding and Smollett, that is, without the coarseness that some readers, including Scott himself, found offensive.[20] One advantage of Scott's coming late to fiction is that he could bring to it a vast amount of reading, as well as experience and learning. *Waverley* is consequently both a criticism of the novel of Scott's day and an attempt to revitalize the form.

The imagery of book-making scattered through *Waverley* betrays the neophyte novelist feeling his way. Scott here takes a more familiar tone with his readers than he assumes in later novels, nudging them along the way to be sure they know what he is doing, alternately confiding in them and gently scolding them. The form of the novel varies from travelogue to exemplary biography to chronicle history, and the author's roles shift accordingly. One of his guises is that of coach driver guiding his readers on a tour into strange new country. The first third of the book, with such chapter headings as "A Horse Quarter in Scotland," "A Highland Feast," and "Highland Minstrelsy," answers more to the "sketch of Scotch manners" that Scott set out to write. He had before him of course the example of Lady Morgan, who exploited quaint Hibernian lore in *The Wild Irish Girl.* Like *Waverley,* it centered about a refined Englishman who discovers the fierce fascination of the hinterlands.

Readers since have complained about the ambling pace of the journey, for Scott does not get "warm in the harness," as he says, until after young Waverley leaves the Mac-Ivors at Glennaquoich (the end of what was originally the first volume). The author anticipates such restiveness, even inviting his passengers to jump off if they wish: "Such as dislike the vehicle may leave it at the next half and wait for the conveyance of Prince Hussein's tapestry, or Malek the Weaver's flying sentry-box."[21] This is to be a real journey, not a magic carpet flight. However, the driver promises "more picturesque and romantic" country ahead for those who stay aboard. At the end, having taken us along with the hero to the battlefields of Bonnie Prince Charlie, he resumes the driver's post to return us safely home. His parting words to his passengers remind them that they do not have to travel to the fabled Orient by means of *Tales of the East* for adventure. Furthermore, the coachman has seen to it that their travel was educational, not merely for rest and recreation.

A concurrent function of the author is that of tutor, suggested by other chapter headings like "Education," "Castle Building," and "Choice of a Profession." Scott indicates in a footnote to the 1829 edition that these chapters "have been a good deal censured as tedious and unnecessary"; they have been no favorites of later readers either. However, apart from their interest as literary history, they place young Edward firmly as the center and point of view of the novel and remind us of its original didactic purpose. Scott treats his hero and his readers alike as naive minds ripe for development. Writer, reader, and hero thus unite in a program of mental growth, the author guiding our reading as well as our travel. He does not approve of young Edward's choice of books any more than he does the favorite stories of his hypothetical "fair readers." Edward loses himself not in tales of terror but in other escapist literature like epics and romances which glorify the dead past and glamorize war. But these romances are not simply deplored as a waste of time. What is more serious to Scott is Edward's lack of discrimination and mental discipline. Turned loose in the "Gothic" library of Waverley-Honour without help or advice from his elders, "Edward was permitted to roam at large . . . young Waverley drove through the sea of books like a vessel without a pilot or rudder" (CH. III). It is obvious from these words that in its time *Waverley* addressed itself as much to parents and guardians as to pliable youth. Scott is quite conscious that his is an age of educational panaceas: "I am aware that I may be reminded of the necessity of rendering instruction agreeable to youth, and of Tasso's infusion of honey into the medicine prepared for a child; but an age in which children are taught the driest doctrines by the insinuating method of instructive games has little reason to dread the consequences of study being rendered too severe" (CH. III). These "instructive games" sound like the "rational toys," such as balloons with maps of the world on their surfaces, described by Miss Edgeworth in her *Moral Tales* and *Practical Education,* which are intended to instruct children at play. Books could also be a form of rational toy, and this was an age of faith in their influence, for good or bad. What concerns Scott about Edward Waverley's reading is that without proper supervision the young man may, to revert to Tasso's image, swallow the honey and reject the medicine.

In Scott's day writers on education generally worried themselves not about whether Johnny could read, but about what Johnny read. Elizabeth Hamilton, a leading educational theorist as well as a popular novelist, warned parents that the imaginations of naturally gifted children "are easily kindled by the flame of enthusiasm. . . . They are like jars filled with electric fluid, ready to explode at the touch of the conductor." This unhealthy condition, according to Mrs. Hamilton, results from exciting the imagination before the reason is properly cultivated; consequently she emphasizes the importance of "turning the attention of the youthful mind to objects, which while they afford exercise to all the powers of the understanding, have a tendency to elevate the imagination and improve the taste."[22] She describes precisely the condition of Edward Waverley in his "Castle-Building" days, who has quick "powers of apprehension," "brilliancy of fancy and vivacity of talent," but who, unfortunately, owing to his overindulgent tutor, was not at the same time acquiring "the art of controlling, directing and concentrating the powers of mind for earnest investigation." Because he has been left so much to his own devices, his "power of imagination and love of literature . . . were so far from affording a remedy to this peculiar evil, that they rather inflamed and increased its violence" (CH. III) .

Another influential treatise, Mrs. Jane West's widely read *Letters to a Young Man, on His First Entrance into Life,* addressed to her son ("My dear Arthur"), anticipates the advice that the author of *Waverley* offers to his fictitious young man. Although Mrs. West expects her son to find his vocation in public life, she strongly advises him to cultivate reading, anticipating that literature may stimulate his mind in moments of weariness and console him in times of sorrow. She suggests, however, that he be selective and discriminating in his choice of books by seeking out "elegant and useful information" both to fill and enlarge his mind and to provide him with that knowledge of his fellow men that "serves as a ballast to keep his vessel steady; while the light, vacant mind, tossed about by every varying inclination, is continually veering towards some new absurdity." On the other hand, he should avoid "a species of reading which renders a vicious enfeebling sensibility . . . which stores the imagination with false images and bewildering ideas, but leaves the mind uninformed and the heart uncorrected." Mrs. West recalls that her own sex has frequently been ridiculed for reading of rubbishy romances, but of late she has been distressed to discover male students lolling about on sofas in dressing gowns and red morocco slippers reading novels to no better purpose than "to kill that monster Time." To her son she recommends works of history, politics, and religion. But she has a better cure still for the cultivated youth with time on his hands. "The tendency to constitutional melancholia would have gained ground had you continued in a retired situation, under the watchful, anxious and participating care of parental tenderness," she reminds young Arthur. "It was happy for us that we decided to send you from us, into those active bustling scenes where necessity requires and example stimulates to action."[23]

This proves to be a happy solution also for Sir Everard

Waverley, to whose care nephew Edward was temporarily consigned. Edward's reading of chivalric romances and his listening to Aunt Rachel's sentimental tales, combined with the old-world atmosphere of Waverley-Honour, threaten to confine him to a dream world which he seems all too willing to exchange for the real one: "Through these scenes it was that Edward loved to 'chew the cud of sweet and bitter fancy,' and like a child among his toys, culled and arranged, from the splendid yet useless imagery with which his imagination was stored, visions as brilliant and fading as those of an evening sky" (CH. IV). Sir Everard is much concerned about his ward's "indolence and habits of abstraction and love of solitude," so Prince Charles' rallying cry comes at the right time, giving Edward a chance to live a heroic life instead of merely reading about it. As Edward himself writes in the fragment of verse he leaves behind:

> So, on the idle dreams of youth,
> Breaks the loud trumpet-call of truth,
> Bids each fair vision pass away,
> Like landscape on the lake that lay,
> As fair, as flitting, and as frail,
> As that which fled the Autumn gale.—
> For ever dead to fancy's eye
> Be each gay form that glided by,
> While dreams of love and lady's charms
> Give place to honour and to arms!   (CH. V)

Both Scott and Sir Everard Waverley seem to concur with Richard Edgeworth that "to inure the mind to athletic vigour is one of the chief objects of education."[24]

The story proper of *Waverley*, where Scott as historian takes over, celebrates, quite understandably, the life of action rather than of thought. At first the outer world seems to Edward, as a mere observer, all beautiful and new. Listening to Rose Bradwardine's account of Fergus Mac-Ivor's forays, he "could not help starting at a story which bore so much resemblance to one of his own day-dreams" (CH. XV). Seated on the banks of the stream that leads him to Fergus' hold, he "had now time to give himself up to the full romance of his situation. Here he sat on the banks of an unknown lake, under the guidance of a wild native [the brigand Donald Bean Lean] whose language was unknown to him, on a visit to the den of some renowned outlaw, a second Robin Hood. . . . What a variety of incidents for the exercise of a romantic imagination, and all enhanced by the solemn feeling of uncertainty, at least, if not of danger!" (CH. XVI).

This romantic cast of mind leads Edward to see events as epics, dramas, and love poems come to life. When he reaches Tully-Veolan and first knocks on the door of the Baron Bradwardine's manor, the echoes make him think that "he had reached the Castle of Orgoglio," and he is "filled almost with the expectation of beholding some 'old, old man with beard as white as snow' whom he might question concerning the deserted mansion" (CH. IX). As for the garden of the Bradwardine home: "The scene, though pleasing, was not quite equal to the gardens of Alcina; yet it wanted not the *'due donzelette garrule'* of that enchanted paradise." The damsels, however, prove disappointing, for they did not, "like the maidens of Armida, remain to greet with harmony the approaching guest" (CH. IX). The Baron's fool Davie Gellatly reminds Edward of one of Shakespeare's clowns. Flora and Fergus Mac-Ivor resemble, to him, Sebastian and Viola in *Twelfth Night*. His relationship with Flora and Rose Bradwardine reminds him of the Romeo-Rosalind-Juliet love triangle.

Frequently Edward's imagination is influenced by literature, but sometimes, through his charmed eyes, scenes present themselves as living paintings. The village girls of Tully-Veolan "somewhat resembled Italian forms of landscape." From these girls "an artist might have chosen more than one model whose features and form resembled those of Minerva" (CH. VIII). Edward's frame of mind is well described by Alan Fairford, the rational hero of *Redgauntlet*, writing to his more imaginative friend Darsie Latimer: " 'Didst ever see what artists call a Claude

Lorraine glass which spreads its own particular hue over the whole landscape which you see through it—thou beholdest ordinary events through such a medium'" (Letter V). One of the most vivid word-pictures in *Waverley,* describing the backdrop for Flora Mac-Ivor's harp minstrelsy, is in effect a Lorraine landscape[25] verbalized and transferred to the Highlands:

> Advancing a few yards, and passing under the bridge which he had viewed with so much terror, the path ascended rapidly from the edge of the brook, and the glen widened into a sylvan amphitheatre, waving with birch, young oaks, and hazels, with here and there a scattered yew-tree. The rocks now receded, but still showed their grey and shaggy crests rising among the copse-wood. Still higher, rose eminences and peaks, some bare, some clothed with wood, some round and purple with heath, and others splintered into rocks and crags. At a short turning, the path, which had for some furlongs lost sight of the brook, suddenly placed Waverley in front of a romantic waterfall. . . . The borders of this romantic reservoir corresponded in beauty; but it was the beauty of a stern and commanding cast, as if in the act of expanding into grandeur.
>
> (CH. XXII)

This "sylvan amphitheatre" where Flora serenades Edward is too close an illustration of Burke's ideas of sublime terror to evoke any sense of place, but it is appropriate to Edward's mood at this time. To be sure, the pibroch that Flora sings is full of the real horrors of feuding and war that Edward comes to know at first hand. But at this time he is hardly aware of what she sings, thinking of himself as a "knight of romance" being regaled by "a fair enchantress of Boiardo or Ariosto, by whose nod the scenery around seemed to have been created, an Eden in the wilderness." As Edward later admits to Flora: "A thousand circumstances of fatal self-indulgence have made me the creature rather of imagination than reason" (CH. XXVI). But Fergus Mac-Ivor, the romantic chieftain, initiates him into the real world: "Come down with me to the court, and you shall see a sight worth all the tirades of your romances," Fergus urges Edward. "An hundred firelocks, my friend, and as many broadswords, just arrived from good friends; and two or three hundred stout fellows almost fighting which shall first possess them" (CH. XXVI). The experience of war in its sordid actuality leads him eventually to recognize as he walks along the shore of the Ullswater that "the romance of his life was ended, and that its real history had now commenced" (CH. LX).

Waverley is a story of misguided rebellion, treachery, and false hope, but above all it exposes that greatest of deceivers—the imagination. At the beginning of Chapter V Scott relates his hero to an earlier one very familiar to his audience:

> From the minuteness with which I have traced Waverley's pursuits, and the bias which these unavoidably communicated to his imagination, the reader may perhaps anticipate, in the following tale, an imitation of the romance of Cervantes. But he will do my prudence injustice in the supposition. My intention is not to follow the steps of that inimitable author, in describing such total perversion of intellect as misconstrues the objects actually presented to the senses, but that more common aberration from sound judgment, which apprehends occurrences indeed in their reality, but communicates to them a tincture of its own romantic tone and colouring.

In *Waverley* Scott is not indeed imitating *Don Quixote* itself but the numerous imitations of that work which were then current. The pattern of the romantic youth maturing into the realistic adult aligns *Waverley* with a type of didactic fiction of this period known as the Anti-Romance.

As a sugar-coated purgative of youthful self-delusion, the Anti-Romance helped make palatable the educational theories of Maria Edgeworth, Elizabeth Hamilton, and Jane West. Although these mock novels varied in the immediate targets of their satire, they had in common a central character whom we might dub, after the best known of them, the "Fair Romance Reader." This heroine, intoxicated by escapist romantic literature of one sort or another, generally goes through a series of ludicrous adventures set off by her desire to imitate the careers of her fictitious models. Eventually she receives a rude awakening which clears her mind and adjusts it to the real world. The great vogues of Sensibility and Terror (frequently fused, of course) soon grew all too ripe for ridicule, so it is no surprise that the Anti-Romance abounded at the end of the eighteenth century and the beginning of the nineteenth. Typical parodies that were widely known among readers at the turn of the century were William Beckford's *Modern Novel Writing; or, The Elegant Enthusiast* (1796) ; Mary Charlton's *Rosella; or, Modern Occurrences* (1799) ; and Maria Edgeworth's delightful "Angelina; ou, l'Amie Inconnue" (1801). During the period just before *Waverley* was published, there appeared, among others, Mrs. Sarah Green's *Romance Readers and Romance Writers* (1810) and what might be regarded as the masterpiece of the genre, Eaton Stannard Barrett's *The Heroine; or, The Fair Romance Reader* (1813).

The prototype of the Anti-Romance, more for its influence than for its originality, was Charlotte Lennox's *The Female Quixote; or, The Adventures of Arabella* (1752). Although Mrs. Lennox conceived her heroine by analogy with Cervantes' knight-errant, Arabella does not mistake windmills for giants, but is subject to "the more common aberration from sound judgment" that Scott speaks of, which is to see life in terms of literature. Arabella is innately bright, sensitive, and imaginative, as children tend to be in learned ladies' books. Unfortunately, she is brought up in a way that, as we read more and more edifying works of this kind, we recognize to be fraught with peril to her mental health. Not only is she left without a mother at an early age, but her father, who is responsible for her education, has retired from society in a fit of misanthropy and insists on keeping her in seclusion. Moreover, her father even refuses to hire a tutor for her, thinking it sufficient to turn her loose in her mother's carefully preserved library. Since the reading of Arabella's mother consisted largely of the romances of Madame de Scudéry (in poor translations, the author hastens to add) the young girl, removed from the real world, loses herself in the pseudo-classical one of *Clélia, Cassandra, Cleopatra,* and *The Grand Cyrus*.[26]

When Arabella finally begins her "entrance into life," her attempts to live by the artificial code of her favorite heroines involve her in absurd complications. She mistakes slight attentions for deep passion, assumes that servants are noblemen wooing her in disguise, and holds off Glanville, her suitor, for an unconscionable length of time under the conviction that the true heroine must affect disdain even toward the man she loves. Her sense of the past being conditioned by Madame de Scudéry, she thinks of Julius Caesar as an effete lover and refuses to believe that Cleopatra was a whore. A rival of her lover, who is himself "up" on all the romances, courts her by disguising himself as an ancient warrior and catering to her fancies. In time, under the tutelage of the long-suffering Glanville, Arabella's "romance" view of her heroes is corrected, like Edward Waverley's, by "history," though she gets her history at second hand, by reading. The continuing vogue of *The Female Quixote* is evident from its republication in 1810 in Mrs. Barbauld's British Novelists series.[27] Maria Edgeworth, Eaton Stannard Barrett, and other anti-romancers refer to it. Scott himself pokes gentle fun at Edith Bellenden in *Old Mortality* for her addiction to the same romances that captivated Arabella.

Among the imitations of *The Female Quixote* contemporaneous with Scott is Mary Charlton's *Rosella; or, Modern Occurrences,* a publication, surprisingly, of the Minerva Press, which apparently was willing to be party to jokes on itself. Indeed, Miss Charlton herself perpetrated the sort of trumpery that she laughs at in this clever little "novel upon novels," which was favorably received in its time.[28] The humor of *Rosella* arises out of a vain search by a mother and daughter after the picturesque, the terrible, and the sublime. Rosella's mother, widowed early in life, has never been "cured of the circulating library mania," which she passes on to her daughter, whom she hopes to see "puzzled in the mazes and perplexed in the errors which had so agreeably tortured the Hermiones, Jacquilinas, Geraldinas, Phillipinas, Gipsey-Duchesses, and beggar-girls of the day."[29] This overstimulated pair take a sentimental journey into Wales, where they expect the primitive countryside to yield them at every turn a terrifying scene, a hair's-breadth escape from danger, a mysterious stranger, or a pastoral lover. Nature and life steadfastly fail to measure up to their expectations.

Maria Edgeworth's "Angelina; ou, l'Amie Inconnue" does not belong with the roisterous Irish tales that gave Scott so much pleasure, but it is akin to *Waverley* as a story of chastened youth. Part of the *Moral Tales* intended for the edification of teen-agers preparing for various professions,[30] "Angelina" differs from the other tales of the group by offering a negative example. The stories that Angelina reads are clearly not of the kind represented by the *Moral Tales* which the author hopes "shall neither dissipate the attention, nor inflame the imagination." Angelina (literary for Anne) Warwick, like Arabella and Edward Waverley, is left too much to her own devices at an impressionable age, her mother and father having cultivated her literary taste but not her judgment. It is her further misfortune to be left an orphan at the age of fourteen and put in the charge of an aunt who is a shallow lady of fashion. In her loneliness, Anne turns to literature for stimulation, and her reading leads her into correspondence with a female author who writes free-flowing and free-thinking Godwinian sentiments under the nom-de-plume of "Araminta." The misadventures of Miss Edgeworth's heroine grow out of her quest after her favorite author, who lives in a cottage in South Wales named "Angelina Bower." On her way to the cottage, Angelina passes a night at an inn in Cardiff, where she is disappointed that the harper who entertains her is not blind or shaggy-haired and sings modern ballads instead of bardic lays. "Angelina Bower" itself proves to be bare, crude, poorly furnished, and cramped, while the "unknown friend" turns out to be not a beautiful shepherdess, as Angelina had expected from her letters, but a coarse, brandy-addicted Amazon.

Angelina eventually is "rescued" by a benevolent aunt who places in her hands a copy of *The Female Quixote* for her chastening. Anne (as she is now content to remain) is moved by her aunt's charity to burst into tears, which we are assured are not tears of sensibility, but "tears of real feeling." The author takes pleasure in assuring the parents among her readers "that it is possible for a young lady of sixteen to cure herself of the affectation of sensibility, and the folly of romance."

Mrs. Sarah Green's *Romance Readers and Romance Writers*, which was published during the year when Scott was first contemplating the publication of *Waverley*, waged a massive assault against the "folly of romance." An ill-humored and heavy-handed piece of invective with as ridiculous a plot as any the author condemns, *Romance Readers* is remembered mainly for its scurrilous preface called "Literary Retrospection—Rudus Indigestiquae" which gives us some idea of who was being read at the time. On its pages Mrs. Green pillories some of her popular rivals, prompted, one gathers, more by envy than by righteous indignation.[31] Most of those she punishes have hardly proved worth the effort: T. Horsley Curteis, whose tumid Gothic tales are considered "dull and tiresome . . . long-winded and loquacious"; Lady Morgan and Charlotte Dacre ("Rosa Matilda"), the "Scylla and Charybdis of Romance"; and the inexhaustible educator-novelist Madame de Genlis, who "has only to foist in a few incidents, the less probable the better, put sentiments and words into the hearts and mouths of people who never felt or uttered them, and then she has conjured up, not with the wand of genius, but with the tool of a literary mechanic, an historical romance." "Monk" Lewis, the one writer mentioned whose notoriety lives after him, had, in Mrs. Green's opinion, fallen into a decline with his translations (those romances "taken from the German" that Scott seems to allude to in the opening paragraph of *Waverley*).

Mrs. Green was convinced that romance in all its varieties—Gothic, sentimental, historical—had had its day:

Romance proved favourable to the cause of gallantry and heroism during the *dark ages,* but we, thank heaven! live in more enlightened days: a lover would find occasion to repent of making such rash oaths as the *inamoratos* of Italy, of Spain, and of Portugal formerly swore to maintain; we are too independent to permit the possibility of it; nor do we frequently take the law into our own hands.

Could she have had any hand in Edward Waverley's upbringing, Mrs. Green would have locked him out of the library of Waverley-Honour. But her most severe censure is reserved for modern imitations of old romances, which to her are "the vermin of literature," and, what is worse, "their spawn creep to our firesides, and cover our tables, our chairs, our sofas and our mantelpieces; we find them in the bed chambers of our daughters; nay, not unfrequently are they placed beneath their pillows to occupy their minds at daybreak, or to beguile a sleepless night."

The story that follows this preface is intended to illustrate "the effects of romance-reading on the weak and ductile mind of youth" and at the same time to counteract these effects "by blending history [i.e. truth] and fiction." The strung-out plot, peppered here and there with prurient incident, follows the fortunes of two daughters of the Reverend Edward Morsham: Mary, who is sensible and natural, and Margaret (or Margaretta, as she styles herself), who is romantic and affected. Margaret reads first tales of dark ruins and castles, ghosts and witchcraft, which derange her imagination, then novels of manners, *Delphine* and *La Nouvelle Héloise,* which corrupt her moral feeling. (Mrs. Green apparently considered French "vermin" more noxious than the English variety.) Mary proves that no evil can happen to one who remains faithful to Richardson and Miss Burney. Although both daughters have the bad taste to fall in love with libertines, Mary succeeds in reforming her rake (by reading to him from *Clarissa*), while Margaret is seduced, and subsequently deserted. At the end, Margaret is ready to settle in the country and bring up her illegitimate daughter on religious poetry and pious fiction.

By far the richest and most ingenious of the Female Quixote tales, and apparently the most popular in Scott's time, was *The Heroine; or, The Adventures of a Fair Romance Reader,* which preceded *Waverley* by a year.[32] The author, a young Irish satirist and polemicist named Eaton Stannard Barrett, varied the formula by having the heroine tell her own story in a series of letters to her governess. The result is a tour de force parodying at once the epistolary manner, the picaresque narrative, and Gothic extravagance of emotion. In content it is a pastiche of such period best-sellers as *The Wild Irish Girl, Ida of Athens, The Novice of St. Dominick, Caroline of Lichfield, The Forest of Mantalbano, The Bravo of Venice, The Children of the Abbey, The Romance of the Forest, The Mysteries of Udolpho,* and *The Italian.* However, Barrett does not confine himself to those mistresses of the false sublime, Mrs. Radcliffe, Regina Maria Roche, Catherine Cuthbertson, and Lady Morgan. Because he is anti-sentimental and anti-heroic as well as anti-Gothic, his caricatures take in Richardson, Fanny Burney, Madame de Staël, Goethe of *The Sorrows of Werther,* and even the Scott of *Marmion* and *The Lady of the Lake.*

The history of Barrett's heroine, the well but not wisely read Cherry Wilkinson, might be described as the pushing of absurd premises to preposterous conclusions, but it is well-sustained foolishness. Cherry,too, finds life at home drab after her immersion in romance. Her reading convinces her, for one thing, that she is not really her father's daughter but the lost heiress of a noble family.[33] She decides, therefore, to lengthen her name to Cherubina de Willoughby (Angelina, Seraphina, and Celestina, we are reminded, have already been pre-empted by other heroines), and runs away from home to seek the adventures proper to an aristocratic young lady of romance. Eventually she is cured of her bibliomania by a sensible young man named Stuart, who takes her in hand as Henry Tilney does Catherine Morland in

Northanger Abbey. But before that happy ending comes about, Cherubina is involved in such gaucheries as mistaking a robber for a villainous knight, whom she routs by blowing up a ruin with gunpowder, furnishing a drafty old castle with odds and ends stolen from an antique shop, and claiming for her own the house of a hostess whom she takes to be an ancestor.

The author of *The Heroine* manages to keep his thin plot spinning by his inventiveness in contriving episodes that seem to conform to Cherubina's daydreams. Among the people she meets is an actor, dressed, as it happens, in the costume of a knight, since he is on his way to a rehearsal, and he is all too willing to humor her. At one house she visits, there is a masquerade ball in progress where her Tuscan costume, modeled on *The Mysteries of Udolpho,* is not at all out of place. At another house, the guests are dressed like fictitious personages, so she gets a chance, as she supposes, to converse with Sir Charles Grandison and Harriet Byron, Lord Mortimer and Amanda, Corporal Trim, Rasselas, and many others.

The denouement of *The Heroine* is as outlandish as that of any romance—it turns out that virtually all the people whom the heroine meets have been partners in a conspiracy instigated by Stuart to restore her to sanity by catering to her absurd notions— but we hardly expect verisimilitude from this elaborate joke. What is important is that common sense wins out over imagination. Cherubina's last letter indicates that she has had more than her surfeit of knights and castles. Her lover presents her with a copy of *Don Quixote* and recommends such antidotes to romance as *The Vicar of Wakefield,* Maria Edgeworth's *Tales of Fashionable Life,* and Hannah More's *Coelebs in Search of a Wife.* Her adventures end in a way proper to a heroine of romance, with a marriage proposal from Stuart, but she goes to the altar as plain Cherry Wilkinson.

The most distinguished reader of *The Heroine* on record was Jane Austen.[34] It has even been suggested that she revised the

opening of *Northanger Abbey* with Cherubina in mind.[35] It is
hard to believe that Scott did not read this burlesque in one of
its three editions, although he does not mention it anywhere.
Whether or not *The Heroine* directly influenced *Waverley,* the
two books are related generically, for at the outset Edward
Waverly is a victim of the same form of mental derangement as
Jane Austen's Catherine Morland. For the "fair romance
reader," Scott substitutes an impressionable young man whose
imagination has been overwrought by an excess of romance
reading. When he goes out into the world, he tends to read into
phenomena notions bred in his mind by fiction. He is finally
cured of his aberration and is well contented to retire from a
heroic life to a domestic one. Mrs. West's *Letters to a Young
Man,* as already noted, provides ample evidence that males could
be as susceptible to the delusions of literature as females. Scott
tells us that through his first hero he was to an extent reliving
aspects of his own youth.[36] Life and literature, Scott's boyhood
experiences, and the vogue of the Anti-Romance thus converge
in his first novel. Scott, however, reduced the exaggeration into
which most anti-romancers were tempted, introduced more credible situations, and generally contributed more substance to the
genre. Whatever its merits, a work like Barrett's *The Heroine*
cannot, in the long run, be admired for more than its virtuosity
because it is never removed from the plane of artifice. *Waverley,*
in its better parts, gives an illusion of real people speaking and
acting and places us in the midst of events as they are taking
place. While Cherubina's adventures are contrived and manipulated, those of Edward Waverley have the actuality of history. In
fact, Scott succeeded in doing what Barrett tried to do—to show
how life may sometimes seem to imitate fiction.

As we know, Scott deliberately set *Waverley* in a period and
section of Scotland where vestiges of old ways of life made for an
atmosphere of quaintness. Without too much forcing, he makes
his hero's first impressions of the Highlands convincingly "romantic." When Edward first approaches the village of Tully-

Veolan, he notices that "the houses seemed miserable in the extreme, especially to an eye accustomed to the smiling neatness of English cottages. They stood, without any respect for regularity. . . ." An old woman, rushing out to rescue one of the children lying about "almost in a primitive state of nakedness," resembles to Edward "a sibyl in frenzy" (CH. VIII). His own disposition leans toward the idyllic as against the primitive and the rugged. He obviously prefers the grounds of the Bradwardine estate: "The solitude and repose of the whole scene seemed almost monastic, and Waverley . . . walked slowly down the avenue, enjoying the grateful and cooling shade, and so much pleased with the placid ideas of rest and seclusion excited by this confined and quiet scene, that he forgot the misery and dirt of the hamlet he had left behind him" (CH. VIII). His experience at Tully-Veolan shows his tendency to escape from sordid reality into a dream world, and at the same time anticipates his disillusionment with the world of romance once he sees it up close.

Most of the characters in the Highlands have the fascination of romance. The people whom Edward meets at first are "originals." The commanding officer of the regiment he joins has been converted to religious enthusiasm, and "this singular and mystical circumstance gave Colonel Gardiner a peculiar and solemn interest in the eyes of the young soldier" (CH. VII). The first person whom Edward happens to encounter at Bradwardine Manor is the "innocent" Davie Gellatley with his "wild, unsettled, irregular expression," in which "the simplicity of the fool was mixed with the extravagance of a crazed imagination" (CH. IX). Davie, while a vivid and convincing character in his own right, stands also as a symbol of the distorted fancy and immature mind of the hero. Among the leading characters, the pedantic, Latin-spouting Baron Bradwardine and the Frenchified Fergus and Flora speak like the literary figures Edward is used to. Prince Charles Edward, with his continental polish, also "answered [young Waverley's] ideas of a hero of romance" (CH. XL). Indeed, with his cavalier manners and his bejeweled weapons, he is the living analogue of the French and Italian knights who have already awakened Waverley's boyish emulation.

In the early episodes Scott represents Edward's adolescent consciousness convincingly by externalizing his impressions vividly enough for the reader to share them. Unfortunately, young Waverley becomes so caught up in the hustle and bustle of the succeeding events that, like the typical Scott hero, he functions as a window where he should be a lens. This objective technique becomes a handicap in representing Edward's emotional growth, which is not adequately visualized through his sensibility but merely described. The two loves of his life—turbulent, rebellious Flora; cheerful, composed Rose Bradwardine—symbolize the conflict in his nature between the wild life of the imagination and the orderly life of the reason. Flora, who adds the element of strangeness to beauty, recognizes the essential incompatibility between them: "The real disposition of Waverley . . . notwithstanding his dreams of tented fields and military honour, seemed exclusively domestic" (CH. LII) .

We must take on faith Flora's testimony as to Edward's "real disposition," since it was beyond Scott's province as a novelist to bring the reader into his hero's mind. But we participate in Edward's disillusionment, thanks to Scott's vivid descriptive power. The empty bluster of Prince Charles Edward in his lost cause, the egoism and opportunism of Fergus Mac-Ivor, and the brigandage of his confederates disenchant us as well as Edward with his heroes. Stark scenes of rapine and destruction contrast with the lush sublimity of the Lorraine landscape: "A brief gleam of December's sun shone sadly on the broad heath [Culloden], which . . . exhibited dead bodies of men and horses, and the usual companions of war—a number of carrion-crows, hawks and ravens" (CH. LX) ; "The avenue was cruelly wasted [at Tully-Veolan]. Several large trees were felled, and left lying across the path; and the cattle of the villagers, and the more rude hoofs of dragoon horses, had poached into black mud the verdant turf which Waverley had so much admired" (CH. LXIII) . Such

sights teach Edward the "real history" of war. His delusions are
purged by life itself, not by books as with other "fair romance
readers." Within his romantic experience is contained the anti-
dote to his romanticism.

The crucial sign of Edward's conversion to the world of reason
is his growing admiration for and aiding of Colonel Talbot, who
stands in *Waverley*, like the Duke of Argyle in *The Heart of
Midlothian*, for the rational, enlightened soldier-statesman-
gentleman. Significantly, Colonel Talbot, who is responsible for
the destruction of Tully-Veolan, with all its romantic associations, eventually restores it to its new estate. Edward's marriage
to Rose Bradwardine thus symbolizes at once his reconciliation
to domestic realism in preference to heroic romanticism, the
union of the two nations that had been embroiled in a destruc-
tive civil war, and the old order yielding place to the new
dispensation. Torn between opposing influences—religious and
political—Edward Waverley is well named. He is not so much an
individual as a cultural archetype representing the transition
from the semifeudal eighteenth century to the civilized nineteenth century. This is what Scott himself represents as a
novelist.[37]

Scott's prescription as an anti-romancer for the cure of the
romantic introvert is to get into the rough and tumble, or into
"active, bustling scenes," as Mrs. West recommended to her
Arthur. But in a less turbulent age one must be satisfied with the
vicarious life of action. So readers are offered a second-best—the
Waverley Novels—the author as historian taking over the reins
of the coach driver. Among other things, young Edward Waverley is an aspiring writer, and he finds a collaborator in that
crotchety but good-hearted amateur antiquarian Baron Bradwardine. Shortly after Edward arrives in Tully-Veolan, the
Baron cordially extends his hospitality to his youthful guest by
guiding him about the countryside, just as Scott pretends to
conduct his readers around the Highlands. This tour also, we are
assured, is educational:

After this ceremony [a stag hunt] he conducted his guest homeward by a pleasant and circuitous route, commanding an extensive prospect of different villages and houses, to each of which Mr. Bradwardine attached some anecdote of history or genealogy, told in language whimsical from prejudice and pedantry, but often respectable for the good sense and honourable feelings which his narrative displayed, and almost always curious, if not valuable, for the information they contained. (CH. XIII)

Baron Bradwardine's tour combines pleasure and instruction in just about the measure that Scott hoped for in his novels. In fact, some of this description—"pleasant and circuitous," "extensive prospect," anecdotes of history or genealogy that are attached to various localities, language "whimsical from prejudice and pedantry," but replete with good sense, charity, and curious information—is applicable to *Waverley* and its successors. In a later novel Scott spoke of his own task as presenting "a lively fictitious picture for which the original anecdote or circumstance . . . only furnished a slight sketch."[38]

Baron Bradwardine's literary taste is staid, as distinguished from Edward's, confined pretty closely to the Latin didactic poets and the Scottish school as represented by Sir David Lindsay and George Buchanan. Even with these, "he would, if the truth must be spoken, have been much better pleased had the pious or sapient apothegms, as well as the historical narratives, which these various works contained, been presented to him in the form of simple prose." The Baron serves, of course, as counterweight to Edward, "warm in his feelings, wild and romantic in his ideas and in his taste of reading, with a strong disposition towards poetry." There is a point where these two opposed temperaments come together:

But although Edward and he differed *toto coelo,* as the Baron would have said, upon this subject, yet they met upon history as on a neutral ground, in which each claimed an interest. The Baron, indeed, only cumbered his memory with matters of fact; the cold, dry, hard outlines which history delineates. Edward, on the contrary, loved to fill up and round the sketch with the colouring of a warm and vivid imagination, which gives light and life to the actors and speakers in the drama of past ages. Yet with tastes so opposite, they contributed greatly to each other's amusement. Mr. Bradwardine's minute narratives and powerful memory supplied to Waverley fresh subjects of the kind upon which his fancy loved to labour, and opened to him a new mine of incident and character. (CH. XIII)

Baron Bradwardine's "matters of fact" supply the exact knowledge and information which, in the opinion of educators of this time, should precede the development of the imagination in the young. His "minute narratives" presumably supersede Sir Everard Waverley's tales of chivalry and Aunt Rachel's sentimental narratives in the interest of young Edward. Baron Bradwardine and Edward Waverley unite historical memory with imaginative temperament, and if Edward finds time to set down on paper any of these "fresh subjects of the kind upon which his fancy loved to labour," we would expect something much like the Waverley Novels to result. Edward's subsequent adventures furnish his mind with still more substantial material to work over, and undoubtedly it gratifies him to learn, when he is reunited with Uncle Everard and Aunt Rachel, that "the imagination of the Baronet and his sister ranked the exploits of Edward with those of Wilibert, Hildebrand, and Nigel, the vaunted heroes of their line" (CH. LXX). The "colouring of a warm and vivid imagination" is a means of bringing "light and life" to "the cold, dry, hard outlines which history delineates." Through the Baron and Edward, Scott may be reconciling his mature self with his youthful self; more to the point, through them he charts his course as a writer of fiction.

Scott was not so much the originator of the historical novel, as he is sometimes called, as he was its improver and developer. In his chapter on Edward's education he deplores the then current practice of making history appealing to young minds by reducing it to a game of cards. Scott prefers graphic description to visual aids. Nor was he fond of potted history for children in the manner of Madame de Genlis' *Tales of the Castle*. On the other hand, he knew well the pitfalls of pedantry. His attempt to complete the unfinished romance of Joseph Strutt, *Queenhoo Hall,* a tale laid in the reign of Henry VI, taught him that mere antiquarian lore did not suffice to bring a past age to life and that archaic language separates the author as well as his characters from readers.[39] Among those who set a direction for Scott in historical fiction was the omnipresent Jane West. She, in fact, took it upon herself to justify this emergent genre in her preface to *Alicia de Lacy,* a romance set in the period of the barons' revolt against King Edward II, where she rationalizes her practice of transforming real people into storybook heroes:

> Whatever objections may be made . . . against the lawfulness of thus bringing out an old worthy in masquerade, it is presumed that they will not be strongly urged by the admirers of Shakespeare's historical plays; or of Marmion, the Lady of the Lake and many other justly popular poems; or even of the epics of Homer and Virgil, which have delighted every age by giving enlarged portraits of those whose miniatures only were exhibited by history. It may surely then be premised, that the majority will, from principle, warmly defend this license as claimed by poetry, and by these the prose fabulist may probably be heard with favour, while urging a claim to the same liberty of building fiction on the basis of truth, and making past heroes and heroines talk in the language of common life, as they have been allowed to do in couplets and blank verse.

Mrs. West could just as well have been speaking for Scott, who was at this time moving into a more colloquial medium from poetry, in which he felt himself being superseded by Byron. "Under which King, Bezonian? speak or die!" reads the epigraph to *Waverley,* the first of a long series of tags from Shakespeare sprinkled through Scott's novels, an indication that he thought of himself as writing prose historical dramas. The reviewer of *Waverley* for the *Scots Magazine,* impressed by its author's lively narrative skill and intimate knowledge of the period covered, expressed the wish that this writer "had carried us through the whole series of the rebellion, in the same manner that he has done through this part of it." This reviewer was convinced that "besides the amusement afforded by such a narrative, it would have formed an important historical document, and would in some degree have supplied the lamentable failure of a poetical historian." The author of *Waverley* obliged subsequently by carrying his readers not only through "the whole series of the rebellion," but back to the Middle Ages, which at first he rejected as material for historical romance.

At the end of the first chapter of *Waverley*, Scott assures his readers that he wishes to avoid quaintness and period manner-isms by "throwing the force of my narrative upon the characters and passions of the actors;—those passions common to men in all stages of society, and which have alike agitated the human heart whether it throbbed under the steel corselet of the fifteenth century, the brocaded coat of the eighteenth, or the blue frock and white dimity waistcoat of the present day." Although he could hardly have been aware of it at the time, Scott was anticipating here a fictional panorama that was to extend from the "steel corselet" (*Ivanhoe, Quentin Durward, The Talisman*) to the "white dimity waistcoat" (*St. Ronan's Well*), taking in along the way the doublet and hose (*The Monastery, The Abbot, Kenil-worth, The Fortunes of Nigel*) and cavalier cape (*Peveril of the Peak, Woodstock*), as well as the "brocaded coat" (*Guy Manner-ing, The Heart of Midlothian, Redgauntlet*). Scott did indeed make up for "the lamentable failure of a poetical historian" so far as his generation was concerned. In this respect *Waverley* was a transition, as indicated some years later in the preface to *Redgauntlet,* in which Scott dealt once more with the Jacobite insurrection. "The Highlanders who formed the principal strength of Charles Edward's army were an ancient and high-spirited race," wrote Scott, "peculiar in their habits of war and peace, brave to romance, and exhibiting a character turning upon points more adapted to poetry than to the prose of real life." With *Waverley,* as Scott seems to have realized in retrospect, he was adapting the historical romance, along with his hero Edward, to the "prose of real life."[40]

Like Jane Austen, Scott ventured into fiction as a scoffer at the art in which he was destined to gain celebrity. Both authors demolished to rebuild. Miss Austen has a character declare in *Northanger Abbey* that the novel at its best is a form of writing where "the greatest powers of mind are displayed." Scott seems to have remained unsure of the dignity of his calling, or so one gathers from his constant pose as annalist, chronicler, or editor—anything but simply a teller of tales—as well as the anonymity he clung to until *The Chronicles of the Canongate* of 1827. "Unstable as water, he shall not excel. . . . He goeth to dancing-houses, and readeth novels—*sat est*," says Saunders Fairford to his son Alan, warning him not to follow in the footsteps of the romantic Darsie Latimer *(Redgauntlet,* LETTER II). But if Judge Fairford speaks for the eighteenth-century gentleman's prejudice against prose fiction, which died hard (to judge by the paucity of reviews of fiction in *The Gentleman's Magazine)*, one has the feeling that in his novels Scott was playing devil's advocate for Darsie Latimer.

Fiction of course remained under attack even while Scott was at the peak of his success, as is evident from the appearance of Anti-Romances like Peacock's *Nightmare Abbey,* Crabbe's *Tales of the Hall,* and an anonymous satire, *The Authoress,* almost simultaneously with the posthumous publication of *Northanger Abbey.* The wheel may be said to have come full circle in 1824 with another diatribe by Mrs. Sarah Green called *Scotch Novel Reading,* in which this time the heroine is cured of an addiction to "the author of Waverley"! This romantic young lady, having steeped herself in the Waverley Novels, dresses in kilts and Highland bonnet with black plumes, curtsies in the style of Helen Macgregor, calls her maid Jenny [sic] Deans, talks in Scotch dialect, and compels her father to eat haggis. She is supposedly purged of the "Caledonian Mania" when her lover disguises himself as a descendant of Rob Roy in sloppy warrior's garb and patch over one eye, and convinces her that Highlanders were a gruff and ugly lot. It is clear that Scotch novels were crowding out Mrs. Green's English novels from popular esteem.[41]

Since the same year of Mrs. Green's attack saw the publication of two more of Scott's Scotch novels, *St. Ronan's Well* and *Redgauntlet*, as well as the production of Edward Boaden's dramatization of *Waverley*, it is obvious that readers in general were not sharing the disillusionment of Alice Fennell, the fair romance reader in *Scotch Novel Reading*. Scott's public remained loyal and enthusiastic, if not always uncritical. After *Waverley* he ceases to be the aggressive anti-romanticist. Having exposed the follies of the "uncorrected" imagination, he continues his readers' education by showing them how imagination well stored with fact can revive past ages and make them yield their exempla for the living as well as for the generations yet unborn.

In our day when Scott is associated with much that is fusty and artificial, it is well to be reminded of what he meant to those who came to him fresh. "Reason neither sleeps nor slumbers at her post while we peruse," observed a reviewer of one of his later novels, "but is perpetually giving us those jogs and shakes which summon us from the dreams of fancy to the dull realities and sober certainties of existence."[42] Scott seems to have an effect, at least on his more alert readers, similar to the impact of the Battle of Culloden upon Edward Waverley. Reality to him, however, was not necessarily dull and sober, as another contemporary critic testifies who described him as a genius at "dramatic or picturesque representations."[43] His well known affinities for painting and theatre led Coleridge to denounce his technique as "false effect and stage trick,"[44] but for Scott they were an approach to literal truth. He envied the ability of the artist to "present a visible and tangible representation of his towns and woods, his palaces and his castles";[45] his frequent graphic analogies indicate his desire to emulate this power.[46] Likewise, he thought it both a handicap and a challenge to the novelist that, unlike the dramatist, he "has neither stage nor scene painter, nor company of comedians, nor dresser, nor wardrobe."[47] It followed for Scott that the writer must supply the verbal equivalent of these crafts. Hence he "sets" his scenes with special care, clothes his characters thoroughly, and even indicates their gestures explicitly. With his penchant for picture and spectacle, Scott was preeminently the writer for the *eye*—at once his strength and his limitation.

The range of Scott's genius was confined mainly to the observable and the verifiable. He leaned largely on portraits and the lore of physiognomy for his characterization. His most successful characters were likely to be those based on life (as with his peasants and professionals) or on history (as with his kings and some of his nobles). His true bent as a writer is revealed in a letter to a friend, the year before *Waverley* was published, where he confides his desire to write a history of *causes célèbres* based on "the criminal records of Scotland." These documents, he points out, "joined to the peculiarity of manners the custom or rule of taking down the whole evidence in writing which prevailed till within these thirty years afforded complete materials for such a selection which by the way I have often thought of."[48] If, with the success of *Waverley*, Scott changed his vocation, the instincts of the lawyer and the antiquarian never left him. Records, evidence, and documents remained the lodestones of his intellectual curiosity, and his return to biography, history, and editing even while busily composing novels indicates that the chronicler dominated over the romancer in him. The most memorable portions of his novels—the panoramic descriptions, the pageants, the living portraits—really move him more in the direction of Macaulay than in that of, say, the Thackeray of *Henry Esmond*. Scott's affinities seem to have been more with Lopez de Ayala, Froissart, and Clarendon than with Cervantes, Le Sage, and Fielding.

The main effect of Scott's accretion of tangible data of all sorts—architectural, sartorial, topographical, legal, medical, and military—was to move the novel into the realm of the actual— "the cumbrousness and temporality . . . in short the materialism which is characteristic of the world," as Walter Bagehot described the texture of the Waverley Novels.[49] Historical fiction deteriorated into rhetoric with Bulwer, melodrama with Ainsworth, antiquarianism with G. P. R. James, and polemics with Charles Kingsley. With a few notable exceptions historical novelists after Scott lacked his eye, ear, historical memory, and precise scholarship. But his documentary technique applied to the contemporary world made for the amplitude and plenitude of the Victorian novel, its spaciousness and populousness and its intense rendering of environment. His great successors, like him, were mockers and improvers, seeking to counteract false fiction with true, bringing art in touch with "common life" by a more detailed notation of experience. With Dickens and Thackeray the novelist enters modern urban life. With Charlotte Brontë and George Eliot we probe aspects of professional life and regions of the mind and psyche that Scott avoided. All of these later novelists also extended the function of the author in various ways. But they built on foundations that Scott laid down. He reestablished the respectability of fiction by bringing to it an erudition that placed it on a level with biography, history, moral philosophy, and sermons and by demonstrating its educational value. Many a Victorian, including all the novelists treated in the following pages, read him in childhood and reread him as adults. As we have recently been reminded, "To have been alive and literate in the nineteenth century was to have been affected in some way by the Waverley novels."[50]

CHARACTERISTIC FICTION CONTEMPORANEOUS WITH *WAVERLEY* (1814)

1796 William Beckford, *Modern Novel Writing; or, The Elegant Enthusiast.*

1799 Mary Charlton, *Rosella; or, Modern Occurrences.*

1800 Maria Edgeworth, *Castle Rackrent.*

1801 Maria Edgeworth, *Angelina; ou l'Amie Inconnue* (in *Moral Tales*).

1805 William Godwin, *Fleetwood.*

1806 Matthew Gregory ("Monk") Lewis, *Feudal Tyrants; or, The Monks of Carlsheim and Sargans.* A Romance. Taken from the German.

Amelia Opie, *Adeline Mowbray; or, The Mother and Daughter.*

Sydney Owenson (Lady Morgan), *The Wild Irish Girl.*

Thomas Skinner Surr, *The Mask of Fashion; A Plain Tale, with Anecdotes Foreign and Domestic.*

1807 Henrietta Rouviere Mosse, *A Peep at Our Ancestors.* An Historical Romance.

Sir Charles Sedley, *The Barouche Driver and His Wife.* A Tale for Haut-Ton.

1808 Mrs. Sarah Green, *The Private History of the Court of England.*

Elizabeth Hamilton, *The Cottagers of Glenburnie.*

Charles Robert Maturin, *The Wild Irish Boy.*

[Anon.] *The Noble Cornutos.* Being a Series of Tales for the Amusement of the Fashionable World.

1810 John Agg, *The Royal Sufferer; or Intrigues at the Close of the Eighteenth Century.*

Peter Middleton Darling, *The Romance of the Highlands.*

Mrs. Sarah Green, *Romance Readers and Romance Writers.*

Ann Hatton (Ann of Swansea), *Cambrian Pictures.*

Jane Porter, *The Scottish Chiefs.*

1812 Mrs. Byron, *The Borderers.* An Historical Romance Illustrative of Manners of the Fourteenth Century.

Charles Robert Maturin, *The Milesian Chief.* A Romance.

Mrs. Jane West, *The Loyalists.* An Historical Romance.

1813 Eaton Stannard Barrett, *The Heroine; or, The Fair Romance Reader.* (In 1814 the subtitle was changed to *The Adventures of Cherubina.*)

1814 Mrs. Frazer (Honoria Scott), *The Castle of Strathmay; or, Scenes in the North Illustrative of Scotch Manners and Society.*

Sydney Owenson (Lady Morgan), *O'Donnell: A National Tale.*

Mrs. Jane West, *Alicia de Lacy.* An Historical Romance.

CHAPTER III

Mansfield Park:

Fanny Price and the Christian Heroine

ONE OF THE EARLIEST readers of Scott's first novel was a then less celebrated genius who had recently brought out her third novel. "Walter Scott has no business to write novels, especially good ones. It is not fair. He has fame and profit enough as a poet, and should not be taking the bread out of the mouths of other people," wrote Jane Austen to a niece. "I do not like him, & do not mean to like 'Waverley' if I can help it, but fear I must."[1] *Mansfield Park,* published two months before *Waverley,* seems to inhabit a wholly different world, but the two novels are equally concerned with proper early lessons and the difficult rites of passage of the young into maturity. Life proves a difficult school for young Fanny Price as for Edward Waverley, although her discipline is a quieter one. The subdued tone and dignity of *Mansfield Park* that distinguish it from Miss Austen's other novels are anticipated in a letter she wrote to her sister Cassandra regarding its predecessor, *Pride and Prejudice:* "The work is rather too light and bright and sparkling; it wants shade; it wants to be stretched out here and there with a long chapter of sense, if it could be had."[2] Having done penance in *Mansfield*

Park for her frivolity in *Pride and Prejudice,* she reverted to the light touch in her next book, but with some misgivings. Her gift copy of *Emma* to the Reverend J. S. Clarke, librarian and chaplain to the Prince Regent, was accompanied by a note of apology: "I am strongly haunted by the idea that to those readers who have preferred 'Pride and Prejudice' it will appear inferior in wit; and to those who have preferred 'Mansfield Park' inferior in good sense."[3]

Miss Austen clearly regarded *Mansfield Park* as something special in her work, as did the Reverend Mr. Clarke, who had written to her shortly before she sent him her gift: "Your late Works, Madam, and in particular Mansfield Park reflect the highest honour on your Genius & your Principles."[4] His respect for the "good sense" in this novel was not universally shared. Comments gathered by Miss Austen from her admiring circle of family and friends when *Mansfield Park* was fresh off the press anticipate some of the reactions of modern readers, particularly toward the hero and heroine. Her brother George disliked Fanny, was in fact "interested by nobody but Mary Crawford." Another brother, Edward, thought Edmund "cold and formal," preferred Henry Crawford, and thought his running off with Mrs. Rushworth "unnatural." Her niece Fanny Knight, on the other hand, was delighted with Fanny Price, but "wanted more love between her and Edmund." Her cousin Anna Lefroy liked *Mansfield Park* more than *Pride and Prejudice* but less than *Sense and Sensibility,* "could not bear Fanny," but was "delighted with Mrs. Norris, the scene at Portsmouth and all the humourous parts." Although presumably addressed to the marriageable generation, *Mansfield Park* seems to have been most appreciated by Miss Austen's older friends. Mr. and Mrs. Cooke sided with their contemporary the Reverend Mr. Clarke, being "very much pleased with it—particularly with the manner in which the Clergy are treated." Perhaps the most significant of these collected "Opinions of Mansfield Park" was that of the lady identified simply as Mrs. Carrick: "All who think deep & feel much will give the preference to Mansfield Park."[5]

Mansfield Park is undeniably the most serious and profound of Jane Austen's six completed novels. Even its wit seems stern, not playful and mocking as in *Sense and Sensibility* and *Pride and Prejudice,* directed at moral flaws, not mere foibles. Among modern critics, Lionel Trilling recognizes the crucial importance in the ethical scheme of the book of the conflict between Fanny and Mary over Edmund's taking orders.[6] The unusual religious emphasis of *Mansfield Park* leads Trilling, quite rightly, to place Fanny Price in the lost tradition of the Christian Heroine, but it is hardly necessary to push back half a century to Richardson's Clarissa and Fielding's Amelia, as he does, to find her literary sisters. Unlike Clarissa, Fanny is being prepared for a Christian life, not a Christian martyrdom, and for her less turbulent fate Jane Austen had many prototypes closer at hand. It is not "the peculiar sanctity of the sick, the weak and the dying," as Trilling assumes, that is lauded in *Mansfield Park,* but the blessedness of the meek—and the firm.[7]

"Miss Austen's way in fiction was not easy, for she moved against the current," according to another critic.[8] The outright parody in *Love and Freindship* and *Volume the First,* the subtler satire in *Sense and Sensibility* and *Northanger Abbey,* and even the irony in *Pride and Prejudice* may move against the current of the eighteenth century of Jane Austen's girlhood, but *Mansfield Park* moves with the current of the early nineteenth century of her mature years. *Northanger Abbey* is best enjoyed after a dosage of Mrs. Ann Radcliffe, Regina Maria Roche, and Eleanor Sleath, just as *Sense and Sensibility* is most fully savored after a dousing in *Tears of Sensibility, Sympathy of Souls,* and *Exhibitions of the Heart. Pride and Prejudice* can be read with reward as an anti-*Evelina* or anti-*Cecilia. Mansfield Park,* however, is rooted in the more hallowed tradition of the religious-didactic novel that raised its peremptory voice during the decade before the Regency. One gets the impression that England then had need of the evangelicals.

The period just before Jane Austen's novels were published is remembered, with good reason, more for poetry than for fiction. The publisher Charles Knight, in his reminiscences, looked back in horror from mid-Victorian times to the bookstalls of this age, which "for the young would offer the worst sort of temptation in sixpenny Novels with a coloured frontispiece; whose very titles would invite to a familiarity with the details of crime—of murder and adulteries, of violence and fraud, of licentiousness revelling in London, and innocence betrayed in the country."[9] Apart from the Penny Dreadfuls which are always among us in some form or other, the bibliography in Dorothy Blakey's *The Minerva Press* gives us a good idea of the sort of literary fare offered to the adult middle-class and upper-class reader of this age. Between the death of Smollett and the emergence of Scott, that astute literary merchant William Lane and his famous press in Leadenhall Street accounted for the greater part of circulating-library fiction: "those scanty intellectual viands of the whole female reading public," as Charles Lamb put it in "The Sanity of True Genius." "Few authors whose reputation has endured until to-day have owned to a connection with the Minerva Press," writes Miss Blakey, even while trying to rescue a minority of the horde of the "forgotten favorites" from total oblivion.

The seven Northanger Novels, we now know, thanks to Michael Sadleir, were all publications of the Minerva Press.[10] Their overwrought romanticism was deflated not only in Jane Austen's satire, but in various other anti-romances we have noticed, such as "Angelina, ou l'Amie Inconnue," and *The Fair Romance Reader* and, incidentally, in *Waverley*. However, the fact that the Minerva Press published one of these satires, Mary Charlton's *Rosella, or Modern Occurrences,* indicates that Lane was not averse to publishing the "improving" sort of fiction. One of his publications in fact was the lofty *Celia in Search of a Husband* (1809) by Medora Gordon Byron, about which a reviewer declared: "All the fashionable absurdities of the day are neatly satirized, and the modern London fine-world is here drawn with exactness, and exhibited, as it ought to be, not as an object of envy, but of disgust; for life in London is, indeed, *wasted*, not *used*."[11] Such writers as Miss Byron directed their crusade against contemporary society, rather than the shadowlands of the Gothic fable.

Mrs. Gore makes the hero of *Cecil; or, The Adventures of a Coxcomb* remark about this period from the vantage point of the 1830's: "If there was little good writing in London during the first half dozen years of the nineteenth century, there was a prodigious quantity of good talking" (CH. III). Some of this alleged "good talking" made its way into the popular scandal chronicles deplored by Scott. The dissoluteness of the society gathered around the Prince Regent was exposed by numerous writers ready to exploit any opportunity to titillate their readers under the guise of edifying them. One of the more notorious books of the time, published in the same year as *Sense and Sensibility*, was Captain Thomas Ashe's *The Spirit of the Book; or, Memoirs of Caroline of Hasburgh: A Political and Amatory Romance*, purporting to be letters from Queen Caroline to Princess Charlotte, defending her conduct. A gossip monger like Henrietta Moriarty, author of *Brighton in an Uproar* (1811) and *Crim-Con* (1812), justified her unsavory subjects by avowing to her readers in a preface that "my best endeavours have been used to promote the cause of Virtue, and to point out the true basis of Domestic Felicity." Mrs. Sarah Green's earlier *A Private History of the Court of England* (1808) made public contemporary court intrigues under the thin veil of a chronicle placed in the reign of Edward IV. Probably this subterfuge was intended for self-protection, but the author makes her work out to be a warning to her own age.

Considering the reputation of London at this time, it is not surprising that the more serious novelists shunned the capital. Their novels seem to have been intended to confirm Cowper's

pronouncement: "God made the country; man made the town."
Maria Edgeworth reflects a typical attitude in her *Tales of
Fashionable Life,* which were intended to expose the artificiality
and hollowness of urban society. Jane Austen was hardly alone in
keeping her heroines in the country. Lucilla Stanley, the ideal
young lady of Hannah More's *Coelebs in Search of a Wife,* is
well protected against the contamination of London in her
Hampshire estate. The heroines of other typical novelists of the
decade like Laetitia Matilda Hawkins and Mary Balfour
Brunton are equally sheltered, so that their belated introduction
to city life becomes almost a shattering experience. A recurrent
theme in these novels that brings us close to *Mansfield Park* is the
disillusionment of the pious, innocent young girl with the way of
life of her supposed social superiors.

Whether or not *Mansfield Park* was an immediate success (it
seems to have been overshadowed in the popular reviews by
Maria Edgeworth's *Patronage* and Fanny Burney's *The Wanderer,* both published almost simultaneously with it), it could
not have seemed out of place either in subject matter or tone
next to what the literate public was then reading. The early
episodes of *Mansfield Park,* in which Fanny Price is plunged into
a program of instruction alongside her more privileged cousins
Maria and Julia Bertram, reflect the strong interest during this
period—in fiction and nonfiction alike—in Female Education. In
Emma Jane Austen refers to establishments "which professed, in
long sentences of refined nonsense, to combine liberal acquirements with elegant morality, upon new principles and new
systems." The age was dominated, as she well knew, by Hannah
More, Mrs. Carter, Sarah Trimmer, Mrs. Barbauld, and Joanna
Baillie, to name only the best remembered system builders. Two
of Miss More's popular titles, *Strictures on the Modern System of
Female Education* (six editions in 1799, the year of its publication) and *Hints towards Forming the Character of a Young
Princess* (1805), indicate the appeal to refined circles of schemes
of mental and moral development. Sometimes these schemes took

the more intimate form of letters of advice, such as Dr. Gregory's much reprinted best seller of 1774, *A Father's Legacy to His Daughters,* whose vogue lasted long enough to be read by Maggie Tulliver. Hester Chapone's *Letters on the Improvement of the Mind,* first published in 1773, was still current in the nineteenth century, as Mrs. Gaskell makes evident in *Cranford.*[12]

Ideas on Female Education inevitably filtered down into the fiction of the period, since much of it was written by educators like Maria Edgeworth, Hannah More, and Jane West. The bluestocking mother of Amelia Opie's heroine Adeline Mowbray becomes infected with the zeal: "All Mrs. Mowbray's ambition had settled in one point, one passion, and that was EDUCATION. For this purpose she turned over innumerable volumes in search of rules on the subject, on which she might improve, anticipating with great satisfaction the moment when she might be held up as a pattern of imitation to mothers, and be prevailed upon, though with grateful reluctance, to publish her system without a name for the benefit of society" (CH. 1). Ironically, while engaged in her system building, she is as neglectful a mother as Lady Bertram: "lost in some new speculations for the good of her child, she would lie in bed all morning, exposing that child to the dangers of idleness." Mrs. Mowbray is the kind of model mother who reads closely reasoned treatises on whether light or heavy shoes are best for a child's development while her Adeline goes barefoot. The "passion" for education that was perverted by Mrs. Mowbray could, by implication, be properly directed. Mrs. Opie is arguing really that what the young primarily need is not rules and principles, but active guidance aided by the living example of their elders—the leading theme of much of the cautionary literature contemporaneous with Jane Austen.

Even the much condemned and satirized Minerva Press authoresses claimed serious didactic purposes. The subtitle of Ann of Swansea's *Cambrian Pictures* is *Every One Has Errors.* Mrs. Parsons, author of one of the "Northanger Novels," *The Castle of Wolfenbach,* is proclaimed on the title page as responsible also

for *Errors of Education* and *Woman as She Should Be.* Eleanor
Sleath, whose *The Orphan of the Rhine* was also read by Isabella
Thorpe and her friend Catherine Morland, later offered her
public *The Bristol Heiress; or, The Errors of Education.* The
youthful Shelley presumed to act as parents' assistant in his two
rather hectic romances. *Zastrozzi,* written in close imitation of
Charlotte Dacre's *Zofloya, or the Moor,* has the avowed moral
purpose of showing the defeat of reason by passion, as illustrated
by the wilful heroine Victoria, nobly born but brought up in
decadent society by her corrupt mother. In his Rosicrucian fable
St. Irvyne, modeled on Godwin's *St. Leon,* we are informed that
the character of the heroine Olympia "has been ruined by a false
system of education."

Among eminent education writers then in vogue, Jane Austen
appears to have been particularly acquainted with Elizabeth
Hamilton, the "respectable Writer" mentioned by her in a letter
to Cassandra.[13] At the time when *Mansfield Park* was in process
of composition, Mrs. Hamilton was emphasizing in her widely
read *Popular Essays* the importance of "extending the benefits of
education to the lower orders of society."[14] She had already
illustrated her thesis in her charming novel *The Cottagers of
Glenburnie,* in which she tried to enlist sympathy for the neglected "lower orders" among the Scottish peasantry. Her educational theories accordingly stress the original powers of the mind
shared by all humanity. Believing that spontaneous curiosity is
more effectual than enforced instruction, Mrs. Hamilton emphasizes the cultivation of the faculties of perception, observation,
and taste in preference to memory. "Will all the wisdom that a
child can gain from books, will all the lessons he can learn from
masters, compensate to him for losing the power of perceiving all
that is placed before his eyes?" she asks her readers. Parents and
teachers are admonished: "In the anxiety for improving the
mind by knowledge, and for storing the memory with facts and
observations, persons of excellent sense are apt to forget, that by

directing the attention exclusively to such objects, they cripple and destroy that faculty on whose exertions their children must ultimately depend for the acquirement of new ideas."[15]

In this respect, Fanny Price clearly has the advantage, from the outset, over her wealthy cousins. If they were well primed with Mrs. Hamilton, readers knew what to think of Maria and Julia Bertram, who lord it over Fanny because they can repeat the chronology of the Roman Emperors and the Kings of England, and perform other such feats of mere memory. Because Fanny is not up to these tasks, her cousins and her tutor think her stupid. Edmund Bertram is more perceptive: "He knew her to be clever, to have a quick apprehension, as well as good sense, and a fondness for reading, which, properly directed, must be an education in itself" (CH. II). Miss Austen stresses not only the greater importance of innate ability over what the age called "accomplishments." She also appears to believe strongly, along with many educators of her time, in the value of exemplary teaching. When she writes, "To the education of her daughters Lady Bertram paid not the smallest attention. She had not time for such cares," she is preparing readers early for the moral flabbiness of the Bertram daughters. Probably the supine Lady Bertram would have done more harm than good had she interfered in her daughters' regimen, but unfortunately she exercises no judgment either in her choice of tutor. Fanny is more fortunate than her cousins: "[Edmund's] attentions were . . . of the highest importance in assisting the improvement of her mind, and extending its pleasures." Miss Austen is not very explicit about the curriculum, but she implies value judgments: "Miss Lee taught her French [the better to enable her to read Marmontel, *La Nouvelle Heloise,* and *Delphine,* which young ladies should not know], and heard her read the daily portion of History [probably straight out of Mangnall's *Questions*]; but he recommended the books which charmed her leisure hours, he encouraged her taste, and corrected her judgment; he made reading useful by talking to her of what she read, and heightened the attraction by judicious praise" (CH. II). So Fanny is encouraged to cultivate her active faculties, thereby, as Miss Hamilton phrased it, "blending the intellectual and moral powers in one simultaneous operation."

Edmund, like Edward Waverley with Rose Bradwardine, takes over the tutelage of his future bride, but he seems more devoted to the task. After Fanny's formal education ceases, he continues to stand by—to "refine" her taste and "correct" her judgment. Fanny's guided reading program, for one thing, proceeds for some time: "How does Lord Macartney go on? [His *Authentic Account of an Embassy to the Emperor of China* is apparently a better way to "extend the pleasures" of the mind than *Tales of the East*]. . . . And here are Crabbe's *Tales* [taken from "real life"][16] and *The Idler,* at hand to relieve you if you tire of your great book" (CH. XVI). The *Quarterly Review* lies about conspicuously in the morning room. Edmund has guided Fanny's taste well, as we note in her revulsion at the play *Lovers' Vows* (by Kotzebue) that so charms the Crawfords and the Bertram girls. She also turns away from *Douglas* and *The Gamester* to take up Shakespeare.

Fanny's reading has a certain practicality about it, not out of keeping with the ideas of contemporary educators, who tended to think of literature as an approach to the appreciation of the everyday world rather than as vicarious pleasure or as stimulus to the imagination. "Mix in the world, copy living instead of imaginary beings, and study the customs of actual, not ideal society," is Stuart's advice to the chastened Cherubina. Edmund is not so extreme, but he tends also to subordinate literature to life, to judge by Fanny's literary taste, which, unlike that of her creator, does not tend much toward novels. Her preference, so far as it is made explicit, seems to be for poetry and biography. If poetry disposes her toward meditation of God's works, biography enhances her appreciation of noble character when she perceives it around her. The main effect on Fanny of the reading she accomplishes under Edmund's tutelage is to make her emulate

her mentor: "She regarded her cousin as an example of everything good and great, as possessing worth, which no one but
herself could ever appreciate. . . ." (CH. IV).

Fanny's education purposely is not confined to books. Whether
or not Edmund read Elizabeth Hamilton, he must certainly have
agreed with her that the proper development of taste "can only
be attained by extensive observation, and an intimate acquaintance not only with the works of genius, but with the nature of
those associations by which the sympathies and affections of the
heart are influenced in the perception of beauty. . . ."[17] Fanny's
famous rhapsody on Nature embarrasses some readers: "Here's
harmony . . . here's repose! Here's what may leave all painting
and all music behind, and what poetry can only attempt to describe! Here's what may tranquilise every care, and lift the heart
to rapture!" (CH. XI). But her speech, if it seems a little childish
in its exuberance, reveals an expanding sensibility. At this point
Fanny is being contrasted with the Bertram daughters and with
Mary Crawford, all of whom show up as immature by comparison. Where their field of vision is contracted within the drawing
room, hers extends outward to take in the whole creation; where
they are dazzled by art and artifice, her eyes are trained directly
on the sources of real beauty. A guiding hand is evident here too,
for in response to Edmund's beaming approval Fanny replies:
"You taught me to think and feel on the subject, cousin."

For Miss More, Mrs. Hamilton, and other female educators,
conversation and mingling in society were of equal value with
reading, if not more valuable, as a source of knowledge about
human nature. Fanny Price's education, significantly, includes
frequent opportunities to observe and discuss the people she
meets: "Well, Fanny, and how do you like Miss Crawford *now?*
. . . How did you like her yesterday? . . . Is it her countenance
that is so attractive? She has a wonderful play of feature! But was
there nothing in her conversation that struck you, Fanny, as not
quite right?" (Edmund, CH. VII); "Since the day at Sotherton,
she could never see Mr. Crawford with either sister without

observation, and seldom without wonder or censure . . . had she been sure that she was seeing clearly and judging candidly, she would probably have made some important communication to her usual confidant" (CH. XII). Here Fanny applies her faculties of observation and perception in a way Elizabeth Hamilton would commend. It is of course her sense of Edmund's worth that gives her the measure by which to judge Henry Crawford and others; in fact, Fanny soon outdistances her teacher in the quick assessment of character, a source of embarrassment to her when Henry Crawford comes wooing.

Not only Fanny and Edmund but practically everybody in *Mansfield Park* seems to be at some time or other a pupil or an amateur educator. As a student Fanny is contrasted first with the Bertrams, then with the Crawfords. We know what to expect of Henry and Mary when we are informed that not only were they the offspring of a second marriage, but they were subsequently brought up by a roustabout seafaring uncle who took a mistress into the house immediately after his wife's death. "The Admiral's lessons have quite spoiled him," is Mary's own comment on her brother (CH. IV). (These are not exactly the kind of "Early Lessons" Maria Edgeworth would have approved.) Shortly afterward Mary's sister Mrs. Grant remarks to her: "Ah! You have been in a bad school for matrimony in Hill Street" (CH. V). Much later, when Fanny complains of Henry Crawford's lack of seriousness, Edmund remarks candidly, if somewhat condescendingly: "How could it be otherwise, with such an education and adviser? Under the disadvantages, indeed, which both have had, is it not wonderful that they should be what they are?" (CH. XXXV).

Obviously Edmund does not consider Henry irretrievable, for he objects not to Henry's attentions to Fanny, only to Henry's approach: "Between us, I think we should have won you. My theoretical and his practical knowledge together, could not have failed. He should have worked upon my plans" (CH. XXXV). So Fanny remains the object of "plans" and "schemes" long after she is out of Miss Lee's supervison. Even Sir Thomas justifies sending Fanny back to Portsmouth as though he were a disciple of Pestalozzi: "It was a medicinal project upon his niece's understanding, which he must consider at present diseased. A residence of eight or ten years in the abode of wealth and plenty had a little disordered her powers of comparing and judging. Her father's house would in all probability, teach her the value of a good income; and he trusted that she would be the wiser and happier woman, all her life, for the experiment he had devised" (CH. XXXVII). The ultimate result of Sir Thomas' "experiment" is that Fanny herself becomes a teacher, passing on the benefits of her education at Mansfield Park to her sister Susan. In the process, Fanny validates Mrs. Hamilton's belief that "Even by the inhabitant of the dusky city, imprisoned as he is by stone walls enveloped in smoke, the emotions of sublimity and beauty may doubtless be experienced in nearly as great perfection as by those who have enjoyed more ample opportunity of contemplating the sublime and beautiful in the works of nature. . . . To every heart in which the affections flow, sources are opened, whence this purest of pleasures may be derived."[18]

Mansfield Park thus becomes a grove of academe with an extension in Portsmouth. Under Edmund's tutelage Fanny is directed to the "works of nature," but she learns also to appreciate how these are enhanced by the works of man. Contemporary educators were fond of drawing an analogy between mental development and the cultivation of land, a correspondence suggested in *Mansfield Park* by polished conversations set against beautifully landscaped parks. Fanny herself, moved by the beauty of the Grants' shrubbery, exclaims to the apathetic Mary: "How wonderful, how very wonderful the operations of time, and the changes of the human mind!" (CH. XXII). She is thinking of the "improvement" that is very much discussed in the novel—improvement of land, improvement of houses, and, by implication, improvement of character. Henry Crawford's "scheme" for Edmund's seat at Thornton Lacey identifies the

owner with his property: "The air of a gentleman's residence
. . . you cannot but give it, if you do anything. But it is capable
of much more. . . .You may give it a higher character. You may
raise it into a *place*. From being the mere gentleman's residence,
it becomes, by judicious improvement, the residence of a man of
education, taste, modern manners, good connections" (CH.
XXV). Edmund looks at once for less and more. He is satisfied
with "rather less ornament and beauty," but, unlike Henry,
expects an estate to accommodate, besides a residence, a farm and
a chapel, and Fanny comes to agree with him. The mind of
Fanny is to Edmund what estates are to Henry Crawford, the
Rushworths, and many another eighteenth-century squire—soil
for "improvement." Contemporaries might have described Edmund's guidance, with particular aptness here, as *husbandry:*
"Having formed her mind and gained her affections, he had a
good chance of her thinking like him." As another religious
gentleman, Hannah More's Coelebs, observed about his Lucilla:
"I had . . . to observe a constant union of feeling as well as a
general consonancy of opinion between us. . . . I had always
considered that a conformity of tastes was as necessary to con-
jugal happiness, as a conformity of principles."

The title *Coelebs in Search of a Wife* enunciates another
theme implicit in *Mansfield Park*—the quest for the ideal life
partner. Fanny Price, as Mary Crawford is quick to observe, is
not "out," but the moral and intellectual discipline she undergoes in training for a Christian Heroine prepares her also for a
sanctified marriage. The opening paragraph of *Mansfield Park*
describes no less than three courtships and marriages:

> About thirty years ago, Miss Maria Ward of, Huntington, with only
> seven thousand pounds, had the good luck to *captivate* Sir Thomas
> Bertram, of Mansfield Park, in the county of Northampton, and to
> be thereby raised to the rank of a baronet's lady, with all the
> comforts and consequences of an handsome house and large
> income. . . . Miss Ward, at the end of half a dozen years, *found*

herself obliged to be attached to the Rev. Mr. Norris, a friend of her brother-in-law, with scarcely any private fortune . . . Miss Frances married, in the common phrase, *to disoblige her family*, and by fixing on a lieutenant of marines without education, fortune or connections, did it very thoroughly. She could hardly have made a more untoward choice. [Italics mine]

The three Ward sisters, Fanny's aunts and her mother, marry respectively men of high, middle, and low degrees—and all three marriages are rash and ill-considered. The marriage which the world would look on as the best is based on nothing more than materialism on one side, superficial enticement on the other. The other marriages are not merely economically imprudent but lack any basis in the affections. Sir Thomas is married for his worth— in the economic sense. The other spouses have neither material nor moral worth. None of the marriages represents that ideal union of the Spirit, Heart, and Understanding that Jane Austen sets forth in her letter of advice to her niece Fanny Knight.[19]

In view of the great vogue of Hannah More at this time, many of the first readers of *Mansfield Park* might well have regarded Edmund Bertram as still another variant of her much imitated hero Coelebs, whose ambition was to convert a Hampshire estate into a modern Eden with a domesticated and Christianized Eve. From all indications *Coelebs* was the most widely read novel of the first quarter of the nineteenth century, running up at least sixteen editions between its first publication in 1808 and 1826 (twelve of these during its first year). It sold out thirty editions in America. Another indication of its phenomenal vogue is the spate of imitations it engendered, such as *Celia in Search of a Husband, Celibia Chusing a Husband,* and *Caroline Ormsby; or, The Real Lucilla.* As one would expect, unauthorized "sequels" also emerged, such as *Coelebs Married* and *Coelebs Suited; or, The Opinions and Part of the Life of Caleb Coelebs, Esq.* Just as inevitably, it was parodied, an anonymous *Coelebs in Search of a Mistress* making its appearance just two years after Miss More's model lover began his courtship. Such was the popular fame of this Grandison figure that Mrs. Sarah Green in her *Scotch Novel Reading* (1824) could refer to the refined flirtation of her priggish young pedant Mr. Hartfield as "a Coelebs-like search."[20]

The hero of *Coelebs in Search of a Wife* is a young man of twenty-two now left free by the death of his mother, to whom he had been devoted, to travel all over England to seek a wife in her image. His story is told in the form of a journal in which he conscientiously records "conversations of interest" that he participates in or overhears in the course of his travels. His intention is to supplement the excellent education that he has gained from his father's library by learning what he can of human character as it emerges in social intercourse. Coelebs' entrance into society is in some ways disillusioning. He is surprised to learn that a supposedly educated young lady prefers the novels of "Rosa Matilda" to the poems of Virgil. At the home of an elegant London gentleman where he had been led to expect "the feast of reason and the flow of soul" he is disappointed that the guests are more preoccupied with physical food and drink. The lady of fashion, Mrs. Fentham, who lures men to her Park Lane mansion to look at her original Titians, confirms him in his contempt for the world, the flesh, and the city. But he does succeed in finding his ideal bride in the person of Lucilla Stanley, daughter of a pious country gentleman.

Coelebs himself is a sexagenarian spinster's idea of the perfect bridegroom. Handsome, wealthy, well-bred, educated, with a sympathetic heart and a refined conscience, he has all a woman could wish for—except flesh and blood. As for Lucilla, we must take the hero's word for it that her features represent "the joint triumph of intellect and sweet temper," since, out of deference to her elders, she rarely says anything. The people whom the hero meets are not so much characters as mouthpieces for the "Observations on Domestic Habits and Manners, Religion and Morals" promised by the subtitle of the book. *Coelebs* is really, strictly speaking, no novel at all, but, as the *Edinburgh Review* rightly called it, "a dramatic sermon."[21] Coelebs himself warns his readers in his prefatory remarks not to expect any excitement in the narrative that follows: "The generality of these characters move in the quiet and regular course of domestic life," he points out. Furthermore, "Great passions . . . and great trials growing out of them . . . I have not attempted to delineate. Love itself appears in these pages, not as an ungovernable impulse, but as a sentiment arising out of the qualities calculated to inspire attachment in persons under the dominion of reason and religion. . . ." Coelebs could not be accused of making false inducements, but he certainly did not discourage readers. The *Gentleman's Magazine* undoubtedly was speaking for a good many of them when it declared: "When pure, sound morality and unaffected benevolence are so pleasingly illustrated, it is sufficient to make us in love with virtue."[22] The contemporary reader is more likely to find himself in agreement with the critic for the *Edinburgh Review* who complained: "Events there are none; and scarcely a character of any interest. . . . Lucilla is totally uninteresting; so is Mr. Stanley . . . and Coelebs is a mere clod or dolt."

If *Coelebs* fails as a novel it can nevertheless command a certain respect as a personified courtesy book. Its author was almost totally devoid of imagination and deficient in a sense of humor, but she was not without caustic wit and common sense. Although her leading characters are little more than bundles of abstract virtues, those figures meant to exemplify various vices and foibles are somehow endowed with personality. One gathers that Miss More was well acquainted not only with true Christians but with the Laodiceans of her day,—as represented in *Coelebs* by nominal, easygoing, churchgoing gentry like the Belfields—and the Pharisees, like the fanatical and rabid Mrs. Ranby, and the gloomy Aston family morbidly obsessed with sin and death. Some social hypocrisies also are neatly touched off: the sparrow-brained Miss Rattle, who "demonstrates the faults of superficial education addressed merely to memory, vanity and love of accomplishment"; the fashionable Lady Denham, who "can detect blemishes in the most perfect," and her counterpart Lady Melbury, who "finds perfections in the most depraved"; the aggressive and wealthy Amazon Miss Sparkes, who is "charitable with her purse, but not with her tongue . . . relieves her poor neighbours, and indemnifies herself by slandering her rich ones."

Coelebs in Search of a Wife, that is to say, for all its longueurs and stiffness, was not intellectually beneath Jane Austen's notice. She was, in fact, aware of it and apparently at least skimmed it, but her recorded remarks on the book are characteristically impish and ambiguous. "You have by no means raised my curiosity after Caleb," she wrote to her sister Cassandra, shortly after this work was first published. "My disinclination for it before was affected, but now it is real; I do not like the Evangelicals." But this sting is followed by a drop of honey: "Of course I shall be delighted, when I read it, like other people, but till I do I dislike it."[23] We do not know what she told Cassandra afterward, but we do know that she had some second thoughts about "the Evangelicals." A few years later she wrote to her niece Fanny Knight, advising her to accept her religious suitor: "I am by no means convinced that we ought not all to be Evangelicals, & am at least persuaded that they who are so from Reason and Feeling, must be happiest & safest."[24] These words were written during the year when *Mansfield Park* was published. Miss More "endeavours to show how religion may be brought to mix with the concerns of ordinary life, without impairing its activity, lessening its cheerfulness, or diminishing its usefulness," as does Miss Austen in *Mansfield Park.*

Certainly the characters of *Mansfield Park* would not feel out of place in the atmosphere of *Coelebs in Search of a Wife.* One notes in both books not only a common interest in religious education and courtship but also in such other themes as the vocation of the ministry, the value of accomplishments in women, the propriety of theatricals and such other entertainments, and the advantages of rural over urban environment. Chapters XXI and XXII of *Coelebs,* for example, are given over to a discourse by Lucilla's father on the ideal clergyman who, in his opinion, should combine with the spiritual virtues the attributes of the scholar and the gentleman. Lucilla's father pleads the importance of the clergyman's being well read and learned, in addition to being pious and understanding of human nature. "Polite literature," he urges, "is within the clergyman's province just so it is not pursued for its own sake, but as a service to Christianity," an attitude very much like Edmund's toward the books he gives Fanny to read. "A pious divine may have as much wit and humour as any other man. . . .Piety does not necessarily involve dullness," affirms Mr. Stanley later on, anticipating Edmund's defense of his future calling to Mary and Henry Crawford. Mary's doubts as to the influence of clergymen over their congregation on the ground that "one scarcely sees a clergyman out of his pulpit," stirs up Edmund:

> "*You* are speaking of London, *I* am speaking of the nation at large" [he says to Mary].
> "The metropolis, I imagine, is a pretty fair sample of the rest" [she replies].
> "Not, I should hope, of the proportion of virtue to vice throughout the kingdom. We do not look in great cities for our best morality" (CH. IX).

Coelebs also disapproves of Londoners, who "attach an ephemeral importance to everything, and a lasting importance to nothing":

> I found too that inhabitants of the metropolis had a standard of merit of their own; that knowledge of the town was held to be knowledge of the world; that local habits, reigning phrases, temporary fashions, and an acquaintance with the surface of manners, was supposed to be knowledge of mankind. (CH. XXXV)

There are other common value judgments in the two books. Among the attributes that Coelebs admires about Lucilla is that "She has a quick perception of whatever is beautiful or defective in composition or in character. . . .Though she has a correct ear, she neither sings nor plays." Admirers of Miss Stanley must have approved of Fanny Price's disdain for Mary Crawford's harp-playing and play acting. They also heard from Mr. Stanley that "A woman whose whole education has been rehearsal, will always be dull, except she lives on the stage, constantly display-ing what she has been sedulously acquiring. Books, on the contrary, do not lead to exhibition. The knowledge a woman acquires in private, desires no witnesses; the possession is the pleasure." Fanny's contempt for the *stage*, note, does not extend to *drama*, which she reads with great pleasure, if we may judge by her love of Shakespeare. She would easily have won the approval of Coelebs, who believes that "The vapid and ignorant are like a bad play; they owe the little figure they make to the dress, the scenery, the music and the company. . . . But an intel-lectual woman, like a well-written drama, will please at home without all these aids and adjuncts" (CH. XXXV) .

Not surprisingly, Coelebs shares with Edmund Bertram a horror of amateur theatricals. His alarm at learning that a family he is visiting is preparing a "Christmas diversion" gives way to relief when he finds out that the entertainment is to consist of a feast for the poor, not a play. Sir Thomas Bertram would have been pleased to overhear Mr. Stanley advising Lady Belfield to add a conservatory to her manor house: "Where a garden and a green-house are to supply to the proprietor the place of the abdicated theatre and ball room, and especially when it is to be a means in her hands of attaching her children to the country and teaching them to love home, I declare myself in favour of the conservatory" (CH. XLV) .

It appears then that, however repelled she may have been by the Evangelical temperament, Miss Austen shared Miss More's ethical views—including the necessity for an extended period of courtship and a rational approach to marriage. (Some of her most delightful parodies in *Love and Freindship* are aimed at such sentimentalities as love at first sight and spontaneous sym-pathy of soul.) Possibly, like the critic for the *Edinburgh Re-view*, she conceded that despite Miss More's prim sententiousness, "her advice is very often characterized by the most amiable good sense, and conveyed in the most brilliant and inviting style. . . ." At any rate she seems to have followed his advice to readers of *Coelebs,* which was to "separate the piety from the puerility."[25]

The shadow of the dedicated author of *Coelebs* hovers over virtually all of the serious fiction read by Jane Austen and her contemporaries. *Celia in Search of a Husband* by Medora Gordon Byron was intended as an "answer" to *Coelebs* from the woman's point of view, offering, according to the author, characters whom ordinary readers could hope to emulate more readily than the "ideal perfections" created by Hannah More.[26] Celia Delacour, Miss Byron's heroine, is a Lucilla Stanley transplanted to London, but well inoculated against its moral pestilence through a careful upbringing by a religious lady.[27] The characters who surround Celia have the easily identifiable attributes of chapbook figures, some of them primitive prototypes of characters we later encounter in *Mansfield Park:* the worldly and effete beauty Lady Townley; Sir Harry Townley, the wealthy baronet, who has married her "as a patron of the arts becomes the owner of a fine picture . . . [and] like some amateurs discovered too late that the picture is not worth the price he paid for it"; Mrs. Welgrave, the prudent domestic economist; Sir Peter and Lady Berton, representative of the enlightened, simple-living, country gentry; their son George, who has deteriorated into a man of fashion under the influence of Oxford and town squires; Danbury the rake, Belford the cynic, and assorted men about town. Celia, needless to say, is much coveted—by the virtuous and the corrupt alike—but eventually settles on the sterling Lord Ellincourt when she becomes convinced that he is "moral, yet cheerful —religious without ostentation—strict in his family; and gives them an example in his own rectitude." These are the virtues also that attract Fanny Price to Edmund Bertram. The environment in general prepares us for Miss Austen's novel. In *Celia* as in *Mansfield Park* we are steeped in a nostalgic kind of cultural atmosphere—the world of the eighteenth-century country gentleman, whose periodicals are not the *Edinburgh Review* but the *Idler* and the *Rambler,* and whose poets, despite the emergence of Wordsworth and Coleridge, are Cowper, Thomson, and Young. It is above all an age that conceives the mind as a *tabula rasa* and believes strongly in the power of "early instructions" to mould character.

There is one best seller of this period that we know Jane Austen read and reread. "I am looking over Self Control again, & my opinion is confirmed of its being an excellently meant, elegantly written Work, without anything of Nature or Probability in it," she wrote late in 1813 to Cassandra.[28] She was referring to a didactic tale then in its fourth edition by Mary Balfour Brunton, the wife of a Scottish clergyman.[29] The author of *Self-Control* also acknowledges indebtedness to *Coelebs* but dedicates the book appropriately to Joanna Baillie, who in her *Plays of the Passions* aimed to teach her generation how to overcome wilful impulse.

Self-Control is probably the novel that Jane Austen was specifically making fun of in her later satirical fragment called *Plan of a Novel.* Its projected heroine sounds like a caricature of Mrs. Brunton's self-righteous, masochistic Laura Montreville: "The Daughter of a Clergyman . . . a faultless Character herself—perfectly good, with much tenderness and sentiment, & not the least Wit—very highly accomplished. . . .Her Person quite beautiful—dark eyes and plump cheeks—Book to open with the description of Father and Daughter—who are to converse in long speeches, elegant Language—& a tone of high, serious sentiment." Mrs. Brunton's Laura is not the daughter of a clergyman; but her father, a retired widower disillusioned by her shallow mother, sees to it that his daughter's education is superintended by a clergyman's wife. As a result Laura lives apart from the world, "conversant with the good and sublime in nature," and learns early how "Christian doctrine, precepts and promises,

warm the heart and guide the conduct, and animate the hopes."
Because of her sheltered innocence she is dazzled momentarily by
the aesthete and libertine Colonel Hargrave. However, knowing
of her religious education, we do not doubt for a moment that it
is the noble and innocuous De Courcy whom she will eventually
marry. De Courcy, however, has to wait patiently through the
heroine's drawn-out ordeals, which include a harrowing ride
through some Canadian rapids strapped in a canoe.[30]

Behind Laura's plight lies an optimistic assumption, obviously
shared by Jane Austen, as to the natural attraction of virtue,
even to the unvirtuous. At first Hargrave's intentions are not
honorable, and when he approaches Laura to make improper
advances, she faints from shock. Her would-be seducer is so
moved at this display of pure innocence that he comes back to
propose—not merely to proposition. Laura refuses him with this
plea:

> "Oh, Hargrave," she cried, clasping her hands in supplication,
> "have pity on yourself—have pity on me—forsake the fatal path on
> which you have entered, that, though for ever torn from you here, I
> may yet meet you in a better world." . . . Colonel Hargrave had
> nothing in himself which made it natural for him to suppose
> passion sacrificed to reason and principle. Had he then deceived
> himself—had she never really loved him?—the suggestion was too
> mortifying to be admitted. . . .

Hargrave, like many a handsome scapegrace in novels of this
period, is a crude copy of Richardson's Lovelace. Through Jane
Austen's more refined art, this figure is transmuted into Henry
Crawford. Readers of *Self-Control* could hardly have been surprised at Henry's pursuit of Fanny Price, but they found Fanny's
love trials less exciting than those of Laura Montreville. Miss
Austen's more urbane "villain" causes her heroine mental, not
physical anguish. Mrs. Brunton's "excellently meant" book
anticipates not only Fanny's love problem but her trouble with
the Bertrams as well. Laura, upon the death of her father, is

received into the house of a wealthy aunt, Lady Pelham, who annoys her by machinations to unite her with Hargrave.[31]

When Jane Austen was writing *Mansfield Park,* serious readers were well used to didactic fiction (really seminovels) in which female education, courtship, and moral conduct were treated in the light of practical Christianity. Another widely esteemed domestic novelist of the day whose work Miss Austen knew was Laetitia Matilda Hawkins, the daughter of Dr. Johnson's first biographer.[32] Jane respected Miss Hawkins while recognizing her considerable failings as a novelist. "Very good and clever, but tedious," was her verdict on Miss Hawkins' *Rosanne; or A Father's Labour Lost* (1814). "There are some very delightful conversations and reflections on religion," she continues, "but on lighter topics I think she falls into many absurdities; and, as to love, her heroine has many comic feelings."[33] These remarks are as aptly descriptive of Miss Hawkins' earlier *The Countess and Gertrude; or, Modes of Discipline* (1811), which one suspects that Jane Austen also read, for it clearly prefigures the central themes of *Mansfield Park.*

The Countess and Gertrude is a ramshackle work—a lumpish mixture of cautionary tale, catechism, and conduct book. "The motive of our undertaking," the author declares in her opening chapter, "originated in the vexation of being compelled to see, in the circuit of an extensive acquaintance with society, very few children made happy by the indulgences lavished on them by their parents, very few parents reaping the expected fruits of indulgence, and very few persons who, on quitting the parental home, can face the realities of life without injury to their temper, shipwreck of conscience, or a lamentable demonstration that fortitude and submission are not amongst the accomplishments they have acquired." *Mansfield Park* is also concerned with indulgent parents, the Bertrams and the Rushworths, and their children who suffer in various ways through being overindulged. The other young people of *Mansfield Park* are shown "quitting the parental home" to "face the realities of life," Fanny and

William Price, the poor, unspoiled pair offsetting Mary and
Henry Crawford, the rich, pampered pair. The trials of Miss
Hawkins' heroine, Gertrude Aubrey, thrown upon society when
her mother is left a widow but remaining steadfastly incorruptible, are similar in outline, though not in detail, to those of
Fanny Price. Little Gertrude's spiritual pilgrimage takes her
from the mansion of Lady Luxmore to the Miss Mendall's
academy with its genteel and trivial curriculum, to the patronage
of the benevolent Mr. Sterling, who launches her on a program of
serious reading, to the tutelage of Miss Bonfoy, who places in her
hands the writings of Miss More, Mrs. Carter, and Mrs. Barbauld. She is thus prepared for marriage with Basil Sydenham,
whose schoolmaster father has taught him "to fix the principles,
to subjugate the passions, to liberate the judgment; every par-
ticle of which endeavours must have their foundations laid in
the simple precepts of religion, pure and mild as it comes from
the source."

Miss Hawkins' fable was intended to illustrate her ideas on
charity as well as on education and on courtship. In her introductory chapter she refers to a contemporary social problem that
could well have suggested to Miss Austen the initial situation of
Mansfield Park. Under the topic, "Protection of Females," Miss
Hawkins takes up the vexed question of "the connection between
the higher and the lower ranks of females," which she feels has
not been given enough serious consideration by the public. She
urges in particular that aristocratic ladies should volunteer "to
take the charge of a young girl on her first quitting her father's
cottage" as part of "the duty of doing all that can be done for
that part of the female youth of this country, who must depend
on their own endeavours for a maintenance." If the "upper
circles" of society do not rise to this responsibility, Miss Hawkins
fears, these poor girls may come under the influence of inferior
women and subsequently carry moral infection into the nurs-
eries. At the same time it is important not only to provide good
homes for the less fortunate, but proper environments also so

that these young blossoms are not nurtured in "corrupt soil."[34] These young girls should learn from their elders to scorn fancy dress and ornament, and the Bible should take precedence over novels in their reading. It is possible that here Miss Hawkins was inspired by one of the episodes of *Coelebs in Search of a Wife* in which Sir John and Lady Belfield adopt a bright but penurious orphan named Fanny (omnipresent name!) and give her a religious education to prepare her for going out into the world. Apparently both ladies, very much of their age, considered the poor to have been placed on earth as a part of God's providential scheme, to give scope to the Christian sympathies of the wealthy. Amusingly enough, we find both of them exhorting their readers to just such "benevolent actions" as the evangelical busybody Mrs. Norris urges on her brother-in-law and sister, the Bertrams, at the beginning of *Mansfield Park*.

To their credit, Sir Thomas and Lady Bertram try to make their poor niece Fanny feel like one of the family. However, the Bertram daughters and their tutor obviously think of her as a creature from a lower order. Mrs. Norris in particular treats her with condescension: "A niece of ours, Sir Thomas, I may say, or at least of *yours,* would not grow up in this neighbourhood without many advantages. I don't say she would be so handsome as her cousins. I dare say she would not; but she would be introduced into the society of this country under such very favourable circumstances as, in all human probability, would get her a creditable establishment." With a beautiful stroke of irony on the author's part, Mrs. Norris now twists about the egalitarian principle to appeal to Sir Thomas' sense of superiority: "You are thinking of your sons but do not you know that of all things on earth *that* is the least likely to happen; brought up, as they would be, always together like brothers and sisters? It is morally impossible. I never knew an instance of it. It is, in fact, the only sure way of providing against the connection." What is morally impossible to Mrs. Norris' smug, narrow soul proves to be quite possible to "The great directing MIND OF ALL."

In the variety of attitudes displayed toward Fanny, the charity
girl, by her social superiors, Miss Austen exposes the streak of
vanity that often runs through human altruism. To Lady
Bertram, Fanny is a pet; to Sir Thomas, the proving ground for
philanthropic schemes; to Mary, a rough diamond to be polished; to Henry, an opportunity for a conquest. Kindliness, we
realize, may be ineffectual, as with Lady Bertram's apathetic
sweetness; obtuse, as with Sir Thomas' "do-goodery"; patronising,
as with Mary Crawford's compliments; insincere, as with Mrs.
Norris' snobbery; unfeeling, as with Tom Bertram's brusque
heartiness; unconsciously cruel, as with the Bertram daughters'
efforts to treat Fanny as an "equal"; misplaced, as with Henry
Crawford's pursuit. Transcending these, of course, is Edmund's
true compassion and genuine love, no less so even when at times
they prove to be misguided. This delicate probing of the motives
behind acts of charity—selfish as well as benevolent—is Jane
Austen's ironical commentary on the gospels of Miss More and
Miss Hawkins.

If Miss Austen read to the end of *The Countess and Gertrude*
—and from all indications she had as much patience as other
novel readers of her time—she came upon this benediction
delivered by an elderly friend of Gertrude and Basil, as the
young couple are joined in holy matrimony: "May the influence
of your example prevail on parents to adopt, not indeed the
severities with which your early years were marked, though even
these have their advantages, but a wholesome, moderate, regular
restraint on their children . . . and may the superior character
of happiness, with which, I hope, your life will be blessed, induce
people to bear patiently that control which the experience of the
present day calls for, and which is meant by the good old term
DISCIPLINE!" Sir Thomas Bertram, for one, is properly chastened.
Looking in dismay upon the "errors of education" of his own
daughters, he muses with regret "that principle, active principle
had been wanting, that they had never been properly taught to
govern their inclinations and tempers, by that sense of duty

which can alone suffice." He is consoled by the happier fate of
Fanny, who proves to him "the advantages of early hardship and
discipline, and the consciousness of being born to struggle and
endure" (CH. XLVIII). Modern readers of *Mansfield Park* who
are taken aback by the abruptness of Edmund's proposal to
Fanny and the summary way in which their marriage is handled
might wish, like Fanny Knight, for "more love between her
[Fanny] and Edmund." But as far as most of Miss Austen's first
readers were concerned, this pair had quite amply demonstrated
already their compatibility, their emotional, moral, and spiritual
character having been tested by experience. Miss Austen, like her
sister novelists, concentrated her attention on courtship, treating
marriage as the "happy ever after."

One understands why *Mansfield Park* appealed to the Reverend J.S. Clarke. Because of the way in which her characters pair
off, Miss Austen might have reverted to her earlier kind of title
and called *Mansfield Park* something like *Self-Love and Selflessness.* Then the Reverend Clarke, or any other reader of 1814,
could have taken Fanny Price's story as a fictional illustration of
Miss Hamilton's thesis that "the benevolent affections" are "the
provision made by the wisdom of Providence, for the counterac-
tion of that spontaneous propensity [magnification of the Self]
which I consider as the origin of all moral depravity."[35]
Perhaps to many of Miss Austen's earliest readers *Mansfield
Park* was of a piece with such edifying fictions as Miss Holcroft's
Fortitude and Frailty, Miss Argus' *Ostentation and Liberality,* or
Mrs. Opie's *Tales of Real Life*—and as quickly to be forgotten.
However, there were happily some who saw in it something more.
"In most novels you are amused for a time with a set of Ideal
People whom you never think of afterwards, or whom you the
least expect to meet in common life," wrote one of them,
"whereas in Miss A[usten]'s works & especially in M[ansfield]
P[ark] you actually live with them, you fancy yourself one of the
family. . . . "[36] This judgment has been confirmed by successive

generations of readers blissfully unaware of Miss Austen's long ignored rival novelists.

Miss Austen's way with the Christian-didactic novel nevertheless is not to be compared with her flippant treatment of Gothicism and sentimentality, for her attitude toward her immediate contemporaries is fundamentally different. Whereas the world of the sentimental, enthusiastic, and terrorist writers was to her unreal and their view of life immature, the moral world of the educator-novelists, much as she may have disapproved of some of its missionaries, was to her basically true and sound. The novelist of *Mansfield Park*, therefore, is no longer the mocker but the improver. She concedes that a book like *Self-Control* is "well meaning," questioning not the validity of its principles but its conformity with "Nature and Probability." It was not the "serious subjects" she objected to in Miss Hawkins' writing, but that lady's heavy-handedness with love and "lighter topics."

Miss Hawkins, Mrs. Brunton, and Miss More were not really novelists at all—and one of them at least quite freely admitted it. Miss Hawkins offered *Rosanne* to her public with "the dejecting consciousness that a subject has been chosen demanding far greater powers, more extensive information, more continuity of thought—in every way more intellect than will be found in it." She betrays the embarrassment of the uneasy venturer into an alien medium, but she consoles herself with the hope of "seeing some abler writer undertake that which has been, in spite of every deficiency, an employment of exquisite delight—the recommendation of the fear and love of God, as an interwoven principle of human actions." Fortunately a genius was at hand to take over. One, at least, of the early admirers of *Mansfield Park* was able to appreciate the difference, praising the novel not only for the "sound sense, Elegant Language & the pure morality with which it abounds," but for "excellent delineation of Character" as well.[37]

Essentially, Jane Austen applied the moral ideals of the evangelical ladies to a real and imperfect world and substituted dynamic characters for their static ones. Miss More, Mrs. Brunton, and Miss Hawkins had a sound enough idea of the Christian Heroine, but, unlike them, Jane Austen could show how such a character is formed. While the Lucillas, the Celias, the Lauras, and the Gertrudes of her generation spring forth from their creators' pens fully armed against the world, Fanny Price develops before our eyes as she is transplanted to "improving soil." The Christian heroines we have encountered suffer at the hands of others but seem to have no difficulty with themselves. In Jane Austen's more complex world we feel the tension of moral choice in Fanny as she wavers in her course, divided within herself. She learns early in life how complicated emotions can be.

At the beginning, upon her arrival at Mansfield Park, Fanny is torn between homesickness and the gratitude Mrs. Norris thinks she should feel, "and her consciousness of misery was therefore increased by the idea of its being a wicked thing for her not to be happy" (CH. II). As the story progresses we realize that she is not immune to the human emotions of pride and vanity, even if they do not overwhelm her as they do Maria and Julia. The headache Fanny acquires from walking in the sun is aggravated by mental depression caused by Edmund's early attentions to Mary Crawford: "She had been feeling neglected, and had been struggling against discontent and envy for some days past" (end of CH. VII). She is capable too of active jealousy. Her objection to Edmund's taking part in *Lovers' Vows* arises not merely out of her superior moral and literary taste: "Alas! it was all Miss Crawford's doing. She had seen her influence in every speech, and was miserable" (CH. XVI). She struggles to conquer her jealousy: "It was her intention, as she felt it to be her duty, to try to overcome all that was excessive, all that bordered on selfishness, in her affection for Edmund." But it is not easy: "She had all the heroism of principle, and was determined to do her duty; but having also many of the feelings of youth and nature, let her not be much wondered at if, after making all these good resolutions on the side of self-government, she seized the scrap of paper on which Edmund had begun writing to her, as a treasure beyond all her hopes. . . . " (CH. XXVII). This is but one sign of the emotional conflict that constantly disturbs Fanny and makes her a fallible human being rather than a perpetual acolyte. Love is no less painful for Fanny and duty no less difficult than they are for others. Just as she struggles between her selfish impulses and benign feelings in her regard for Edmund, so her disdain for Henry Crawford is tempered by her gratitude toward him. Her attitude toward her own family is also complex; she finds it difficult to avoid condescension toward them as she reminds herself of her filial obligations.

In a letter written to her niece shortly before her death, Jane Austen defended her mode of characterization. Miss Knight had shown some of her aunt's writing to an admirer and passed on his remarks for comment. The young man, it appears, was disappointed that Miss Austen's heroines were less than ideal. "Have mercy on him, tell him the truth & make him an apology," Jane advised. "He and I should not in the least agree of course, in our ideas of Novels and Heroines;—pictures of perfection as you know make me sick & wicked—but . . . I particularly respect him for wishing to think well of all young Ladies; it shows an amiable & a delicate Mind.—And he deserves better treatment than to be obliged to read any more of my Works."[38] She generally avoids "pictures of perfection" also with her heroes. Even Edmund has a fault—obtuseness. He is human enough to be attracted to Mary Crawford's surface appeals and blind enough to be misled by Henry. His conflict of values is most strikingly dramatized in that episode where he leaves Fanny gazing out the window at the open skies and moves toward Mary to listen to her perform glees on the harp (CH. XI). His temptation continues even after the unpleasant interview with Mary in London, when he must exert self-command to keep from returning to her after he has taken his final farewells (CH. XLVII). But with an especially delicate touch, Miss Austen makes Edmund's error of judgment proceed from one of his supreme virtues—his universal sympathy.

Henry Crawford also has a disturbing effect on Fanny, despite herself. She is caught off guard through the faculty that Edmund does so much to cultivate—her sensitivity to great poetry. Listening to Henry Crawford reading a speech from Shakespeare's *King Henry VIII:* "She could not abstract her mind five minutes; she was forced to listen; his reading was capital, and her pleasure in good reading extreme. . . . It was truly dramatic.—His acting had first taught Fanny what pleasure a play might give, and his reading brought all his acting before her again; nay, perhaps with greater enjoyment, for it came unexpectedly and with no such drawback as she had been used to suffer in seeing him on the stage with Miss Bertram." Ironically it is just this reaction, as sensed by Edmund, that leads him to suppose that Fanny could be won by Henry, and causes him to encourage Henry to pursue his courtship:

> Edmund watched the progress of her attention, and was amused and gratified by seeing how she gradually slacked in the neddle-work, which, at the beginning, seemed to occupy her totally; how it fell from her hand while she sat motionless over it—and at last, how the eyes which had appeared so studiously to avoid him throughout the day, were turned and fixed on Crawford; fixed on him for minutes, fixed on him in short till the attraction drew Crawford's upon her, and the book was closed, and the charm was broken. Then she was shrinking again into herself, and blushing and working as hard as ever. . . . (CH. XXXIV)

Part of Fanny's willing penance for her momentary lapse is to turn away from Shakespeare, once the hypnotic effect of Henry's dramatic reading is dispelled, and to give greater attention to Edmund's subsequent discourse on sermon reading. Forever after, the Church replaces the Theatre for her.

If Fanny and Edmund have the faults of their virtues, Mary and Henry have the virtues of their faults. Miss Austen's sister novelists tended to paint their ladies of fashion and libertines so black that one could not imagine anybody's being even temporarily drawn to them. Miss Austen manages to make hers attractive, despite their deficiencies of character, and thereby more insidious. Her success is proved by the hold they continue to exert on readers who to this day side with them against the less faulty characters. However, much of their appeal, as Miss Austen makes clear, is theatrical. While reading *Mansfield Park* we may be disposed to think Henry a "good fellow," but sober judgment ought to lead us to second thoughts about the sort of man who plays on women's feelings like an actor on an audience. It is true that he is capable of right feelings and decent acts, but he is meant to demonstrate the instability of natural good sense without "fixed principles," as the educators of the day would diagnose it. Miss Austen's superior taste preserves Henry from the usual fate of the libertine—suicide from remorse or death from dissipation. "That punishment, the public punishment of disgrace, should in a just measure attend *his* share of the offence is, we know, not one of the barriers society gives to virtue," the author tersely observes. "In this world the penalty is less equal than could be wished . . ." (CH. XLVIII). She is content to leave Henry, like his sister Mary, to live out his life in a vague state of regret over his imprudence and the loss of one who might have redeemed him.

The defense of Mary Crawford rests on flimsy ground, but readers will hold to it as perversely as they profess a preference for Rosamond Vincy over Dorothea Brooke in *Middlemarch.* Lionel Trilling is not one of these, although he has written that "to outward seeming Mary Crawford is another version of Elizabeth Bennet." Elizabeth Bennet does not gossip about her uncle to strangers, run down the clergy, or condone adultery. Again Miss Austen means us to recognize in Mary a creature who is not vicious but erring because she too lacks "fixed principles." She is not *immoral* but *indelicate.* "She would not voluntarily give unnecessary pain to any one," as Edmund observes, but she can involuntarily wound feelings. Like Edmund we are taken in by her charms, but, as Hannah More's Mrs. Stanley says, "being entertaining does not make amends for everything."

"We have all been more or less to blame . . . every one of us, excepting Fanny. Fanny is the only one who has judged rightly throughout, who has been consistent." Edmund is speaking here (CH. XX) to Sir Thomas specifically about the embarrassing business of the rehearsals for *Lovers' Vows*. But generally speaking, Fanny, no more than the others, can be said to have "judged rightly throughout." Whereas in some situations she proves to be more acute than Edmund, in others she lacks Edmund's compassion and delicacy of perception. Even at the end, Fanny is still receiving moral instruction from her cousin. They have occasion to discuss Mary once more, when Edmund has told Fanny of his disillusioning meeting with her in London. Fanny learns that Mary has dismissed in a cavalier fashion Henry's misconduct with Maria Bertram:

> "Cruel!" said Fanny, "quite cruel. At such a moment to give way to gaiety and to speak with lightness, and to you!—Absolute cruelty."
> "Cruelty do you call it? [replied Edmund] We differ there. No, her's is not a cruel nature. I do not consider her as meaning to wound my feelings. The evil lies yet deeper; in her total ignorance, unsuspiciousness of there being such feelings. . . . Her's are not the faults of temper . . . Her's are faults of principle, Fanny, of blunted delicacy and a corrupt, vitiated mind. . . . Gladly would I submit to all the increased pain of losing her, rather than have to think of her as I do. I told her so." (CH. XLVII) [39]

Edmund's moral influence on Fanny is very much like that of the Duke on Isabella in *Measure for Measure*. To her natural piety he adds the towering Christian virtue of charity, the power to understand and to forgive.[40] As the union of Fanny and Edmund is finally brought about, Miss Austen, were she given to such tags, might have appended these lines from Cowper, one of her favorite poets, that in fact introduce Miss Hawkins' *Rosanne:* "There is no virtue more amiable in the softer sex, than

that mild and quiescent spirit of devotion, which without en-
tangling itself in the dogmas of religion, is melted by its charities
and exhilarated by its hopes." But she had the tact to let her
readers infer this for themselves.

In *Mansfield Park,* then, Jane Austen created the one masterpiece of a dead early nineteenth-century genre—the Christian
didactic novel. From the episode where Fanny is momentarily
beguiled by Henry's readings, we may infer that, like Miss More,
Mrs. Brunton, and the others, she had a lingering fear of the
seductions of fiction, but in the novel itself she seems to be
endeavoring to justify fiction by proving that it can be at once
edifying and diverting.[41] Probably the Reverend Edward
Morsham of Mrs. Green's *Romance Readers and Romance
Writers* pretty well sums up Miss Austen's attitude. Complaining
of the excessive religiosity of *Coelebs,* Morsham offers his own
prescription for fiction:

> Let the writers of the modern novels . . . like the excellent
> Richardson, Fielding and Smollett, hold up a faithful picture of
> the times they live in; lash vice, in whatever shape it may appear,
> and applaud virtue in every-one, while they make their heroes not
> demi-gods, but mere erring man; and let them, like those incom-
> parable authors, intersperse their works with only those *few*
> religious sentiments, which may serve to shew the orthodoxy of
> their own principles, and prove to their readers that there is no
> trust to be placed on mere moral rectitude and philosophy without
> the aid of Omnipotence; these serious interspersions . . . are quite
> sufficient for a work which is only meant to unbend and recreate
> the mind; and make those read who are not fond, naturally, of
> study; and who, if they find these works too serious, will close the
> book not read at all, or else fly to the dangerous rubbish of
> licentious publications.

The sobriety of mood that sets *Mansfield Park* apart from Miss
Austen's previous novels suggests that she was at least touched by
the Evangelical Movement, but perhaps the change is no more
than is to be expected from the once precocious young author

now grown up. *Northanger Abbey, Sense and Sensibility,* and *Pride and Prejudice* were late revisions of work originally conceived in her teens and twenties; *Mansfield Park* was first set down in her late thirties. A year before it was published she confided to her sister: "By the bye, as I must leave off being young, I find many Douceurs in being a sort of Chaperon for I am put on the Sofa near the Fire & can drink as much wine as I like."[42] She has incidentally described her new function both in art and life, but she was far from a passive chaperon. By this time she is Aunt Jane advising another Fanny on love and courtship. It is a tempered humorist who writes to her niece a year later urging her to marry the pious "Mr. J. P.": "Do not be frightened from the connection by your Brothers having most wit. Wisdom is better than Wit, & in the long run will certainly have the laugh on her side."[43] The chaperon had merged with the female educator. Her favorite theme—marrying and giving in marriage—dominates her last novels, with religion in abeyance. Here she tends to mock the chaperon, such as Lady Russell in *Persuasion,* as a busybody, preferring to leave the young to find their own way to the altar by trial and error. Emma Woodhouse and Anne Eliot do not marry clergymen, but in their choice of mates she tries to balance the claims of wit and wisdom.[44]

At a time when Sir Walter Scott was turning the novel outdoors, Jane Austen kept it indoors. Scott considered himself the master of the broad stroke ("the Big Bow-wow strain") rather than the light touch, but he thought of both himself and Jane Austen as novelists of manners. Her province, he indicated in a review, was "the paths of common life," while he, by implication, celebrated "uncommon events, arising from the consideration of minds, manners and sentiments greatly above our own."[45] He implies here that he was a writer of epic and she of domestic novels, a distinction that became a commonplace and tended for some time to keep his prestige at a level above hers. His most ardent admirers, when they were not comparing him with Shakespeare, thought of him as the Scotch Homer, while

Miss Austen was frequently coupled with his countrywoman Susan Ferrier. "He has scarcely a competitor in painting the rougher and more savage lineaments of our nature, and unfolding the elemental strife of the passions during unsettled and turbulent periods," declared a contemporary reviewer of Scott, but added, "We doubt whether his pencil is equally skilled in the portraiture of those less unquiet feelings, which grow up in the shade of domestic privacy."[46] As far as this reader was concerned, fiction needs its rovers and its stay-at-homes, but in Scott's time and through the mid-Victorian period his large voice reached farther than Jane Austen's quiet one, his histories of rebellions making more of an impact on the large public than her histories of fine consciences.

The balance has swung the other way since critics came to appreciate Miss Austen's art, style, and delicacy of feeling more, and Scott's picturesqueness, grandioseness, and erudition less. But both were appreciated more for matter than for art by their first and subsequent generations of readers. Of the various forms of fiction that emerged in the Victorian period, Scott's impress is most marked on the *bildungsroman,* Jane Austen's on the *familienroman.* The Scott hero gets his education from the world, then gladly returns to his manor house for an early retirement. The Austen heroine is confined to a home study course, like Anne Eliot in *Persuasion,* aspiring to no more than "that profession which is, if possible, more distinguished in its domestic virtues than in its national importance." Not until her very last novel, in fact, is a young wife disturbed by anything like "the dread of a future war" that "could dim her sunshine." George Henry Lewes, one of her greatest admirers among Victorians, complained that "she never stirs the deeper emotions, . . . never fills the soul with a noble aspiration, or brightens it with a fine idea, but at the utmost, only teaches us charity for the ordinary feelings of ordinary people, and sympathy with their goodness."[47] That was sufficient for her. It was left to Charlotte Brontë and George Eliot to depict what Lewes describes as "the more stormy and energetic activities which find vent in every day life." Like Scott, Jane Austen believed that reason and restraint made for civilization. A certain decorum also kept her from probing too far into her characters' secret lives. Character for her was subsumed under "personal and mental endowments,"[48] those qualities that present themselves in the drawing room. Morals as illuminated by manners and exhibited in conversation—all that is implied by *courtesy* in its fullest social and spiritual sense—was her span of observation. She was not as much preoccupied with physical detail as Scott, nor with cultural history or movements of thought, as those who came after her. Her heritage to her successors in the Victorian Age was the elevation of "common life" and the "domestic virtues."[49] Later novelists put more furniture in their houses, but she established the home as the sanctuary of affection and piety, love of man, and love of God.

Such certainly is the impression that her family wished to leave of her. Her brother, the Reverend Henry Austen, in his memoir considers her spiritual graces more important than her literary ones. The inscription on her grave in the north aisle of Winchester Cathedral indicates that she died after a long illness, "supported with the patience and hopes of a Christian." Tribute is paid to "the benevolence of her heart, the sweetness of her temper and the extraordinary endowment of her mind." Her family are consoled by "a firm though humble hope that her charity, devotion, faith and purity have rendered her soul acceptable in the sight of her Redeemer." Nothing is said of her having been a novelist.

CHARACTERISTIC FICTION CONTEMPORANEOUS
WITH *MANSFIELD PARK* (1814)

1801 Maria Edgeworth, *Moral Tales for Young People.*
1801–9 Maria Edgeworth, *Early Lessons.*
1805 Charlotte Dacre (Rosa Matilda, pseud.), *The Libertine.*
    Amelia Opie, *Adeline Mowbray; or, The Mother and the Daughter.*

1806 Medora Gordon Byron, *Anti-Delphine: A Novel.*

1808 Hannah More, *Coelebs in Search of a Wife.*

1809 Medora Gordon Byron, *Celia in Search of a Husband.*

Robert Torrens, *Coelibia Choosing a Husband.*

[Anonymous], *Caroline Ormsby; or, The Real Lucilla.* (Variously attributed to Jane West, Grace Kennedy, and Barbara Hofland, but authorship remains unestablished.)

1809–12 Maria Edgeworth, *Tales of Fashionable Life* (*Ennui, Almeria, Madame de Fleury, Dun, Manoeuvering, Vivian, Emilie de Coulanges, The Absentee*).

1810 Mary Balfour Brunton, *Self-Control. A Novel.*

Percy Bysshe Shelley, *Zastrozzi. A Romance.*

1811 Captain Thomas Ashe, *The Spirit of "The Book"; or, Memoirs of Caroline of Hasburgh: A Political and Amatory Romance.*

Henry Card, *Beauford; or, A Picture of High Life.*

Charlotte Dacre (Rosa Matilda, pseud.), *The Passions.*

Laetitia Matilda Hawkins, *The Countess and Gertrude; or, Modes of Discipline.*

Percy Bysshe Shelley, *St. Irvyne; or, The Rosicrucian. A Romance.*

1812 Amelia Opie, *Temper, or Domestic Scenes.*

1813 Amelia Opie, *Tales of Real Life.*

1814 Bridget Bluemantle (Mrs. Elizabeth Thomas), *The Prison-House; or, The World We Live In.*

Fanny Burney, *The Wanderer; or, Female Difficulties.*

Maria Edgeworth, *Patronage.*

Laetitia Matilda Hawkins, *Rosanne; or, A Father's Labour Lost.*

1815 Mary Balfour Brunton, *Discipline.*

CHAPTER IV

Oliver Twist:

The Fortunate Foundling

OLIVER TWIST ANNOUNCES HIS ENTRANCE into life with a lusty cry. As Dickens says, had little Oliver known what awaited him, he would have cried louder. Without the social status of Edward Waverley, or the family connections of Fanny Price, "he was badged and ticketed, and fell into his place at once—a parish child—the orphan of a workhouse—the humble, half-starved drudge—to be cuffed and buffeted through the world—despised by all, and pitied by none." Despite his low status, however, he is subjected no less than Fanny Price to educational schemes: "a systematic course of treachery and deception" at the parish workhouse, the "parental superintendance" of that efficient domestic economist Mrs. Mann; the "experimental philosophy" tried out by the board of the "brick and mortar elysium" which serves Oliver, for lack of better, as his nursery and elementary school. Because of Oliver's peculiar circumstances, his formal education is brief, perfunctory, and rather hit-or-miss, but he somehow manages to acquire perfect manners and faultless grammar.

In Jane Austen's time, as we have observed, bluestockings like

Hannah More, Laetitia Matilda Hawkins, and Elizabeth Hamilton dedicated their pens to the cause of the education of the poor, but by the 1830's the issue was being debated in the halls of Parliament. The New Poor Law, a familiar part of the background of *Oliver Twist,* raised the nagging problem of the schooling of workhouse wards.[1] By now the need for educating the children of paupers and abandoned or orphaned children was widely recognized, but there was no agreement as to who was responsible for it. The farming-out system employed for Little Oliver and his fellow inmates was certainly obsolete by this time. Dickens, a legislative reporter, was undoubtedly aware of the bill proposed by John Arthur Roebuck in 1833 calling for the establishment of an infant school in every parish.[2] But this was before the concept of state education had taken root, and Roebuck's scheme came to naught. In May 1835 Lord Brougham, addressing the House of Lords, declared it inexpedient to establish parish schools; he suggested instead "voluntary effort" by the philanthropic and civic-minded.[3] It may have been he whom Dickens lampooned a few years later in a sketch as "the Radical . . . of the utilitarian school . . . having many ingenious remarks to offer upon the voluntary principle and various cheerful disquisitions connected with the population of the country."[4] Most of Dickens' examples of volunteer educators in *Oliver Twist,* at any rate, are far from heartening. Mrs. Mann is one. Fagin is another, offering to Oliver the seminary for youth where he is such an inept pupil. Oliver eventually proves more fortunate than Fagin's other pupils by falling in with Mr. Brownlow, who furnishes the home-school so congenial to Dickens' ideals of education. But first he—and the reader—undergo the rigorous regimen of the streets.

Oliver Twist is not only tossed between the Old Poor Law and the New Poor Law, but bandied about from guardian to guardian. Nor does there seem to have been much agreement as to what waifs thrown on "the tender mercies of churchwardens and overseers" were supposed to learn. The red-faced "philosopher" in the white waistcoat who interviews Oliver in the workhouse assumes that he is to be "taught a useful trade," but depends on unsupervised volunteers to carry out the program. Evidence from other sources indicates that vigorous efforts were being made during these years to protect helpless boys from the real-life Gamfields and Sowerberrys. Barbara Hofland, a popular children's writer, pointed to her native Sheffield as a model for the administration of poor relief. In this large manufacturing town, she proudly proclaimed, even though the poor are numerous, funds are ample and the overseers are "men of property and benevolence, alike liberal and conscientious"—more like Mr. Brownlow, one supposes, than Mr. Bumble. She contrasts the wealthy city with "petty villages" where "the poor are at the mercy of the mean and tyrannical who conceive that they oblige their neighbours by curtailing the comforts of the poor."[5] Among Oliver Twist's misfortunes is being born in the "petty village" of Mudfog.

Bill Sikes, of all people, is our source of information about another institution that was trying to ease the "parish boy's progress." The master thief complains that the Juvenile Delinquent Society is encroaching on his "occupation" when it takes a vagrant boy in hand, "teaches him to read and write, and in time makes a 'prentice of him." But things could be worse. "If they'd got money enough (which it's a Providence they have not), we shouldn't have half a dozen boys left in the whole trade, in a year or two" (CH. XIX). That threat seems indefinitely averted. Dickens had, however, a more encouraging example before him in the Foundling Hospital, located in Great Coram Field near Doughty Street, where he lived while he was writing *Oliver Twist*. He took an active interest in this institution, regularly attending chapel there during the few years that he lived in the neighborhood, and in this connection became acquainted with a namesake of Oliver's benefactor—John Brownlow.[6] At the time when Dickens met him, Brownlow was in charge of the placement of boys and had succeeded in reforming the policy of the

Foundling Hospital with regard to apprenticeship after bringing to light cases of cruelty by masters. In other respects too Brownlow showed up the "experimental philosophers" of Mudfog, effecting improvements in the physical care and the diet of the inmates of the Foundling Hospital.[7] Brownlow himself was living proof of the benefits of this institution; he had originally entered it himself as a charity boy. As will be shown later, Dickens' association with this asylum, rooted in eighteenth-century paternalism and hallowed by missionary zeal, is closely linked to the theme and tone of *Oliver Twist*.

To its first readers, *Oliver Twist* had the glare of an exposé. Serial publication allied it with topical journalism; Cruikshank's illustrations made the characters leer, simper, glower, and beam right out of its pages. In the playbill of a "serio-comic burletta" hacked out of the tale while the press ink was hardly dry, the author was applauded for " 'Holding the mirror up to nature' albeit in its worst light." Dickens, according to this playsmith, was "opening one of the darkest volumes of life, and revealing facts that must startle the more strongly, from the previous total ignorance of their existence, even by those persons residing in the very heart of the scenes in which they are daily and nightly passing."[8] Dickens was not, of course, introducing his readers to the seamy side of London life for the first time. Some of the *Sketches by Boz Illustrative of Every-Day Life and Every-Day People,* which first appeared in newspapers, germinated characters and episodes in *Oliver Twist.* The first of the sketches, "The Parish," begins ominously: "How much is conveyed in those two short words—'The Parish.' And with how many tales of distress and misery, of broken fortune, and ruined hopes, too often of unrelieved wretchedness and successful knavery are they associated." Bumble is anticipated in the portrait that follows of the Beadle "in his state-coat and cocked hat with a large-headed staff for show in his left hand, and a small cane for use in his right" officiously marshaling the urchins in his charge. The master of the workhouse and the parish schoolmaster are among others sketched. "A Visit to Newgate" takes in juvenile delinquents and a school for pickpockets. Among the "Scenes" transferred in part to *Oliver Twist* are "The Streets—Morning," "The Streets— Nights," "Gin-Shops," "Criminal Courts," "The Prisoners' Van," and "The Drunkard's Death." In Dickens' first book, parish boys, charity schools, apprenticeship, and crime are brought together between covers but not yet amalgamated into a novel.

In the Preface to the Second Edition of the *Sketches,* the youthful "Boz," pleased with the success of his "pilot balloon," promises his faithful readers "fresh sketches, and even connected works of fiction of a higher grade, [for which] they have only themselves to blame." Connection, indeed, is what he particularly insists upon in many of the chapter headings of his first plotted novel: "Treats of a very poor Subject. But is a short one; and may be found of some Importance in this History" (CH. XXIV—the death of the hag who stole the locket from Oliver's mother) ; "In which a mysterious Character [Monks] appears upon the Scene; and many things inseparable from this History are done and performed" (CH. XXVI) ; "Is a very short one, and may appear of no great importance in its Place, but it should be read notwithstanding, as a Sequel to the last, and a Key to one that will follow when its Time arrives (CH. XXXVI—the parting of Rose Maylie and Harry) . His description of his new book as a "history" in itself stresses causal sequence. Dickens was struggling against the serial publication of the story, its picaresque tendency and particularly the association of his name in readers' minds with trivial comedies and ephemeral journalism. His problem was complicated by the concurrent appearance of *Pickwick Papers* and the reissue of *Sketches by Boz* in monthly parts.[9] Probably, however, Dickens was most concerned about his reputation with critics who had questioned his ability to sustain a long narrative and were already predicting the exhaustion of his sparkling vein.[10] The highly cultivated style of the book, which contributes to its satirical effect, also indicates, together with his self-conscious exposure of his artistry, that he was trying to convince the snobbish gentlemen of the press that he was something more than "the literary Teniers of the metropolis."[11]

Dickens, moreover, was making a bid for consideration as an interpreter of life, not merely a reporter of it. The playbill of the burletta that was the first of numerous efforts to extend his message to the semiliterate who attended the theatre hailed the author of *Oliver Twist* as a "Hogarth [who] has raised a beacon on the basis of truth to warn the erring, guide the inexperienced, instruct the ignorant to avoid the shoals by which they are surrounded." Dickens' tale was reduced here to "a great moral lesson" proving that vice is eventually punished and virtue rewarded. Dickens himself, though disavowing this dramatization,[12] echoed its program note in his first public pronouncement on his first novel, the Preface to the Third Edition of 1841, where he invoked the spirit of Hogarth, "the moralist and censor of his age."[13] Too many readers, to Dickens' annoyance, had become so engrossed in the low life of his novel that they had missed its high purpose. The Princess Victoria for one, reading it in *Bentley's Miscellany*, confided to her mother that she found it "too interesting" and was promptly scolded for indulging in light literature.[14] Thackeray, his greatest rival, while ridiculing *Oliver Twist* in his mock-novel *Catherine*, admitted that "the reader at once becomes [Dickens'] captive, and must follow him whithersoever he leads."[15] But Thackeray did not like where he was being led. Against critics who had condemned *Oliver Twist* as salacious and immoral, Dickens felt compelled to defend his choice of characters, "from the most criminal and degraded of London's population." "I have yet to learn," he continues, "that a lesson of the purest good may not be drawn from the vilest evil." Out of Oliver's adventures in the underworld he extracted a fable of incorruptible innocence, as wholesome as *Sandford and Merton* or *The Shepherd of Salisbury Plain:* "The principle of Good surviving through every adverse circumstance, and triumphing at last."

The serial publication of *Oliver Twist* tended to leave the outcome of "the principle of Good" in suspense as Oliver was shunted between malefactors and benefactors. The three-volume publication, which antedated the conclusion of the serial, also left the survival of innocence in doubt, since the first volume ended with Fagin's turning over Oliver to Bill Sikes, and the second with the rendezvous between Oliver's evil half-brother Monks and the corruptible Bumble. But Dickens' intention was finally fixed indelibly in the readers' minds with the edition in numbers which, contrary to normal practice, came out five years after the three-decker.[16] Here the front wrapper designed by Cruikshank sets out in a series of panels Dickens' conception of Oliver's "progress" as a modern morality—at the top Oliver embracing a benign lady inside a cottage, at the bottom Fagin shivering in his cell, while flanked on the right and left between "heaven and hell" are Oliver's tormentors and tempters. To us, the survival of Good "through every adverse circumstance" seems a matter of Oliver's being in the right place at the right time, but we need to put ourselves in the frame of mind of Dickens' generation, who more readily assumed that God helps the helpless. Many years later, in a letter to Wilkie Collins, Dickens expressed his own conviction as to "the ways of Providence, of which all art is but a little imitation."[17]

In his 1841 Preface Dickens emphasizes the pathos of his tale, for the benefit of children and his more delicate adult readers. A careful reading of his pronouncement prepares one for the full blend of sensation, satire, and sentiment that he was working up into his formula, but he shrewdly understates the first two elements. During the serial publication of *Oliver Twist* and afterward, he was plagued by invidious comparisons with the so-called "Newgate" school of fiction. The coupling of his novel with *Jack Sheppard* was inevitable, since the Ainsworth melodrama also appeared in *Bentley's Miscellany* (under Dickens' editorship) and was illustrated by Cruikshank. A reviewer of *Jack Sheppard* recognized the essential moral seriousness of

Dickens' story but candidly added, "We are certain that it is far less the under-current of philosophy which has sold his book, than the strong flavour of the medium, in which he has disguised the bitterness of its taste."[18] Thackeray, despite a "sneaking kindness" for the book, lumped it—largely on the basis of the sentimental treatment of Nancy—with Ainsworth's stories and with Bulwer's *Paul Clifford* and *Eugene Aram* in his parody *Catherine,* where he denounced the glorifying of crime. Dickens does his best to dissociate himself from this company, writing in the Preface: "Here are no canterings on moonlit heaths, no merry-makings in the snuggest of all possible caverns, none of the attractions of dress, no embroidery, no lace, no jack-boots, no crimson coats and ruffles, none of the dash and freedom with which 'the road' has been, time out of mind, invested." Instead, like Cervantes, he attempts "to dim the false glitter surrounding something which really did exist, by showing it in its unattractive and repulsive truth." So his criminals are city thieves and murderers, not glamorous highwaymen, wear greasy flannel, frayed velveteen, soiled breeches, and disport themselves in dark, filthy taverns. Little Oliver, no more attracted by crime in literature than in life, flings away the lurid history of the lives and trials of great criminals that Fagin gives him, just as readers are supposed to do.

The pumped-up Gothic atmosphere of some scenes in *Oliver Twist* suggests a lingering memory of Dickens' childhood reading in other crime fiction. Old Sally, the midwife who attends Oliver's mother, is a stereotype of the literary witch: "Her body was bent by age, her limbs trembled with palsy, and her face distorted into a mumbling leer" (CH. XXIV). As Dickens admits, she "resembled more the grotesque shaping of some wild pencil than the work of Nature's hand," perhaps a concession that he got her out of an illustration from a penny dreadful. Oliver's elder brother, with his "dark figure," "trembling hands," "grim laughs," "excited imagination," and obsession with demons is straight out of the literature of "the awful and the terrific." The nocturnal meeting between this villain and the Bumbles takes place in a noisome swamp near the river, amidst a cluster of abandoned huts and a dilapidated old factory where they are interrupted occasionally, and predictably, by peals of thunder and flashes of lightning. Here Dickens transforms the props of the Gothic romances—ruined castles, abbeys, murky tarns, and crashing storms—to suit a modern urban setting. His giving the nickname Monks to his malevolent schemer is a lame joke that has generally gone unappreciated.

His true wit comes out in his handling of a more contemporaneous realistic genre. A contemporary of Dickens, accounting for the success of *Oliver Twist,* recalled that "he arose at a time when the novels of England were both vicious and snobbish, when one set of writers was producing the Satanic school of literature, and another, like those poor things whom we name to forget, the Countess of Blessington and Lady Charlotte Bury, was cultivating what was appropriately called the silver-fork school."[19] In "London Recreations," one of the *Sketches by Boz,* Dickens pokes gentle fun at "the small gentility—the would be aristocrats—of the middle classes, . . . tradesmen and clerks, with fashionable, novel reading families." One of the early reviewers of *Oliver Twist* was pleased that its author took the novel out of the drawing room into the streets. Dickens' popularity, he observes, "has been fairly earned without resorting to any of the means by which most other writers have succeeded in attracting the attention of their contemporaries. He has flattered no popular prejudices and profited by no passing folly; he has attempted no caricature sketches of the manners or conversation of the aristocracy; and there are few political or personal allusions in his works."[20] Dickens himself declared in his 1841 Preface:

I saw no reason, when I wrote this book, why the dregs of life, so long as their speech did not offend the ear, should not serve the purpose of a moral, at least as well as its froth and cream. Nor did

I doubt that there lay festering in Saint Giles's as good materials towards the truth as any to be found in Saint James's.

These words have usually been taken at their face value, but the alert reader can catch the sly author winking between the lines. Such a reader is best able to savor the irony of Dickens' description of the infant Oliver in his swaddling clothes: "What an excellent example of the power of dress, young Oliver Twist was! Wrapped in the blanket which had hitherto formed his only covering, he might have been the child of a nobleman or a beggar; it would have been hard for the haughtiest stranger to have assigned him his proper station in society" (CH. I). Dickens does not mean here merely to anticipate Oliver's refined parentage. The barbed chapter headings scattered through the novel suggest that, but for the grace of God, Oliver "might have been" the hero of a "Silver Fork" novel. His apprenticeship in particular suggests an unlike likeness with the career of the dandy. Chapter III, which introduces Gamfield, "Relates How Oliver Twist was very near getting a Place, which would not have been a Sinecure"—like a seat in the House of Lords or a commission. Oliver's situation at this point could also have been contrasted with that of the hero of another Bentley novel advertised in the first edition—*Melton de Mowbray; or, The Banker's Son*.[21] The next chapter, where Oliver meets Sowerberry, headed "Oliver, being offered another Place, makes his first Entry into public Life," suggests the fortunes of Disraeli's Young Duke. This vein is sustained by ambiguous chapter summaries that ape the *ton*: "How Oliver passed his Time in the improving Society of his reputable Friends" [Jack Dawkins and Charlie Bates]; "Atones for the Unpoliteness of a former Chapter; which deserted a Lady [Mrs. Corney] most unceremoniously"; "An old acquaintance of Oliver's [Noah Claypole], exhibiting decided Marks of Genius, becomes a public Character in the Metropolis"; "Comprehending a Proposal of Marriage [Harry and Rose Maylie] with no Word of Settlement or Pin-money."[22]

Through Noah Claypole in particular Dickens parodies the peacocks who strut through *Almacks* and *The Exclusives*. As a charity-boy, Noah is one rung up the social ladder from Oliver, a mere workhouse orphan: "No chance-child was he, for he could trace his genealogy all the way back to his parents, who lived hard by; his mother being a washerwoman, and his father a drunken soldier." Noah, himself derided by the shop-boys, follows the pecking order by abusing Oliver, "now that fortune had cast in his way a nameless orphan, at whom the meanest could point the finger of scorn." Among other things, Dickens is writing the poor man's *Book of Snobs*. As he observes of the relationship between Noah and Oliver: "It shows us what a beautiful thing human nature is, and how impartially the same amiable qualities are developed in the finest lord and the dirtiest charity-boy" (CH. V).

Bill Sikes, hiding out in a dingy tenement after an unsuccessful "expedition" to Chertsey, bears a faint resemblance to Beau Brummell: "The house-breaker was lying on the bed, wrapped in his white greatcoat by way of a dressing gown"; "Nor were there wanting other indications of the good gentleman's having gone down in the world of late, for a great scarcity of furniture, and total absence of comfort, together with the disappearance of all such small movables as spare clothes and linen, bespoke a state of extreme poverty" (CH. XXXIX). Bill's overdressed accomplice Toby Crackit, with his "smartly cut snuff-coloured coat, with large brass buttons; an orange neckerchief," and his red-dyed hair "tortured into long corkscrew curls," is a grotesque version of a Regency fop, and at the same time neatly hits off Bulwer's gentleman thieves (CH. XXII). His speech also is pseudo-Holland House: "I can't talk about business till I've eat and drank; so produce the sustanance, and let's have a quiet fill-out for the first time these three days!" (CH. XXV).[23] Dickens has indeed kept his promise to his readers not to "offend the ear." Crackit is ashamed to be seen playing cribbage with Tom Chitling, "a gentleman so much his inferior in station and mental endowments," but is pleased to take the easy money. Chitling is too much dazzled by Crackit's gentility to care about his loss. Their creator cannot help interposing that "there are a great number of spirited young bloods upon town who pay a much higher price than Mr. Chitling for being seen in good society, and a great number of fine gentlemen (composing the good society aforesaid) who establish their reputation upon very much the same footing as flash Toby Crackit" (CH. XXXIX). He depicts two such, Lord Frederick Verisopht and Sir Mulberry Hawk, in his next novel, *Nicholas Nickleby*.

In "London Recreations" Dickens had observed: "The wish of persons in the humbler classes of life to ape the manner and customs of those whom fortune has placed above them is often the subject of remark, and most frequently of complaint." He furnishes plenty of examples among Oliver's "improving friends." The Artful Dodger, Jack Dawkins, a "young gentleman," introduces Oliver to Fagin, a " 'spectable old gentleman." Fagin lives up to the role. When Oliver first meets him, "the Jew grinned; and making a low obeisance . . . took him by the hand, and hoped he should have the honour of his intimate acquaintance" (CH. VIII). Everybody to him is "my dear"; Oliver is taught manners ("Make 'em your models, my dear—make 'em your models . . . do everything they bid you, and take their advice in all matters—especially the Dodger's, my dear. He'll be a great man himself, and will make you one, if you take pattern by him"); he is avuncular toward Nancy ("Why . . . you're more clever than ever tonight. Ha! Ha! my dear, you are acting beautifully [giving her a basket]. Carry that in one hand, it looks more respectable, my dear"); he attempts to polish her uncouth companion ("Come, come, Sikes . . . we must have civil words—civil words, Bill."). Bill proves somewhat refractory, but Nancy knows how to lay out "tea things" in the garret after he has finished a bout of debauchery, and Oliver takes time out for "making his toilet" before accompanying him on a pre-dawn burglary expedition.

But Dickens' satire is double-edged. Most of the episodes
involving Fagin, Bill Sikes, their "associates" and their "protégés"
have their counterparts in the "Exclusivism, fashionable novel-
ism, Nashism, and fifty other fribbleisms of the West-end" recalled by one of Mrs. Gore's retired gentlemen.[24] For the schools
of deportment and the dancing academies, substitute the public
house in Saffron Hill where Fagin puts his "dear boys" through
their paces. For the faro and gaming tables, substitute the whist
matches of the Artful Dodger, Toby, and Tom. In Fagin's
household the magazine is not the *Journal des Modes* but the
Hue and Cry. In place of the elegant shopping districts of Bond
Street and Regent Street, readers are escorted to Field Lane, the
"dismal alley" leading to Saffron Hill, in whose "filthy shops are
exposed for sale huge bunches of second-hand silk handkerchiefs,
of all sizes and patterns; for here reside the traders who purchase
them from pickpockets," and are invited to peer inside ware-
houses where "stores of old iron and bones, and heaps of mildewy
fragments of woollen-stuff and linen, rust and rot in the grimy
cellars" (CH. XXVI) .

Among their other "London Recreations" Dickens' would-be
aristocrats of the lower classes like to "get up tavern assemblies in
humble imitation of Almack's and promenade the dingy 'large
room' of some second-rate hotel with as much complacency as the
enviable few who are privileged to exhibit their magnificence in
that exclusive haunt of fashion and foolery." Peer, parvenu, and
poor come together in that low-life Almack's, the Three Cripples
Inn. This euphemistically styled, smoke-laden "establishment"
has its "chairman with a hammer of office in his hand" and its
exclusive membership like "a professional gentleman, with a
bluish nose and his face tied up for the benefit of the toothache,
[who] presided at a jingling piano in a remote corner." Soon the
distinguished company join voices in a ribald ballad. A few years
earlier, Bulwer had proclaimed proudly in *England and the
English* that the clubs which "form a main feature of the social
system of the richer classes of the metropolis" were no longer

"merely the resort of gamblers, politicians or bon vivants." He ventured to predict, completely without tongue in cheek, that these institutions would infiltrate the lower levels of society, for their atmosphere of "moral dignity" and "intellectual relaxation" "contain the germ of a mighty improvement in the condition of the humbler classes."[25] This improvement obviously has not reached that hideout, the Three Cripples, to judge by the music of the establishment and the conversation, which turns mainly on such topics of the day as police news and the affairs of Fagin, Sikes, and Company. The membership as a whole has reached this stage of enlightenment: "Cunning, ferocity and drunkenness in all its stages were there, in their strongest aspects . . . presenting but one loathsome blank of profligacy and crime."

One has the feeling that in this Hogarthian scene Dickens was not merely exposing his more privileged readers to the cesspools of London but showing them their own reflections there. Certainly the society mirrored in some of the novels of the day was not the shining example visualized by Bulwer. The hero of the anonymous *Russell; or, The Reign of Fashion* shuns "that too numerous class of idle, useless, worthless fools of fashions, whose studies and anxieties are devoted to cravat-tying, whisker-pruning, opera-lounging, actress-hunting, dinner-eating, tobacco-smoking, prize-fighting, billiard-playing." Another disenchanted member of the Silver-Fork set recalls a Grosvenor Street soirée where "I, of course, met with some of my Oxford contemporaries, of whom I recognized some dandies and dissipated idlers transformed into legislators and official personages; others sustaining their original characters, and matured into gamblers, jockeys, patrons of tailors, and opera-girls—in a word, men of fashion."[26] Dickens, it appears, had not really separated the "dregs" of society from its "froth and cream," but homogenized them. His fictitious inhabitants of St. Giles could just as well be the inhabitants of St. James in masquerade. When all is said and done, both groups are engaged in the same occupations—drinking, gambling, idling, and whoring. Presumably the criminal poor of *Oliver Twist* are no more parasitic either than the wastrels of high society. Of all the early reviews of *Oliver Twist,* the youthful Dickens must have been particularly gratified by one which compared it with *The Beggar's Opera* and *Jonathan Wild* for "the boldness with which the writers have stripped society of its disguises, and exhibited the shallowness of those conventionalities which varnish the vices of fashionable life, the falsehood of its pretences, the hypocrisy of its assumptions of decency and propriety."[27]

A modern reader of *Oliver Twist* might prefer the bitter without the sweet, but the story was undoubtedly most palatable to its first audience as the *Parish Boy's Progress,* promised by its original label. The universal appeal of the orphan in fiction, the topicality of the workhouse and private charity, along with Dickens' own identification with the plight of oppressed children—these suggested to him the foundling story as a vehicle for his parable of society. The tradition of the orphan eventually rescued from poverty by revelation of his respectable birth extends well back into the eighteenth century. Its central theme is announced in the title of Eliza Haywood's once popular *The Fortunate Foundlings* (1744). Literary historians customarily trace Oliver Twist back to *Tom Jones* and *Humphry Clinker,* which are among the books read by young David Copperfield. However, waifs and strays abounded in the early nineteenth century—Charlotte Brooke's *Emma; or, The Foundling of the Wood* (1803); the anonymous *Amasina; or, The American Foundling* (1804); Elizabeth Somerville's *Aurora and Maria; or, The Advantages of Adversity* (1809); Mary Pilkington's *Sinclair; or, The Mysterious Orphan* (1809); Charles Lucas' *Gwelygordd; or, The Child of Sin* (1820); Dorothy Kilner's *Edward Neville; or, The Memoirs of an Orphan* (1823); and the perennial and much pirated *Fatherless Fanny; or, A Young Lady's First Entrance into Life.*

A foundling story in vogue during Dickens' childhood, Agnes Maria Bennett's frequently reprinted *The Beggar Girl and Her Benefactors* (1797), may be taken as seminal in its mixture of philanthropy with picaresque adventure.[28] Mrs. Bennett apologizes, exactly forty years before Dickens, to her "polite readers, supposing she should be honoured with any such," for "the vulgar people and low scenes to which perforce the memoirs of a beggar must introduce them" (I, CH. VI). With gentle mockery she twists humility into subtle indignation:

> But notwithstanding no creature living has a more due and profound respect for the higher order of society which all ranks know they merit . . . yet, as, to the eternal disgrace of the police, which, to be sure, should order these things better, there are such things as little folk, who have the presumption to breathe the same atmosphere with the greatest of the great, and by the up and down jumble of chance, not only mingle their paltry interests in the grand movement of high life, but sometimes actually swim on the surface, like common oil on the richest wines. . . .

Presumably, the fact that Mrs. Bennett's beggar girl Rosa Wilkins turns out, like Oliver Twist, to be derived from rich wine rather than common oil does not negate her egalitarian philosophy.

The Beggar Girl and Her Benefactors probably did much to fix in the minds of early nineteenth-century readers the stereotypes of the outcast waif and benevolent gentleman. The ingredients of Dickens' fable are laid out here: the specter of the parish workhouse (Rosa is rescued from its jaws by the wealthy Colonel Buhanun, who takes her to live with him), the career of persecution and exploitation, the flight to the city, the long-delayed reunion (Rosa proves to be not the daughter of a prostitute, as was supposed, but the natural daughter of her benefactor). There is also satire, if somewhat crude, of the world of fashion through such figures as Mrs. Modely, Lady Gauntley, and Mrs. Wouldby, with whom little Rosa gets involved during her London adventures.

The prestige of a commendation from Coleridge in one of his rare remarks on the fiction of his times has kept the name of Mrs. Bennett flickeringly alive. "*The Beggar Girl* is the best novel, *me judice,* since Fielding," he scribbled on the flyleaf of one of his books. "I should like, therefore, to read the others."[29] At a time when the ranks of female novelists were headed not by Jane Austen but by Jane West, such a remark may not have seemed outlandish. Agnes Maria Bennett might be described as a self-taught writer, but she schooled herself in masters. Such figures as the semiliterate maid Betty Brown, whom Coleridge enjoyed, the tenderhearted hypochondriac Colonel Buhanun, and the scoundrelly Sir Solomon Mushroom bear the stamp of Smollett; elsewhere she echoes Fielding's banter. Her loosely woven tale is eked out with much padding (she was paid by the volume and had a large family to support by her pen), but its good spirits and warm humanity carry one over dull stretches.[30] Whether Dickens knew it directly or not is uncertain, but he was acquainted with many a tale influenced by it. In "Astley's," one of the *Sketches by Boz,* he chafes at the popularity of estranged fathers and children in the theatre:

> By the way, talking of fathers, we should very much like to see some piece in which all the dramatis personae were orphans. Fathers are invariably great nuisances on the stage, and always have to give the hero or heroine a long explanation of what was done before the curtain rose . . . Or else they have to discover, all of a sudden, that somebody whom they have been in constant communication with, during three long acts, without the slightest suspicion, is their own child, in which case they exclaim, "Ah! What do I see! This bracelet! That smile! These documents! Those eyes! Can I believe my senses?—It must be!—Yes—it is—it is—my child!" "My father!" exclaims the child, and they fall into each other's arms, and look over each other's shoulders; and the audience give three rounds of applause.

He followed through with a piece in which virtually "all the dramatis personae were orphans," but he was not above bringing in his own variant of a stage father to effect a happy ending.

The 1830's in particular saw a proliferation of orphan tales, bounded at one end of the decade by *Elizabeth and Her Three Beggar Boys* and *The Stolen Boy; An Indian Tale,* at the other by *Oliver Twiss,* a parody-sequel of Dickens' novel by a hack named Thomas P. Prest, who signed himself "Bos." In the year when *Oliver Twist* was being serialized in *Bentley's Miscellany,* there appeared one of the numerous reprints of *Fatherless Fanny.* Again, that enterprising hawker of literary wares, Newman, points to an important vogue. It is significant that after 1820, "Minerva Press," with which he had long been associated from his partnership with William Lane, was dropped from his imprints and his catalogues began to feature very prominently "Juvenile and Prize Books." Some of these were of the fanciful and pretty sort, such as *Angelina; or, Conversations of a Little Girl with her Doll* and Miss Selwyn's *Fairy Tales,* but his staple was the true adventure story. Superseding the romantic, didactic fables of the last century—such as Fénelon's *Télémaque,* Lucy Peacock's *The Adventures of the Six Princesses of Babylon in Their Travel to the Temple of Virtue,* and the twice-told ancient legends that were supposed to edify Sandford and Merton— were the pious, polemical tales of the times toward which Hannah More had led the way. One of the most popular and fertile producers of this "improving" fiction for youth during the 1820's and 1830's, and one of Newman's stars, was the "amiable and ingenious writer of tales for young and old alike," Mrs. Barbara Hofland. Her titles bristle with the moral virtues—*Decision, Energy, Self-Denial, Fortitude, Patience,* and virtually all of them, like *Young Crusoe; or, The Shipwrecked Boy,* follow the tribulations of young vagabonds whose characters are strengthened rather than toughened by the buffets of the cruel world.

One of Mrs Hofland's fiction-sermons, *Elizabeth and Her Three Beggar Boys* (ca. 1830) , adapted from her earlier *Tales of the Priory* (1820) ,[31] attaches the foundling tale to the social agitation that preceded the enactment of the New Poor Law. Like many of Mrs. Hofland's books, this is a "Tale Founded on

Fact." It concerns the progress of a parish boy, William Warren, from rags to riches, as he passes from the workhouse into the rough hands of a cruel farmer, thence into the kinder hands of a religious farmer's wife. She has him apprenticed to a pottery manufacturer, who makes him a partner. The fact is based on the career of the charitable Elizabeth Linley, a cottager's wife from Wakefield, who, despite her poverty, devoted her life to the care of homeless children. The purpose is made explicit in the preface:

> To shew the poor, that even in their poverty they may do much good, and to prove to the rich, that the poor are capable of displaying those virtues which circumstances render extremely difficult, and thus to bring both parties into that contact which their common nature admits, and the religion they alike profess insists upon, wherever faith or morals are concerned, is the especial object of the writer. In her own opinion she has never offered to the world a narrative more true to nature, or better calculated to move the rich to benevolence, and the poor to exertion; and this belief must be her apology for rewriting and re-offering to the young and amiable a "twice-told tale."

Mrs. Hofland defines here the role of emissary of good will among the classes that was being assumed by some of the more social-minded writers at this time. The humbler format of this new condensed version of her tale is an emblem of her humanitarianism—stately half-calf giving way to paper wrappers in order to insure it wider circulation. She reaches simultaneously up and down, involving high and low in a sense of mutual obligation, anticipating Dickens' moral scheme in *Oliver Twist*. In other ways too Mrs. Hofland's tale for her times prepares us for Dickens' fable. Both their parish boys are miraculously preserved from sickness and starvation, despite the workhouse, are saved from criminal careers, are brought up on the New Testament, *The Pilgrim's Progress*, and hymn books. With Mrs. Hofland, as with Dickens, Good Works is the hero and Public Charity the villain. With both authors the pastoral scene is sentimentalized and sacramentalized. Oliver inherits wealth, un-

like William Warren, but like William he becomes the benefactor of the next generation of poor. Sympathy and benevolence
lubricate the wheels of society.[32]

Another tale of the day, although it is placed in the previous
century, is *Hans Sloane: A Tale Illustrating the History of the
Foundling Hospital* (1831), written by Dickens' friend John
Brownlow. Brownlow's sole venture into fiction rather awk-
wardly interweaves a rudimentary tale of a fortunate foundling
with a memorial to Captain Coram, the founder of the hospital
that employed Brownlow. *Hans Sloane* went generally unnoticed
in its time, but there is every evidence that Dickens was familiar
with it. Brownlow's story, with its lurid intrigue joined to sentimental humanitarianism, seems to have influenced *Oliver Twist*
even more than his real-life career.

Hans Sloane begins in the summer of 1740, about a year after
Captain Coram's establishment of the Foundling Hospital. The
young hero is legitimate and of a well-to-do family, but becoming
orphaned at birth, he falls into the hands of an unscrupulous
uncle. The uncle, now sole heir to the strictly entailed family
estate, is worried about the eventual claim of his brother's
surviving child. He refuses to adopt the infant, as his wife
wishes. Refraining from murdering him only out of fear of the
law, he orders his wife to leave the child at the newly established
Foundling Hospital, where it can be brought up in ignorance of
its birth. Reluctantly she brings the infant to the home in the
dead of night, concealing her own identity. But, contrary to her
husband's instructions, she ties around the baby's neck an amulet
containing a miniature portrait of his mother. Here is the germ
of the much deplored Monks' plot of *Oliver Twist*, which
Dickens complicated by making his infant illegitimate, the villainous relative a half-brother instead of an uncle (though
preserving his motivation), and by having him seek out the child
and rather implausibly plan its moral destruction. Above all,
Dickens conceals the whole relationship from the reader until the
end to invest the story with an air of mystery.

To return to the misadventures of little Hans Sloane—he is named by the nurses at the hospital after one of its great benefactors, the distinguished Chelsea doctor who also endowed the British Museum.[33] After baptism, little Hans is sent out to be reared by cottagers and then comes back to the hospital, where he spends his childhood. Despite the constricted spiritual and physical fare of this institution, Hans, like Oliver, grows into a sprightly, alert lad. He is, however, spared one of Oliver's ordeals. As a "private" child he remains up to the age of twelve under the protection of the hospital instead of being sent out to work. It is then his good fortune to be adopted by a kindly childless couple, the Reverend Mr. Humphries and his wife. By a contrived quirk of destiny the miniature portrait around his neck is recognized by Mrs. Humphries as that of her dead sister. All comes to light when Mr. Humphries attends the death bed of a strange woman at an inn; she proves, of course, to be Hans' aunt, who had deposited him at the Foundling Hospital years before. Upon seeing the amulet she confesses all and dies; and the unscrupulous uncle, his treachery now discovered, commits suicide, leaving the family estate clear for Hans. The Humphries feel thankful "for the miraculous interposition by which they were restored to a relative of whom they had every reason to be proud," and young Hans is determined to use his new-found wealth for the benefit of less fortunate orphans.

Allowing for additional complications introduced by Dickens to unravel his more whorled plot, the conclusion of this crude fable anticipates the dénouement of *Oliver Twist,* with the function of Mr. and Mrs. Humphries dispersed among Mr. Brownlow, Dr. Losberne, Rose Maylie, and her adopted mother. *Hans Sloane* is basically a prose hymn of praise to the Foundling Hospital and to its benefactors. In *Oliver Twist* Dickens retains the eighteenth-century moral atmosphere—faith in human benevolence and divine providence (the key, probably, to his much denounced sentimentalism and "outrageous" use of coincidence), along with the assumption of the original virtue and innocence of children. But he updates his story to bring it into line with then current interests in the New Poor Law and juvenile crime.

The historical essays and lay sermons that interlard Brownlow's desultory tale concern perils that Little Hans escapes, but to which Little Oliver is exposed. The initial situation of *Oliver Twist,* for example, may well have been suggested by the account of Captain Coram's encounter with a victim of seduction who had abandoned her infant, an experience which led him to establish the hospital. Brownlow's animadversions on the education of foundlings in the last century prefigure, in turn, the "school" for thieves. He relates that Doctor Johnson, horrified during a visit to the Foundling Hospital to discover that the inmates were not receiving religious instruction, exclaimed: "To breed children in this manner is to rescue them from an early grave, that they may find employment for the gibbet; from dying in innocence that they may perish by their crimes." With his particular interest in apprenticeship, Brownlow denounces the bonus system introduced by Parliament during Captain Coram's time to induce employers to take on homeless boys and relieve the towns of the burden of rearing them. He cites good as well as bad examples, but leaves the impression that Gamfield and Sowerberry were more typical than the unnamed farmer who supervises the regeneration of Charley Bates. All of these issues are revived by Dickens in contemporary settings. The Reverend Mr. Growler, the cynical friend of Mr. Humphries, who predicts a bad end for little Hans, has his counterpart in Mr. Grimwig, the friend of Oliver's benefactor, Mr. Brownlow. Another parallel is Paul Pipkin, an unscrupulous tavern keeper of Eastcheap, whom Bill Sikes resembles.

Dickens' imagination seems particularly to have been stirred by one of Brownlow's moral digressions in which he pleads for sympathy for the unwed mother, urging his readers to abandon their smugness in favor of "a compassionate estimate of the weaknesses of humanity, and a just measure of relief to voluntary repentance":

> This lesson of mercy was eminently taught by the Founder of Christianity Himself, when he bade the Jew who was without sin cast the first stone at the repentant adulteress, and then calmly dismissed her with the charge to *sin no more*. It was not that her crime was venial, but He who desired not the death of a sinner, but rather that she should repent and live, saw perhaps in this wretched criminal sufficient of remorse to be the object of a lesson to mankind,—that the rigour of human law should not be exercised without a human regard to the circumstances under which the crime may have been committed, and the sincerity which may have followed. (CH. X)

For the character of Fagin, Dickens is now believed to have drawn upon a notorious Jew named Ikey Solomon, a fence and a seducer of boys into crime. His "fallen woman," Nancy, presumably could have been based on numerous Cheapside prostitutes. But Brownlow's allusion suggests the biblical analogy that Dickens intended the Fagin-Nancy relationship to convey. Fagin, forgetting that he is responsible for her downfall, flings stones at Nancy for her profession, as the unenlightened reader might also be disposed to do. Dickens' frequent reference to Fagin by the generic term "the Jew" indicates that he may have conceived him in the image of the sanctimonious Pharisee of the New Testament. Certainly Nancy is a modern incarnation of the penitent Magdalen, the aspect of her character that Dickens emphasizes in her meeting with the innocent Rose Maylie (CH. XL), and reiterates with scriptural eloquence in his preface to the 1841 edition, where he felt called upon to defend her portrayal:

> IT IS TRUE. Every man who has watched these melancholy shades of life, knows it to be so. . . . It is emphatically God's truth, for it is the truth He leaves in such depraved and miserable breasts; the hope yet lingering behind; the last fair drop of water at the bottom of the dried up, weed-choked well. It involves the best and worst shades of our common nature; much of its ugliest hues, and

something of its most beautiful; it is a contradiction, an anomaly, an apparent impossibility; but it is a truth.

In naming Oliver's benefactor Mr. Brownlow, Dickens seems to have been paying an early tribute to one of the most dedicated social servants of his age.[34] John Brownlow must be counted among Dickens' unsung progenitors, but it is probable that a far more distinguished foundling than Hans Sloane is to be included among Oliver's literary brothers—Professor Diogenes Teufelsdröckh. Among the first critics of *Oliver Twist,* the young George Henry Lewes was virtually alone in noting that Dickens' works "are volumes of human nature, that have a deep and subtle philosophy in them, which those who read only to laugh may not discover."[35] As early as *Oliver Twist* we may discern the allegorizing tendency of Dickens' imagination, particularly in his attempts to invest his sordid characters with moral—even biblical—significance. But the moral that draws together all his characters—genteel and pseudo-genteel—grows out of the initial episode where Little Oliver, "enveloped in the old calico robes which had grown yellow in the same service . . . was badged and ticketed, and fell into his place at once—a parish child. . . . " The whole novel, as well as Oliver himself, is "an excellent example of the power of dress." Incogruities of wearing apparel, as we have seen, figure in the satire of the book—Fagin in his greasy coat teaching his ragamuffins how to filch silk handkerchiefs, the elaborate getup of the housebreaker Toby Crackit, Nancy's passing herself off as Oliver's mother by means of a shawl and basket. Dickens also uses the device seriously to connote character. Bill Sikes' "black velveteen coat, very soiled drab breeches . . . dirty belcher handkerchief around his neck" are the fitting garments of his obscene soul, just as the "powdered head and gold spectacles . . . bottle-green coat with a black velvet collar, . . . white trousers, and . . . smart bamboo cane" appropriately deck out Mr. Brownlow's fairy-godfather elegance of character.

However, the idea Dickens wished to convey in his novel was

that clothes do not really make the man except in the eyes of the beholder. So he hints in his pointed Preface of 1841, when he defends his choice of characters from St. Giles to his more squeamish readers:

> But there are people of so refined and delicate a nature, that they cannot bear the contemplation of these horrors. Not that they turn instinctively from crime; but that criminal characters, to suit them, must be, like their meat, in delicate disguise. A Massaroni in green velvet is an enchanting creature; but a Sikes in fustian is insupportable. A Mrs. Massaroni, being a lady in short petticoats and a fancy dress, is a thing to imitate in tableaux and have in lithograph on pretty songs; but a Nancy, being a creature in a cotton gown and cheap shawl, is not to be thought of. It is wonderful how Virtue turns from dirty stockings; and how Vice, married to ribbons and a little gay attire, changes her name, as wedded ladies do, and becomes Romance.

Accordingly, in the novel itself he scrambles clothes and characters to illustrate the arbitrariness of distinctions based on dress. Rags cover Nancy as well as Bill Sikes and Fagin. Bill Sikes and Mr. Brownlow both wear black velvet. To outward seeming, Monks and Mr. Brownlow are both gentlemen. Oliver changes clothes as he moves from thieves' den to country cottage and back again, but he does not change character. A facetious illustration of the accidents of attire is Bumble's fall from beadledom after his marriage to Mrs. Corney:

> The laced coat, and the cocked hat, where were they? He still wore knee-breeches, and dark cotton stockings on his nether limbs; but they were not *the* breeches. The coat was wide-skirted, and in that respect like *the* coat; but, oh, how different! The mighty cocked-hat was replaced by a modest round one. Mr. Bumble was no longer a beadle.

Bumble's downfall leads Dickens to philosophize on mankind in general:

> There are some promotions in life, which, independent of the more substantial rewards they offer, acquire peculiar value and dignity from the coats and waistcoats connected with them. A field-

marshal has his uniform, a bishop his silk apron, a counsellor his
silk gown, a beadle his cocked hat. Strip the bishop of his apron, or
the beadle of his hat and lace; what are they? Men. Mere Men.
Dignity, and even holiness, too, sometimes, are more questions of
coat and waistcoat than some people imagine. (CH. XXXVII)

These observations were not new. A few years before, some, at
least, of the first readers of *Oliver Twist* had been startled also by
passages like:

Has not your Red hanging-individual a horsehair wig, squirrel-
skins, and a plush-gown; whereby all mortals know that he is a
JUDGE?—Society, which the more I think of it astonishes me the
more, is founded upon Cloth.

Aprons are Defences; against injury to cleanliness, to safety, to
modesty, sometimes to roguery. . . . How much has been concealed, how much has been defended in Aprons! Nay, rightly
considered, what is your whole Military and Police Establishment,
charged at uncalculated millions, but a huge scarlet-coloured, iron-
fastened Apron, wherein Society works (uneasily enough) . . . . But
of all Aprons the most puzzling to me hitherto has been the
Episcopal or Cassock. Wherein consists the usefulness of this
Apron? The Overseer (*Episcopus*) of Souls, I notice, has tucked-in
the corner of it, as if his day's work were done: what does he
shadow forth thereby?

Lives the man that can figure a naked Duke of Windlestraw
addressing a naked House of Lords? Imagination, choked as in
mephitic air, recoils on itself, and will not forward with the
picture. The Woolsack, the Ministerial, the Opposition Benches?—
infandum! infandum! And yet why is the thing impossible? Was
not every soul, or rather every body, of these Guardians of our
Liberties, naked, or nearly so, last night; 'a forked Radish with a
Head fantastically carved'? And why might he not, did our stern
fate so order it, walk out to St. Stephens's, as well into bed in that
no-fashion; and there, with other similar Radishes, hold a Bed of
Justice?

Thomas Carlyle's Professor Diogenes Teufelsdröckh was, of
course, after bigger game than parish beadles, but his caustic
wisdom encompasses Mudfog. The life and opinions of this

abandoned waif, who grew up to occupy the Chair of Things-in-General at the University of Weissnichtwo, appeared in book form in 1838, while *Oliver Twist* was still running serially, but they had burst forth five years earlier in the pages of *Fraser's Magazine*. Dickens' long-lived (and generally unrequited) adulation of Carlyle's writings apparently began even earlier than *The French Revolution*.[36] *Oliver Twist* takes over from *Sartor Resartus* not only Professor Teufelsdröckh's Philosophy of Clothes, but his scorn for the dismal science of political economy as well. Herr Teufelsdröckh's "Liberals, Economists, Utilitarians . . . European Mechinisers" are Dickens' "experimenters" and "well-fed philosophers" anonymously and mysteriously responsible for Oliver's plight. Carlyle, in addition, overtly denounces what Dickens implicitly parodies—the "buck, or Blood, or Macaroni, or Incroyable, or Dandy."[37]

Of all Dickens' immediate contemporaries it was Carlyle who raised the orphan tale to the level of metaphysical and moral fantasy. *Oliver Twist* echoes the transcendentalism as well as the satire of *Sartor Resartus*. Entepfühl embraces Eastcheap, particularly in Teufelsdröckh's recollection of his obscure origins, as recorded in the chapter pointedly entitled "Genesis":

> Ever, in my distresses and my loneliness, has Fantasy turned, full of longing, to that unknown Father, who perhaps far from me, perhaps near, either way invisible, might have taken me to his paternal bosom, there to lie screened from many a woe. . . .
> And yet, O Man born of Woman . . . wherein is my case peculiar? . . . The Andreas and Gretchen, or the Adam and Eve, who led thee into Life, and for a time suckled and pap-fed thee there, whom thou namest Father and Mother; these were, like mine, but thy nursing-father and nursing-mother; thy true Beginning and Father is in Heaven, whom with the bodily eye thou shalt never behold, but only with the spiritual.

So Dickens reminds us about his orphan hero. In one of the more sentimental episodes he shows us Little Oliver, after suffering in silence from the corporal punishment of Mr. Sowerberry and the brutal taunts of Noah, finally giving vent to his repressed emotion: "But now when there were none to see or hear him, he fell upon his knees on the floor, and hiding his face in his hands, wept such tears as, God send for the credit of our nature, few so young may ever have cause to pour out before Him!" (CH. VII). This cloys because we feel removed from the situation and flatter ourselves that we don't need to be reminded, as Dickens assumed that his first readers needed to be, that the high and the humble have a common origin. Oliver's angelic appearance, his preternatural virtue and piety, his general aura of "clouds of glory" are all intended to recall his eternal home.

At a remove of more than a century we are especially likely to squirm over Oliver's farewell to the dying orphan Dick:

> "Yes, yes, I will [stop] to say good-bye to you," replied Oliver. "I shall see you again, Dick, I know I shall! You will be well and happy!"
>
> "I hope so," replied the child. "After I am dead, but not before. I know the doctor must be right, Oliver, because I dream so much of Heaven, and Angels, and kind faces that I never see when I am awake. Kiss me," said the child, climbing up the low gate, and flinging his arms round Oliver's neck. "Good-bye, dear! God bless you!"
>
> The blessing was from a young child's lips, but it was the first that Oliver had ever heard invoked upon his head; and through the struggles and sufferings and troubles and changes of his after life, he never once forgot it. (CH. VII)

But no reader of Wordsworth had difficulty believing in children who see angels. A reader of Carlyle besides, like Dickens, could see the orphan as representative of man's estrangement from his creator—Diogenes Teufelsdröckh's vision of the human condition. Little Oliver and Little Dick are best regarded not as real children but as symbolic children moving in a world that seems real but is reality transfigured.

Dickens provided a kind of postscript to *Oliver Twist* in his letter, "Crime and Education," contributed to the *Daily News* several years after the novel was first published.[38] Here he comments on the Ragged Schools he had visited, charity schools where overworked volunteers attempted to teach the poor, children and adults, "and show them some sympathy and stretch a hand out, which is not the iron hand of Law, for their correction." He conveys a lesson he carried away from a fetid classroom in Saffron Hill, where *Oliver Twist* takes place:

> This, Reader, was one room as full as it could hold; but these were only grains in sample of a Multitude that are perpetually sifting through these schools; in sample of a Multitude who had within them once, and perhaps have now, the elements of men as good as you or I, and maybe infinitely better; in sample of a Multitude among whose doomed and sinful ranks (oh, think of this, and think of them!) the child of any man upon this earth, however lofty his degree, must, as by Destiny and Fate, be found, if, at its birth, it were consigned to such an infancy and nurture, as these fallen creatures had!

Such a "fallen creature" is Oliver Twist, who "might have been the child of a nobleman or a beggar." Unlike Nancy and Little Dick, he is rescued from this multitude because Dickens has singled him out for a special mission. Dickens was critical of the Ragged Schools, particularly of their overemphasis on religious mysteries beyond the comprehension of their pupils, but he urges his readers to support them. He would especially like to see funds that have been contributed by the wealthy toward the building of new churches diverted to these impoverished classrooms, "as an appropriate means of illustrating the Christian Religion." He suggests, moreover, that they do not remain aloof, but "go themselves into the Prisons and the Ragged Schools, and form their own conclusions." Through Oliver Twist, in effect, he enables his readers to be reborn. With Oliver they live among the "doomed and sinful ranks," the Ragged Schools writ large in the dens of Eastcheap. They even descend with him into the cells of the condemned. What we might have expected to be a shattering, traumatic experience for Little Oliver—his witnessing of Fagin's last night alive—instead brings out the depth of his human sympathy. "Oh! God forgive this wretched man!" are his words as his most fiendish tormentor is led to the gallows. So high and low, old and young, virtuous and villainous, are brought together in a common bond.[39]

Sensationalism, satire, and sentiment—those disparate and sometimes discordant elements of Dickens' genius—tend toward the same goal—to make humanity recognize what they have in common. Depending on Dickens' mood, all men are criminals, fops, or angels. As early as *Oliver Twist* we recognize a tension between the tender-minded and the tough-minded Dickens. "Men who look on nature, and their fellow men, and cry that all is dark and gloomy, are in the right," he observes halfway through his story, "but the sombre colours are reflections from their own jaundiced eyes and hearts. The real hues are delicate and need a clearer vision" (CH. XXXIV). To us he seems to see more powerfully out of his "jaundiced eyes" than with his "clearer vision." In *Oliver Twist* his "sombre colours," the murky city scenes, somehow impress themselves on our memory, while the "delicate hues," the idyllic country scenes, remain a roseate blur. The vividness that Dickens gives to the world of darkness has led Graham Greene mistakenly to call him a Manichean. Dickens really means for "the principle of Good" to survive, but the principle of Evil engaged both his imagination and his sense of humor more. Whereas his irony and caustic wit come into play in his treatment of the thieves, he leaned on stock associations of the good, the beautiful, and the pathetic in representing Rose Maylie and her family.[40] His own representation of humanity, therefore, may seem out of focus; but a balanced picture, he reiterates in his various prefaces to *Oliver Twist,* includes "the best and worst shades of our nature; much of its ugliest hues, and something of its most beautiful."

Although we tend to think of *Oliver Twist* as a novel about the poor, it really contains in essence the novel of society that Dickens developed with greater amplitude in *Bleak House, Little*

Dorrit, and *Our Mutual Friend,* where all classes are reciprocally involved not merely symbolically but literally. The pattern of the well-born descending to the lower depths tends to reverse itself in the mature novels, with the low-born moving up and discovering their new-found wealth to be a curse rather than a blessing. With his growing cynicism Dickens also was to stress the acquisitiveness rather than the kindliness of the wealthy. But he continued to lodge his faith in the hearts of men rather than in institutions. The motiveless benignity of a Mr. Brownlow and the Cheeryble Brothers counted for more than a parish work-house, a Bible Institute, or organized philanthropy as represented by Mrs. Jellyby and Mrs. Pardiggle. If distrust of institutions accounts for some of his most effective satire, trust in man accounts for some of his most mawkish sentimentality. At the beginning of his career he could glance back nostalgically at an ideal eighteenth-century vision of the benevolent gentleman carrying on God's work in the world. This is the tradition inherited by Oliver Twist and Rose Maylie, who—temporarily fallen from their true places—are restored to them; "tried by adversity, [they] remembered its lessons in mercy to others, and mutual love and fervent thanks to Him who had protected and preserved them." Humanity is joined in a circle of empathy and an apostolic succession of benevolence.

Of all the popular types of fiction that Dickens wove into this children's story for adults, he had a special affinity, in these early years, for the foundling tale. A true story that his first readers did not know—as remarkable in its way as the Parish Boy's Progress—was his own progress from Baynham Street and Camden Town to Regent's Park. *Oliver Twist* was the first of what was to be a series of projections of his own situation as the *arriviste.* It is not a mere accidental detail, surely, that Oliver sees his gentleman-savior for the first time in front of a bookstall. It was, after all, to literature that Dickens owed his own "rescue" from obscurity. Mr. Brownlow's library plays as important a part in Oliver's rehabilitation as the village church. Oliver rejects the crime thrillers of Fagin in favor of the Bible, *The Pilgrim's Progress,* and those numerous unnamed books given him by Mr. Brownlow, at the time when Dickens was leaving behind mere amusement and entertainment and dedicating himself to "improving" literature. Mr. Brownlow, in a way, stands for the reading public that made possible Dickens' rise from reporter to novelist-prince. This public Dickens was later to visualize as Abel Magwitch, in terms of Frankenstein's monster pursuing his creator—but that, of course, is another story.

CHARACTERISTIC FICTION CONTEMPORANEOUS WITH *OLIVER TWIST* (1837–39)

1820 Edward Lytton Blanchard, *The Life of George Barnwell; or, The London Apprentice of the Last Century.*

1821 Pierce Egan, *Life in London; or, The Day and Night Scenes of Jerry Hawthorn, Esq. and Corinthian Tom.*

The Affecting History of Tom Bragwell, wherein are strikingly delineated the rise, progress, and fatal termination of juvenile delinquency.

1823 [Dorothy Kilner], *Edward Neville; or, The Memoirs of an Orphan.*

1824 Barbara Hofland, *Decision: A Tale.*

———, *Patience: A Tale.*

1826 Benjamin Disraeli, *Vivian Grey.*

Mrs. Hudson (Marianne Spencer Stanhope) , *Almack's.*

1827 Barbara Hofland, *Self-Denial: A Tale.*

Lady Charlotte Bury, *Flirtation.*

1828 Edward Bulwer-Lytton, *Pelham; or, The Adventures of a Gentleman.*

Charles White, *Almack's Revisited.*

Lady Charlotte Bury, *A Marriage in High Life.*

1829 Lady Charlotte Bury, *The Exclusives.*

1830 Barbara Hofland, *Elizabeth and Her Three Beggar Boys.* (Abridged from *Tales of the Priory* [1820].)

Edward Bulwer-Lytton, *Paul Clifford.*

W. Massie, *Sydenham; or, Memoirs of a Man of the World.*

1831 John Brownlow, *Hans Sloane; A Tale Illustrating the History of the Foundling Hospital.*

1832 Edward Bulwer-Lytton, *Eugene Aram.*

1834 William Harrison Ainsworth, *Rookwood.*

Lady Charlotte Bury, *The Disinherited and the Ensnared.*

1835 Barbara Hofland, *Fortitude: A Tale.*

1837 Theodore Hook, *Jack Brag.*

Fatherless Fanny; or, A Young Girl's Entrance into Life. (One of numerous reprints of this anonymous children's story, first published ca. 1818.)

Barbara Hofland, *Humility: A Tale.*

1838 William Henry De Merle, *Melton de Mowbray; or, The Banker's Son.*

1839 Thomas Peckett Prest ("Bos"), *Oliver Twiss.*

1840 William Harrison Ainsworth, *Jack Sheppard.* (Appeared serially in *Bentley's Miscellany* from January, 1839 through March, 1840.)

Frances Trollope, *The Life and Adventures of Michael Armstrong, the Factory Boy.*

CHAPTER V

Pendennis:

Arthur Pendennis and the
Reformed Coxcomb

THACKERAY, like Dickens, moved into the novel from "maga-
zinery," but his apprenticeship lasted longer, for he did not have
his chief rival's good fortune to leap into fame with a bound.
Though he was an unsuccessful applicant for the job of illustrating the *Posthumous Papers of the Pickwick Club,* he owed his
start in fiction to Dickens, who accepted his first story, "The
Professor," for *Bentley's Miscellany.*[1] Both made their debuts as
novelists with rogue tales, but Thackeray's unpleasant "cathar-
tic," *Catherine,* lay buried in *Fraser's Magazine,* a failure with
both critics and public, while *Oliver Twist,* one of the novels it
lampooned, enjoyed new life both in boards and wrappers.
Dickens felt sufficiently established to break free of the "Bent-
leian bonds" at a time when Thackeray, practically unknown in
his own country, was pleased to get a glimmer of recognition in
America in N. P. Willis' *The Corsair.* In 1841, when Dickens
could boast five successful novels, Thackeray ventured to predict
in the preface to his *Comic Tales and Sketches* that he was

marching to "the very brink of immortality" with Michael
Angelo Titmarsh, Charles Yellowplush, and Major Gahagan, but
he had to mark time for six years more. Early in 1844 in an issue
of *Fraser's Magazine,* where his second novel, the cynical *Barry
Lyndon,* was running, generally unappreciated, he praised "A
Christmas Carol," expressing his gratitude to its author for "the
harmless laughter, the generous wit, the frank, manly human
love which he has taught us to feel."[2] With *Vanity Fair,* his less
genial picture of humanity finally seized hold of the large public,
and Thackeray suddenly found himself "all but at the top of the
tree . . . and having a great fight up there with Dickens."[3]
With his next novel he was indeed competing with Dickens, the
two novelists having arrived at the same stage—the one "dismiss-
ing some portion of himself into the shadowy world" with *David
Copperfield,* the other feeling free to "lay bare his own weaknesses, vanities, peculiarities" in *Pendennis.*[4]

By now the two authors have changed their moods—Dickens,
the "sentimentalist," describes an unhappy childhood, while
Thackeray, the "cynic," reveals a relatively happy one. While
working on *Pendennis,* Thackeray confided to a friend: "I am
beginning to see the folly of my ways & that people are a
hundred times more frank, kind and good-natured than a certain
author chooses to paint them. He shan't wear yellow anymore: it
is he who is jaundiced and not the world that is bitter: in fine
. . . I will have my next book in rose colour and try to amend."[5]
Thackeray's mutation quite possibly was induced by his friend
Lewes' complaint: "In *Vanity Fair* . . . how little there is to
love! The people are all scamps, scoundrels, or humbugs."[6] At
any rate, Lewes, when reviewing *Pendennis,* pointedly observed
that the new novel was "a very decided advance" upon its
predecessor "with respect to a broader and more generous view of
humanity, a larger admixture of good with what is evil, and a
more loving mellowed tone throughout."[7] Juvenal has given way
to Horace. Now accepted by the public that had ignored or been
indifferent to him, Thackeray could relax his indignation. Also,

having put more of himself into his new novel, he shifts his mental position from detached ironist to engaged moralist.

Thackeray's subject, as before, is "erring man" viewed against the large "canvas of humanity,"[8] but this time he focuses his light not on an anti-hero but on a semi-hero in whom vice and virtue are more subtly blended. As Becky Sharp is a "civilized" Catherine, practicing a more refined husband-murder, so Arthur Pendennis is a more intelligent Barry Lyndon, worming his way into society like that scapegrace with the aid of false genealogy and a scheming uncle, but spared his predecessor's disgrace by a saving conscience. Although to an extent he was reliving his own childhood and youth in Pendennis, Thackeray was really transmuting himself into one of the representative "gentlemen of our age," as he says in his Preface, "no better nor worse than most educated men." Parents had been reading of life among young men in the barracks in Charles Lever's *Confessions of Con Creagan, the Irish Gil Blas,* and in midshipman's quarters in James Hannay's books such as *A Claret Cup for Naval Messes.* Thackeray would have them know at close hand "what moves in the real world, what passes in society, in the clubs, colleges, messrooms—what is the life and talk of your sons." So we are invited once more to witness the maturing of a naive young man by home, school, and society, under the guidance and misguidance of a variety of mentors. Unlike Oliver Twist, Arthur Pendennis is tested by prosperity rather than adversity. As Thackeray hints in his Preface, he was more familiar with refined depravity than with "the manners of ruffians and gaol-birds." Arthur Pendennis grows up amidst surroundings at once more rarefied than Little Oliver's, more opulent than Fanny Price's, and more worldly than Edward Waverley's.

The leading interest of *Pendennis* in the "gentlemen of our age" and "the notorious foibles and selfishness of their education" is borne out even by some of the commodities advertised in the original monthly parts: Rowland's Macassar Oil; The Gentleman's Real Head of Hair, or Invisible Peruke; Doudney's

Royal Registered Cloak for Gentlemen; Nicoll's Registered Pale-
tot; Ford's "Eureka" Shirts. Some of the books promoted are
Douglas Jerrold's *Punch's Letters to His Son* and *A Man Made of
Money;* Frank Smedley's *Frank Fairlegh, or Scenes from the Life
of a Private Pupil;* a new and cheap edition of Bulwer's *Pelham;
or, The Adventures of a Gentleman;* a reprinting of Hogarth's
The Rake's Progress, and Lady Ponsonby's *The Discipline of
Life.* Conspicuous among publishers' offerings is John Leech's
series of lithographs from *Punch* called *The Rising Generation.*
Had Thackeray not been equally skilled with the pencil and pen
himself, Leech's drawings could have served well to illustrate
Pendennis, with their young gentlemen ogling heiresses at the
piano, cutting each other out in the ballroom, passionately
declaring themselves on their knees before ethereal beauties,
holding forth on metaphysics and literature, arguing with "the
Governor" over the weekly allowance.

Thackeray's own allegorical wrapper designed for the monthly
parts, depicting a young man flanked on one side by sprites, on
the other by innocents, proclaims immediately the theme of
youth at the crossroads. Pen is described as a bivalent character
with a potential for good: "very weak as well as very impetuous,
very vain as well as very frank, and if of a generous disposition,
not a little selfish in the midst of his profuseness" (CH. XVIII).
This motif is repeated by some of the illustrations, like "Youth
Between Pleasure and Duty" (CH. III, Pen with Foker on one
side and his schoolmaster, Dr. Smirke, on the other), and the
picture of Pen as the Prodigal Son that originally decorated the
title page of Volume II. The historiated initials, a more sophisticated form of Thackeray's schoolboy doodling in copy books,
gloss the moral fable of the text with their emblems of life as a
school (the child on lead strings, CH. XVIII; the child in cap and
gown, CH. XVII; the child in a dunce cap, CH. XXII; the child
being trained in music by Pan, CH. XXXI), or as a battlefield
(the child as a warrior, CH. XXI; the child confronting a dragon,
CH. XXIX; the young man riding off on a charger, CH. XXX).

The temptations of youth in society are also depicted graphically (a nymph draped about a wine cup, CH. XIX; a tavern assignation, CH. XXXV; gluttony, CH. XLI; a snake wrapped around a tree, CH. LXV) .[9]

In the 1830's while Dickens, among others, was casting aspersions on the education of the lower classes, there was plenty of evidence that all was not well with upper class education either. Henry Beazley's *The Oxonians* (1830) opens with this anonymous poem:

> Who wouldn't send a son to college
> To gather there all kinds of knowledge
> To stuff his head with Greek and Latin
> Till the classics he is pat in;
> To hunt, to swear, to drink and dine
> And fit him for a grave divine.

Beazley uses the novel itself as a platform to denounce the curricula of Eton and Oxford, which launch youth "from the learned ignorance of a college into the great world," where he "falls prey to the villainy of others or his own intemperance." The only worthy education, in his opinion, is "that knowledge of life which assists us in our progress through it; which enables us to stem the tide of our passions, to resist temptation, and to make the best use of every opportunity which presents itself." The choice before youth, according to Beazley, seems to be the Rake's Progress or the Pilgrim's Progress, and he regrets the false direction given them by parents and schoolmasters early in life when they are most pliable.

At the end of the decade, Mrs. Gore in *The Cabinet Minister* (1839) shows us an educated young aristocrat idling about town with the "harum scarum schoolboys" of his set and complains that despite his great abilities ripe for development, "the tares implanted at public schools and fashionable colleges were overruning the generous soil, to the extermination of all hope for harvest." The Cruikshank drawings for *Frank Fairlegh* that advertise this school tale in one of the monthly parts of *Pen-*

dennis indicate that in some ways the situation had not improved in ten years. Glowering over the scene is a dissipated-looking goblin in mortar board, wine glass in hand, long pipe dangling from his mouth. Decorating the border are students engaged in such academic pursuits as horseback riding, coaching, playing billiards, and dancing. But the picture is not all bad. One young man is shown studying by a lamp, and crowning the page is a wedding group.

Near the time when Thackeray began writing *Pendennis,* George Henry Lewes, in his novel *Ranthorpe* (1847) , expressed a somewhat more sanguine outlook than most other writers:

> Parents are needlessly alarmed at the wildness of their sons. Look at the young Cantabs and Oxonians, who, after getting deeply into debt, learning more slang than Greek, becoming first rate "dragsmen" or incomparable scullers, instead of senior wranglers, are pronounced by parents worthless scamps for whom no hope is possible. What do these young men become? Scamps? No: good, upright manly Englishmen; specimens of the finest race in the world—English gentlemen . . . interrogate their youths, and see from what youthful extravagances these men have emerged to become the first of citizens. (Book V, CH. III)

Lewes urges that bad early lessons are not necessarily indelible and that up to a point one has control over his moral destiny. His novel, like *Pendennis,* is concerned with the "critical period in the young man's life when he may be turned into anything that is good." "Give the young men their pleasures," affirms Major Pendennis, Pen's experienced uncle. "I'm not one of your strait-laced moralists, but an old man of the world, begad; and I know that as long as it lasts, young men will be young men!" This is one point of view. The author, momentarily siding with the "strait-laced moralist," adds: "And there were some young men to whom this estimable philosopher accorded about seventy years as the proper period for sowing their wild oats: but they were men of fashion" (CH. XLI). As for his young hero's improvement with time, Thackeray oscillates between optimism

and pessimism. The suspense is kept up even by Thackeray's
cover drawing, which came out in two versions. In the monthly
parts, Pen looks in the direction of the good woman; by the time
the story is published in book form Pen's eyes have shifted
toward the sea nymph. In the novel itself, the issue is complicated and diversified by the various young men with whom Pen's
destiny is interwoven: Henry Foker, the spoiled buck, his rival
for Blanche Amory; Sam Huxter, the coarse young medical
student who wins Fanny Bolton; Warrington, the bohemian
intellectual who sadly relinquishes Laura to Pen. Then too there
is the pampered young brother of Blanche Amory, and to offset
him, that country earl's grandson, Mr. Pynsent, "going to set up
as a Parliament man." So Thackeray draws his "gentlemen of our
age" from a wide circle—town and country; decadent aristocracy,
rural gentry; nouveaux riches, middle class; leisured and professional.

With its emphasis on the problems of youth, *The History of
Pendennis* indicates that Thackeray was shifting from the "cynical and sentimental history" that he labeled *Vanity Fair* to a
domestic history, setting Jane Austen's miniatures of home life
against Scott's pageants of social life and manners. He maintains
his intimacy with his audience—the "confidential talk between
writer and reader" promised in the Preface—but his tone this
time is mellower and less supercilious. Readers are brought into
contact with a sophisticated man of the world who is at the same
time "one of them." "There is no writer of the present day who
has established such friendly relations between himself and the
public—none whom the reader seems to know so well, and with
whom he feels so familiar," testified one of the first reviewers of
Pendennis. "We think, somehow, that we have often met him—
that we are in the habit of dining with him—that he has often
come to take a bed in our house, or been housed with us beneath
other men's roofs." So easy is this "alliance" between Thackeray
and his readers, affirms this particular reader, that "We think
that we have often spent a day in pleasant converse with him—

no high discourse about 'fixed fate, free-will, foreknowledge absolute' but common everyday talk about worldly topics. . . ."[10]

In keeping with this pose of family friend, Thackeray addresses his "confidential talk" to all members of the household. He offers advice to sons and daughters on matters of the heart: "It is best to love wisely no doubt; but to love foolishly is better than not to be able to love at all. Some of us can't; and are proud of our impotence too" (CH. VI). He spares the feelings of young ladies not particularly well endowed by nature when he passes up a chance to praise Laura: "I am not good at descriptions of female beauty; and, indeed, do not care for it in the least (thinking that goodness and virtue are, of course, far more advantageous to a young lady than any mere fleeting charms of person and face) " (CH. XXII). Now and then he turns to their parents to nudge them with a gentle irony: "But these circumstances [Pen's rakish days at Oxbridge] . . . took place some years back, when William the Fourth was king. Young men are much better behaved now, and besides, Saint Boniface was rather a fast college" (CH. XVIII). Mothers who, like Helen Pendennis, hesitate about letting their sons loose on the Babylon of London are admonished: "Temptation is an obsequious servant that has no objection to the country, and we know that it takes up its lodging in hermitages as well as in cities. . . ." (CH. XXVIII). At the end of the novel, for the benefit of wives and daughters who might be disposed to ask: "And what sort of a husband would this Pendennis be?," the author ventures to predict that Laura can look forward to a reasonably happy marriage. Thackeray's first readers looked to their author for advice on child rearing, education, marriage, and domestic relations, following the fortunes of the Pendennis family eagerly as variations on their own.

To extend the education of his readers, the narrator of *Pendennis* calls the attention of the older generation in particular to social change, such as new styles in dress and household furnishing (illustrated by the advertisements in the monthly parts) , and the coming of the railway (as Major Pendennis trundles to Fairoaks in the cramped, stuffy mail-coach: "Eight miles an hour, for twenty or five-and-twenty hours, . . . a hard seat, a gouty tendency, a perpetual change of coachmen grumbling because you did not fee them enough, a fellow-passenger partial to spirits-and-water,—who has not borne with these evils in the jolly old times? and how could people travel under such difficulties? And yet they did and were merry too" CH. VII). In connection with the marriage market, he reminds them that they are living through an age of leveling, as indicated by the social success of the illiterate parvenu Lady Clavering: "This fact shows our British independence and honest feeling—our higher orders are not such mere haughty aristocrats as the ignorant represent them: on the contrary, if a man have money they will hold out their hands to him, eat his dinners, dance at his balls, marry his daughters, or give their own lovely girls to his sons, as affably as your commonest roturier would do" (CH. XXXVIII). "Rank and buth," to quote Charles Yellowplush, are disappearing. "We are grown doosid republican," remarks Major Pendennis to Lady Clavering's affected daughter Blanche. "Talent ranks with birth and wealth now, begad: and a clever man with a clever wife may take any place they please" (CH. XLV). It is not, of course, so much Blanche's talent that the Major is interested in as her money, which he is eager to secure for nephew Arthur, but he shows himself to be a sound observer of the passing social parade none the less.

The author's course of instruction, moreover, takes in the loftier as well as the lighter "topics-of-the-day," as he warns his readers in the Preface when he identifies "the story-teller" with "graver writers or thinkers" as conveyors of truth. He indicates much later that his novel is not merely about his hero's "Fortunes and Misfortunes," as the title states, but an attempt "to follow out, in its progress, the development of the mind of a worldly and selfish, but not ungenerous or unkind or truth avoiding man" (CH. LXII). Because Thackeray is charting his hero's mental as well as moral growth, intellectual history is superimposed upon social history.[11] The religious events of the 1840's cast their shadows over this novel of the 1830's. Helen Pendennis, on a continental tour with her family, feels a shock of revulsion at the "Barefooted friars in the streets; crowned images of Saints and Virgins in the churches before which people were bowing down and worshipping, in direct defiance, as she held, of the written law" (CH. LVII). She represents one extreme. At the other is a cousin of Henry Foker's, one of the daughters of the Earl of Rosherville, who has converted her cupboard into an oratory and fasts on Fridays (CH. XL), and Blanche Amory preparing altar covers for the Reverend Mr. Smirke, who moves high enough to read the Roman Hours and "intimated that he was ready to receive confessions in the vestry" (CH. LXIV). The first readers of *Pendennis* were presumably following the controversies over the Ritualist Movement, and in 1850, the year *Pendennis* was first published in book form, occurred the so-called Papal Aggression, when Father Wiseman was created Cardinal and a Roman Catholic hierarchy was established in England.[12] While attending Oxbridge, Pen does not sound like the kind of student who would have been sensitive to the rumblings of the Oxford Movement, but he pontificates on it to Warrington: "Make a faith or a dogma absolute, and persecution becomes a logical consequence. . . . Make dogma absolute, and to inflict or to suffer death becomes easy and necessary" (CH. LXII). Such sacrifices do not appeal to this relativist and hedonist any more than the Monastic Revival then being preached across the Channel by Montalembert and Lacordaire, of which he seems also to be aware: "Were the world composed of Saint Bernards or Saint Dominics, it would be equally odious. . . . Would you have every man with his head shaved and every woman in a cloister,—carrying out to the full the ascetic principle?" He even looks ahead to "that man, who, driven fatally by the remorseless logic of his creed, gives up everything, friends, fame, dearest ties, closest vanities, the respect of an army of churchmen, the recognised position of a leader, and passes over, truth-impelled, to the enemy in whose ranks he will serve as a nameless private soldier." "That man," to Pen's readers if not to Warrington, his immediate audience, was of course Newman, whose conversion of 1845 was retold in fictional guise in *Loss and Gain* (1848), a novel they could have been reading in between the installments of *Pendennis*.

Pen doesn't seem to have shone in the Debating Union at Oxbridge either, but his discourses on politics with Warrington also reveal unusual foresight: "The fiercest reformers grow calm, and are fain to put up with things as they are; the loudest Radical orators become dumb, quiescent placemen [Chartists]; the most fervent Liberals when out of power, become humdrum Conservatives or downright tyrants or despots in office. Look at Thiers, look at Guizot, in opposition and in place![13] [The guns of the Revolution of 1830 were echoing in the ears of Pen and Warrington; for the readers of *Pendennis* it was the Revolution of 1848]. Look at the Whigs appealing to the country, and the Whigs in power! [Lord John Russell and his temporizing cabinet, for example]." Politics and religion give the iconoclasm of young Pen something substantial to batten on.

Primarily, however, *Pendennis* is about the development of a writer; therefore, appropriately, literary life is very much in the foreground. Quite possibly because he had more of a struggle for success than did Dickens, Thackeray gives us more of a sense of the vagaries and vicissitudes of the early Victorian literary market place than we get in *David Copperfield*.[14] Through Bacon and Bungay (generally identified with the rival publishers Colburn and Bentley, who had begun their careers as partners), Thackeray exposes the huckstering that too often had pegged the prices in this market. The impecunious Captain Shandon (said to be based in part on William Maginn) is only too vivid evidence of the precariousness of the career of literary journalism that had supported Thackeray himself so fitfully before *Vanity Fair*. With Percy Popjoy, the would-be novelist, Mr. Wagg, the shallow popular favorite, and Miss Bunion, the poetaster, he shows that literature's rewards can be as undeserved as they are capricious. At one point he even questions the basis of Pen's (and by implication his own) success:

> If Mr. Pen's works have procured him more reputation than has been acquired by his abler friend [Warrington], whom no one knows, George lives contented without the fame. If the best men do not draw the great prizes in life, we know it has been so settled by the Ordainer of the lottery. We own, and see daily, how the false and worthless live and prosper, while the good are called away, and the dear and the young perish untimely. . . . (CH. LXXVI)

However, it is not only at Mr. Bungay's dinner and in Captain Shandon's prison cell that authors and authorship are conspicuous. Whereas we are hardly aware that David Copperfield is a practicing writer, Arthur Pendennis is in constant preparation for his vocation. His poems to Miss Fotheringay and Blanche Amory, *Sturm und Drang* effusions though they are, amount to his literary apprenticeship. He begins his first novel, *Walter Lorraine,* in college. Later his colloquies with Warrington consider the career of literature as well as "topics of the day." At the end of the novel Pen, along with his public duties, is still on the staff of the *Pall Mall Gazette* and presumably is able to give some of his time to writing the sort of novels Laura approves of: "good books, kind books, with gentle kind thoughts . . . such as might do people good to read." Through Pen, Thackeray traces his own metamorphosis from journalist to novelist-philosopher.

In recounting Pen's literary development from apprentice to author, Thackeray, like Sir Walter Scott before him, acts as a readers' advisor to his hero, to the other characters in the novel, and, by extension, to his audience. No believer in "free" reading, he takes Pen to task as a little boy because "he never read to improve himself out of school-hours, but, on the contrary, devoured all the novels, plays and poetry, on which he could lay his hands" (CH. II). The author is explicit here: "He devoured all the books at home from Inchbald's Theatre [Mrs. Inchbald was, among other things, a translator of Kotzebue, who is in Miss Fotheringay's repertoire] to White's Farriery [the better to emulate the sporting buck]. . . . He found at Clavering an old cargo of French novels [Mme. de Genlis? Mme. de Staël? Chateaubriand? Paul de Kock?]" (CH. III). It is true that at other times Pen "would sit for hours perched upon the topmost bar of Doctor Portman's library steps with a folio on his knees, whether it were Hakluyt's Travels, Hobbes's Leviathan, Augustini Opera, or Chaucer's Poems," which bodes well for his intellectual and spiritual development. At this point unfortunately, like Edward Waverley, Arthur Pendennis gobbles up his reading without digesting it properly. Dr. Smirke, more interested in courting Helen than in guiding Arthur, proves as lax a tutor as Sir Everard Waverley's chaplain from Oxford.

The classical poetry Arthur reads with Dr. Smirke sets him off on the writing of bombastic tragedies and Ovidian verses addressed to Miss Fotheringay. He would take the love sentiments and let the wisdom go. As for modern poetry, Thackeray is by implication just as critical of exuberant romantics like the authors of *The Corsair* and *Lalla Rookh,* Pen's favorites, as he is of lacrimators like Bishop Heber and Felicia Hemans, who cause Helen Pendennis "to melt right away, and be absorbed into her pocket-handkerchief" (CH. III). The compromise between poetry and morality is reached, we gather, with *The Christian Year,* in which verse is wedded to liturgy: "The son and the mother whispered it to each other with awe—faint, very faint," we are told in words clearly meant to be taken seriously, "and seldom in after-life Pendennis heard that solemn church-music: but he always loved the remembrance of it, and of the times when it struck his heart, and he walked over the fields full of hope and void of doubt, as the church-bells rang on Sunday morning." This passage is accompanied by drawings showing Pen's mother pointing out a church to him from their balcony. Close thy Byron, open thy Keble![15]

The women in *Pendennis* are for the most part not particularly sophisticated in their reading taste, nor, it would follow for
Thackeray, in their reading of life. Madame Fribsby, the milli-
ner, is an especially avid reader of romances, "and by a perpetual
perusal of such works (which were by no means so moral or
edifying in the days of which we write, as they are at present) she
had got to be so absurdly sentimental that in her eyes life was
nothing but an immense love match; and she never could see two
people together, but she fancied they were dying for one another" (CH. XVI). That latter-day *précieuse* Blanche Amory also
is in love with love. Lamartine is her poet, while her novelists are
Balzac (presumably as author of *Modeste Mignon* rather than
Eugénie Grandet) and George Sand. As a result, "however little
she sympathised with her relatives at home, she had friends, as
she said, in the spirit-world, meaning the tender Indiana, the
passionate and poetic Lelia, the amiable Trenmor, that high-
souled convict, that angel of the galleys,—the fiery Stenio,—and
the other numberless heroes of the French romances" (CH. XXIV) .[16]
The temperament in particular of George Sand seems to have
transferred itself to her idolatress Miss Amory—an overheated
fancy joined to emotional frigidity.

The low-class Fanny Bolton, no less than the haughty Blanche
Amory, has been sheltered between rose-colored book covers.
Vauxhall, where Pen begins his rather tame flirtation with the
porter's daughter, is presented to us first through her immature
fancy: "'. . . O-O-law, how beautiful!' She shrank back as she
spoke, starting with wonder and delight as she saw the Royal
Gardens blaze before her with a hundred million of lamps, with
a splendour such as the finest fairy tale, the finest pantomime she
had ever witnessed at the theatre, had never realised" (CH.
XLVII). Pen notices in her "a great deal of dangerous and
rather contagious sensibility." Later we learn: "Many novels had
Fanny read, in secret and at home in three volumes and in
numbers." This was during the mid-1830's before the *Penny
Story Teller*, *Lloyd's Penny Sunday Times*, and *Reynolds'*

Weekly Newspaper. "Periodical literature had not yet reached the height which it has attained subsequently, and the girls of Fanny's generation were not enabled to purchase sixteen pages of excitement for a penny, rich with histories of crime, murder, oppressed virtue and the heartless seductions of the aristocracy." But every age has its vicarious roses and thorns, and consequently Fanny "had had the benefit of the circulating library which, in conjunction with her school and a small brandy-ball and millinery business, Miss Minifer kept,—and Arthur appeared to her at once as the type and realisation of the heroes of all those darling greasy volumes which the young girl had devoured" (CH. XLVIII). Thackeray refers here of course to the numerous pomade-streaked spawn of Vivian Grey and Pelham.

The reading of the female characters of *Pendennis* runs to the three S's—Sensationalism, Sentimentality, and Sensibility—that Thackeray habitually scorned. Like the plays performed by the illiterate actress Miss Fotheringay, these novels prettify or romanticize life. However, most of the male characters with their humdrum tastes offer no better examples to Arthur. Major Pendennis' respectful distance from great literature is suggested by his attribution of "Whatever is, is right" to Shakespeare. His favorite novelist seems to be Paul de Kock. Blanche Amory's stepfather Sir Francis Clavering turns to Bell's *Life in London* (edited by Pierce Egan) in his abundant leisure. Foker's room is lined not with bookshelves but with French prints of odalisques and likenesses of Conkey Sam and the Worcestershire Nobber in action. At the other extreme is the grind Paley, buried in his law books at the Temple, who "could not cultivate a friendship or do a charity, or admire a work of genius, or kindle at the sight of beauty or the sound of a sweet song. . . . All was dark outside his reading lamp. Love, and Nature, and Art (which is the expression of our praise and sense of the beautiful world of God) were shut out from him" (CH. XXX).[17] Thackeray tries to move his men and women, along with his readers, out of the hothouse environments of theatre, sports ring, circulating library, and study chamber into "the beautiful world of God" and His works.

The student whom Pen is expected to emulate is not Paley but Warrington, who interests himself in "all higher thoughts, all better things, all the wisdom of philosophers and historians, all the thoughts of poets; all wit, fancy, reflection, art, love, truth altogether." Therefore, once Helen Pendennis has supervised Pen's moral education, Smirke has started him on his academic study, and Major Pendennis has indoctrinated him in the ways of society, Warrington takes over as his literary mentor. Pen has come to admire Warrington's articles with their "strong thoughts and curt periods, the sense, the satire, and the scholarship." He is gratified by his older and wiser friend's encouragement: "Those little scraps and verses which I have seen of yours, show me, what is rare in these days, a natural gift, sir" (CH. XXXII). Pen and Warrington are apt counterfoils. "I am a prose labourer," Warrington says to Pen at one point, "you, my boy, are a poet in a small way, and so, I suppose, you are authorised to be flighty" (CH. XXXIII). Thackeray may seem to be using Warrington rather immodestly as an indirect self-tribute, but actually he splits himself in two here to represent two complementary aspects of his literary imagination—its mercurial nature, reflected in Pen, held in check by its more practical nature, reflected in Warrington. Where Pen is the dilettante, Warrington is the philosopher; where Pen is the romantic, Warrington is the realist; where Pen is the worldly skeptic, Warrington is the idealist. Moreover, the colloquies between them in effect allow Thackeray to have a dialogue with himself—the sympathetic moralist in him correcting the would-be dandy and cynic.[18]

Warrington, appropriately, guides Pen's hand as he rewrites his novel-in-progress, *Walter Lorraine*. Pen would write a serious study of society. By now he has moved out of his *Sturm-und-Drang* mood, "the Byronic despair, the Wertherian despondency, the mocking bitterness of Mephistopheles of Faust," that empurpled the part of the novel he wrote at Oxbridge (CH. XLII). As with Edward Waverley, the romance of his life is ending and its history is about to begin—but it is to be a contemporary history. The impecunious journalist Captain Shandon had aroused his interest by speaking of "the characters of the day, and great personages of fashion, with easy familiarity and jocular allusions, as if it was his habit to live amongst them" (CH. XXXIII). Yet he is not contented with the "flood of fashionable talk" that Mr. Wagg likes to pour out (CH. XXVI) and would not like to be in the situation of the hack Finucane, "in tattered trousers and dingy shirtsleeves, cheerfully describing and arranging the most brilliant *fêtes* of the world of fashion" (CH. XXXVI). He would be one with the "world of fashion," but he would prefer that their talk have some significance beyond mere gossip.

We do not learn much about the published version of *Walter Lorraine* apart from Percy Popjoy's promotion statement that it is "full of wit, genius, satire, pathos, and every conceivable good quality" (CH. XLII). Nor is Helen Pendennis' description of it as "a happy mixture of Shakespeare and Byron, and Walter Scott" very helpful. Pen was writing, we are informed, "at the period when the novel called 'The Fashionable' was in vogue among us, and Warrington [in trying to sell Pen's novel to Mr. Bungay] did not fail to point out . . . how Pen was a man of the very first fashion himself, and received at the houses of some of the greatest personages in the land." Thackeray could be referring to Lady Charlotte Bury's *The Exclusives*, first published in 1829 (followed, like *Vivian Grey*, by a "Key" identifying the persons of note represented). Or he may have intended a composite of this and other gossip novels like *Memoirs of a Lady of Fashion*, *The Fashionables and the Unfashionables*, *English Fashionables Abroad*, and *Russell; or, The Reign of Fashion*.

Thackeray himself commented on a later novel of Lady Charlotte Bury's called *Love* (1837): "If this is exclusive love, it should be a lesson to all men never to marry a woman beyond the rank of milkmaid and vice-versa."[19] In his lampoon, "The Fashionable Authoress," appears a mock review of *Heavenly Chords, a Collection of Sacred Strains,* edited by one Lady Frances Juliana Flummery. (Lady Charlotte had published a book of religious verse called *Suspirium Sanctorum, or Holy Breathing,* which might have been one of Helen Pendennis' favorites.) The reviewer does not mince words with Lady Frances: "Her poetry is mere wind; her novels, stark naught; her philosophy sheer vacancy."[20] On Lady Charlotte Bury's anonymously published *Diary of a Lady-in-Waiting at the Court of George IV* (1838), Thackeray has Charles Yellowplush comment: "O *trumpery!* O *morris!* as Homer says: this is a higeous pictur of manners, such as I weap to think of . . . . As for believing that Lady Sharlot had any hand in this book, Heaven forbid! she is all gratitude, pure gratitude—depend upon it."[21]

As was Jane Austen's way with the religious didactic fiction of her time, Scott's with the Gothic and historical romance, and Dickens' with the edifying foundling tale, Thackeray at once parodied, imitated, and improved the so-called Silver Fork novel, a leading genre at the time when he was trying to make his way as a fiction writer. Unlike Dickens, who inverted the society novel for his own satiric purposes, Thackeray was temperamentally drawn to the type, recognizing early in life its educative value, whatever he may have thought of elegant scandal mongers like "Lady Sharlot." As a schoolboy he read and enjoyed one of the first, best, and most serious of the novels of fashion, Thomas Henry Lister's *Granby* (1826).[22] *Granby* is remembered, if at all, for its portrait of Beau Brummell, but he is not Lister's hero. With its high-minded youth, tempted but not corrupted by high society, this novel anticipates the basic moral conflict of *Pendennis.* Young Granby, like Arthur Pendennis, eventually rejects a society belle and settles down in the country with an unaffectedly charming and virtuous girl and his family legacy. Of Miss Darrell, the Mayfair princess, a character in the novel observes: "She has more shining than sterling qualities . . . in one

word, she is not domestic." This wise man, Mr. Duncan, comments further to his wife as he watches a group of young people
at a ball:

> 'But you are not to judge of the real feelings of young men in
> general, by the temporary admiration and attention which they
> bestow in a ball-room. They generally select a partner for life,
> upon very different principles from those upon which they single
> out their partner for the next quadrille. Nay, they will even,
> sometimes, display the most outward gallantry to those whom in
> their hearts they esteem the least.' (III, CH. VIII)

Lister, who felt that Jane Austen was being unduly neglected in
favor of more lurid novelists like Mrs. Shelley, brought something of Miss Austen's moral sense to the fashion novel.[23]
Basically, like his Mr. Duncan, he favors the parlor and nursery
over the ballroom, as does the author of the later *Russell; or, The
Reign of Fashion,* who denounced the "tinsel splendours or
meretricious pleasures, those gilded vapours which perpetually
dance before the eyes of the Fashionable world" and "decoy its
votaries from the heart-cheering and heart-soothing comforts of
HOME."

Many of the authors of society novels regarded themselves as
amateur "parents' assistants," like Maria Edgeworth in her *Tales
of Fashionable Life,* warning susceptible youth away from the
modern Gomorrah. Henry Beazley describes his *The Oxonians* as
"a history of those passions and follies that fill up and give their
colour to the scenes of life; with an attempt to give those passions
and follies their true names, and to strip them of that false
varnish, with which youthful imagination and the sophistry of
the times, are too apt to conceal their tendency and to gloss over
their deformity." The corruptness of high society is the burden of
Alaric A. Watts' *Scenes of Life and Shades of Character,* whose
titles also appear to be directed to immature beaux and belles:
"Schlemihl the Second," "Miseries of a Ball-Room," "Decline
and Fall of the British Empire," "The Child of Impulse,"
"Pleasure Parties," "The Heir Presumptive." A few years later,

Tales of Fashion and Reality, the joint product of two spinster sisters, Caroline Frederick and Henrietta Mary Beauclerk, offer more sermons and soda water to youth: "Journal of a Chaperon," "Journal of a Debutante," "The Honey Moon; or, Why Did I Love?", "Match-Making," and "The Detrimentals; or, The Younger Sons." Their contemporary Winthrop Mackworth Praed neatly touches off these "improving" gossip chronicles in "April Fools":

> Next I announce to hall and hovel
> Lord Asterisk's unwritten novel.
> It's full of wit, and full of fashion
> And full of taste and full of passion.
> It tells some very curious histories,
> Elucidates some charming mysteries,
> And mingles sketches of society
> With precepts of the soundest piety . . . .

Vanity Fair has been called the culminating work of the Silver Fork novel.[24] In some respects, however, *Pendennis* is more characteristic of the type as it eventually developed. *Vanity Fair* grew out of fictional tableaux like the tales of Alaric Watts and the Misses Beauclerk, Beazley's *The Oxonians* (subtitled *A Glance at Society*) and particuarly Mrs. Gore's *The Sketch Book of Fashion*. *Pendennis* resembles more the extended memoir in which a sobered bachelor looks back over his youth with the hindsight of matured wisdom. A motto for all of these could be supplied from a comment in *The Oxonians:* "The general history of mankind is, that the last half of life is passed in repentance for the manner in which the first half of it has been wasted" (I, CH. VI). Bulwer's *Pelham; or, The Adventures of a Gentleman,* which was conceived as Etherege and Congreve *moralisé,* was by no means the first of such novelized journals, but it undoubtedly did much to establish the vogue. Its lineage includes: W. Massie's *Sydenham; or, Memoirs of a Man of the World* (1830), with its sequel *Alice Paulet* (1832); Theodore Hook's *Gilbert Gurney* (1835); Mrs. Gore's *Cecil; or, The Adventures of a Coxcomb*

(1841) ; John Mills' *D'Horsay; or, The Follies of the Day* (1844) ; and some of Lady Blessington's works, such as *Meredith* (1843) ; *Strathern; or, Life at Home and Abroad* (1845) ; *Lionel Deerhurst; or, The Days of the Regency* (1846) ; and *Marmaduke Herbert; or, The Fatal Error* (1847) .[25]

The literary prototype of many of these heroes is mentioned in *Pendennis* when Thackeray comments on young Arthur's evil associates at Oxbridge:

> Are there five in the hundred, out of the hundreds and hundreds of English schoolboys, brought up at our great schools and colleges, that must not own at one time of their lives to having read and liked *Don Juan?* Awful propagation of evil!—The idea of it should make the man tremble who holds the pen, lest untruth, or impurity, or unjust anger, or unjust praise escape it. (CH. XIX) [26]

Don Juan, however, started out properly. Like Arthur Pendennis, he had a doting mother, described, somewhat anachronistically, by her son:

> In short, she was a walking calculation,
>   Miss Edgeworth's novels stepping from their covers,
> Or Mrs. Trimmer's books on education,
>   Or "Coelebs' Wife" set out in quest of lovers,
> Morality's prim personification,
>   In which not Envy's self a flaw discovers;
> To others' share let "female errors fall,"
> For she had not even one—the worst of all.
>
> (Canto I, 16)

Moreover, his education, except for the Catholic reference, also sounds pretty close to that of a child in an early nineteenth-century English evangelical household, such as that of Arthur Pendennis:

> Young Juan wax'd in goodliness and grace,
>   At six a charming child, and at eleven
> With all the promise of as fine a face
>   As e'er to man's maturer growth was given.
> He studied steadily and grew apace,
>   And seem'd, at least, in the right road to heaven,

For half his days were pass'd at church, the other
Between his tutors, confessor, and mother.
              (Canto I, 49)

The mock-epic career of Byron's hero is followed by the young
rakes of the Silver Fork novels—travel, romances, mingling in
high society, whose celebrities they ridicule even while they bask
in their adulation. The creator of Don Juan himself frequently
hovers in the background of these novels. Lady Blessington
exploits her friendship with him in her writings. Pelham wor-
ships at his shrine. Gilbert Gurney takes pride in having been
born in the very same month and year as Lord Byron. The poet
actually appears in *Cecil,* accompanying Mrs. Gore's hero on part
of his Mediterranean tour. But there is an important difference.
We can only conjecture as to Don Juan's eventual fate, since
Byron never completed the story of his adventures. In a letter to
his publisher John Murray, Byron left the outcome indeterminate: "I had not quite fixed whether to make him end in Hell, or
in an unhappy marriage, not knowing which would be the
severest."[27] The imitation Don Juans of some of the society
novelists, on the other hand, end up as tamed social lions, like
Cuthbert Bede's Mr. Verdant Green, "Married and Done For."

Thackeray's sources are relatively easy to spot because of his
delightfully perverse habit of planting them in his works. Theodore Hook, creator of that pseudo-Byron, Gilbert Gurney, turns
up as Mr. Wagg in both *Vanity Fair* and *Pendennis.*[28] Having
recovered from his defeat in a parley of wit with Becky Sharp, he
calls on the widow Pendennis at Fairoaks. Helen Pendennis is
her usual gracious self to this famed writer, even to the extent of
concealing her opinion of him: " 'My brother, Major Pendennis,
has often mentioned your name to us . . . and we have been
very much amused by some of your droll books, sir,' Helen
continued, who never could be brought to like Mr. Wagg's
books, and detested their tone most thoroughly" (CH. XXVI). She
speaks undoubtedly for a certain refined segment of the reading
public, including, we may easily gather, Thackeray himself.

Wagg is represented in this scene as a name-dropping snapper-up of trivia and an unctuous fawner with "the soul of a butler who had been brought from his pantry to make fun in the drawing room" à la Charles Yellowplush. But to naive young Pen he is an object of envy: "He believed fondly, as yet, in authors, reviewers and editors of newspapers. Even Wagg, whose books did not appear to him to be masterpieces of human intellect, he yet revered as a successful writer."[29] Laura is convinced that Pen can do better than Mr. Wagg—one reason why she urges Helen to permit him to go to London and seek his fortune.

Young Thackeray no less than young Pen (or, for that matter, young Dickens) emulated this "successful writer." Thackeray's apprenticeship to Hook began early as his Cambridge days with the *Ramsbottom Papers* in *The Gownsman*. Tales of come-uppance like "Barber Cox" and "The Fatal Boots," as well as rogues' exploits like "Diamond Cut Diamond," tap the Hook vein of hardboiled farce. The moral fables *The Great Hoggarty Diamond* and *A Shabby Genteel Story* (later expanded into *The Adventures of Philip*) resemble a a type of didactic story popularized by Hook in his three volumes called *Sayings and Doings* (1824-28), in each of which some proverbial saying is illustrated by a suitable action. Some of the chapter headings in *Pendennis* carry over this device: "Shows How First Love May Interrupt Breakfast"; "Contains Both Love and War"; "More Storms in the Puddle"; "Prodigal's Return"; "In Which the Major Neither Yields His Money Nor His Life"; "In Which Pendennis Counts His Eggs." One entire episode of *Pendennis*—the hero's infatuation for Miss Fotheringay—can be traced back to a story in the third series of *Sayings and Doings* entitled "Gervase Skinner; or, The Sin of Economy." Pen's inamorata betrays kinship with Gervase's idol Amelrosa Fuggleston, an actress whom this wealthy but stingy bachelor meets and woos, contrary to his father's wishes, when he entertains a band of provincial players (in hope of getting free tickets to their performances). Miss Fuggleston, like Miss Fotheringay, plays Ophelia and farce roles

on the same bill, with equal aplomb and equal lack of understanding. She is glamorous on stage, vulgar and insensitive off it,
loves to cook tripe, and displays her ignorance at every turn.[30]

However, *Pendennis* owes most to Hook's autobiographical
novel *Gilbert Gurney,* a remarkably close antecedent in both
plot and characterization. Both authors recreated their own
youth in the mould of a Regency rake, while recalling their
struggles for literary recognition. Gilbert Gurney's grandfather
(like Pen's grandfather and father) was an apothecary who
called himself a doctor. Gurney's father (like Pen's) is a parvenu, marries to improve himself socially, and is very much
concerned with lineage. (Pen's father and Gilbert's father both
give it out that they are descended from Norman families.) In
both novels the hero is sent to study law, but is really interested
in literature and the theatre, to the despair of his mother. Mrs.
Gurney, who has a horror of actors and actresses, expresses her
revulsion in words that Helen Pendennis would approve: "It will
be ruinous to associate with a class of men and women whose
whole existence is one tissue of artificiality; who see nature not in
her proper colours, but through the darkened medium of the
theatrical lamp-light" (I, CH. I). Mrs. Gurney is convinced that
law and the stage do not mix. Gilbert tries to convince her
otherwise by following for a time the route of Goldoni, from law
to the theatre, though without that jolly Venetian's success.

Gilbert Gurney's literary life diverges from that of Arthur
Pendennis, since it is colored by Hook's own experiences as a
hack writer of comedy and melodrama (which later furnished
him with plots for his novels) and as an actor of sorts.[31] But
both, while studying at Inns of Court, come under the influence
of a fellow student who dabbles in literature and encourages
their early efforts. Gilbert anticipates Pen, too, in taking part in
a dinner party attended by various famed litterateurs of the day.
He also finds out how little of their discussion concerns literature
(II, CH. I). There are further parallels. Gurney's mother dies,

leaving him contrite—with a modicum of financial independence. At first he plans a *mariage de convenance* with a wealthy
heiress, loses out on this venture, and eventually marries a
parson's daughter. (Laura Bell is the daughter of the curate who
could not afford to marry Helen Pendennis.) A good many of
Gilbert Gurney's adventures, it appears, were repeated by Arthur
Pendennis a generation later.[32]

Pen's character fuses Theodore Hook's literary picaro with the
intellectual dandy developed by Lister and taken over notably
by Mrs. Gore. This most prolific, popular, and brilliant society
novelist of the 1840's has survived principally in Thackeray's
parody "Lords and Liveries," one of his famous *Punch's Prize
Novelists* series, which gives a misleading impression of his
attitude toward her. If one reads only the opening words, extoll-
ing the debutante Amethyst Pimlico: " 'Corbleu! What a lovely
creature that was in the Fitzbattleaxe box tonight,' said one of a
group of young dandies, who were leaning over the velvet-
cushioned balconies of the Coventry Club—smoking their full-
flavoured Cubs (from Hudson's) after the opera," Mrs. Gore
sounds like all frippery. But "Lords and Liveries" should be read
with care, particularly the description of its hero:

> Alured de Pentonville, eighteenth Earl of Bagnigge, Viscount Paon
> of Islington, Baron Pancras, Kingscross, and a Baronet, was, like
> too many of our young men of *ton,* utterly *blasé,* although only in
> his twenty-fourth year. Blest, luckily, with a mother of excellent
> principles (who had imbued his young mind with that Morality
> which is so superior to all the vain pomps of the world!), it had
> not been always the young Earl's lot to wear the coronet for which
> he now in sooth cared so little. His father . . . left little but his
> sword and spotless name to his young, lovely, and inconsolable
> widow, who passed the first years of her mourning in educating her
> child in the elegant though small cottage in one of the romantic
> marine villages of beautiful Devonshire. Her child! What a gush of
> consolation filled the widow's heart as she pressed him to it! How
> faithfully did she instil into his young bosom those principles
> which had been the pole-star of his gallant father.[33]

Except for the title and the fabulous wealth, the foregoing could serve as a fair summary of the opening chapters of Arthur Pendennis' story—with its cottage in Devonshire and the widow who finds consolation in overmothering her child. Thackeray scaled down young Arthur's social and economic status to bring it more into conformity with his own background. Above all, he wished to make high comedy out of Arthur's pretensions, as well as those of Major Pendennis. Arthur is not a young earl but comports himself like one.

Thackeray treated Mrs. Gore with his characteristic eclecticism. Among other *Punch's Prize Novelists,* for example, he found Charles Lever's humor, if not his sentimentality, worthy of imitation in *Barry Lyndon* and ransacked his pages for such Irish types as the O'Dowds of *Vanity Fair* and Captain Costigan in *Pendennis.* He made fun of Bulwer's grandiloquence and G. P. R. James' antiquarianism, but, as he later showed, he was not averse to philosophy and history in novels. Mrs. Gore was actually the novelist of his time with whom Thackeray felt the closest affinity. After his success with *Vanity Fair* he enjoyed a close social and literary friendship with this "full blown rose of a woman" (as Disraeli called her) and salon hostess. Thackeray's most recent biographer has written: "She regarded the life around her with an absorbed but disillusioned gaze, and Thackeray found the fashion in which she bowed to fashionable standards in her life, while exposing them in her novels and conversations, a fascinating subject for study."[34] Aside from "Lords and Liveries," Thackeray shows the greatest respect for her. After he was firmly established, he admitted in a letter to Mrs. Gore that "it was only a secret envy & black malignity of disposition" that had prompted his parody.[35] He was not offended when her novel *Cecil* (1841) was mistakenly attributed to him, only sorry that he had not in fact written it.[36] His admiration of her work goes back even earlier. A youthful entry in his Diary reads: "Went to see Black-eyed Susan [by Douglas

Jerrold] at Miss Inverarity's benefit—read part of a novel called
the Fair of Mayfair—a sensible book enough."[37]

The Fair of Mayfair (1832) has a sternness of tone appropiate
to the tags from Pope and other eighteenth-century didactic poets
that head its chapters. The tales themselves, such as "The Flirt of
Ten Seasons," "The Separate Maintenance," "Hearts and Diamonds" and "A Divorcee" introduce us to such future citizens of
Vanity Fair as the shallow debutante, the maneuvering mother,
the philandering husband, the adulterous wife, the ignorant
parvenu, and the corrupt peer engaged in all manner of stylish
dissipation.[38] Mrs. Gore makes it quite evident in her introduction that these revels in the upper regions of the damned are not
intended for mere entertainment.[39] She thinks of herself as a
modern Juvenal, castigating her contemporaries as Pope and
Johnson did theirs, but in less lofty tones. She would re-dress that
neglected muse Satire, "long accustomed to the graceful array of
poetry," in "the homely garment of prose," to make her accessible
to a new generation:

> It is plain that in this prosiest of centuries when oratory is valued
> by the hour, and books by their length, breadth and thickness, the
> terseness of poetical satire will ensure its condemnation by the
> gaugers of literature. Like Esop's diamond, it is derided as useless
> by the heroes of the barndoor. Modern science, however, can
> decompose the gem; and, by reducing it to charcoal, render it
> available to household purposes.

In the targets of her invective as well as in her authorial tone—
compounded of cynicism and moral indignation—Mrs. Gore
prepares the way for Thackeray. Her very titles are premonitory.
Put together some of these—*The Fair of Mayfair, The Sketch
Book of Fashion, Sketches of English Characters*—and one has
just about arrived at the original title of Thackeray's first
masterpiece: *Vanity Fair: Pen and Pencil Sketches of English
Society.* Moreover, the epigraph that begins Mrs. Gore's best
novel, *Cecil: or, The Adventures of a Coxcomb* (1841), is:
"Vanitas—vanitatis!"

Apparently Thackeray borrowed a feather or two from Cecil's tuft when he created his own coxcomb some years later. At any rate, their paths run parallel. Cecil suffers through the cycle of tormented school days (the "preparatory purgatory" at Chiswick; an "excruciating" residence at Eton), the corrupting influence of young rakes at Oxford, the round of high society, the Grand Tour, ending up with a seat in Parliament. As for his love life, Cecil also is torn between a guileless innocent and a Frenchified pseudosophisticate, though unlike Pen he remains a bachelor. Arthur Pendennis shares Gilbert Gurney's literary life, but his education and social life are more those of Cecil Danby.

Cecil is linked in tone with *Pendennis* by a certain wistful air of time remembered[40] and in plot by the pattern of the worldly youth chastened. Moreover, the subtitle of *Pendennis*—"His Fortunes and Misfortunes His Friends and His Greatest Enemy" —epitomizes Cecil's own conviction that school and society alone are not responsible for the corruption of the young:

> But Youth has another and still bitterer enemy than its Masters— ITSELF! Of all the mockeries it has to dread, those most fatal in the creation of mistrust are its own. The generous glow, the fervid impulse, are, in truth, vouchsafed by nature. But the curious in casuistry are requested to decide whether, of the spirits of good and evil assigned to each of us as our companions through life, the good have not the ascendancy over our material, and the evil over our moral nature!—The flush of joy, the thrill of horror, so instinctive in our early years, at the relation of wicked or virtuous actions,—the gushing tears, or uncontrollable smiles, evincing our sympathies of affection, are far more independent of our will than we care to own; whereas most of our evil deeds are the result of deliberation.
> (I, CH. VII)

This passage reads like the text for the allegorical drawing designed by Thackeray for the first edition of *Pendennis,* its young man, hand on his chin, deliberating, his head slightly turned in the direction of the evil sprites.[41] With both Cecil and Pen, social sophistication perverts natural affections, and their careers illustrate the conflict between innocence and worldliness.

Cecil's good nature convinces him that the good, sweet Emily Barnett, the equivalent of Laura in Pendennis' life, is an angel, "but it would have been a bore to produce in good company a wife who seems to have been educated for a governess" (I, CH. VII) —just as Pen temporarily neglects Laura to pursue Blanche Amory. The character of Blanche is anticipated both by Lady Harriet Vandeleur, Cecil's London inamorata, and by a young lady named Thérèse de St. Barthélemy whom Cecil meets during a stay in Paris. Thérèse, like Blanche, is a *"femme incomprise."* Both have an insatiable appetite for the literature of sensibility, keep thought diaries, enjoy self-torment, alternately contemplating suicide and incarceration in a nunnery. Eventually Blanche Amory, with her factitious emotions and histrionic tears, is banished to her proper element. She becomes a member of the *petite noblesse*, Madame la Comtesse de Montmorenci de Valentinois, and thus enters the social circle of her literary sister Thérèse de Barthélemy, Madame la Comtesse de la Vrillière. Pen has a happier fate than his literary brother. Cecil becomes disillusioned with society, but Emily dies before he gets around to proposing to her. Pen gets a second chance.

Among the guests at Mr. Bungay's dinner is Lady Violet Lebas, editor of Annuals for refined young ladies. One of Thackeray's close friends and correspondents at this time was the popular *bas bleu* Lady Blessington, friend of Lord Byron, society queen by marriage, diarist, journalist, mediocre novelist, and platonic mistress of Count D'Orsay. Disposed as he may have been to poke gentle fun at the literary countess, Thackeray moved comfortably in her genteel literary world, even deigning to contribute to one of her Keepsakes.[42] Lady Blessington specialized in the confession-memoir type of fiction, which sometimes took the form of candid diaries by retired servants like *Memoirs of a Femme de Chambre* (1846), but more often allowed the upper classes to betray themselves. Characteristic titles are *The Confessions of an Elderly Gentleman* (1836), *The*

Confessions of an Elderly Lady (1838), and *Desultory Thoughts and Reflections* (1839). Nearer to the time when Thackeray began *Pendennis,* she published two more fictitious journals, *Meredith* (1843) and *Marmaduke Herbert; or, The Fatal Error* (1847). In these novels we encounter, along with the familiar young coxcomb, the old roué, also immortalized in *Pendennis.*

In *Meredith* a middle-aged reformed coxcomb passes on to the rising generation the lessons gleaned from his misadventures. Young Meredith, like Arthur Pendennis, is pulled in two directions. His mother is a tender, affectionate woman, unhappily married, who spoils him through compensatory overdevotion. When she dies, young Meredith is left for a time in the care of her relative, Lord Lymington, a cynical, selfish epicure, who detests any show of affection or sentiment. Meredith is initially attracted to his patrician guardian. "So bland were his manners, and so even seemed his temper, that he was, on first acquaintance, sure to captivate the good will of those with whom he came in contact," the hero recalls. But he learns better: "Nor did they discover how much too favourably they had judged him, until, on a greater intimacy, encouraged by his urbanity, they ventured to appeal to his sympathy while labouring under some of the trials from which none are exempt" (I, CH. XX). Lady Blessington's later *Marmaduke Herbert* repeats the formula of the hero torn between the opposing influences of a sentimental, religious mother and a worldly, cynical uncle.[43] Both of these uncles seem to have sat for Major Pendennis, but Thackeray shades and deepens the character, giving him some modicum of tenderness and courage, and eventually making him a pitiable rather than a contemptible figure.[44] Moreover, Thackeray's superannuated roué, no less than his jaded coxcomb, is reborn, spending his unenviable retirement being read to by Laura.

The follies of adolescence, misspent youth, the overindulgence and undersupervision by elders, mistakes of education, as we have seen, were the burden of much of the fiction that Thackeray grew up with. The main problem of the young man in these

didactic comedies of manners is wrenching himself free of bad
influences and finding his own direction. Wrong as he may be in
other respects, Major Pendennis proves to be right when he
assures Helen about her son: "Boys will be boys. . . . If he has
sown his wild oats, and will stick to his business, he may do well
yet" (CH. XXIX). We get the impression that young Arthur,
after sowing his wild oats, is content to graze in the green
pastures of Devonshire. He follows out the pattern, notably, of
Frank Grenfell, hero of Mrs. Gore's *The Cabinet Minister*
(1839), who, after his claret parties, carousing, and time-serving
at Carleton House, settles down with his boyhood sweetheart to
become "the patient, plodding lawyer—the happy husband—the
cheerful father." For Pen, journalism and writing take the place
of law, but eventually, when Lord Clavering leaves the world he
never graced, Pen finds his vocation in the hallowed halls of
Parliament along with Vivian Grey and Cecil the Peer.

In the fictional debate that raged through this decade over
whether parents of young Oxonians and Cantabs should tighten
the lead strings or loosen them, Thackeray seems to have sided
with his friend Lewes, who argued in *Ranthorpe* that "Dissipation, though an evil, is an evil best got through in youth."
Ranthorpe, like *Pendennis,* traces the development of a young
writer from *Sturm-und-Drang*-ism through the temptations of
quick success as a social lion to his dedication of his pen to the
service of humanity. As a novel about vocation it involves also a
young surgeon, Harry Cavendish, who settles into respectability
after a somewhat rakish early youth. Lewes comments:

> Is this a defence of dissipation? No; it is simply saying, that as
> youth is foolish and exuberant, its acts will be folly; but when
> youth passes away, it carries with it the cause of all this folly, and
> parents should not despair. Instead of despairing, they should
> observe. There is a critical period in the young man's life, when he
> may be turned into anything that is good. It is then that his future
> profession or vocation will have power to wean him from his
> habits. It is then that his character begins to consolidate. Of all
> influences capable of directing him into the right path, none is

more powerful as that exercised by women. If he loves, he is saved.

Harry was saved by love. . . . (*Ranthorpe*, Book V, CH. III)

So, we gather, was Arthur Pendennis. As he says to Laura's patron, Lady Rockminster, who would have preferred that her ward marry Warrington: "And if you mean that I am not worthy of Laura, I know it, and pray Heaven to better me; and if the love and company of the best and purest creature in the world can do so, at least I shall have these to help me" (CH. LXXV). Most of the other youths settle down in one way or another—Mr. Pynsent raises himself through his Lady Diana; the young surgeon Sam Huxter somewhat lowers himself with Fanny Bolton, but they both appear to realize their ambitions. Others find themselves, but without benefit of a woman's love. Warrington remains saddled with his backward young wife—having had no Major Pendennis, as he says, to save him from a youthful misalliance—but consoles himself with his writing and his platonic admiration for Laura. Foker apparently remains a bachelor after getting Blanche Amory out of his system, living elegantly and indolently on his inherited brewer's fortune. Only young Amory remains irretrievably corrupted by his pampered youth, but perhaps he is intended to remind us, as Lewes remarked, that "A few turn out badly, but they are the exceptions." If, in the long run, Thackeray does not fully answer the questions he poses, he at least does not simplify them.

From *Catherine*, his first novel, where he exposed the criminality latent in us all, Thackeray has arrived in *Pendennis* at a view of man as a coxcomb with a potentiality for genuine nobility. *Pendennis*, like all the great novels we have discussed, has an ethical plot—the molding of character by the plastic force of experience—but with Thackeray character tends to be more "open-ended" and indeterminate than with his predecessors. Some critics were disturbed by Thackeray's "mixed characters." One of them, while observing that novelists had progressed since

Scott in "the delineation of the changes and fluxes of a character," and conceding that Scott may have oversimplified the
conflict between good and evil in the world, nevertheless feared
that "the subtle psychological activity" of writers like Thackeray
"is apt to entangle their readers in a variety of moral problems,
the suggestion of which in a half-solved state gives dimness and
uncertainty to their moral picture of life." He considered
Dickens' conception of man in *David Copperfield* and elsewhere
"idealized as it undoubtedly is . . . by far the more complete
and the more healthy, and therefore in the higher sense more
true," and by implication accused Thackeray of a "morbid
weakness of moral fibre."[45] Lewes, already the student of psychology, exploring in his own novels the duality and contradic-
toriness of human character, found Thackeray's ambivalence a
sign of his greatness. To him Thackeray was not a mere "mocking Mephistopheles" as alleged by his detractors, but a "Janus
Bifrons" endowed with the power to see things from opposing
viewpoints. Furthermore, a certain "tendency to antithesis" in
Thackeray's mind, he points out, makes him able to detect at
once "a soul of goodness in things evil, as well as the spot of evil
in things good."[46]

Lewes was one of the first to appreciate Thackeray's bifocal
view of his men and women, which makes us see not only the
good and bad in them, but the amusing and the sad together. He
can with one breath laugh at Miss Fotheringay for her ignorance
and with the next praise her for her native shrewdness, just as he
manages to make her father Captain Costigan likable for his
warmth and good heart, with all his blarney and bluster. Lady
Clavering is at one moment comic with her solecisms and mala-
propisms, at another pathetic, as a disappointed and ineffectual
mother. A rogue like Ned Strong redeems himself in our eyes by
his loyalty to Blanche Amory's down-at-the-heels father Colonel
Altamont, and even that outlaw proves to be not so much a
villain as a weakling, and one capable at times of genuine feeling
for his estranged daughter as well as a sense of humor about his

own pretensions. Thackeray's supreme example of what he calls "flowers of good blooming in foul places" is that mixture of humbug and Dutch uncle, Major Pendennis, who can stoop to blackmailing Lord Clavering, and yet rise to his firm confrontation of the unscrupulous Morgan; who tries to win Pen to the "practical" way of life, only himself to succumb to the "sentimental" way.

The opposite end of Thackeray's moral spectrum, "in the most lofty and splendid fortunes, flaws of vice and meanness, and stains of evil," is amply illustrated through his hero and his associates in Oxbridge and Mayfair, but most remarkably in some of his female characters, who are outwardly the souls of virtue. Fanny Bolton, for example, is far from the innocent victim of seduction that she would be in a Dickens novel. She does her part in leading Pen on, and her loving husband, Sam Huxter, expresses some doubt as to her faithfulness. That paragon of mother love, Helen Pendennis, is not entirely without sin. Like Amelia in *Vanity Fair,* she shows that selflessness can be a subtle form of pride asserting itself in possessiveness. Her shock at Arthur's flirtation with Fanny Bolton is prompted at least as much by "sexual jealousy" (in the nineteenth-century sense of the word) as by moral indignation.[47] Even Laura, of whom Thackeray is least critical, is occasionally caught off guard. Her virtue at times shades off into self-righteousness in her treatment of Pen. Like Fanny Price, she is tainted with feminine vanity, as revealed in her jealousy first of Miss Fotheringay, then of Blanche Amory, and she shows up no better than Helen Pendennis in the Fanny Bolton affair, which brings out the streak of smugness and snobbery in her nature.[48] Thackeray's acute sensitivity to the good in the worst of us and the bad in the best of us made for that urbanity of tone that some of his contemporaries took for mere pococurantism.

As with Wilde and Shaw later in the century, Thackeray disturbed readers by occasionally making his heroes and villains exchange roles or by questioning conventional notions of good and evil. His mind for antinomy asserts itself also in situations that reflect, echo, or even parody each other. Major Pendennis' "sacrifices" to make Pen a man of the world provide the interlude to Helen Pendennis' tragedy of maternal martyrdom. Miss Fotheringay acts great drama with bland insensitivity, while Blanche Amory makes a pageant of her minor woes. Blanche's tears of sensibility make the tears of sentiment shed so readily by Helen and Laura refreshing in their genuineness. Captain Costigan travesties the military code of honor upheld by Major Pendennis, just as the peripatetic and philandering Colonel Altamont ridicules the Don Juan ideal worshiped by Pen at Oxbridge. Class snobbery is viewed from opposing standpoints in Pen's priggish treatment of the chef Mirabolant and Major Pendennis' foiling of the upstart valet Morgan. Finally, to offset Lord Clavering, there is Laura's patron, Lady Rockminster, reminding us that the aristocracy is not all decadent.[49]

Thackeray's agile and perverse wit shifts his readers' angles of vision on life and character, even juxtaposing illusion and reality. Pen's disenchantment with the lachrymose poetess Miss Bunion, who proves to be "a large and bony woman in a crumpled satin dress . . . creaking into the room with a step as heavy as a grenadier's" (CH. XXXV), is typical of the "bumps" experienced by other characters as they move out of fiction into life.[50] Blanche Amory's *petite noblesse* husband is something less than a "fiery Stenio" out of George Sand. Colonel Altamont is effectively shaved down from the swashbuckling figure Lady Clavering had conjured up from her adventure stories. Fanny Bolton takes the gruff Sam Huxter on the rebound, when Pen fails to be the Prince Charming of her favorite fashion novels. Even Laura is a little let down by life. Blanche Amory gives her a "first lesson in the Cynical philosophy," but "something like this selfishness and waywardness, something like this contrast between practice and poetry, between grand versified aspiration and every-day life, she had witnessed in the person of our young friend Mr. Pen" (CH. XXV). With their respective sentimental-isms tempered by reasonable cynicism, Laura and Pen presumably are well matched.

The main effect of Thackeray's mental legerdemain, however, is to awaken his readers' minds to the range of human possibility. Their excursion into society is intended to bring them, along with Arthur, to a new sophistication—the true sophistication, that is, of the tolerant, the open-minded, and the forward-looking, as opposed to the false sophistication of the blasé and the snobbish, the dilettante, and the pedant. Time, like character, is viewed relatively in *Pendennis;* childhood and youth are seen from the vantage point of maturity, making this a novel simultaneously about growing pains and the pleasures of memory. Life and people are in a constant state of flux in this "chronicle of Fate's surprises. . . . Of chances, changes, ruins, rises," to quote from one of Thackeray's poems.[51] Even one of the clubs Pen visits is called The Wheel of Fortune. Inherent in this atmosphere of change and transition, with its fluid characters, its fusion of past and present, its shifting perspectives on reality, is the consciousness of a world of becoming. Arthur Pendennis, as a man of the new generation, seems to be moving with the turn of the wheel, while Major Pendennis, clinging to an age that the younger generation knew only through Jesse's *Life of Beau Brummell* (1844), is being left behind. Unlike the Major, Pen is aware of a world teeming outside of the gentleman's club. He agrees with Percy Popjoy that the old dandies framed in the window of Bays' Club "ought to be cast in wax, and set up at Madame Tussaud's."

Thackeray could not confine himself to St. James' Street either, and with Pen he moves the society novel out of the salon and the drawing room. Pen seems to be combining his vocation with his avocation in the Royal Gardens of Vauxhall, where he mingles with entertainers and spectators, old and young, grave and gay, respectable and social outcast. "Of this sympathy with all conditions of men Arthur often boasted," we are assured; "he was pleased to possess it and said that he hoped thus to the last he should retain it." He regards human "anthropology as his favorite pursuit; and had his eyes always eager to its infinite varieties and beauties." The author has evolved from novelist of manners to cultural historian. "All sorts of places and men" come within his span, together with their haunts and habitations—lodging houses, inns of court, mansions, manor houses, clubs—and their resorts—taverns, ballrooms, and parks. We are presented with a variegated world as well as a changing one.

Primarily, however, it is a workaday world. Pen's gay youth is finished along with his literary apprenticeship under Warrington. He agrees with his wise friend that the author can enclose himself neither in Mayfair nor in a Palace of Art. As Thackeray puts it, Pegasus must put on the harness like a dray horse (CH. XXXVI). Major Pendennis is unhappy about the disappearance of the "lounging guardsmen and great lazy dandies"; "there's no use for 'em," he sighs, "they're replaced by a parcel of damned cotton spinners and utilitarians, and young sprigs of parsons with their hair combed down their backs." This is the Major's contemptuous bow to the new Puritanism of morality, industry, and utility. Pen does not share the Major's disdain for "the *canaille* of today with their language of the cabstand, and their coats smelling of smoke," or "today's Lady Lorraine—a little woman in black silk gown, like a governess, who talks astronomy, and labouring classes, . . . and lurks to church at eight o'clock in the morning" (CH. LXVIII). He would involve himself with the *"canaille"* and with Lady Lorraine together, as he affirms to Warrington:

"But the earth where our feet are, is the work of the same Power as the immeasurable blue yonder, in which the future lies into which we would peer. Who ordered toil as the condition of life, ordered weariness, ordered sickness, ordered poverty, failure, success . . . Look, George . . . look and see the sun rise: he sees the labourer on his way a-field; the workgirl plying her poor needle; the lawyer at his desk, perhaps; the beauty smiling asleep upon her pillow of down; or the jaded reveller reeling to bed; or the fevered patient tossing on it; or the doctor watching by it, over the throes of the mother for the child that is to be born into the world;—to be born and to take his part in the suffering and the struggling, the tears and laughter, the crime, remorse, love, folly, sorrow, rest." (CH. XLV)

So the Silver Fork is exchanged for pewter. The novel of fashion is absorbed into the world of works and days, along with Pen's rediscovering his boyhood home at Clavering, "the once quiet and familiar fields of which were flaming with the kilns and forges of the artificers employed on the new railroad works" (CH. LXXVI). Thackeray remains essentially the "sceptical philosopher," as he characterized himself before he became a novelist, but like Pen in Vauxhall he now observes people "with a satiric humour that was not deprived of sympathy," uniting the spirit of charity with the muse of wit. With his immense sartorial, decorative, culinary, and social detail, Thackeray sharpened the novel as register of the immediate world of actuality, while the sliding lenses that he placed between that world and his readers flashed with a busy, mercurial intelligence making them constantly aware of time's mutations. The sensitive mind becomes an even more active agent in the fiction of two of Thackeray's most enthusiastic admirers, Charlotte Brontë and George Eliot.

Thackeray's moral significance to his times is attested by one of his other fellow novelists, John Cordy Jeaffreson. "He is the true gentleman of our generation, who has appealed to our best and most chivalric sympathies," wrote Jeaffreson, "and raising us from the slough and pollution of the Regency, has made us once more a nation of gentlemen."[52] Thackeray passed through childhood while the century was, as at the beginning of *Vanity Fair,* "in its teens." In *Pendennis,* as at the end of *Vanity Fair,* he urges his generation to put away their gew-gaws and close up their toy boxes. The *"couleur de rose,"* as Mrs. Gore's Cecil puts it, was fading into the *"couleur de bleu."* Thackeray, his hero Arthur—and the century—were all entering middle age as the Regency was sobering into the Age of Victoria. Colonel Esmond and Colonel Newcome, not Major Pendennis, are to be the gentlemen of that age.

CHARACTERISTIC FICTION CONTEMPORANEOUS WITH *PENDENNIS* (1848–50)

1825 Robert Plumer Ward, *Tremaine; or, The Man of Refinement.*
1826 Thomas Henry Lister, *Granby.*
1826–27 Benjamin Disraeli, *Vivian Grey.*
1827 Robert Plumer Ward, *De Vere; or, The Man of Independence.*
1828 Edward Bulwer-Lytton, *Pelham; or, The Adventures of a Gentleman.*
      Thomas Henry Lister, *Herbert Lacy.*
1829 Lady Charlotte Bury, *The Exclusives.*
1830 Henry Beazley, *The Oxonians; A Glance at Society.*
      Catherine Gore, *Women as They Are.*
      W. Massie, *Sydenham; or, Memoirs of a Man of the World.*
      Russell; or, The Reign of Fashion.
1831 Benjamin Disraeli, *The Young Duke.*
      Catherine Gore, *Pin Money.*
      W. Massie, *Alice Paulet; A Sequel to Sydenham.*
      Society; or, The Spring in Town.
      Alaric A. Watts, *Scenes of Life and Shades of Character.*
1832 Catherine Gore, *The Fair of Mayfair.*
      Thomas Henry Lister, *Arlington.*
1833 Catherine Gore. *The Sketch Book of Fashion.*
1834 Catherine Gore, *The Hamiltons.*
1835 Theodore Hook, *Gilbert Gurney.*
1836 Caroline Frederika and Henrietta Mary Beauclerk, *Tales of Fashion and Reality.*
      Lady Blessington, *The Confessions of an Elderly Gentleman.*
      Catherine Gore, *The Diary of a Désennuyée.*
1838 Lady Blessington, *The Confessions of an Elderly Lady.*
1839 Catherine Gore, *The Cabinet Minister.*
1841 Catherine Gore, *Cecil; or, The Adventures of a Coxcomb.*
      ———, *Cecil; or, The Peer.*
      Robert Plumer Ward, *De Clifford; or, The Constant Man.*
1842 Lady Blessington, *The Lottery of Life.*
1843 Lady Blessington, *Meredith.*

1844 Benjamin Disraeli, *Coningsby.*
    [John Mills], *D'Horsay; or, The Follies of the Day.* By a Man
      of Fashion.
1845 Lady Blessington, *Strathern; or, Life at Home and Abroad.*
    Benjamin Disraeli, *Sybil; or, The Two Nations.*
1846 Catherine Gore, *Sketches of English Characters.*
    Lady Blessington, *Memoirs of a Femme de Chambre.*
    ——, *Lionel Deerhurst; or, The Days of the Regency.*
1847 Lady Blessington, *Marmaduke Herbert; or, The Fatal Error.*
    Benjamin Disraeli, *Tancred.*
    George Henry Lewes, *Ranthorpe.*
1848 John Henry Newman, *Loss and Gain.*
1849 Frank Smedley, *Frank Fairlegh; or, Scenes from the Life of a
      Private Pupil.*

CHAPTER VI

Villette:

Lucy Snowe and the Good Governess

CHARLOTTE BRONTË, like Thackeray, first caught the attention of the general public with a novel about a governess who marries above her station. That is about all that Jane Eyre and Becky Sharp have in common, but the two authors continued in literary association. The title of *Vanity Fair* was taken from one of Miss Brontë's favorite books, and she saw its author more as the lion of Judah than the social lion, a lay prophet "terribly in earnest in his war against the falsehoods and the follies of 'the world.'"[1] In the preface to the second edition of *Jane Eyre* she visualized him as hurling "the Greek fire of his sarcasm" and flashing "the levin-brand of his denunciation" over the palaces of the mighty. She spoke of him repeatedly in such hyperbolic terms: "the legitimate high priest of Truth"; "a Titan, so strong that he can afford to perform with calm the most herculean feats"; "an intellectual boa-constrictor."[2] Thackeray's wisdom made a deeper impression on her than his wit, particularly his vision of society as a modern Babylon. Partially through his influence, she enlarged her conception of the novel after *Jane Eyre*. In her next novel, *Shirley,* she attempted his panoramic method with a retrospective view of her native Yorkshire, setting the home life of her two provincial heroines against the background of the Napoleonic Wars and the Industrial Revolution. Her last novel, *Villette,* based on her Brussels experiences, is, like Thackeray's semiautobiographical *Pendennis,* the *bildungsroman* of a writer. Some commentators—Mrs. Gaskell and later Mrs. Humphry Ward, for example—have seen a closer connection. Once falsely accused of being the original of Mr. Rochester in *Jane Eyre,* Thackeray went on to share honors with Constantin Heger as the prototype of Monsieur Paul Emanuel in *Villette.*[3] Although this influence is probably exaggerated, it is true that Monsieur Paul affects Lucy with the "blended feelings of admiration and indignation" which Miss Brontë experienced from Thackeray's writing and combines just those diverse traits, "harsh and kindly, wayward and wise, benignant and bitter," that she found in her "first of modern masters."[4]

Miss Brontë certainly shared Thackeray's view of the world as a hard university. Lucy Snowe of *Villette,* like Caroline Helstone of *Shirley,* is plunged early into the "humbling, crushing, grinding" initiation process of "the school of Experience." Lucy herself makes the analogy early in the novel: "A very unique child," she muses over the bed of little Polly. "How will she get through this world, or battle with this life? How will she bear the shocks and repulses, the humiliations and desolations, which books and my own reason tell me are prepared for all flesh?" (CH. III). However, it is Lucy's "battle with life" that we follow, not Polly's. Lucy supposes at this point that she will be a mere nursemaid-governess sheltered from "shocks and repulses, humiliations and desolations," but circumstances force her into the heat of combat.[5] At the outset she has, as she says, only "books and my own reason" as guides, but these are supplemented in time by other resources. In *Shirley* Caroline Helstone has an imported Belgian tutor. Lucy has to travel abroad to find hers; and Labassecour, Monsieur Paul, along with Experience—of which she writes: "No other mentor . . . wears a robe so black,

none bears a rod so heavy, none with hand so inexorable draws
the novice so sternly to his task"—teach her what she could not
learn in sheltered Bretton.

At the time she was writing *Villette,* Charlotte Brontë observed in a letter to her friend and former teacher Miss Wooler:
"Schools seem to be considered almost obsolete in London.
Ladies' colleges, with Professors for every branch of instruction,
are superseding the old-fashioned Seminary. How this system will
work, I can't tell: I think the College classes might be very useful
for finishing the education of ladies intended to go out as
Governesses; but what progress little girls will make in them—
seems to me another question."[6] Her own novel harks back to
the "old-fashioned Seminary," recalling for a new generation a
system of education then in process of being superseded by
institutions like Queens College.[7] Like Fanny Price before her
and Maggie Tulliver after, Lucy Snowe is "going out" as a
governess, but we see her actually practicing her vocation.

Some chapters (particularly those entitled "Madame Beck"
and "Isidore") are so packed with detail about school administration and classroom procedure that they read like source material for Matthew Arnold's *Popular Education in France* and
Schools and Universities on the Continent. There were abundant
novels about English schools, such as Harriet Martineau's *The
Crofton Boys,* Mrs. Marsh-Caldwell's *The Previsions of Lady
Evelyn,* Mrs. Gore's *Peers and Parvenus,* and Frank Smedley's
Frank Fairlegh—and many more to come. But the foreign school
was relatively new fictional territory. Charlotte Brontë was not
the first writer to set a tale in a continental school—the popular
Julia Kavanagh had, as we shall notice later, already taken
readers inside a girls' school in Normandy in *Nathalie* (1850)—
but she had the advantage of first-hand knowledge of the school
she represented.

Villette, as is well known, grew out of Miss Brontë's renewed
and again unsuccessful attempts to publish her first-written
novel, *The Professor.* Her return to the scene of that novel

happened to coincide with new concerted efforts to establish
national schools in England, efforts which caused educational
reformers to look with envy across the Channel. A book much
discussed at this period, particularly in George Henry Lewes'
The Leader, which Miss Brontë was reading, was her friend Sir
Joseph Kay-Shuttleworth's *The Social Condition and Education
of the People in England and Europe* (1850). Kay-Shuttleworth,
then Secretary to the Committee of the Privy Council on Education, pointed to continental countries, particularly France and
Germany, as models for the establishment of liberal education
for children. In his opinion, the governments of European countries had advanced far beyond England in their recognition of
man's fundamental needs, "food for the body, intelligence for
the soul," because they had not allowed internal religious differences to interfere, as in England, with the provision of basic
education for all.[8] Lucy Snowe pointedly observes that the
Pensionnat Beck, where she does her practice teaching, is "a
foreign school, of which the life, movement and variety made it a
complete and most charming contrast to many English institutions of the same kind" (CH. VIII). However, one gathers that
private schools, in Labassecour at least, are not particularly
enlightened. Madame Beck is an efficient administrator, to be
sure, but the bigotry Lucy encounters among her students, along
with their resistance to learning, make this particular school fall
somewhat short of Kay-Shuttleworth's ideal. And we also have
Ginevra Fanshawe's testimony: "Oh, the number of foreign
schools I have been at in my life! And yet I am quite an
ignoramus" (CH. VI).

Another immediate appeal of *Villette* to its own generation
certainly was its intimate account of a young woman finding her
vocation: "I know not that I was of a self-reliant or active nature,
but self-reliance and exertion were forced upon me by circumstances, as they are upon thousands besides," writes the heroine
(CH. IV). A book like *Education as a Means of Preventing
Destitution,* advertised in the first edition of *Villette,* crystallized

Lucy's situation. Ironically, Charlotte herself was without a settled place at the time *Villette* was published. "I only wish my chance of being useful were greater," she complained to Miss Wooler in the very letter announcing its publication.[9]

Some years before, her editor, W. S. Williams, had sought her advice on a career for his daughter Louisa, then about to enter Queens College. "Believe me—teachers may be hard-worked, ill-paid and despised—" she wrote to him, "but the girl who stays at home doing nothing is worse off than the hardest-wrought and worst-paid drudge of a school."[10] On the basis of a character sketch of his daughter that Williams sent her, Charlotte tried to judge Louisa's qualifications for the career of a governess: "Of pleasing exterior (that is always an advantage—children like it)," she observed, "good sense, obliging disposition, cheerful, healthy, possessing a good average capacity, but no prominent master talent to make her miserable, by its craving for exercise, by its mutiny under restraint—Louisa thus endowed will find the post of governess comparatively easy." On its surface, *Villette* is a projection of this letter of advice—the experience of one educated woman "going out as a governess" retold for the benefit of others in a like situation. Lucy Snowe lacks "pleasing exterior," "obliging disposition," and other characteristics that Charlotte set down for the ideal governess. Besides, like her creator, she is endowed with a "prominent master talent to make her miserable, by its craving for exercise." Lucy, however, subdues this perverse instinct and overcomes her other personal handicaps to establish her own Pensionnat de Demoiselles, aided by the parting gift of Monsieur Paul. Miss Brontë herself did not achieve her heroine's success.

Villette, whatever its superficial resemblance to such period inspirational literature as Mrs. Burbury's *Florence Sackville; or, Self-Dependence* (which also chronicles a young lady's obstacles in "finding herself"), is of course something more than the career-woman's vade mecum. Lucy's course of teacher training involves an education of her mind, sensibility, and imagination, and these

expand in a large environment of events and ideas. "You will see
that 'Villette' touches on no matter of public interest," she wrote
to George Smith late in 1852.[11] "I cannot write books handling
the topics of the day; it is no use trying." She was contrasting her
forthcoming novel specifically with a current best-seller called
Uncle Tom's Cabin, but undoubtedly was thinking also of her
difficulties in assimilating military, economic, and social history
in her previous novel *Shirley.* She had been aware of her deficiencies in this direction as early as *Jane Eyre,* which she feared
would not impress the critics of the serious journals: "It has no
learning, no research, it discusses no subject of public interest. A
mere domestic novel will, I fear, seem trivial to men of large
views and solid attainments."[12]

In *Shirley,* Miss Brontë made conscientious efforts to enlarge
her views. She envied Thackeray and Dickens their "varied
knowledge of men and things."[13] Her friends Mrs. Gaskell and
Harriet Martineau had incorporated "subjects of public interest"
into fiction. Probably influenced by Lewes' advice "not to stray
too far from the ground of experience,"[14] she confined her scene
to her local village and "got up" her history through newspaper
research. But Lewes complained this time that *Shirley* was too
"disconnected in its attempt at panorama, lacking the standing
point of individual experience . . . the fire of one passion" that
in *Jane Eyre* "fused the discordant materials into one mould."[15]
Returning to her own recent history for her next novel, as well as
to the autobiographical point of view of *Jane Eyre,* she forged
the "passionate link" that Lewes missed in *Shirley.* She did not,
however, despite her disclaimer, abandon "topics of the day."

Charlotte gives the impression sometimes that she was as
indifferent as the three young curates of *Shirley* to the march of
mind. When the manuscript of Thackeray's *Henry Esmond* was
passing through her hands, she wrote to George Smith that she
wished its author "could be told not to care much for dwelling
on the political or religious intrigues of the times. Thackeray, in
his heart, does not value political or religious intrigues of any age

or date. He likes to show us human nature at home, as he himself daily sees it."[16] By implication one gathers that Miss Brontë was interested principally in "human nature at home." But elsewhere she shows that she was quite aware of the political and religious intrigues of her own times, and *Villette* reverberates with the current rumbles of Church and State.

The years immediately preceding the publication of *Villette* were particularly turbulent ones for the English Church, when so many adherents of the Oxford Movement seemed to be following Newman to Rome. In the rather heavy-handed banter that introduces *Shirley,* readers are assured: "It is not positively affirmed that you shall not have a taste of the exciting, perhaps towards the middle and close of the meal, but it is resolved that the first dish set upon the table shall be one that a Catholic—ay, even an Anglo-Catholic—might eat on Good Friday in Passion Week."[17] In 1850, just after the publication of *Shirley,* anti-Catholic feeling was aggravated by the so-called "Papal Aggression," when the Roman hierarchy was restored to England with the appointment of Cardinal Wiseman as Archbishop of England by Pope Pius IX. This move, intended to unify and inspire English Catholics, was popularly interpreted as a campaign of proselytism. Newman, now established at the Oratory of St. Philip Neri in Birmingham, published his *The Present Position of Catholics in England* in an attempt to clarify the significance of the Pope's decision. Lewes, in *The Leader,* welcomed the "Aggression" as a challenge to his countrymen. Charlotte Brontë took particular interest in his editorial "The Pope, or Free Thought?," in which he attacked "the passive Indifferentism, the reckless Don't Carishness" among the clergy of the English Church and asserted that "Every man really anxious about Truth should rejoice at the present commotion in the religious world," for the opposition between Catholics and Protestants "will have the effect of rousing men from lazy acquiescence, and force them to reconsider the grounds of their acquiescence."[18] She wrote to congratulate him on the article, confirming his conviction that religion must be active in men's hearts and affairs and expressing her own belief that the Church can do its work "quite as well in a curate's plain clothes as in a cardinal's robes and hat."[19]

Much of the tension in Lucy Snowe's situation derives from her being a Protestant in a Catholic country. In Labassecour she is beset by a "Papal Aggression" in miniature:

> The opinion of my Catholic acquaintance concerning my spiritual prospects was somewhat naively expressed to me on one occasion. A *pensionnaire,* to whom I had rendered some little service, exclaimed one day as she sat beside me,—
>
> "Mademoiselle, what a pity you are a Protestant!"
>
> "Why, Isabelle?"
>
> "Parce que, quand vous serez morte, vous brûlerez tout de suite dans l'enfer."
>
> "Croyez-vous?"
>
> "Certainement que j'y crois; tout le monde le sait; et d'ailleurs le prêtre me l'a dit."
>
> Isabelle was an odd, blunt little creature. She added *sotto voce*—,
>
> "Pour assurer votre salut là-haut, on ferait bien de vous brûler tout vive ici-bas."
>
> I laughed, as, indeed, it was impossible to do otherwise. (CH. IX)

Lucy is subjected later, and in a darker mood, to the blandishments of Père Silas, who affirms: "You were made for our faith. Depend upon it, our faith alone could heal and help you. Protestantism is altogether too dry, cold, prosaic for you" (CH. XV). Readers, aware of the recent conversions to Rome, undoubtedly sensed danger when Lucy, dazed and disconsolate, wanders into Père Silas' church to relieve her misery by confession.[20] But she makes it clear that the Church of St. Jean Baptiste attracted her for the same reason that in London she was moved by the sight of St. Paul's—as a religious sanctuary considered apart from denomination: "Any solemn rite, any spectacle of sincere worship, any opening for appeal to God was as welcome to me then as bread to one in extremity of want. I knelt down with others on the stone pavement." At this point

Lucy is in the perplexed state of the heroine of Elizabeth Sewell's *Margaret Percival* (1847) upon stepping inside the cathedral of Rouen. Here Miss Sewell comments: "We live in an age when the unity of the Church of Christ is considered unattainable. . . .We have even ceased to lament over its absence; and the greatness of our loss is seldom understood or appreciated till we find ourselves in a foreign country shut out in spirit from the temples which ought to open to us as our homes" (CH. XI).[21] Both Margaret Percival and Lucy Snowe have highly developed spiritual feelings, but both cast the Scarlet Lady behind them. Lucy assures those who might have questioned her firmness: "Did I, do you suppose, reader, contemplate venturing again within that worthy priest's reach? As soon should I have thought of walking into a Babylonish furnace." At the same time she warns them of the lures of Rome to the susceptible, for had she allowed Père Silas to continue to play on her religious emotions: "I know not how it would all have ended. We all think ourselves strong in some points; we all know ourselves weak in many."[22] This episode, "The Long Vacation," ends what was originally the first volume of *Villette*. By the end of the second volume ("The Hôtel Crécy") Lucy leaves no doubt of her Protestantism by comparing her "discipline" of Ginevra Fanshawe to the preaching of John Knox to Mary Stuart.

With all of Lucy's talk of "Popish superstition," "the pomp of Rome," the "ecclesiastical millinery," and "celestial jewelry" that "struck me as tawdry, not grand," it is not surprising, as she confided to Miss Wooler two months after *Villette* was published, that "Currer Bell's remarks on Romanism have drawn down on him the condign displeasure of the High Church party."[23] Her friend Harriet Martineau, though herself a Dissenter, was also offended by the way Catholicism was "violently reprobated" in *Villette*. "We do not exactly see the moral necessity for this," Miss Martineau complained, ". . . and we are rather sorry for it, occurring at a time when catholics and protestants hate each other quite sufficiently; and in a mode which will not affect conversion."[24] On the other hand, at least one reviewer commended Miss Brontë for tolerance, observing of her treatment of the Jesuit influence on Monsieur Paul that "the system of intrigue is properly denounced, but without any bigotry or ranting against Catholicism."[25] He recognized the ecumenical spirit that informs *Villette* at its close, where sympathy of soul overcomes the religious barriers that separate Lucy and Paul. They exert a reciprocal influence on one another, no longer divided by dogma but united by the fundamental of faith. "At ease with him," Lucy discovers, "I could defend my creed and faith in my own fashion. . . . He was made to comprehend something of their [the Protestants'] mode of honouring the Light, the Life, the Word." Furthermore, she comes to respect Paul's faith: "I thought Romanism wrong, a great mixed image of gold and clay; but it seemed to me that *this* Romanist held the purer elements of his creed with an innocency of heart which God must love" (CH. XXXVI). She wrote this at a moment when a prominent religious journal was calling for novels that could assimilate religion "as a principle of conduct, a moving force influencing external circumstance, not as a theological system or a didactic code."[26] Lucy and Paul, at least, effect a *modus vivendi* at this time when "catholics and protestants hate each other sufficiently."

Alongside the pulpit war of the early 1850's a war of the pen was being waged on the political front more directly involving England with France. In one of the issues of *The Leader* that debated the Catholic question, Sir Francis Head's alarmist book *The Defenceless State of England* was reviewed. The reviewer referred to this book, in which Sir Francis contended that England was an open prey to a rapacious France, as a "new romance." It was taken seriously enough, however, to elicit a protest from the President of France that the French Navy had in late years been contracted to a mere defensive force.[27] Nevertheless, Louis Napoleon's *coup d'état* of December 1851 revived the

rumors of aggression. Miss Brontë commented to Miss Wooler in
1852:

> As to the French President—it seems to me hard to say what a man
> with so little scruple and so much ambition will *not* attempt. I
> wish, however, the English Press would not prate so much about
> invasion; if silence were possible in a free country—would it not be
> far better to prepare silently for what *may* come—to place the
> national defences in an effective state and refrain from breathing a
> word of apprehension? Doubtless such is the thought of practical
> men like the Duke of Wellington—I can well conceive his secret
> impatience at the mischievous gabbling of the newspapers. Won-
> derful is the French Nation![28]

Conflicts of State as well as Church enter, not surprisingly, into
Lucy's adventures in Labassecour. With a playfulness aimed no
doubt at the Francophobia of some of her readers, Miss Brontë
magnifies the Pensionnat Beck into a political battlefield.

Madame Beck, to Lucy, seems to have been intended for
greater things than a Pensionnat de Demoiselles: "That school
offered for her powers too limited a sphere; she ought to have
swayed a nation; she should have been the leader of a turbulent
legislative assembly. . . . In her own single person, she could
have comprised the duties of a first minister and a superinten-
dent of police" (CH. VIII). Her stealth and furtiveness in prying
into the affairs of her staff is likened to secret diplomacy. Later,
in preparing Lucy for her first encounter with her pupils, she
adopts the tone of the chauvinist: "Bon! But let me tell you that
these are not quiet, decorous English girls you are going to
encounter. Ce sont des Labassecouriennes, rondes, franches,
brusques, et tant soit peu rebelles." The bellicose language is
taken up by Lucy as she faces the fierce second division class,
which "was considerably the largest, and accommodated an
assemblage more numerous, more turbulent, and infinitely more
unmanageable than the other two." As for the students:
"Mesdemoiselles Blanche, Virginie, and Angélique opened the
campaign by a series of twitterings and whisperings; these soon

swelled into murmurs and short laughs, which the remoter
benches caught up and echoed more loudly. This growing revolt
of sixty against one soon became oppressive enough, my command of French being so limited, and exercised under such cruel
constraint" (CH. VIII) .[29] The ease by which Lucy quells this
classroom war should have effected a comic catharsis for those of
her readers who had feared another attempted Napoleonic invasion.[30]

A state of armed truce prevails through Lucy's relations with
the Labassecouriennes, breaking out now and then into altercation. On the day of Madame Beck's *fête*, Lucy is forced by
Monsieur Paul to assume the role of a fop in a *vaudeville*. When
taunted by a colleague for her gaucherie, Lucy becomes angry:
"and I could not help turning upon her and saying that if she
were not a lady and I a gentleman, I should feel disposed to call
her up." The Master interposes: " 'After the play, after the play,'
said M. Paul. 'I will then divide my pair of pistols between you,
and we will settle the dispute according to form. It will only be
the old quarrel of France and England' " (CH. XIV) . Later, and
more crucially, Lucy's confrontation of Paul Emanuel in class on
the day of his *fête* is carried on as a mock war. Lucy describes
how, irritated at what he supposes is her neglect of his birthday,
he goes out of his way to embarrass her in class. "I don't know
how, in the progress of his *discours*, he had contrived to cross the
Channel and land on British ground; but there I found him
when I began to listen." Monsieur Paul's verbal "invasion" of
England consists of a lengthy blast against English women. At
first Lucy is determined to ignore this tirade, and not to betray
any reaction to it, but her equanimity wavers:

> I grieve to say I could not quite carry out this resolution. For
> some time the abuse of England and the English found and left me
> stolid. I bore it some fifteen minutes stoically enough; but this
> hissing cockatrice was determined to sting, and he said such things
> at last—fastening not only upon our women but upon our greatest
> names and best men, sullying the shield of Britannia and dabbling

the Union Jack in mud—that I *was* stung. With vicious relish he brought up the most spicy current Continental historical false-hoods, than which nothing can be conceived more offensive. Zélie and the whole class became one grin of vindictive delight, for it is curious to discover how these clowns of Labassecour secretly hate England. At last, I struck a sharp stroke on my desk, opened my lips and let loose this cry—

"Vive l'Angleterre, l'Histoire et les Héros! A bas la France, la Fiction et les Faquins!" (CH. XXIX)

With this jingoistic outburst on Lucy's part, the Professor's bombardment of insults ceases. But Lucy realizes that she has played into his hands: "Little monster of malice! He now thought he had got the victory, since he had made me angry." Fortunately, this literary saber rattling ends on a conciliatory note, with mutual apologies and exchanges of gifts. In fact, it leads to a new admiration on Lucy's part for Monsieur Paul—a breakdown of her habitual fear and disdain of him—that even-tually ripens into love. Whatever it might bode for future inter-national relations, the Battle of Labassecour is settled amicably. Since it takes place in Belgium it might be called Lucy Snowe's victory at Waterloo (a battle that had been revived in readers' minds recently by *Vanity Fair* and her own *Shirley*). Indeed, not too long after this episode Lucy likens Monsieur Paul to Napo-leon himself (CH. XXX).

Villette assimilates the social and intellectual history of its time to the burning consciousness of Lucy Snowe, who has something of Dorothea Brooke's faculty for converting ideas into feelings. Through Lucy's wit and intelligence, problems of Church and State are reduced to homely terms for the benefit of her more sheltered readers. A more important function that Lucy's story served for the average reader of the time is suggested by a reviewer who, after praising *Villette* for its powerful plot and dramatic delineation of character, pointed out that "the interest of the tale is metaphysical and subjective rather than external, and evinces a clear perception of the causes of mental suffering in a highly sensitive and conscientious mind."[31] He likened its effect on the reader to the spell cast by the glistening eye of the Ancient Mariner over the wedding guest.

Practically speaking, *Villette* is a reliving of a mental and moral ordeal, "the actual thoughts and feelings of a strong, struggling soul . . . the cry of pain from one who has loved passionately, and who has sorrowed sorely," as Lewes wrote in a review.[32] Answering an objection that her editor, W. S. Williams, raised while he was reading the story in manuscript, Charlotte wrote: "You say that she [Lucy] may be thought morbid and weak, unless the history of her life be more fully given. I consider that she *is* both morbid and weak at times; her character sets up no pretension to unmixed strength; and anybody living her life would necessarily become morbid."[33] Some of her letters to Miss Wooler enter with painful detail into aspects of psychopathology that are explored in *Villette*—loneliness, hypochondria, living with an elderly cripple (in her case her invalid, nearly blind father, the Reverend Patrick Brontë). In one letter she describes a state of profound melancholia that she herself experienced: "I can never forget the concentrated anguish of certain insufferable moments and the heavy gloom of many long hours—besides the preternatural horror which seemed to clothe existence and Nature—and which made Life a continual waking Night-mare."[34] This "waking Night-mare" is transferred to Lucy Snowe and objectified into a universal despair.

To her "studies of character," as she describes Lucy's psychological probings, Miss Brontë brings an insight into human nature that she thought Jane Austen lacked. "The Passions are perfectly unknown to her," she commented after reading *Emma*. "Her business is not half so much with the human heart as with the human eyes, mouth, hands and feet; what sees keenly, speaks aptly, moves flexibly, it suits her to study, but what throbs fast and full, though hidden, what the blood rushes through, what is the unseen seat of Life and the sentient target of death—*this* Miss Austen ignores."[35] As the Reverend Mr. Brontë's daughter, however, imbued with *The Pilgrim's Progress* and the Bible, she was hardly indifferent to the character of the Christian Heroine. But she tended to see the struggle for holiness as a war within the self, and the passions therefore interested her as human instincts to be conquered rather than indulged. She appears never to have forgotten the lessons taught in Isaac Watts' *The Doctrine of the Passions Explained and Improved,* a treatise she read in her youth at Haworth Parsonage,[36] which bears the motto, attributed to Solomon: "He that hath no Rule over his own Spirit is like a City that is broken down and without Walls." Watts' book is an aid to the religious toward the understanding of the Passions, "the sudden and secret turns and windings of them through the heart," for the purpose of "forming proper rules for their better management, and the bringing these active and restless promoters, or disturbers, of our happiness, under a moral and religious discipline; and without this, we can neither be men of wisdom nor piety." Such is the wisdom transmitted to her readers by Lucy Snowe, the Christian Heroine incarnated in the Good Governess.

The governess-heroine, a fictional type who emerged in the late 1830's and 1840's alongside the spoiled lady of fashion, was one whom Charlotte Brontë could readily re-create in her own image. Like William Crimsworth, the hero of *The Professor,* her heroines have to work for a living and "master at least half the ascent of 'the Hill of Difficulty.'" So the Silver Fork heroine, as represented by Blanche Ingram or Ginevra Fanshawe, is relegated to a subordinate role. Charlotte Brontë moved the female teacher into the limelight in place of the female pupil—a trend that had been gathering momentum for some time. The lady tutors of the Female Education novels of the early nineteenth century tended to be unobtrusive, like Madame de Rosier, the genteel émigrée of Maria Edgeworth's "The Good French Governess," described as "a lady of good family, excellent understanding and most amiable character," but something of a human catalyst, stimulating others but remaining unaffected herself.[37] Miss Taylor, who has served Emma Woodhouse for sixteen years "less as a governess than as a good friend," retires into matrimony on the first page of the novel. The governess of the Bertram girls and Fanny Price is barely mentioned. Many ladies seem to have assumed, along with Mrs. Murray, one of the employers of Agnes Grey, that: "The judicious governess knows . . . while she lives in obscurity herself, her pupil's virtues and defects will be open to every eye; and that, unless she loses sight of herself in the cultivation, she need not hope for success" (*Agnes Grey*, CH. XVIII). "Having said what she wished," Anne Brontë's heroine confides to the reader, "it was no part of her plan to await my answer: it was my business to hear, and not to speak." But she speaks out in her quiet but firm tone to her public.

The governess had been speaking out for her rights as a human being at least as far back as Lady Blessington's *The Governess* (1839), a society novel turned social tract. Lady Blessington's story, concerned with an orphaned heroine struggling for security, shows the governess novel emerging out of the "Fatherless Fanny" tradition. Here the author, who had herself met with frustration in her status seeking, tries to enlist sympathy for the much put-upon heroine, while arousing contempt for the vulgar rich. Clara Mordaunt, the heroine, actually has no vocation for the governess's life, having been forced into what she regards as a servile career. She is glad to be rescued from it by a timely legacy and a proposal from a lord. Other governess heroines are more dedicated. Emily Morton, in Elizabeth Sewell's *Amy Herbert* (1844), sublimates her frustrations and humiliations in her devotion to guiding young Amy in Christian thought and conduct. The heroine of Mrs. Sherwood's *Caroline Mordaunt* (1845) is also a teacher of "vital Christianity" to her young charges. Agnes Grey expresses mainly disillusionment with her profession, but her stoicism and moral courage make her narrative a kind of conduct book and guide to the novice entering the field.[38] Jane Eyre is no more the pattern governess than she was the model Edgeworth-Hofland-Sherwood child at Lowood Hall.[39] The moral of her story is that she is a woman first and a governess second, and we almost forget her original vocation after she meets Mr. Rochester. Probably a greater shock to Lady Eastlake's generation than Jane Eyre's boldness in declaring her love to Rochester was her rejection of St. John Rivers, because the reward for the governess's trials, including Agnes Grey's, was generally marriage to a clergyman. From Lady Blessington's porcelain doll, Clara Mordaunt, to plain Jane Eyre we seem to have traveled almost the distance from *Gorboduc* to *Hamlet,* but Jane too gets her legacy and her lord. To be sure, Rochester is no handsome prince and Thornton Hall is no castle in the air; nevertheless, a certain vestige of the romantic heroine clings to Miss Brontë's first governess heroine.

With Lucy Snowe, Charlotte Brontë reverts to the rugged path that she had set out for William Crimsworth in *The Professor,* who, she had determined, should not only work his way through life, but:

> that he should never get a shilling he had not earned; that no sudden turns should lift him in a moment to wealth and high station; that whatever small competency he might gain, should be won by the sweat of his brow; . . . that he should not even marry a beautiful girl or a lady of rank. As Adam's son he should share Adam's doom, and drain throughout life a mixed and moderate cup of enjoyment.

As William Crimsworth, ascending the "Hill of Difficulty," is a latter-day incarnation of Bunyan's Christian, so Lucy Snowe is Christiana. She is Eve's daughter who is allowed one moment in Eden and lives on the memory of it. She is never rescued from the necessity of earning her own bread. The only money she inherits is a hundred pounds from her deceased mistress Miss Marchmont, not her entire fortune, as she would have if somehow she had stumbled into the world of Lady Blessington and the Annuals.[40] The love of her life is an ugly middle-aged man, and nothing, practically speaking, comes of it.

In *Villette,* then, Miss Brontë tries to follow William Crimsworth's advice that "Novelists should never allow themselves to weary of the study of real life," with no concession to wishfulfillment. Contributing to the reality of her last novel is its density of concrete detail not only of people but of places and interiors, much of which, as has been pointed out, was based on her own experience.[41] *Villette* conveys an unusual sense of actuality because it is pervaded by its author's recent recall of her London adventures, as well as her experiences in Brussels, which are transferred to Labassecour, her country of the mind.[42] Many critics attribute the intense realism of the book to the intimacy with which Charlotte Brontë reveals herself in Lucy Snowe.[43] Certainly in Lucy we find the governess-heroine completely deglamorized. Also, her role significantly changes.

Among literary governesses Lucy Snowe is closer to Maria Young of Harriet Martineau's *Deerbrook* (1839) than to Lady Blessington's Clara Mordaunt, who appeared in the same year. Maria Young is intellectual but morbidly shy, concealing strong emotions and an intense inner life beneath an unattractive appearance and a diffident manner. She is an aspiring spirit who finds her teaching career unrewarding and stultifying. She has her pathetic moment in the novel when it is revealed that she is in love with Philip Enderby, who eventually marries one of the two heroines, Margaret Ibbotson. As tutor to Margaret, Miss Young is in a position to bring the two together, and she acts with altruism. Keeping her secret forever locked up inside her, she counsels Margaret and her sister Hester on love, drawing on the knowledge of her own heart.

The germ of a memorable character is contained in Maria Young; unfortunately Harriet Martineau did not develop her. It was left to Charlotte Brontë to move the self-sacrificing young spinster from the periphery to the center of the story. *Deerbrook* foreshadows to an extent the mood of *Villette,* a cry of the heart, a reaching out of one anguished soul to others. The character of Maria Young helps also to define the function of the narrator of *Villette*.[44] Lucy Snowe, like Maria Young, is a counsellor of the heart, but she carries her moral wisdom beyond the walls of her *externat de demoiselles*. In other ways too she moves beyond Maria Young, for she finds release and fulfillment. Almost midway in the novel Lucy makes an important decision. Offered a chance by Mr. Home to become his daughter Polly's tutor-companion:

> I declined. I think I should have declined had I been poorer than I was, and with scantier fund of resource, more stinted narrowness of future prospect. I had not that vocation. I could teach, I could give lessons; but to be either a private governess or a companion was unnatural to me. Rather than fill the former post in any great house, I would deliberately have taken a housemaid's place, bought a strong pair of gloves, swept bedrooms and staircases and cleaned stoves and locks, in peace and independence. Rather than be a companion, I would have made shirts and starved. (CH. XXVI)

Once contented with a recluse's existence, Lucy now exchanges "small pains" for "great agonies." Moreover, her declaration of independence signifies a new freedom for the governess.

With Lucy Snowe, the Good Governess develops into the traveling Instructress. The reading public had already made her acquaintance in a popular novel that Charlotte Brontë knew well, Julia Kavanagh's *Nathalie* (1850). This story is a forerunner of *Villette* in a number of respects—its continental school setting, its rebellious heroine subdued by religion and love, and particularly its principal romance. Nathalie Montolieu, the heroine, is a lovely, headstrong young schoolmistress from Provence, unhappily placed in a position in a bleak Normandy village. Nathalie's southern French origin is supposed to suggest a volatile temperament, even if in Miss Kavanagh's genteel hands she emerges as a rather decorous English schoolgirl. However, her clashes with the stony northern disposition of the tyrannical headmistress Mademoiselle Dantin are a kind of rehearsal for

Lucy Snowe's altercations with Madame Beck. Dismissed from her school, Nathalie is befriended by a neighboring aristocratic family, who take her to live in their chateau. Here she spurns the affections of the scion of the family in favor of his uncle, a cultivated, middle-aged cynic. The love of Nathalie and Monsieur de Sainville develops out of mutual reserve and distrust, proving that antitypes may be transformed into elective affinities, as with Lucy and Monsieur Paul.

Miss Kavanagh favored Miss Brontë with an autographed copy of this romance, for which Miss Brontë wrote to thank her.[45] She was generally fascinated with the book, offering only minor reservations. "Nathalie's perverseness as well as her final submission struck me as a little exaggerated—as did some of the traits in M. de Sainville's character," she demurred, "but I said I would not criticise; the contrast in their natures, and the *kind* of contrast is a happy thought; the mutual attraction to which it leads would—I doubt not, be exactly paralleled in nature and real life." And who should know better?[46] Charlotte read *Nathalie* at the beginning of the year when she began writing *Villette*. The lesser and the greater novel alike show cultural barriers broken down by a sympathy of souls, but *Villette* covers far more ground, encompassing politics and religion as well as temperamental differences.[47] And—more in keeping with her own life—Miss Brontë's heroine never settles down with her Monsieur. Nor does she retire from teaching, as does Nathalie Montolieu.

Although Charlotte Brontë did not sign herself "A Clergyman's Daughter" on her title pages, as did many another contemporary authoress aiming to impress Mudie's more pious subscribers, *Villette* could easily have been taken in its time as another example of exemplary biography by a governess evolved into religious educator. One of its most enthusiastic reviewers commended the author for "a strong sense of the meaning of Life, and an earnest striving 'upwards and onwards.' "[48] Inevitably the devout governess was caricatured by the irreverent,

like Marmion Savage, whose Miss Stanley, lady tutor to the
Spread family, "thought of nothing but the church, church,
church, from Monday to Sunday, and from Sunday back, corrected her pupils with the collects, and punished them with the
psalms."[49] Thackeray offset Becky Sharp with his Maria Theresa
Wigglesworth, "Governess in families of the highest distinction,"
who peers out from the title page of "The Orphan of Pimlico,"
prim and severe in black coif, sparrow-beaked and bespectacled,
and carries the imprimatur of "the Reverend W. Oriel, the
Reverend W. Thurifer and other revered Clergy of the district"
for the strictness of her character and principles.[50] But even
Becky Sharp, it will be remembered, becomes a regular church-
goer and composer of hymns in her retirement at Bath and
Cheltenham.

Certainly Lucy Snowe has the audience for pulpit novels,
among others, in mind when she defends her lapse into despair
during her lonely Long Vacation ordeal at the Pensionnat Beck:
"Religious reader, you will preach to me a long sermon about
what I have just written; and so will you, moralist, and you,
stern sage. . . . Perhaps you are all right, and, perhaps, circum-
stanced like me, you would have been, like me, wrong." She
shows her readers the way of the Christian but makes it clear that
the path is a thorny one. But her detailed recording of mental
anguish is meant as a spiritual catharsis for her readers, Lucy's
lay sermon reaching out to the disconsolate as well as to those
disappointed in love.

Villette, considered as religious fiction, is a series of steps-along-
life's-way, a kind of secular pilgrimage. In purpose it is not far
removed from Sarah Stickney Ellis' much read and influential
moral treatise of the early 1840's, *The Daughters of England,*
addressed to the "Christian woman [who] has made her decision
not to live for herself, so much as for others; but, above all, not
to live for this world, so much as for eternity." Mrs. Ellis offers
her wisdom to the neophyte "just as an experienced traveller,
who had himself often stepped aside from the safest path, and

found the difficulty of returning, would be anxious to leave directions for others who might follow in order that they might avoid the dangers with which he had already become acquainted, and pursue their course with greater certainty of attaining the end desired."[51] This scheme of the seasoned and weatherbeaten voyager helping on those who are just setting out was imitated in novels. Another example, read and enjoyed by Charlotte as well as many others of her generation, was a first novel, *Passages in the Life of Mrs. Margaret Maitland* (1849), in which the twenty-one-year-old author Margaret Wilson (later Mrs. Oliphant), speaking with the voice of a Scottish spinster and daughter of a minister of the Kirk, "of discreet years and small riches," writes for the edification of "young folk":

> It is a troublous water—the water of life, and it has often given me a sore heart to see young things launched upon it, like bairn's boats, sailing hither and thither in an unpurpose-like manner, and having no thought of who it is that sends both the lown wind and the storm and if they have need of various instruments and a right pilot-man to guide ships over that constant uncertainty, the sea (as I have read in books), I think not but there is far greater need of all manner of helps to win safely through that greater uncertainty—life. Uncertainty I call it, looking at it as the young folk I have mentioned do, with the short-sighted vision of a frail mortal; and though we know that to one Eye there is in it no matter of dubiety, yet I will not therefore change my word, for that is too great a thing for the like of me, seeing I profess to nothing but a common share of understanding, to make or meddle with.[52]

The heroine of another novel that Charlotte Brontë knew, Mrs. Burbury's *Florence Sackville; or, Self-Dependence* (1852), recalls: "My friends have generally been among the aged. There is something in their wise and passionless calmness that has always been inexpressibly delightful to me. . . . One listens with reverence to their experience, learning lessons of wisdom from their lips."[53] Lucy Snowe is in such a relationship with Miss Marchmont, who "gave me the originality of her character to study, the steadiness of her virtues . . . the power of her

passions, to admire; the truth of her feelings to trust" (CH. IV).
She becomes in turn the sage old lady: "My hair, which, till a
late period, withstood the frosts of time, lies now at last white,
under a white cap, like snow beneath snow," she puns (CH. V).
Her thirty-seven-year-old creator sets the action back to a vague
"time gone by" to give her words a venerable air.

As a reminiscence of an elderly spinster now at peace with the
world looking back over early years of frustration and sorrow,
Villette bears an especially suggestive resemblance to a religious
novel that preceded it by a year, Elizabeth Sewell's *The Experience of Life* (1852). Miss Sewell was an educator-writer like Miss
Brontë.[54] Both conceived in their own images precocious, refractory young girls moulded and subdued by religious teaching
as well as unattractive, strong-spirited young women of intellect
and scrupulous conscience who settle into lives of quiet self-
abnegation. The title of Miss Sewell's book suggests a spiritual
autobiography rather than a work of fiction, and she in fact
disclaims any intention to write a tale which is "only a vignette,
a portion of the great picture of life," preferring something closer
to "a real representation of human existence." Sally Mortimer,
the narrator, makes no claim to being a heroine in the sense of
having lived a striking or exciting life. She is rather one of those
who "are born unthought of beyond their own immediate circle,
and die lamented only by a few; and we pass over their names in
the obituary of the day with the strange indifference with which
we hear the aggregate amount of deaths in a battle; forgetting
that for each individual soul in the vast multitude there has been
a special day of trial, a special providence and guidance; and
there will be a special day of reckoning and doom."

Among the obscure anonymous is Lucy Snowe: "If I failed in
what I now designed to undertake, who, save myself, would
suffer? If I died far away from—home I was going to say, but I
had no home—from England, then, who would weep?," she
ponders as she embarks for the continent (CH. VI). Lucy stresses
her drabness and ordinariness. The unromantic Sally Mortimer

describes herself in words that could apply as well to Lucy: "Sickly, plain and indifferently educated, what better could I expect than to live in shade, whilst others glittered in sunshine? . . . What pleasure could I anticipate, but such as might be obtained from the reflected enjoyments of my more fortunate sisters?" (*The Experience of Life*, CH. IV). The unheroic heroine of *Villette*, together with the minimal amount of "incident" (in comparison with *Jane Eyre*), suggests that Miss Brontë, like Miss Sewell, was trying to move away from the conventions of fiction and in the direction of the true life history. The structure of *Villette* for the most part is loose and "open," giving the illusion of the "flow of time" (as Lucy phrases it) rather than of manipulated events.[55] Even the coincidences—such as Lucy's falling in with the Brettons and Polly on the continent—are attributable, in this scheme of things, to providence. Like *The Experience of Life*, *Villette* attempts "a great picture of life," encompassing childhood, youth, and old age, related to the grander scheme of *The Pilgrim's Progress*. Christiana, Everywoman, and ordinary woman fuse in Lucy Snowe and her experiences.

This self-effacement answers to Miss Brontë's purpose in *Villette*, which, like *The Professor*, is addressed to "the man of regular life and rational mind" and is a sermon against despair. The ordeals that test such a man's spirit, according to Crimsworth, are just those faced by Lucy:

> He loses his property—it is a blow—he staggers a moment; then, his energies, roused by the smart, are at work to seek a remedy; activity soon mitigates regret. Sickness affects him; he takes patience—endures what he cannot cure. Acute pain racks him; his writhing limbs know not where to rest; he leans on Hope's anchors. Death takes from him what he loves; roots up and tears violently away the stem around which his affections were twined—a dark, dismal time, a frightful wrench—but some morning Religion looks into his desolate house with sunrise, and says, that in another world, another life, we shall meet his kindred again. (*The Professor*, CH. XIX)

Lucy identifies her plight with the human condition, and from time to time she invites her readers to participate in an act of resignation and humility:

> These struggles with the natural character, the strong native bent of the heart, may seem futile and fruitless, but in the end they do good. They tend, however slightly, to give the actions, the conduct, that turn which Reason approves, and which Feeling, perhaps, too often opposes. They certainly make a difference in the general tenor of a life, and enable it to be better regulated, more equable, quieter on the surface; and it is on the surface only the common gaze will fall. As to what lies below, leave that with God. Man your equal, weak as you, and not fit to be your judge, may be shut out thence. Take it to your Maker; show Him the secrets of the Spirit He gave; ask Him how you are to bear the pains He appointed; kneel in His presence, and pray with faith for light in darkness, for strength in piteous weakness, for patience in extreme need. (CH. XVII)

Whether or not Charlotte Brontë read Miss Sewell, one is aware of a shared ambience of religious ideas and feeling in the two writers, both of whom grew up in clerical households. One of Miss Sewell's heroines, Margaret Percival, is cautioned by her mentor: "The world which we bear about with us must differ widely from the world in which we appear to dwell. It is in this contrast between the visible and the invisible, the seen and the felt, that lies the trial of our daily life." The trial of daily life, the world as a testing ground for the endurance of the soul, are themes central to the novels of Miss Brontë as well as Miss Sewell. Lucy Snowe, like Miss Sewell's heroines, seeks signs of God's providence through this harsh world. She shows that those hidden from men's eyes are not hidden from His eyes. Lucy burns with a fiercer flame than Sally Mortimer and she is allowed her time for love; but she too remains unmarried, dedicating her life to imparting her hard-won wisdom to new generations. The governess has moved out of the nursery and the schoolroom to reach a larger and wider ranging audience.

Villette has the intimacy and immediacy of a diary, expanding on the "small, thick book" in which Louis Moore confides his thoughts: "It is pleasant to write about what is near and dear as the core of my heart: none can deprive me of this little book, and through this pencil, I can say to it what I will—say what I dare utter to nothing living—say what I dare not *think* aloud" (*Shirley*, CH. XXIX). However, it is a confession released from a private world to bring solace to other living beings. But there is another tale to be considered in *Villette*—the anti-romance embedded in the life history. Self-examining and self-dramatizing as she is, Lucy recognizes that she is torn between a vivid inner life and a drab real life, "and provided that the former was nourished with a sufficiency of the strange, necromantic joys of fancy, the privileges of the latter might remain limited to daily bread, hourly work, and a roof of shelter" (CH. VIII). Despite her avowal, "Of an artistic temperament I deny that I am" (CH. VII), Lucy betrays this temperament at every turn with her literary allusions and her intense "studies of character" of the people she meets. "Is not the real experience of each individual very limited?" Miss Brontë asked Lewes in discussing her writing. "Then, too, imagination is a strong, restless faculty, which claims to be heard and exercised; are we to be quite deaf to her cry and insensate to her struggles?"[56] Obviously not, for we soon notice that although Lucy Snowe lives externally in the world of the domestic, didactic novel, mentally she dwells in the world of romance and the tale of terror. Superimposed upon the story of how Lucy found peace of mind and her vocation is an allegory of the imagination coping with the world outside itself. And with the purgation of the soul comes the exorcising of the imagination.

Certain arabesque and Gothic elements in the story betray

Lucy's susceptibility to "the strange necromantic joys of fancy."
When she awakens from a stupor to find herself once more with
the Brettons, who, unknown to her, have also moved to Villette,
she momentarily thinks that she is back in England, like "Bed-
reddin Hassan, transported in his sleep from Cairo to the Gates
of Damascus" (CH. XVI). Later, as she gropes about the dark
streets of the old Basse-Ville, she is reminded of a city petrified
"as if by Eastern enchantment," and the ancient church with its
"dark, half ruinous turrets" evokes in her mind "the venerable
and formerly opulent shrine of the Magi." The hunchback
Madame Walravens looks to Lucy like Malevola, the evil fairy
(CH. XXXIV).

Knowing the good use to which Miss Brontë put the story from
A Sicilian Romance of the concealed wife in a castle, one is not
surprised that Lucy's imagination is tinged also with Radcliffian
shades. The house on the Rue des Mages where Madame Walravens lives seems to have been moved out of Udolpho; the
drugged potion given by Madame Beck to Lucy to calm her
nerves (CH. XXXVIII) recalls the noxious brews served to many
a Gothic heroine. Of all the Radcliffe romances, *The Italian; or,
The Confessional of the Black Penitents* seems to hover most in
the background of *Villette,* with its confession chamber and its
meddling Father. Père Silas is not the sinister figure that Mrs.
Radcliffe's Italian priest is, but he and Madame Beck, like their
counterparts Rafaelle Schedoni and Marchesa Vivaldi, plot to
separate two lovers. However, these are mere echoes used for
anticlimactic effect, for *Villette* is a story in which the fancy
cheats itself.[57] So the evil castle turns out to be just a house, and
"Malevola" is the grandmother of Monsieur Paul's dead beloved
Justine Marie. Père Silas and Madame Beck, who had appeared
so ominous to Lucy, are not assassins like the Radcliffian characters they superficially resemble, but merely send Paul off to
Guadaloupe to claim Madame Walravens' real estate, ironically
achieving their dire ends by quite ordinary means. In her wry
way, Miss Brontë makes her readers recognize that evil is at once

more subtle and less glamorous than the Gothic tales would lead
them to believe. The nun's "apparition," that vestige from the
Minerva Press thrillers of her girlhood, is best appreciated as a
similar kind of prank by which she deceives her readers with the
truth.[58]

The Arabian Nights and *Tales of the East* were still amusing
Victorian children as they had their Georgian forebears, and
Mrs. Radcliffe's tales of terror were then available in cheap
reprints with lurid covers; but Miss Brontë's satire was probably
aimed equally at the New Gothicism of Joseph Sheridan
Lefanu's *Ghost Stories and Tales of Mystery* (1851), and the
outré narratives of Catherine Crowe. Mrs. Crowe in particular
startled mid-Victorian readers with *The Night-Side of Nature;
or, Ghosts and Ghost Seers* (1848), a series of alleged eyewitness
accounts of such phenomena as premonitory dreams, apparitions,
revenants, poltergeists, and spectral lights. Her *Light and Darkness; or, The Mysteries of Life* (1850), tales based on the
hallucinations of criminal or diseased minds, includes some
nocturnal adventures of a somnambulistic monk.[59]

In that intensely hallucinatory episode of the midnight *fête* in
the Haute-Ville, where Lucy wanders delirious and opium-dazed,
she leads readers to expect the "nun" to reveal herself, but lets
them down: "Ah! when imagination once runs riot, where do we
stop?" she warns her readers. "What winter tree so bare and
branchless . . . that Fancy, a passing cloud, and a struggling
moonbeam will not clothe it in spirituality, and make of it a
phantom?" (CH. XXXIX). Lucy would dispense with all phantoms. "So much for ghosts and mystery," is her reaction (and
presumably the reader's) when the supposed ghost of the nun
proves to be but a "buxom and blooming . . . *bourgeoise
belle*." The unholy spirits that had been driven out of the temple
of fiction by Jane Austen and Sir Walter Scott are exorcised once
more at midcentury. Miss Brontë's last word on the Gothic
romance is a laugh and a laugh that liberates. It signalizes also a
new life for her heroine. Lucy, as a living captive nun, had

identified herself with fictitious ghostly nuns.[60] In burying the empty religious vestments under her pillow she becomes the "new" realistic heroine sloughing off the trappings of the sheltered romantic heroine. At the same time, Madame Beck's drug runs its course; the "Night-Side of Nature" is dispelled, and in the natural light of day Lucy's reason gains control over her "imagination run riot."

Lucy Snowe then represents, among other things, the conflict in the creative imagination between the "night-side" and the "day-side" of nature. She makes clear which side wins: "All falsities! all figments! We will not deal in this gear," she declares about the fantasies that momentarily deranged her mind. "Let us be honest, and cut, as heretofore, from the homely web of truth" (CH. XXXIX). Instrumental in her rehabilitation is her tutor, and eventually her fiancé, Monsieur Paul Emanuel. His character, like much of the experience related in *Villette,* is distilled from literature and life. He probably derives at least as much from the French novels that Charlotte read in the 1840's and 1850's as from her real tutor, Monsieur Constantin Heger. In Balzac's *Illusions Perdues,* which she read and admired for "analysis of motives" and "subtle perception of the most obscure and secret workings of the mind," a learned French priest awakens the mind of a sensitive provincial young lady to the humanities and the secular learning of the Enlightenment. Her favorite George Sand novel, *Consuelo,* begins with the heroine's tutelage under the imposing and irascible but tenderhearted Maestro Porpora, who discovers and nourishes young Consuelo's genius for song.[61]

Among the gifts which Charlotte received and treasured from Monsieur Heger after she left Brussels was a set of the works of Bernardin de Saint-Pierre (the author whom Shirley Keeldar reads with Louis Moore).[62] Her naming of the ship on which Paul Emanuel sails out of the life of Lucy Snowe the *Paul et Virginie* indicates how much Saint-Pierre's once popular pastoral-idyll was on her mind in composing the main love story of *Vil-*

lette. Its reissue in English translation in Bentley's Standard Novels the very year when *Villette* was published would have reminded her first readers of a classic of their childhood that even the Emperor Napoleon was said to have kept under his pillow. The echoes of *Paul et Virginie* in *Villette* are more than verbal. The Faubourg Clothilde in which Lucy and Paul enjoy their final rendezvous is a replica of the exotic paradise that surrounds Saint-Pierre's innocent young lovers: "The air was still, mild, and fresh. Above the poplars, the laurels, the cypresses, and the roses looked up a moon so lovely and so halcyon, the heart trembled under her smile" (CH. XLI). Their repast suggests a primitive utopia: "Our meal was simple. The chocolate, the rolls, the plate of fresh summer fruit—cherries and strawberries bedded in green leaves—formed the whole; but it was what we liked better than a feast." The Faubourg Clothilde, like Saint-Pierre's lush gardens of Mauritius, is a preserve from man's first estate. Lucy's parting from Paul brings together the *précieuse* and the *religieuse* in her nature:

> We walked back to the Rue Fossette by moonlight—such moonlight as fell on Eden—shining through the shades of the great garden, and haply gilding a path glorious for a step divine, a presence nameless. Once in their lives some men and women go back to these first fresh days of our great sire and mother, taste that grand morning's dew, bathe in its sunrise.[63]

And once only indeed for Lucy and Paul, whose paradise is destined to be lost, as with Paul and Virginie. However, the ending of *Villette* exactly reverses that of Saint-Pierre's romance —with Paul instead of Virginie drowning at sea and Lucy joining the mourners on the shore.[64]

Lucy is denied reunion with her beloved, but he leaves her an important heritage. When Monsieur Paul supersedes Dr. John Bretton in her heart, Lucy, as she says, gives up a love "born of beauty" for a love "venturing diffidently into life after long acquaintance, furnace-tried by pain, stamped by constancy, consolidated by affection's pure and durable alloy," and furthermore one that "laughed at Passion, his fast frenzies and his hot and hurried extinction" (CH. XXXIX). Lucy's transference of her affections, far from being capricious, as some have alleged, symbolizes at once her harmony of soul and the conversion of the creative imagination from romance to reality. Monsieur Paul introduces to her what Bernardin de Saint-Pierre brought to her creator.

Paul et Virginie was originally part of a series called *Études de la Nature,* so that not the least significant feature of Monsieur Paul's last lessons is that they are conducted out of doors under open skies. The tales he reads in *"les bois et les petits sentiers"* are noteworthy for their artlessness, told in "such a diction as children love and learned men emulate." Monsieur Paul in effect supersedes the world of the book and the aesthetic life for Lucy: "His mind was indeed my library, and whenever it was opened to me, I entered bliss"; so great are his descriptive powers that "such a picture I have never looked on from artist's pencil" (CH. XXXIII). Monsieur Paul's spontaneity of emotion and intuitive grasp of phenomena counteract Lucy's tendency to escape from actuality into the "necromantic dreams of fancy." He leads her from literature into nature, from vicarious experience into real experience, from imitations of life into life itself. Lucy Snowe's *éducation sentimentale* at the Pensionnat Beck is completed.

The book that Lucy eventually writes is, appropriately, an autobiography, a direct rapport between writer and readers, giving them a sense of life as it is being lived, intermittently using the artifices of fiction only to scorn them. "Here, at any rate, is an *original* book," wrote Lewes, taking due note of its paucity of conventional novelistic devices. "Every page, every paragraph is sharp with *individuality*. It is Currer Bell speaking to you, not the Circulating Library reverberating echoes."[65] Lucy is motivated to write by a desire to commemorate her master as much as to unburden herself, and her work therefore mingles confession with memoir. As a literary lady, she is in the paradoxical position of denigrating literature and of writing a book about one who, as she tells us, "was not a man to write books; but I have heard him lavish with careless, unconscious prodigality, such mental wealth as books seldom boast" (CH. XXXIII). It is this "mental wealth" that Lucy dispenses in her own book, where her literary skills are employed to enhance her mentor's oral wisdom: "I used to think what a delight it would be for one who loved him better than he loved himself to gather and store up those handfuls of gold dust, so recklessly flung to heaven's reckless winds" (CH. XXXIII).

With *Villette*, Charlotte Brontë was all the more "determined to take Nature and Truth as my sole guides," as she once wrote Lewes in accounting for the blandness of *The Professor,* her first novel intended for the general public.[66] Her last novel is the culmination of her campaign to free herself from Angria. "I doubt whether the regular novel-reader will consider the 'agony piled sufficiently high' (as the Americans say) or the colours dashed on to the canvas with proper amount of daring," she wrote her editor, W. S. Williams, while the manuscript was passing through his hands. "Still, I fear, they must be satisfied with what is offered; my palette affords no brighter tints; were I to attempt to deepen the reds, or burnish the yellows, I should but botch."[67] *Jane Eyre* had been her one compromise with the demands of the "regular novel-reader" and publishers for "the wild, wonderful and thrilling—the strange, startling and harrowing."[68] *Shirley* pinned her down to actuality, confined her imagination, toned down her exuberance, and engaged her mind with ideas and issues. But it was in *Villette* more than anywhere else in her writing that she succeeded in reconciling the conflicting elements in her imagination—passion and reason, fantasy and reality, art and nature.

In *Villette* we follow not only the curve of Charlotte Brontë's literary development, but the course of the nineteenth-century novel. Lucy Snowe would have been quite contented, she confesses early in the novel, to remain all her life a domestic companion. When she was shut off from society with Miss

Marchmont, "Two hot, close rooms thus became my world. . . . I forgot that there were fields, woods, rivers, seas, an ever-changing sky outside the steam-dimmed lattice of this sick-chamber" (CH. IV). With Lucy's expulsion from her cramped chambers, the domestic novel breaks out of its confining walls and engages itself with man's larger moral and spiritual struggles. Charlotte Brontë thought that her métier, like Thackeray's, was "human nature at home," but the epical scope and sweep of *Villette* indicate that she was following her "high priest of Truth" in opening the windows of the sitting room out on the world. At the same time, as a parable of the imagination, Lucy Snowe's autobiography recapitulates her readers' literary experience of the past half-century—romance and domestic history, the tale of terror and the tale "founded on fact," the novel of society and the religious-didactic novel commingled. The French and English novel also are joined in a unique wedding of sensibility and mid-Victorian realism.

A year after *Villette* was published, Charlotte Brontë was married to a curate, Arthur Bell Nicholls, conforming in the long run more closely to the pattern of the Good Governess than any of her heroines. "My husband is not a poet or a poetical man—and one of my grand doubts before marriage was about 'congenial' tastes and so on," she confided in a letter to a friend written during the honeymoon. But she found him considerate of her sensibility and love of nature. "So far he is always good in this way—and this protection which does not interfere or pretend is I believe a thousand times better than any half sort of pseudo sympathy. I will try with God's help to be as indulgent to him whenever indulgence is needed."[69] The marriage appears to have been reasonably happy, but it was not destined to last long. Ten months later she joined the "well-loved dead" whose passing she alludes to in a veiled way in *Villette*.[70] Thackeray published the fragment of another novel she left behind her (carefully concealed from her husband during their marriage) in *Cornhill*

Magazine. In his introduction, which served as an epitaph, he probably best summarized what Miss Brontë meant to her generation: "Who that has known her books has not admired the artist's noble English, the burning love of truth, the bravery, the simplicity, the indignation at wrong, the eager sympathy, the pious love and reverence, the passionate honour, so to speak of the woman?"[71]

Lewes, before her death, had stressed her more purely literary significance, calling attention in reviews to her "strange power of subjective representation," her faculty for "the psychological interpretation of material phenomena," her "mental analysis," her "passionate heart to feel," coupled with a "powerful brain to give feeling shape."[72] This union of heart and brain was noticed especially by one of the most enthusiastic admirers of *Villette,* a journalist and translator, Marian Evans, who wrote to a friend that she thought this novel "a still more wonderful book than Jane Eyre. There is something almost preternatural in its power."[73] This *mélange* of diary, memoir, devoir, and *lecture pieuse* wrung from the anguished heart of Lucy Snowe undoubtedly brought peace of soul to many of her contemporaries. It also opened up the subconscious to later novelists. Looking simultaneously backward and forward, *Villette* is at once an ancestral voice and a prophetic voice in the house of fiction, speaking of what was past and passing and to come.

CHARACTERISTIC FICTION CONTEMPORANEOUS WITH *VILLETTE* (1853)

1839 Lady Blessington, *The Governess.*
  Harriet Martineau, *Deerbrook.* (New ed., 1843.)
1842–43 George Sand, *Consuelo.* (English tr., 1847.)
1844 Honoré de Balzac, *Modeste Mignon.*
  Elizabeth Missing Sewell, *Amy Herbert.*
1845 Geraldine Jewsbury, *Zoe: The History of Two Lives.*
  Martha Mary Sherwood, *Caroline Mordaunt; or, The Governess.*
  Elizabeth Missing Sewell, *Gertrude.*

1847 Anne Brontë, *Agnes Grey.*

Elizabeth Missing Sewell, *Margaret Percival.*

1848 Catherine Crowe, *The Night-Side of Nature; or, Ghosts and Ghost Seers.*

Geraldine Jewsbury, *The Half-Sisters.*

Julia Kavanagh, *Madeleine.*

1849 *Grace Dermott; A Help for the Afflicted* (Religious Tract Society Pamphlet).

Margaret Oliphant, *Passages in the Life of Mrs. Margaret Maitland of Sunnyside.*

Elizabeth Missing Sewell, *Laneton Parsonage.*

1850 Catherine Crowe, *Light and Darkness; or, The Mysteries of Life.*

Julia Kavanagh, *Nathalie.*

Harriet Martineau, "The Old Governess," *Sketches from Life* (published in *The Leader*, November 9, 1850; reprinted in book form, 1856.)

1851 Mrs. E. J. Burbury, *Florence Sackville; or, Self-Dependence.*

Joseph Sheridan Le Fanu, *Ghost Stories and Tales of Mystery.*

Grace Overton; or, The Service of the Heart.

1852 *The Nun, A Recital of the Convent.* Adapted from Diderot [*La Religieuse*].

Elizabeth Missing Sewell, *The Experience of Life; or, Aunt Sarah.*

1853 Bernardin de Saint-Pierre. *Paul and Virginia.* (English tr., published in Bentley's Standard Novels Series. Originally published in 1787.)

CHAPTER VII

The Mill on the Floss:

Maggie Tulliver and the Child of Nature

"WHAT I WANT, you know . . . is to give Tom a good eddication; an eddication as'll be a bread to him," are the first words we overhear Mr. Tulliver saying to Mrs. Tulliver as we move into their parlor. *The Mill on the Floss,* like *Villette,* recalls an earlier age—the Duke of Wellington is the Prime Minister and Theodore Hook is the novelist read by Tom's tutor Mr. Stelling behind his Latin tomes—but it too comments indirectly on "eddication" of the 1850's. Had Mr. Tulliver been able to read, he would not have lacked for counsel in this enlightened day, when professional educators, clerical and lay, turned more and more to fiction to advocate specific institutions and programs. Thomas Hughes' perennial favorite *Tom Brown's School Days* (1857) and *Eric; or, Little by Little* (1858) by the Reverend Frederic William Farrar are the best remembered of a run of titles like *Godfrey Davenant, a Tale of School Life* (1848) by the Reverend W. E. Heygate; *Edgar Clifton; or Right and Wrong: A Tale of School Life* (1852) by Charlotte Adams; *The Grammar-School Boys* (1854) by Mrs. E. J. Burbury; and *Basil the Schoolboy; or, The Heir of Arundel* (1856) by the Reverend Edward

Monro. Tom Tulliver, alas, was educated, as George Eliot wryly reminds us, "in those dark ages when there were no schools of design—before schoolmasters were invariably men of scrupulous integrity, and before the clergy were all men of enlarged minds and varied culture" (Book Second, CH. IV).

There were plenty of books about schoolgirls as well as schoolboys by 1860, on the order of Agnes Loudon's *Tales of School Life* (1850), Dorothy Richmond's *Amy Carlton; or, First Days at School* (1855), and Mrs. Oliphant's *Agnes Hopetoun's Schools and Holidays* (1859). George Eliot herself remarks, in excusing her heroine's naiveté about gypsies:[1] "Maggie Tulliver, you perceive, was by no means that well-trained, well-informed young person that a small female of eight or nine necessarily is in these days" (Book First, CH. XI). Ironically, although Maggie is more ripe for learning than Tom and eventually becomes a teacher, nobody is much concerned about a school for her. This "wild thing" and "Bedlam creature," as Mrs. Tulliver calls her, is left pretty much to her own devices but seems to soak up learning through her pores. One of the first reviewers of *The Mill on the Floss* noted that the author's "delight in depicting strong and wayward feelings, shows that she belongs to the generation of Currer Bell, and not to that of the quiet authoress of *Emma*."[2] Unlike the indrawn Charlotte Brontë, George Eliot had little inclination toward fantasy or romanticism (Maggie Tulliver quickly becomes disillusioned with the gypsies and later gives up Scott's *The Pirate* for religious reading), but she too looked back on the female education of pre-Victorian days to underscore the frustration of the gifted woman of her own age. The novels of both can be read particularly in the light of the then omnipresent "Woman Question." *Villette,* as we have seen, touched on issues close to Miss Brontë's own situation, such as the status of the governess and the insecurity of the educated spinster. *The Mill on the Floss,* like its predecessor *Adam Bede,* drew partially on George Eliot's childhood memories, but both undoubtedly owed much of their initial appeal to their topical relevance.

Lewes' journal, *The Leader,* to which George Eliot contributed before she turned to fiction, gave prominent attention at this time to the problem of female professions. Announced early in 1858 was the first number of a new shilling "Literary and Domestic Magazine," *The Englishwoman's Journal,* which promised to devote itself to "The present industrial employments of women, both manual and intellectual, the best mode of judiciously extending the sphere of such employments, and the laws affecting the property and condition of the sex."[3] The initial number of this new Female Companion suggested that in view of the "social misery produced by the overcrowding of the teacher's profession," women might consider turning to less intellectual pursuits, such as business. Daughters, according to this journal, should be encouraged to assist their brothers and fathers as accountants and clerks. "Mr. Bull has an unusually fair share of what is termed 'good common sense,' " affirmed the editors. "Has Mrs. Bull no feminine counterpart to these fine sterling qualities?"[4]

Mrs. Bull as incarnated in "healthy, fair, plump and dull-witted" Mrs. Tulliver finds sufficient outlet for her energies in domestic economy. The more alert young Maggie, who could "read almost as well as the parson" according to Mr. Tulliver, has time on her hands, but it would be difficult to visualize her in the counting house with Tom. Work for the mind rather than for the hands was the subject of another book glowingly advertised in *The Leader* this same year: Miss Mulock's *A Woman's Thoughts about Women.* The author of the phenomenally popular *John Halifax, Gentleman* (1856) was equally successful with this book of prudence culled from her polemical journalism, in which she shifted public attention from the self-made gentleman to the neglected woman struggling for social recognition. "A book of sound counsel . . . one of the most sensible works of its kind, well-written, true-hearted and altogether practical," read the quoted review, with the added recommendation that "whoever wishes to give advice to a young lady may thank the author for means of doing so."⁵ Although such comment suggests another *Daughters of England,* far from echoing conventional platitudes or sentimentalities, *A Woman's Thoughts about Women* was intended to shock sheltered girls and their mothers out of their complacency.

The titles of the essays that make up *A Woman's Thoughts* indicate its range of interests, economic, social, psychological: "Self-Dependence," "Female Professions," "Female Friendships," "Gossip," "Lost Women." The last-named chapter, urging an enlightened attitude toward what the age called the "straying woman," has a bearing on Hetty Sorel's plight in *Adam Bede.*⁶ More relevant to Maggie Tulliver's situation is the opening chapter, "Something to Do," which deplores the intellectual poverty forced on the daughters of England by the obtuseness of parents and an absurd social code. One passage in particular is best read alongside Book First ("Boy and Girl") and Book Second ("School-Time") of *The Mill on the Floss:*

> Herein I refer, . . . not to those whom ill or good fortune . . . has forced to earn their bread; but to "young ladies," who have never been brought up to do anything. Tom, Dick and Harry, their brothers, each has had it knocked into him from school-days that he is to do something, to be somebody. Counting-house, shop or college, afford him a clear future on which to concentrate all his energies and aims. He has got the grand *pabulum* of the human soul—occupation. If any inherent want in his character, any unlucky combination of circumstances nullifies this, what a poor creature the man becomes!—what a dawdling, moping, sitting-over-the-fire, thumb-twiddling, lazy, ill-tempered animal! And why? "Oh, poor fellow! 'tis because he has got nothing to do!"
>
> Yet this is precisely the condition of woman for a third, a half, often the whole of their existence.
>
> That Providence ordained it so—made men to work, and women to be idle—is a doctrine that few will be bold enough to assert openly. Tacitly they do, when they preach up lovely uselessness, fascinating frivolity, delicious helplessness—all those polite impertinences and poetical degradations to which the foolish, lazy, or selfish of our sex are prone to incline an ear, but which any woman

of common sense must repudiate as insulting not only her woman-
hood but her Creator.

Mr. Tulliver makes no secret of his opinion on the question.
Daughter Maggie to him is "too 'cute for a woman"; as far as he
is concerned, "It is as I thought—the child 'ull learn more
mischief nor good wi' the books" (Book First, CH. II, III). So
Maggie stays home while brother Tom is sent off to school and
must content herself with whatever crumbs of learning she can
lick up on visits with him during term time. Miss Mulock was
not what came to be known later in the century as a suffragette.
She was making the plea, later echoed more stridently by Eliza
Lynn Linton and others, not that women go out into the world
to compete with men, but that they make better use of their time
at home. She believes that women should emulate men only in
occupying their brains and souls. As it is, "Tom, Dick and
Harry . . . leave school and plunge into life; 'the girls' likewise
finish their education, come home and stay at home." Furthermore, "Nobody thinks it needful to waste a care upon them.
Bless them pretty dears, how sweet they are! papa's nosegay of
beauty to adorn his living room." It does not seem to bother
papa that his daughters have "not one definite object of interest
or employment; flattery or flummery enough, but no solid food
whatever to satisfy mind or heart—if they happen to possess
either—at the very emptiest and most craving season of both."

Flattery and flummery may suffice for cousin Lucy, but Maggie
obviously requires solid food. However, Maggie has other needs
that are not satisfied, and Miss Mulock, inevitably, offers advice
also to the love-starved. Many a "shipwrecked life," she observes,
has resulted from a young lady's falling in love to fill the void in
her soul, for all too often "the object is generally unattainable or
unworthy." What is the consequence? "A long, dreary season of
pain, real or imaginary, yet not the less real because it is
imaginary, of anger and mortification, of impotent struggle—
against unjust parents, the girl believes, or, if romantically

inclined, against cruel destiny." This suggests Maggie Tulliver's love problem in the last part of *The Mill on the Floss*.

Miss Mulock is sympathetic to young ladies frustrated in love, but her main concern, as she makes clear in Chapter II of *A Woman's Thoughts* ("Self-Dependence") , is to reconcile them to living without men. In this "curious phase of social history, when marriage is apparently ceasing to become the common lot, and a happy marriage is the most uncommon lot of all," Miss Mulock believes that parents and teachers are obligated to educate girls to lean more upon their inner resources, to be less self-indulgent, and not to look to the material world for their satisfactions:

> And here, piercing the Foundation of all truth—I think we may find the truth concerning self-dependence, which is only real and only valuable when its root is not in self at all; when its strength is drawn not from men, but from that Higher and Diviner Source whence every individual soul proceeds, and to which alone it is accountable. As soon as any woman, old or young, once feels *that*, not as a vague sentimental belief, but as a tangible, practical law of life, all weakness ends, all doubt departs: she recognises the glory, honour and beauty of her existence; she is no longer afraid of its pains; she desires not to shift one atom of its responsibilities to another. She is content to take it just as it is, from the hands of the All-Father; her only care being so to fulfil it, that while the world at large may recognise and profit by her self-dependence, she herself, knowing that the utmost strength lies in the deepest humility, recognises, solely and above all, her dependence upon God.

"I've been a great deal happier . . . since I have given up thinking about what is easy and pleasant, and being discontented because I couldn't have my own will," says Maggie to Philip Wakem, the first suitor whom family loyalty forces her to reject. "Our life is determined for us—and it makes the mind very free when we give up wishing, and only think of bearing what is laid upon us, and doing what is given us to do" (Book Fifth, CH. I) . Later, in the face of the "great temptation" represented by Stephen Guest, she declares: "We can't choose

happiness either for ourselves or for another; we can't tell where
that will lie. We can only choose whether we will indulge ourselves for the present moment, or whether we will renounce that,
for the sake of obeying the divine voice within us—for the sake of
being true to all the motives that sanctify our lives" (Book Sixth,
CH. XIV). So the formerly willful, wayward Maggie Tulliver
comes to agree with Miss Mulock after all. She learned this
wisdom from Thomas à Kempis' *Imitation of Christ.* Miss
Mulock sends her readers to Thomas' source—the New Testament.

Early in 1860, annoyed to find her name coupled with Miss
Mulock's in a Parisian literary review, George Eliot wrote to a
friend that "the most ignorant journalist in England would
hardly think of calling me a rival of Miss Mulock—a writer who
is read only by novel readers, pure and simple, never by people of
high culture. A very excellent woman she is, I believe—but we
belong to an entirely different order of writers."[7] Probably nobody in her day any more than in ours would have disputed this
statement, especially if they compared Tom Tulliver with Miss
Mulock's version of a country boy, John Halifax. When George
Eliot assured her readers that Tom was not "moulded on the
spooney type of the Industrious Apprentice" (Book Fifth, CH.
II), she undoubtedly had Miss Mulock's Bible-reading young tan-
ner in mind, for Tom's "practical shrewdness" and calculated
virtue effectively offset the sanctimoniousness of John Halifax.
Moreover, it must have been something of a jolt to readers of
both ladies to turn from the David-Jonathan friendship of John
Halifax and the crippled Phineas Fletcher to Tom's thoughtless,
even at times sadistic, treatment of the hunchbacked Philip
Wakem.[8] But if George Eliot was not much impressed with Miss
Mulock as a novelist or with her knowledge of young men, she
appears to have shared some of her thoughts on women, for the
source both of Maggie's frustrations and of her solace is anticipated
in Miss Mulock's case histories. Although in fiction Dinah Mulock may have tended, as Henry James once observed, to look at

life "through a rose-colored gauze curtain,"[9] in *A Woman's Thoughts about Women* she looked with unglazed eyes at social realities, providing that ballast of fact that George Eliot believed should always weigh down works of imagination. Feeling a commitment, as Miss Mulock did, to edify and awaken the moral sympathies of the mass of readers, George Eliot was elated to discover that " 'The Mill' . . . has found its way to the great public."[10] This "great public" presumably included "novel readers pure and simple" as well as "people of high culture."[11]

George Eliot's awareness of the ordinary novel reader is apparent in a letter she wrote to Blackwood when she was beginning her next novel, *Silas Marner:* "It seems to me that nobody will take any interest in it but myself, for it is extremely unlike the popular stories going."[12] *The Mill on the Floss* was at once like and unlike "the popular stories going." Along with much of the didactic fiction of the time, it is child-centered. At the beginning of the novel, as we have noticed, Mr. Tulliver is seeking advice about the proper school for Tom. Mrs. Tulliver, in turn, is worried about Maggie's perverseness and "comical" ways. It is also family-centered, in line with the domestic chronicles in vogue at the time, such as Miss Mulock's *The Ogilvies,* Bulwer's *The Caxtons,* Thackeray's *The Newcomes,* and Mrs. Oliphant's *The Athelings.*[13] The narrator brings us immediately into the family circle: "Before I dozed off, I was going to tell you what Mr. and Mrs. Tulliver were talking about, as they sat by the bright fire in the left-hand parlour, on that very afternoon I have been dreaming of" (CH. I) . Some of the chapter headings— "Tom Comes Home," "Enter the Aunts and Uncles," "Mrs. Tulliver's Teraphim," and "The Family Council"—suggest another series of vignettes on the order of *Domestic Scenes* or *The Family Picture Gallery* that appealed to the enlarged middle-class public and the hearthside reading circle.

George Eliot later called her form of novel "the Home Epic," the culmination of the tendency of early Victorian writers to

extol the domestic virtues. We have noticed that even some of the
fashionable novelists of the 1830's were votaries of the lares and
the penates. In the next decade, Thackeray and Charlotte Brontë
both reflect a shift of reader interest from exclusive to ordinary
society. In the preface to her *The Daughters of England* (1842)
Mrs. Ellis attributes the new prestige of the commonplace to the
sympathetic and homelike image of the reigning monarch:
"Thus while the character of the daughter, the wife and the
mother, are so beautifully exemplified in connection with the
dignity of a British Queen, it is the privilege of the humblest, as
well as the most exalted of her subjects, to know that the heart of
woman, in all her tenderest and holiest feelings, is the same
beneath the shelter of a cottage, as under the canopy of a
throne."

The domestic novel grew up in reaction against the artificial
glamorizing or heightening of life in fiction, counteracting first
the "Silver Forks," then the rattling militarism of Lever and
Gleig, the pageantry and pretentiousness of Bulwer, and the
historicism of that latter-day Scott, G. P. R. James. Harriet
Martineau, in her quiet rural drama of conscience, *Deerbrook*
(1839), pointedly declares to her readers: "The universal, eternal, filial relation is the only universal and eternal refuge. It is
the solace of royalty weeping in the inner chambers, and of
poverty drooping beside its cold hearth" (CH. XXXIII). Fundamentally, to her, king, aristocrat, warrior and peasant are one:
"If they be poor in spirit, it matters little what is their external
state, or whether the world which rolls on beside us or over them
be the world of a solar system, or of a conquering empire, or of a
small-souled village." Miss Martineau meant not to denigrate
heroes so much as to celebrate the unsung heroism of the hamlet.
Others joined in: "Heroism!—To those who consider rightly, a
far nobler thing now: when it is no longer a sound to mark the
glowing excitement, the lofty enthusiasm," writes Anne Marsh-
Caldwell at the beginning of *Emilia Wyndham* (1846)," . . .
but the slow, silent death-struggle of the soul in solitude, dark-

ness and obscurity; against the heavy, wearying, every-day evils of every-day actual life." George Eliot, too, assures her readers a place in the grand scheme of things: "The suffering, whether of martyr or victim, which belongs to every historical advance of mankind, is represented in this way in every town, and by hundreds of obscure hearths; and we need not shrink from this comparison of small things with great" (Book Fourth, CH. I). She magnifies the "small-souled village" of St. Ogg's into a theatre of tragedy ("Mr. Tulliver had a destiny as well as Oedipus"), and the obscure filial devotion and frustrated love of Maggie Tulliver is elevated into a moral martyrdom comparable to the fate of Antigone. She gives what she calls an "epic breadth" to her story of a brother and sister alienated in life but united in death by an intense rendering of their various environments—nature, home, school, and society. Of all of these, nature is the primal influence of the young seedlings and the one to which they eventually return.

One of George Eliot's contemporaries recognized this affinity when he praised her for her exposure of the "bare naturalism of human life."[14] *The Mill on the Floss* carries on the migration, then already well under way, of readers and writers back to "virgin soil." "Civilization has two contrary movements," observed Marmion Savage in *The Bachelor of the Albany* (1848), as the Spread family prepares to retire to the country; "its first impulse is out of the woods townwards, turning swains into citizens and burghers; its second direction is back into the woods and fields, changing the citizen into the swain again" (CH. II). Miss Mitford had awakened nostalgia for the pre-Industrial Revolution countryside in *Our Village* (1824-32) and *Belford Regis; or, Sketches of a Country Town* (1835). Across the Irish Sea, the Banims, William Carleton, and Gerald Griffin memorialized turf and bog. G. R. Gleig in *The Country Curate* (1830) invited his readers to return with him to the wilds of Kent to enjoy "uncultivated nature." George Eliot of course read and absorbed the more distinguished regional novels of the Brontës and Mrs. Gaskell. However, the strongest current of influence on her probably came from across the Channel.

During the 1840's and early 1850's George Sand had stimulated fresh interest in the pastoral scene with such stories as *Le Meunier d'Angibault, La Mare au Diable, La Petite Fadette,* and *François le Champi.* In particular, *Le Meunier d'Angibault,* which George Eliot read,[15] removes its readers "far from the madding crowd." The narrator recalls a past age to a later generation, expatiating on old customs, quaint social types, outmoded means of travel, peasant superstitions, and here and there interrupting her story to describe a particularly striking rural scene. The attitude of George Sand toward her reader is much like that of George Eliot, who also seems to speak to us from places removed and across the gulf of years: "The rush of the water, and the booming of the mill, bring a dreamy deafness, which seems to heighten the peacefulness of the scene. They are like a great curtain of sound, shutting one out from the world beyond. And now there is the thunder of the huge covered wagon coming home with sacks of grain" (CH. I). St. Ogg's is a town "familiar with forgotten years"; "In old-fashioned times an 'independence' was hardly ever made without a little miserliness as a condition, and you would have found that quality in every provincial district, combined with characters as various as the fruits from which we extract acid" (Book First, CH. XII).

In *François le Champi,* which George Eliot praised in one of her letters as "simplicity and purity itself,"[16] George Sand justified her writing a pastoral novel in modern times. Largely because of its association with young Marcel of *Swann's Way,* whose mother reads it to him at bedtime, *François le Champi* has survived mainly as a child's story, although it was certainly not so intended by the author. In an introductory dialogue that precedes the tale itself, the fictitious narrator explains to a friend that the pastoral, properly conceived, can act as a universal solvent, breaking down barriers between rich and poor, city man and country man, intellectual and illiterate, old and young—

uniting all in a bond of common sympathy. The writer of pastorals, he affirms, should not be too consciously "literary," but should draw his material from common life, enhancing it only sufficiently to make it comprehensible to the general reader. He reconciles art and life by offering what is alleged to be a tale originally narrated by a peasant but retold in the language of civilization.

In her first two novels, George Eliot brings the country to her readers by allowing her simple folk to speak for themselves as much as possible.[17] In *Adam Bede* she sets the scene: "With this drop of ink at the end of my pen, I will show you the roomy workshop of Mr. Jonathan Burge, carpenter and builder, in the village of Hayslope, as it appeared on the eighteenth of June, in the year of our Lord 1799." Shortly afterward, the author's cultured tone disappears and the Warwickshire dialect of Adam and Seth Bede takes over. In *The Mill on the Floss* the narrator seems to be in more immediate contact with the life she is describing, writing not so much fiction as reminiscence: "How lovely the little river is, with its dark changing wavelets! . . . I remember those large dipping willows. I remember the stone bridge"; "I have been pressing my elbows on the arms of my chair, and dreaming that I was standing on the bridge in front of Dorlcote Mill, as it looked one February afternoon many years ago." Almost immediately the recollecting mind fades into the scene recollected and we hear the voices of Mr. and Mrs. Tulliver in conversation.

Like George Sand, George Eliot revivified nature and country life, at the same time attempting to free them from artificial literary conventions. The narrator of *François le Champi* finds evidence in the timeworn tradition of pastoral poetry of man's instinctive desire to return to nature, but he is determined to show peasants and shepherds as they truly exist, not the bucolic lovers of *Daphnis and Chloe*. George Eliot's classical allusions in her early novels, which strike some readers as pedantic, were undoubtedly intended at the time to be purposely incongruous, with their juxtapositions of poetic and actual country life: "When Tityrus and Meliboeus happen to be on the same farm they are not sentimentally polite to each other" (*Adam Bede,* Book Sixth, CH. LIII, referring to the laborers on Mrs. Poyser's farm) ; "a simple farmer's girl [Hetty Sorel], to whom a gentleman with a white hand was dazzling as an Olympian god" (*Adam Bede,* Book First, CH. IX).[18] She is more sarcastic in *The Mill on the Floss* in her description of the port of St. Ogg's, "where the black ships unlade themselves of their burthens from the far north, and carry away, in exchange, the precious inland products, the well-crushed cheese and the soft fleeces, which my refined readers have doubtless become acquainted with through the medium of the best classic pastorals" (Book First, CH. XII). George Eliot seems to have felt it necessary to remind her "refined readers" that farms and meadows are places for work, not merely for love and sport.

Above all, George Sand, like George Eliot after her, preserves rural childhood in its essence, evoking the empathy of the young with all creation and the pristine beauty of nature as seen by the child's innocent eyes. In an early chapter of *François le Champi,* the young waif-hero disports himself like a young animal—diving in water like a fish, taming the horses, climbing poplars to grab magpies' nests. His childhood resembles that of young Tom and Maggie Tulliver, fishing in the Round Pool, raising rabbits, playing house under the chestnut tree, gathering purple plumes from the tops of reeds, romping among the peacocks, pigeons and guinea-fowls at Garum Firs. Among Maggie's favorite childhood reading, along with Aesop's *Fables* and *The Pilgrim's Progress,* is an illustrated book, *Animated Nature.* She feels a kinship with the world of nature which she never loses, reminding us of Marcelle Blanchemont, the heroine of George Sand's *Le Meunier d'Angibault,* of whom the author writes: "Youth cannot curse the time of its blossoming, nor those years so charming and so cherished, though charged with storms and tempests."

Little Maggie looks ahead to country picnics with brother

Tom, stretched out endlessly in time: "They trotted along and sat down together, with no thought that life would ever change much for them; they would only get bigger and not go to school, and it would always be like the holidays; they would always live together and be fond of each other" (Book First, CH. v). But school interrupts this idyll. Tom, who is not fond of books, is sent on from the games of Mr. Jacob's academy to the intellectual discipline of King's Lorton and the Reverend Walter Stelling. One gathers that the bookish Maggie, who, as a member of the "inferior" sex, is deprived of this learning, gains more from nature and her own sensibility than Tom does from his academies, a sign that George Eliot did not look on the classroom as the exclusive province of learning. This period, as has been noted, was rich in school novels, but the educator-novelists considered the main function of the school to carry over the early lessons of "Nature . . . wisest, gentlest, holiest of teachers," as the Reverend Mr. Farrar put it, describing young Eric's childhood in the Vale of Ayrton.[19] Thomas Hughes, author of *Tom Brown's School Days* (1857), insisted that the students of Rugby "lose nothing of the boy that is worth keeping, but build up the man upon it."[20] The early chapters of his novel, which recapture Tom's fledgling years amidst the green fields and open skies of White Horse Vale, illustrate a fundamental theme of these didactic novels—how nurture builds upon nature.

Tom Tulliver, in Mr. Stelling's view, is "rather a rough cub," a creature to be treated "with uniformity of method and independence of circumstances, which distinguish the actions of animals understood to be under the immediate teaching of nature." We watch the taming and civilizing process at work: "He was of a very firm, not to say obstinate disposition, but there was no brutelike rebellion and recklessness in his nature: the human sensibilities predominated" (Book Second, CH. I). Mr. Tulliver's intentions for his son Tom are vaguely utilitarian— "an eddication as'll be a bread to him"—but Tom undergoes the rigorous regimen of the *literae humaniores,* the only curriculum

available to him. As we feel Tom's brain being strained with incompatible learning, we recognize that George Eliot had notions
of her own about the "Young Idea" not entirely in conformity
with those that prevailed in the more influential education
novels.

Didactic novelists of Jane Austen's and Scott's day, as we have
observed, emphasized private tutelage and individual influence,
but the schoolmaster-writers of the 1850's tended to think of students as a group to be moulded by a collective ideal. Hughes
holds up young East, Tom Brown's mentor, as "a genuine specimen [of the lower-school boy]—frank, hearty, and good-natured,
well satisfied with himself and his position, and chock full of life
and spirits, and all the Rugby prejudices and traditions." The
motto from the *Rugby Magazine* that appears on the title page of
Tom Brown's School Days reads: "As on the one hand it should
be remembered that we are boys, and boys at school, so on the
other hand we must bear in mind that we form a complete social
body . . . a society, in which . . . we must not only learn, but act
and live not only as boys, but boys who will be men." Mr. Farrar,
more concerned with the spiritual than the social body, declares
that his *Eric; or, Little by Little* was written "with but one single
object—the vivid inculcation of inward purity and moral
strength." Their contemporary Charlotte Yonge has a character
remark, quite aptly: "Most of the men you have seen have been
rounded into uniformity like marbles, their sharp angles rubbed
off against each other at school."[21]

George Eliot's publisher, John Blackwood, for one, had an eye
for "sharp angles." He observed with pleasure to his brother
William, as he was reading the manuscript of *The Mill on the
Floss*, that "the hero is a wonderful picture of a boy and lifelike
contrast to the sort of Tom Brown ideals of what boys are."[22]
Stressing Tom Tulliver's boyish weakness and immaturity—his
resistance to learning, his malingering, his taunting of Maggie
for her fumbling efforts at Latin, his patronizing of Philip—
George Eliot models him no more on the Rugby Boy than on

"the spooney Industrious Apprentice" John Halifax. She takes more pride in Tom's individuality, which remains steadfast against systems of learning. "I say nothing against Mr. Stelling's theory: if we are to have one regimen for all minds, his seems as good to me as any," she remarks as Tom's schoolmaster foists the Eton Grammar on him. "I only know it turned out as uncomfortably for Tom Tulliver as if he had been plied with cheese in order to remedy a gastric weakness which prevented him from digesting it" (Book Second, CH. I). Moreover, Tom stands as a living refutation of *tabula rasa* theories of learning. Despite Mr. Stelling and the stifling environment of King's Lorton, "there was a visible improvement of Tom under this training; perhaps because he was not a boy in the abstract, existing solely to illustrate the evils of a mistaken education, but a boy of flesh and blood, with dispositions not entirely at the mercy of circumstances" (Book Second, CH. IV).[23] "Education was almost entirely a matter of luck—usually of ill-luck in those distant days," she remarks at one point, adding later that Tom "compared with many other British youths of his time who have since had to scramble through life with some fragments of more or less relevant knowledge, and a great deal of strictly relevant ignorance, was not so very unlucky" (Book Second, CH. IV). The young heroes of *Tom Brown* and *Eric* are "rescued" from village private schools, such as Tom Tulliver attends, and transferred to the guidance of public school headmasters. Readers are left to judge for themselves whether their own sons, being educated in the enlightened 1850's by clergy of "enlarged minds and varied culture," have fared any better than Tom Tulliver.

The authors of school novels of the period, eager to get their young people off to school as soon as possible, generally do not linger long in the parlor. "It is not within the scope of my book to speak of family relations," Hughes apologizes in an early chapter of *Tom Brown's School Days*, "or I should have much to say on the subject of English mothers—aye, and of English

fathers, and sisters and brothers too." Needless to say, this gap
was amply filled by many of his contemporaries, for whom apron
strings took precedence over school ties. In the early 1840's the
family novels of the Swedish writer Frederika Bremer, such as
*The Neighbours, A Story of Every Day Life; The Home; or,
Family Joys and Family Cares;* and *Brothers and Sisters: A Tale
of Domestic Life,* reached a wide public in England through
Mary Howitt's translations. Subsequently there was no end of
titles like *Family Secrets: or, A Page from Life's Volume; Home
Happiness; Mothers and Sons;* and *A Mother's Recompense.*
Grace Aguilar, author of one of the most popular domestic
novels of this period, the significantly titled *Home Influence*
(1847), speaks for many of these authors in her preface, where
she declares that her aim is "to assist in the education of the
HEART, believing that of infinitely greater importance than the
mere instruction of the MIND, for the bright awakening of the
latter, depends far more on the happy influences of the former
than is generally supposed."

Home Influence stresses, in addition to the education of the
morals and the affections, the heroism of the hearth. Subtitling
her novel, "A Tale for Mothers and Daughters," Miss Aguilar
reminds both that the world needs its Marthas as well as its
Marys: "Opportunities to evince the more striking virtues women
may never have, but for the cultivation of the lesser, they are
called upon each day." Among these virtues is self-abnegation.
Like many another chimney-corner *familienroman* of the day,
Home Influence follows the fortunes of a sister and brother, the
one sensitive and selfless, the other callous and selfish. Miss
Aguilar's Ellen Fortescue is more spotless and muslin-draped
than Maggie Tulliver, and Edward Fortescue more corrupt than
Tom, but her story of the dog-like devotion of a sister to an
undeserving brother and sibling love tested by misunderstanding
and sorrow foreshadows one we are more familiar with.

Maggie Browne, the heroine of Mrs. Gaskell's *The Moorland
Cottage* (1850), is a close prototype of Maggie Tulliver, even to

her brown complexion. She also has a brother whom she adores, although he constantly teases her and treats her with condescension as she tries to pick up some scraps of his learning. Edward goes off to school, leaving Maggie alone with her lively imagination, which accompanies her, as with Maggie Tulliver in the Red Deeps, "over moor and fell, into the hollows of the distant mysterious hills, where she imagined all strange beasts and weird people to haunt" (CH. III). Maggie Browne's mother fears that she is growing too introverted and dreamy, but that danger is averted by religious education. Her brother becomes a prize pupil; unfortunately, his moral education is neglected. As a result, he grows more arrogant and spoiled, while Maggie's spiritual faculty develops as she learns to admire female saints and martyrs and recognizes the holiness possible in common life.[24] Mrs. Gaskell, like Miss Aguilar, makes her sister and brother too much angel and devil, but then she too was writing a moral tale addressed principally to children.

"Home influence" is pervasive in Charlotte Yonge's *The Daisy Chain; or, Aspirations, A Family Chronicle* (1856), described in its preface as "a domestic record of home events, large and small, during those years of early life when the character is chiefly formed, and as an endeavour to trace the effects of those aspirations which are a part of every youthful nature." *The Daisy Chain* is an involved "Family Chronicle," following the mingled paths of no less than nine children and their widowed father, but it is dominated by the benign presence of one of the daughters, Ethel May, probably *the* Christian heroine to many a mid-Victorian reader. Miss Yonge perpetuates Miss Austen's tradition of the home as sanctuary, but religious instruction is more prominent in *The Daisy Chain,* a reminder of its origin in a series called *Conversations on the Catechism* written for a Sunday-school magazine.[25] Though an earnest Christian, she was not a gloomy one. *The Daisy Chain* is irradiated with a warm vitality, recreating for all time the bustle of a middle-class Victorian country household with its round of prayers, lessons, meals, and wholesome sports. Ethel May is introduced at an early age, like Maggie Tulliver eager for knowledge and brimming over with animal spirits. She too is frustrated by her desire to keep up intellectually with her favorite brother, but eventually gives up her pursuit of "men's studies" to fulfill herself in dedication to her young pupils and elderly father. Both heroines read Thomas à Kempis and retain their family loyalty, instilled in them as children, which eventually makes them renounce marriage. Ethel May, while a less turbulent heroine than Maggie Tulliver, who never wholly succeeds in subduing her natural energies, gives us some idea of what Maggie might have become had she survived the flood. Maggie's last words before the flood are: "O God, if my life is to be long, let me live to bless and comfort. . . . "

A common fount and source for all these writers who were preoccupied with child development is suggested by Thomas Hughes at the beginning of a chapter of *Tom Brown's School Days:* "As that venerable and learned poet (whose voluminous works we all think it is the correct thing to admire and talk about, but don't read often) most truly says, 'the child is father to the man'; *a fortiori,* therefore, he must be father to the boy" (CH. II) . As Poet Laureate, Wordsworth enjoyed a belated respect and influence beyond what he had known during his more creative years. His poems glorifying Nature and immortalizing childhood are echoed by many besides Hughes. The "Ode to Duty" forms the epigraph to Anne Marsh-Caldwell's widely read and reread *Emilia Wyndham,* which is dedicated to the poet. Particularly after his death in 1850, Wordsworth's lines adorn many a tale of real life. In Mrs. Gaskell's *The Moorland Cottage* Maggie Browne's lover extols her natural beauty with a passage from one of the Lucy poems (CH. V) . Wordsworth is among the most quoted poets (along with Tennyson and Longfellow) in *The Daisy Chain.* The motto of a chapter of *Eric; or, Little by Little* is his line "Give to the morn of life its natural blessedness," which the author glosses fulsomely in his account of his hero's salad days. George Eliot joined the throng of the dead laureate's disciples, as indicated by the quotations on the title pages of *Adam Bede* and *Silas Marner*.[26]

The "Ode on Intimations of Immortality" and other nature lyrics of Wordsworth undeniably had a strong impact on the early Victorian literary imagination, but by the middle of 1850, with the posthumous publication of *The Prelude*, Wordsworth's most extensive treatment of the theme of "irrecoverable child innocence" (as Elizabeth Barrett Browning called it in *Aurora Leigh*) was available. Oddly enough, despite its affinities with popular novels of country childhood, *The Prelude* went largely unappreciated by both readers and writers of that generation. One of its few admirers, however, was George Eliot, whose letters are sprinkled with quotations from this literary autobiography.[27] Moreover, echoes of it are not confined to an epigraph in *Daniel Deronda*. As *Adam Bede* looked back to *The Excursion*, *The Mill on the Floss* draws its inspiration from *The Prelude*.

The Prelude anticipates *The Mill* most obviously in its psychological ideas—the impingement of sensory experience on the sensitive mind, the storing of associations, the persistence of childhood memories into adult life:

> Fair seed-time had my soul, and I grew up
> Fostered alike by beauty and by fear. . . .
> > (Book First, 11. 300–01)

> From Nature and her overflowing soul,
> I had received so much, that all my thoughts
> Were steeped in feeling. . . .
> > (Book Second, 11. 397–99)

The Prelude also suggests the scheme of *The Mill*—the intellectual progress from childhood to formal education (Book Second of both works is entitled "School-Time") to completion of moral education by friendship, love, and society. Both show how sympathy for mankind develops out of love of nature and the lower creatures. Both represent the moral sense growing out of a heightened emotional sensitivity and the maturing of the imaginative powers. In *The Mill on the Floss* as in *The Prelude* the child in effect leads the man back to his grass roots, and the cycle of nature ends with its beginnings. The opening situation of *The Prelude,* the narrator recalling his first home through the stirring up of memory by imagination, is very much like that of the beginning of *The Mill.* The poet is :

> . . . escaped
> From the vast city, where I long had pined
> A discontented sojourner; now free,
> Free as a bird to settle where I will. . . .
>
> (Book First, 11. 6–9)

Soon a familiar scene presents itself:

> . . . . Many were the thoughts
> Encouraged and dismissed, till choice was made
> Of a known Vale, whither my feet should turn,
> Nor rest till they had reached the very door
> Of the one cottage which methought I saw.
> No picture of mere memory ever looked
> So fair. . . .
>
> (Book First, 11. 70–76)

The Prelude is linked to *The Mill on the Floss* explicitly in George Eliot's touching *Brother and Sister* sonnets, registering the childhood devotion between her and her brother Isaac, which abound with Wordsworthian images:

> Long years have left their writing on my brow,
> But yet the freshness and the dew-fed beam
> Of those young mornings are about me now,
> When we two wandered toward the far-off stream.
>
> (Sonnet II)

> Thus rambling we were schooled in deepest lore,
> And learned the meanings that give words a soul,
> The fear, the love, the primal passionate store,
> Whose shaping impulses make mankind whole.

Those hours were seed to all my after good;
My infant gladness, through eye, ear and touch;
Took easily as warmth a various food
To nourish the sweet skill of loving much.

(Sonnet V)

The wide-arched bridge, the scented elder-flowers,
The wondrous watery rings that died too soon,
The echoes of the quarry, the still hours
With white robe sweeping-on the shadeless noon,

Were but my growing self, are part of me,
My present Past, my root of piety.

(Sonnet VI)

The *Brother and Sister* poems at the same time recall *The Mill on the Floss* in compressed form—the rediscovery of childhood, the innocent love of brother and sister faintly overcast with the pall of "the dire years whose awful name is Change," the reuniting of the two through memory.[28]

The originality of *The Mill on the Floss* lies not in its setting or subject matter, which, as we have seen, were the staple of much of the domestic fiction of this period, but in a more penetrating treatment of the by then hackneyed themes of "natural piety" and "recollections of early childhood." Children here do not trail clouds of glory, and nature too is seen plain. George Eliot brought to her "bare naturalism of human life" a unique combination of poet's vision and biologist's eye. Ecological analogies point up the interconnection of all living things. St. Ogg's is "one of those old, old towns which impress one as a continuation and outgrowth of nature, as much as the nests of the bower-birds, or the winding galleries of the white ants" (Book First, CH. XII). Much later, its people are described as "part of a gross sum of obscure vitality, that will be swept into the same oblivion with the generation of ants and beavers" (Book Fourth, CH. I). Philip Wakem is moved with "the pity of it, that a mind like hers [Maggie's] should be withering in its very youth, like a young forest-tree, for want of the light and space it was formed to flourish in!" (Book Fifth, CH. I). As the author herself observes: "In natural science, I have understood, there is nothing petty to the mind that has a large vision of relations, and to which every single object suggests a vast sum of conditions. It is surely the same with the observation of human life" (Book Fourth, CH. I).

We know how George Eliot became interested in natural science and her contemporaries guessed. One early reviewer of *The Mill*, annoyed by the author's use of scientific terminology, went so far as to accuse Lewes of interpolating it.[29] He was hardly doing justice to George Eliot's esemplastic power. Nowadays Lewes' formative influence on her thought and writing is generally assumed;[30] in connection with *The Mill* one can pin it down with some precision. George Eliot's letters and a journal kept by Lewes record their reading and thinking from the autumn of 1859 to the spring of 1860, the period of the writing of *The Mill on the Floss*. We know that before this time she studied mills in Dorsetshire and perused back issues of the *Annual Register* for cases of inundation to insure the documentary accuracy of her book.[31] While writing the novel she stimulated her imagination by rereading some of her favorite books, whose titles hardly come as a surprise—*Aurora Leigh, The Excursion, The Imitation of Christ*. Meanwhile Lewes was pursuing a program of reading on his own, taking in some less familiar works, such as Schroeder van der Kolk's *Über den Unterschied zwischen todten Naturkräften, Lebenskräften und Seele*, Von Kolliker's *Handbuch der Gewebenlehre des Menschen*, Gegenbaur's *Grundzüge der vergleichenden Anatomie* and Moreau's *Psychologie Morbide*.[32] He was, apparently, mastering the new knowledge of comparative anatomy, psychosomatic medicine, and genetics then being disseminated by continental biologists and psychologists.[33]

Much of this research was incorporated into Lewes' *The Physiology of Common Life*, the book he was working on while

George Eliot was writing *The Mill on the Floss*. In the midst of strolls with "Polly," he read proof for "Feeling and Thinking," and rewrote "The Mind and the Brain" (which became respectively Chapters Eight and Nine of his book). There is more than this casual connection between their two works. Some of the topics of these two chapters, such as "The General Stream of Sensation," "The Whole World Kin" (note the literary reference), and "The Qualities We Inherit from Our Parents," could be transferred to *The Mill on the Floss*. Like Lewes, in her novel George Eliot describes the continuum of sensation and experience, the influence of feeling on thinking, the affinities between man and animals, and the transmission of both physical features and character from parent to child.

Lewes' *Physiology* was intended primarily as an introduction for laymen to the science of the body,[34] but it also had a polemical purpose. To judge from the belligerent tone with which he argues them, some ideas advanced in this treatise ran counter to traditional beliefs held by English biologists. One of these ideas was that the nerves can serve as their own stimulus independently of the brain. In the chapter called "Feeling and Thinking," Lewes was at pains to establish facts about human behavior that we take for granted today—that some nervous reactions are involuntary and that at times man acts from unconscious or subconscious impulse. As he puts it: "Knowledge cannot exist without consciousness; but consciousness may, and often does, exist without knowledge." Lewes here anticipates modern psychologists in distinguishing *passive* from *active* environment.

To enliven his subject for the general reader Lewes draws upon familiar experience for illustration. In proof of his assertion that consciousness may exist without knowledge, he points out how we gradually become so accustomed to the sounds about us—such as the rustle of trees, the twittering of birds, and the roll of vehicles—that we become oblivious to them. However, Lewes insists, our awareness of these phenomena does not cease.

Here is one of his more extended examples of the operation of subliminal influence:

> The mill-wheel, at first so obtrusive in its sound, ceases at length to excite any attention. The impressions on our auditory nerves continue; but although we hear them, we cease to think about them: the same reflex-feelings are no longer excited. It is held, indeed, that we cease to hear them, in ceasing to be 'conscious' that we hear them; but this is manifestly erroneous. (If the sound ceases, we are aware of it; even if we are asleep, we awake; if movement slows down, we are at once aware of it.) . . . The truth seems to be that at first the sound of the wheel was *obtrusive*— excited reflex feelings—gave determinate direction to our thoughts. It afterwards ceased to excite these feelings, and the sensations became *merged* in the general sum of sensations which make up our total Consciousness. (*Physiology*, Ch. 8)

Both George Eliot and George Henry Lewes obviously were impressed by their observations of Dorsetshire mills. Lewes points up the focal significance of the Dorlcote Mill in the novel. It is the center of Maggie's world during her childhood and remains on the periphery of her consciousness throughout her short life. The flooding of the mill brings economic ruin on Mr. Tulliver; its loss hastens his death; glancing at "the silvery breadth of the dear old Floss" brings tears to Maggie's eyes in later years when "the sight of the old scenes had made the rush of memories so painful" (Book Sixth, CH. II); instinct drives her back to the Mill during the fatal flood; the rebuilding of the Mill after the flood symbolizes the restoration of harmony in both natural and human relations. The Mill is indeed pervasive in Maggie's "total Consciousness."[35]

In the early episodes of the novel we are plunged into the "general stream of sensation" that makes up Maggie's subliminal environment, and we absorb the world of phenomena along with her:

> The resolute din, the unresting motion of the great stones . . . the meal for ever pouring, pouring—the fine white powder softening all surfaces, and making the very spider-nets look like a faery lace-

work, the sweet pure scent of the meal—all helped to make Maggie feel that the mill was a little world apart from her outside everyday life. (Book First, CH. IV)

There was nothing to mar her delight in the whispers and the dreamy silences, when she listened to the light dipping sounds of the rising fish, and the gentle rustling, as if the willows and the reeds and the water had their happy whisperings also. (Book First, CH. V)

Not only nature but food also is endowed with vivid sensuousness, as in the family Christmas dinner seen through Tom Tulliver's eyes:

The plum-pudding was of the same handsome roundness as ever, and came in with the symbolic blue flames around it, as if it had been heroically snatched from the nether fires into which it had been thrown by dyspeptic Puritans; the dessert was as splendid as ever, with its golden oranges, brown nuts, and the crystalline light and dark of apple jelly and damson cheese. (Book Second, CH. II)

Maggie and Tom both demonstrate Lewes' observation that "the ebullient energy which one day exalts life, and the mournful depression which the next day renders life a burden almost intolerable, are feelings not referable to any of the particular sensations; but arise from the massive yet obscure sensibilities of the viscera" (*Physiology*, Ch. 8). In their childhood and adolescence visceral response naturally predominates over cerebral, but George Eliot shows how their cumulative subconscious reactions to nature and sensory stimuli affect their minds and characters. The acuity of her insight into their learning processes undoubtedly grew out of Lewes' studies in the psychology of association and the conditioned response, in which he anticipated some of the discoveries of Pavlov.

"Habits, Fixed Ideas, and what are called Automatic Actions, all depend on the tendency which a sensation has to discharge itself through the readiest channel," wrote Lewes. "We have all our tricks of phrase or gesture, which no effort can prevent. . . . The same is observable in the region of ideas. Old associations, old beliefs, are not to be displaced" (*Physiology,* Ch. 8). So George Eliot recognized with the Tulliver children when she foresees, as they play alongside the Floss with no thought for the morrow: "Life did change for Tom and Maggie; and yet they were not wrong in believing that the thoughts and loves of these first years would always make part of their lives." She refers to "all the subtle inextricable associations the fleeting hours of our childhood left behind them." Furthermore, "Our delight in the sunshine on the deep-bladed grass to-day, might be no more than the faint perception of wearied souls, if it were not for the sunshine and the grass in the far-off years which still live in us, and transform our perception into love" (Book First, CH. v).

In both Tom and Maggie, George Eliot shows the arbitrariness and subjectivity along with the persistence of associative memory. Tom, for example, prefers dark December to sunny August because he first connected winter with the closing of school and return home. His love of his home is traced to its source: "where the pattern of the rug and the grate and the fire-irons were 'first ideas' that it was no more possible to criticise than the solidity and extension of matter." The furniture of our first home may look ugly to outsiders, she continues, and the improved taste of adulthood might scorn it, "But heaven knows where that striving might lead us, if our affections had not a trick of twining round those old inferior things—if the loves and sanctities of our life had no deep immovable roots in memory" (Book Second, CH. I). She thus shows us Tom's conventionality and bourgeois pride in their incipient development.

Of a more sensitive and aesthetic temperament than Tom, Maggie responds more to beauty and things of the intellect and the imagination. We learn in later chapters that her "tranquil, tender affection for Philip, with its root deep down in her childhood" continues to evoke her pity for him, and that Stephen Guest calls up in her soul "the half-remote presence of a world of love and beauty and delight, made up of vague mingled images from all the poetry and romance she had ever read, or had ever woven in her dreamy reveries" (Book Sixth, CH. VII, III). But interlaced with these memories are ineffable ties to her home and family, as with Tom. In an earlier chapter the author comments on how the affections may attach themselves to a plant not so much for its beauty as for its familiarity: "And there is no better reason for preferring this elderberry bush than that it stirs an early memory—that it is . . . the long companion of my existence, that wove itself into my joys when joys were vivid" (Book Second, CH. I). So Maggie—when confronted with moral choices in adult life—clings to the perennial companions of her existence, the Floss and Dorlcote Mill, her brother, and her parents. In her early years we see how affection—for Tom, her father, Philip Wakem—becomes associated in her mind with mental anguish and self-sacrifice. In the climactic episodes of the novel, faced with another conflict between love and kinship, Maggie acts in accordance with her habitual pattern of response and rejects her lover Stephen to avoid wounding her cousin Lucy.

The mental development of Maggie and Tom, as it unfolds in the early episodes, grows out of their relations to outdoor life, including the animal world. Little Maggie tries to interest the illiterate mill hand Luke in her favorite picture book, *Animated Nature:* "That's not Dutchmen, you know [Luke has not taken to Pug's *Tour of Europe*], but elephants, and kangaroos, and the civet cat, and the sun-fish, and a bird sitting on its tail. . . . There are countries full of those creatures, instead of horses and cows, you know. Shouldn't you like to know about them, Luke?" (Book First, CH. IV). He seems apathetic to "those creatures," but they were of utmost importance to George Henry Lewes, who, at the time these words were being written, was working on his *Studies of Animal Life.* The section of his *Physiology* called "The Whole World Kin" records some of his initial findings on this subject. His Shakespearean title reveals his obsession with the unity of living creatures (the burden also of Darwin's forthcoming work),[36] a provocative issue at this time, when, as Lewes pointed out, most biologists tended to overemphasize *differentiae:*

. . . a naturalist admits the difference between two animals, admits that a monkey is very unlike an oyster, and that the two should never be confounded; but while they differ, they also agree: he classifies them according to their differences, but their fundamental agreements make him range both under the general conception of an Animal. Various as animals are, he knows that underlying all diversities there are certain uniformities; all animals belong to the grand division of *Animalia,* and obey the same biological laws.

In the childhood episodes of *The Mill on the Floss,* which might themselves be called "Animated Nature," so bounding are they with flora and fauna of all sorts, Maggie and Tom bring out the kinship of living things by their close identification with the animal world. Maggie is first presented to us tossing her head to keep her hair out of her eyes, "an action which gave her very much the air of a small Shetland pony" (Book First, CH. II). Later, Maggie and Tom are described as "very much like young animals, and so she could rub her cheek against his, and kiss his ear in a random, sobbing way" (Book First, CH. V). Maggie and her cousin Lucy huddled together suggest "the contrast between a rough, dark, overgrown puppy and a white kitten" (Book First, CH. VII). Maggie, Tom, and Lucy, released from parental control, "scampered out among the budding bushes of the garden with the alacrity of small animals getting from under a burning-glass" (Book First, CH. VII). Of the grown-up Maggie's aspirations after higher things, her creator observes that "she often strove after too high a flight, and came down with her poor little half-fledged wings dabbled in the mud" (Book Fourth, CH. III). Animal analogies are applied occasionally to the older generation—the "emmet-like Dodsons and Tullivers," the resemblance of Mrs. Tulliver's brother-in-law Mr. Moss to "the depressed, unexpectant air of a machine-horse," and Mr. Tulliver's lumping together of rats, weevils, and lawyers as creations of "old Harry" (Book First, CH. III, VII, VIII). Generally, however, George Eliot's animal imagery is to be distinguished from that of "naturalistic" novelists like Zola, for it is not deliberately reductive.

She points out that Maggie is "gifted with that superior power of misery which distinguishes the human being, and places him at a proud distance from the most melancholy chimpanzee" (Book First, CH. VI). Tom, we have already noticed, displays a certain mulishness at King's Lorton, but eventually "the human sensibilities predominated." Tom and Maggie in different ways represent the emergence of the rational man out of "the grand division of *Animalia*," the real objective of Lewes' studies in comparative anatomy. [37]

Lewes' studies in zoology were extended to genetics, an interest reflected in the vivacious description of the fowl and livestock at the Deanes' farm, Garum Firs:

> All the farmyard life was wonderful there—bantams, speckled and top-knotted; Friesland hens, with their feathers all turned the wrong way; Guinea fowls that flew and screamed and dropped their pretty-spotted feathers; pouter-pigeons and a tame magpie; nay, a goat, and a wonderful brindled dog, half mastiff, half bulldog, as large as a lion. Then there were white railings and white gates all about, and glittering weathercocks of various design, and garden-walks paved with pebbles in beautiful patterns—nothing was quite common at Garum Firs. (Book First, CH. IX)

The fine precision of this passage owes much to Lewes' preoccupation with mutants and varieties, or what Hopkins was to refer to as "all things counter, original, spare, strange."

Ultimately, however, as in his anatomical investigations, Lewes was concerned about the vagaries of the human species. Mr. Tulliver has his opinions on this subject too:

> "It seems a bit of a pity . . . as the lad should take after the mother's side i'stead o' the little wench. That's the worst on't wi' the crossing o' breeds: you can never justly calkilate what'll come on't. The little un takes after my side, now; she's twice as 'cute as Tom. Too 'cute for a woman, I'm afraid. . . . It's no mischief much while she's a little un, but an o'er 'cute woman's no better nor a long-tailed sheep—she'll fetch none the bigger price for that." (Book First, CH. II)

The "crossing o' breeds" is very prominently displayed in the Tulliver heritage. Here George Eliot brings to her exposition of the popular subject of "Home Influence" an exact knowledge not available to her fellow writers. In the section of his book entitled "The Qualities We Inherit from Our Parents," Lewes, once more flouting tradition, refuted the theory then current that parents each transmit definite characteristics to their offspring according to a set pattern. He insists, as Gregor Mendel was to verify afterward, that heredity is mixed and variable, pointing to families where some children resemble the father, some the mother, and some both parents. Tom's resemblance to his fair-complexioned mother and Maggie's to her dark-complexioned father illustrate Lewes' hypothesis that parents transmit not only physical but also psychological traits to their children. "We inherit the temperament, the longevity, the strength, the susceptibility of one or both parents," he declares. "We inherit the nervous system, no less than the muscular and bony" (*Physiology,* CH. 12) . Accordingly, George Eliot subtly mixes the temperaments of Mr. and Mrs. Tulliver in their son and daughter. Maggie is sensitive, tender-hearted, irritable, and stubborn like her father, but at times reverts to her mother's docile and submissive disposition. Tom inherits his mother's plodding unimaginativeness and practicality, but has a latent sensitivity which responds now and then to Maggie's influence.[38]

Lewes' researches carried him into the complications of dominant and recessive traits, exemplified in the Tulliver children's various aunts, uncles, and cousins. The Dodson or maternal streak of practicality, subdued in Tom by more ingratiating traits, dominates in Mrs. Tulliver's smug sisters Aunt Glegg and Aunt Pullet. Mr. Tulliver's sister, Mrs. Moss, on the other hand, had the Tulliver trait of sensitivity in recessive form. Her face, bearing a "faded resemblance to her brother's," is akin to Maggie's, but she lacks Maggie's intelligence and bookishness. Her daughter Lizzie is reputedly "sharp" like Maggie, but "she was inferior enough to Maggie in fire and strength of expression, to make the resemblance between the two entirely flattering to Mr. Tulliver's fatherly love" (Book First, CH. VIII). Lewes points out other fortuities of physical and psychological inheritance. Two parents may be highly intelligent, for example, "yet because their nervous systems have been developed at the expense of their nutritive systems, their children may be susceptible but puny and feeble." George Eliot illustrates with the crippled aesthete Philip Wakem.[39] Lewes was particularly fascinated with the phenomenon of atavism, or the tendency of family characteristics to skip a generation, demonstrated in opposite ways in the Tulliver children. On the one hand, writes Lewes, "a man of highly susceptible nervous organization" married to "a woman of powerful organization, but of rather inferior brains," may produce a child who is "healthy, vigorous and commonplace." The result is a Tom Tulliver. On the other hand, "parents of ordinary capacity [may] produce a child of extraordinary power." Maggie Tulliver's intelligence, it is made clear, emerged out of latent Tulliver ancestral influence.

George Eliot and George Henry Lewes, then, were both, in their respective spheres, physiologists of common life. The novelist's imagination was stirred by a new insight into the relations of body and mind and the dynamics of heredity that invigorated such stereotypes of mid-Victorian fiction as children of nature, country life, home influence, and school days. Nature and man are seen for the first time in English fiction as under a microscope rather than solely by intuition or by the speculative reason.[40] Wordsworth's nature and vision of childhood seem sentimental and idealized next to the world displayed in *The Mill on the Floss*. Sir Walter Scott's Claude Lorrain paintings, Jane Austen's landscaped parks, Dickens' country idylls, Thackeray's Constable landscapes, and Charlotte Brontë's Rousseau-St. Pierre Eden are related to Dorlcote Mill and Garum Firs as the artificial to the real. The environment of Maggie and Tom Tulliver is revealed in all its plenitude, inanimate nature, animal nature, and human nature bound together by a subtle and intricate system of laws. With her mixture of caprice and control, Maggie is at one with this world. Like nature, she is alternately turbulent and harmonious. Like the lower animals, she has irrational instincts. These are subdued but not removed by the influence of Thomas à Kempis: "That new inward life of hers, notwithstanding some volcanic upheavings of imprisoned passions, yet shown out in her face with a tender soft light that mingled itself as added loveliness with the gradually enriched colour and outline of her blossoming youth" (Book Fourth, CH. III). Before her meeting with Philip in the Red Deeps, "one has a sense of uneasiness in looking at her—a sense of opposing elements, of which a fierce collision is imminent" (Book Fifth, CH. I). It is, however, when Stephen Guest enters Maggie's life that the opposing elements in her character clash most painfully.

A contemporary of George Eliot's, one of her most admiring and at the same time severest critics, described *The Mill* in its original three-decker publication as "a masterly fragment of fictitious biography in two volumes, followed by a second-rate one-volume novel."[41] A more recent critic has remarked that *The Mill* is "among the major English novels, but it holds that position in spite of grave defects."[42] The sections of the book entitled "The Great Temptation" and "The Final Rescue" have generally been regarded as a falling off, even by George Eliot herself, but the reasons for dissatisfaction vary.

The last "volume," which is really Maggie Tulliver's "entrance into life," completes her education by introducing her to society, and it brings her moral principles to a test. Modern critics tend to stress the technical faults of these climactic episodes. The crisis in Maggie's life is precipitated neither by Tom nor Philip, but by an entirely new character, Stephen Guest, whose mind we enter on insufficient acquaintance and who is never sufficiently developed as a personality so that we can believe in his impact upon the heroine. Moreover, the tragic ending is really only catastrophic, growing out of natural, not human, causes. George Eliot's main regret was that she lingered so long over the childhood of Maggie and Tom that she could not give due attention to their adult years, and Books Sixth and Seventh indeed strike us as cramped and cursory after the *"epische breite"* of the nature and family scenes. When we come to Book Sixth, the walls of the Deanes' "well-furnished dining room" shut us out from the fresh air, and the genius of the author seems suddenly stifled in a hothouse. Still, the romance of *The Mill* is not to be dismissed as a failure so much as an interesting attempt at a candid treatment of love, which for various reasons George Eliot was unable to bring off with complete success.

The reactions of some of George Eliot's contemporaries to this portion of the novel, as compared to our reactions, reveal an interesting shift of attitude. Where our generation remains unconvinced, George Eliot's was left uneasy. To some of her first readers, ironically, she succeeded all too well in just the situations where to us she seems to falter. We are disposed to ask what Maggie could "see" in such a pallid image of a coxcomb as Stephen Guest. But Dinah Mulock, for one, was disturbed at "this passionately drawn picture of temptation never conquered."[43] Stephen Guest, as drawn, seems insufficient to us to stir up much agitation in Maggie's soul, but the eminent critic Richard Holt Hutton thought that the moral effect of the novel was spoiled by "the mere physiological attraction felt by the heroine . . . and all but yielded to."[44] The colloquies between Stephen and Maggie that strike us as somewhat bombastic and repetitious were denounced as "indelicate and repulsive" by the *Saturday Review*.[45] Bulwer wrote to Blackwood regarding Maggie's "great temptation" that "the *indulgence* of such a sentiment for the affianced of a friend under whose roof she was, was a treachery and a meanness according to the Ethics of Art, and nothing can afterwards lift the character to the same hold on us."[46] George Eliot's famous defense of her *intention*—she conceded only that its *execution* was faulty—was a reply specifically to Bulwer's criticism, but answers objections of other shocked readers as well. "If the ethics of art do not admit the truthful presentation of a character essentially noble, but liable to great error—error that is anguish to its own nobleness," she declared, "then, it seems to me, the ethics of art are too narrow, and must be widened to correspond with *a widening psychology.*"[47]

By "a widening psychology," she meant a psychology rooted in man's physiological nature. For her the tragedy of the human condition—man's proneness to "error"—grew not only out of free will but out of the passions and appetites of our animal nature. Love and the pain of loving are the subject of the last part of *The Mill on the Floss,* as of the earlier parts, but here George Eliot applies to sexual love the new insight that had enlivened her treatment of sibling and family love. Here, too, involuntary responses, subliminal stimuli, and conditioned associations exert their insidious influences. A "slight pressure of the hands, and momentary meeting of the eyes" sets off a relationship between Stephen and Lucy that Maggie comes to regard as a bond with the strength of an engagement. The infatuation of Maggie and Stephen for each other also is conveyed by such ineffable physical signs: "For one instant Stephen could not conceal his astonishment at the sight of this tall dark-eyed nymph with her jet-black coronet of hair." And Maggie "felt herself, for the first time in her life, receiving the tribute of a very deep blush and a very deep bow from a person towards whom she was herself conscious of timidity. This new experience was very agreeable to her—so agreeable that it almost effaced her previous emotion about Philip. There was a new brightness in her eyes, and a very becoming flush on her cheek, as she seated herself" (Book Sixth, CH. II).

Further on, when Stephen is reading to Lucy, Maggie responds with a reflex action: "she sat looking at him, leaning forward with crossed arms, and with an entire absence of self-consciousness, as if he had been the snuffiest of old professors, and she a downy-lipped alumnus." Stephen, in turn, "was so fascinated by this clear, large gaze, that at last he forgot to look away from it occasionally towards Lucy" (Book Sixth, CH. II). Later, while in a boat with Stephen and Lucy, Maggie is sufficiently stirred by "the rhythmic movement of the oars" to abandon the reserve which had kept her from meeting Stephen's gaze. George Eliot, moving into the drawing room that had been Jane Austen's province, exposed the undercurrents of primitive instinct rustling beneath the decorum of genteel manners. Her treatment of love is franker and more biological too than Charlotte Brontë's symbolical lyricism. Today we have come to take the description of sexual stimulation so much for granted in fiction that we hardly notice George Eliot's quiet hints and implications, but they were sufficiently jarring to disturb some of her first readers.

Stephen's appeal to Maggie, however, is not merely physical. He represents, as does Henry Crawford for Fanny Price, the temporary displacement of morality by aesthetics. Her first impression of Stephen comes through his singing voice. Maggie's susceptible temperament thrills to art as formerly it had to nature: "It was not that she thought distinctly of Mr. Stephen Guest, or dwelt on the indications that he had looked on her with admiration; it was rather that she felt the half-remote presence of a world of love and beauty and delight, made up of vague mingled images from all the poetry and romance she had ever read, or had ever woven in her dreamy reveries." The laws of association operate in Maggie's fanciful as in her real life. The memory of Stephen's singing draws her for a fleeting instant from Thomas à Kempis: "The music was vibrating in her still—Purcell's music, with its wild passion and fancy—and she could not stay in the recollection of that bare, lonely past" (Book Sixth, CH. III). Clearly, we are supposed to rejoice in the triumph over Maggie's animal nature of her spiritual nature along with the victory of ethical principle over aesthetic hedonism.

One reader who encouraged George Eliot to carry out her intention for "Sister Maggie" was John Blackwood. Having been concerned over "the want of the hurrying on interest of a taking

narrative" in the first half of the manuscript, he wrote enthusi-
astically to the author as he was looking over the final portion.
"The moment I saw Stephen Guest and Lucy sitting together I
felt that there was the element which I had missed in the
probable form of the coming tragedy. This third volume will be
perfectly fascinating."[48] He was probably speaking for the ordinary reader of the day with his demand for "story interest."

Such a reader would not have been likely, as we are, to regard
Maggie's "tragedy" as masochism. Self-denial and renunciation
were upheld in novel after novel. "How the honest heart glows
with new aspirations after better things to come for its own inner
life—as the loveliness of virtuous self-sacrifice, the grandeur of
true heroism," declared Anne Marsh-Caldwell in the preface to
Emilia Wyndham. One heroine of the period, Maggie Browne of
Mrs. Gaskell's *The Moorland Cottage,* who is a sister to Maggie
Tulliver physically and temperamentally, is also involved in a
similar dilemma when the hero Frank Buxton transfers his
affections from his frivolous cousin Erminia to her. Maggie
Browne is prepared to renounce Frank both out of moral com-
punction and out of loyalty to a brother who is in disgrace, but
circumstances bring about a happy ending in her case.[49] Lewes'
two novels, which also belong to this period, bring us even closer
to Maggie's moral crisis. In *Ranthorpe* (1847) a young lady
admired by the hero is persuaded during his long absence on the
continent to become engaged to another suitor, although she is
not sure of her love for the rival. When the hero unexpectedly
returns and renews his courtship, she refuses him in spite of
herself, considering her previous pledge sacred. In the face of the
hero's importunings, she remains adamant: "My duty! . . . I
may be miserable—I shall be so—but I shall be innocent—my
conscience will be light." In *Rose, Blanche, and Violet* (1848),
one of the heroines, learning that her lover had once courted her
stepmother, who still loves him, writes in farewell: "I renounce
the hope of happiness, I have only now to bear with fortitude my
wretched fate. . . . Life has other purposes than love; other pur-

poses even than happiness; let these occupy you. . . . I must weep for my heart is breaking, Marmaduke; but I shall not flinch." "O hard, when love and duty clash!" exclaims Tennyson in *The Princess*. We might reply with R. L. Stevenson: "There is no duty we so much under-rate as the duty of being happy," but not George Eliot, or her mentor Lewes, for whom moral imperatives took precedence over the affections.[50]

To appreciate Maggie's "tragedy," one must sympathize with a Calvinistic scrupulousness and sense of sin that to us seem to verge on the morbid. But George Eliot is also looking ahead with some foreboding to an age of relativistic ethics whose spokesman is Philip Wakem. He implies at one point that Maggie has a wilful drive towards self-torture. "You will be thrown into the world some day, and then every rational satisfaction of your nature that you now deny will assault you like a savage appetite," he warns her (Book Fifth, CH. III). We may side with Philip, but the author does not mean us to. When Philip says to Maggie: "No one has strength to do what is unnatural. It is mere cowardice to seek safety in negations," he is not to be taken as the voice of wisdom but as the spirit of hedonism proclaiming that what is natural is right.[51] *The Mill on the Floss* reveals that at this point George Eliot, with all her "free thinking," had not strayed far from her evangelical early education. What she learned about nature and human psychology from Lewes' researches confirmed rather than upset her conviction that man's nature is something to be wrestled with and conquered.

Once accommodated to George Eliot's moral bias, we can accept Maggie's act of renunciation and the value of renunciation itself, although we may still be dissatisfied with what Maggie is renouncing. The fact that Stephen Guest was a more vivid figure to the first readers of the novel than he seems to us suggests that George Eliot was evoking a popular stereotype. The "diamond ring, attar of roses, and air of nonchalant leisure . . . the graceful and odoriferous result of the largest oil-mill and the most extensive wharf in St. Ogg's" were part of the alphabet of charm available to any writer of mid-Victorian magazine tales. Unfortunately, Maggie's admirer remains little more than the "clothier's block" that Leslie Stephen aptly called him. The vitality of the novel seems diminished at this point because we are no longer appropriating Maggie's world simultaneously with her. Whereas during her early years we were borne along with her by instinctive associations, in the romantic part of the novel George Eliot leaned too much on conventional literary associations. In the language of the psychologists that George Eliot was learning, when Maggie reacts to nature, home, school, and family, we get her stimuli together with her responses. When she falls in love, we get her responses without her stimuli.

Whatever its faults of presentation, the "story" of *The Mill on the Floss,* as apart from its life history, is best appreciated as a case of conscience. George Eliot here explores the avenues to moral decision—the slow, subtle cumulation of instinct, appetite, nervous reaction, association, rationalization, and reason that influence human motivation. In her later and more profound "experiments in life" (as she called her novels),[52] the moral dilemma becomes more prominent and is posed against a larger social and cultural environment. Society, as expressed through collective morality, which occupies the foreground in *Romola* and *Middlemarch,* is a dimly felt force in the latter third of *The Mill on the Floss.* Much of the pain that Maggie suffers for her innocent rendezvous with Stephen Guest on the boat can be blamed on the wagging tongues of her fellow villagers (Book Seventh, CH. II, "St. Ogg's Passes Judgment"). Miss Mulock also addressed herself to this social evil in a chapter of *A Woman's Thoughts about Women* entitled "Gossip," where she vehemently denounces Dame Rumour and all the harm she produces. Of all forms of gossip, Miss Mulock writes, "this tittle-tattle about love affairs is the most general, the most odious, and the most dangerous." As a result of "unhappy loves made cruelly public," she continues in anger as well as sorrow, it may happen that "families [are] set by the ears, parents against children, brothers against brothers—not to mention brothers and sisters-in-law. . . .Friendships [are] sundered, betrothals broken, marriages annulled—in the spirit, at least, while in the letter kept outwardly, to be a daily torment, temptation and despair." Miss Mulock describes well how St. Ogg's and the Tulliver clan are rocked by Maggie's minor indiscretion. She also understands the spiritual state from which Maggie is providentially rescued by the flood. To the self-righteous, Miss Mulock pleads: "Do your neighbour good by all means in your power, moral as well as physical—by kindness, by patience, by unflinching resistance against every outward evil—by the silent preaching of your own contrary life," but never, she urges, by overt preaching "in a self-satisfied, super-virtuous style." The Reverend Dr. Kenn, who alone among the citizens of St. Ogg's brings a sympathetic insight to Maggie's troubled conscience, stands also as a model of the unsanctimonious spiritual counsellor commended by Miss Mulock. George Eliot herself praises his "spirit of minute discrimination," just the attitude she was seeking in her own reading of human affairs. Her studies in physiology were leading her on to a finer anatomy of the soul and a new conception of the author's function.

Important as was Maggie's "great temptation" to George Eliot's design for her novel, it does not appear to have engaged her imagination as completely as the brother-sister relationship, the first love of Maggie's life, temporarily interrupted by Stephen Guest as well as Philip Wakem. It is to this love that Maggie returns at the moment of her death. "Brother and sister had gone down in an embrace never to be parted: living through again in one supreme moment the days when they had clasped their little hands in love, and roamed the daisied fields together." This death is caused by outside forces, it is true, but these are the manifestation of the inner forces that had rent Maggie's soul. The ending of *The Mill on the Floss*, if it is really catastrophic rather than tragic, performs a poetic justice. The flood reveals that Maggie and Tom, who each had inherited different strains of the Tulliver-Dodson line, have grown toward one another, Maggie becoming more practical and circumspect, Tom made aware just before his death of "a new revelation to his spirit, of the depths in life that had lain beyond his vision"[53] (Book Seventh, CH. v). By the end, harmony in all relations, natural and human, has been re-established:

> Nature repairs her ravages—repairs them with her sunshine, and with human labour.

> Dorlcote Mill was rebuilt. And Dorlcote churchyard . . . had recovered all its grassy order and decent quiet.

> "In their death they were not divided."

Never far from George Eliot's mind was her estrangement from her own brother, owing to her unconventional union with Lewes. Through Maggie's renunciation, George Eliot satisfied herself that she could not approve any merely self-indulgent love, especially one that might wound others. She was at peace with herself as to the morality of accepting life with Lewes, but she remained an outcast from her brother's house until almost the end of her life.[54] It is this loss that she laments in the plangent close to the *Brother and Sister* sonnets:

> School parted us; we never found again
> That childish world where our two spirits mingled
> Like scents from varying roses that remain
> One sweetness, nor can evermore be singled.

> Yet the twin habit of that early time
> Lingered for long about the heart and tongue:
> We had been natives of one happy clime,
> And its dear accent to our utterance clung,

> Till the dire years whose awful name is Change
> Had grasped our souls still yearning in divorce,
> And pitiless shaped them in two forms that range
> Two elements which sever their life's course.

> But were another childhood-world my share,
> I would be born a little sister there.

The Mill on the Floss enabled George Eliot to be "born a little sister" again and carried her readers back to the early morn of their lives, bathed in a new light. Like Dickens, she relived childhood for her generation, universalizing it into the childhood of humanity, but for her it was regarded as a stage in the life of man and in the evolution of human culture, traced through its later development in her succeeding novels. With Thackeray, she recognized the mixture of good and evil in us all, but her closer knowledge of man's physiological and nervous composition led her to a subtler insight into motivation. She brought, therefore, a new precision to the analysis of the irrational that Charlotte Brontë recognized as a phase of the human condition. Lewes applied physiology to common life; she gave life to physiology, revealing man in his totality as a subtle knot of instinct, emotion, reason, and conscience. George Eliot is the most "modern" of Victorian novelists in her psychosomatic representation of character and yet very much of her age in her elevation of ethics above aesthetics. *The Mill on the Floss* in its ennobling of domestic life and its preoccupation with "natural piety," family love and loyalty, is rooted in the social and literary milieu of its times, but its poetry rises above them and its thought and psychology moved ahead of them.[55] In her second novel she reveals early that genius for imaginative assimilation of science and new learning displayed most amply in *Middlemarch,* where human nature is examined against a grander and broader background of civilization.

CHARACTERISTIC FICTION CONTEMPORANEOUS WITH *THE MILL ON THE FLOSS* (1860)

1845 George Sand, *Le Meunier d'Angibault.* (English tr., 1853.)
1846 Anne Marsh-Caldwell, *Emilia Wyndham.*
     George Sand, *La Mare au Diable.* (English tr., 1850.)
1847 Grace Aguilar, *Home Influence; A Tale for Mothers and Daughters.*
     George Henry Lewes, *Ranthorpe.*

1848 Frederika Bremer, *Brothers and Sisters: A Tale of Domestic Life.*
(English tr., by Mary Howitt.)

Rev. W. E. Heygate, *Godfrey Davenant. A Tale of School Life.*

George Henry Lewes, *Rose, Blanche and Violet.*

George Sand, *La Petite Fadette.* (English tr., 1850.)

1849 Dinah Maria (Mulock) Craik, *The Ogilvies.*

1850 Dinah Maria (Mulock) Craik, *Olive.*

Elizabeth Cleghorn Gaskell, *The Moorland Cottage.*

Holme Lee (Harriet Parr), *Kathie Brande.*

Agnes Loudon, *Tales of School Life.*

George Sand, *François le Champi.*

1851 George Borrow, *Lavengro.*

1852 Charlotte Adams, *Edgar Clifton; or, Right and Wrong.* A Tale of
School Life.

1853 Elizabeth Cleghorn Gaskell, *Ruth.*

Charlotte Mary Yonge, *The Heir of Redclyffe.*

1854 Mrs. E. J. Burbury, *The Grammar-School Boys.* A Tale of Schoolboy Life.

1855 D[orothy?] Richmond, *Amy Carlton; or, First Days at School.* A
Tale for the Young.

1856 Dinah Maria (Mulock) Craik, *John Halifax, Gentleman.*

Rev. Edward Monro, *Basil the Schoolboy; or, The Heir of
Arundel.*

Charlotte Mary Yonge, *The Daisy Chain; or, Aspirations.* A
Family Chronicle.

1857 M. M. Bell, *Eda Morton and Her Cousins; or, School-Room Days.*

George Borrow, *The Romany Rye.*

Elizabeth Barrett Browning, *Aurora Leigh.*

R. J. Dixon, *Home and School.*

Margaret Oliphant, *The Athelings; or, The Three Gifts.*

1858 Rev. Frederick William Farrar, *Eric; or, Little by Little.*

Julia Wedgwood, *Framleigh Hall.*

1859 Margaret Oliphant, *Agnes Hopetoun's Schools and Holidays.*

CHAPTER VIII

Middlemarch:

Dorothea Brooke and the Emancipated Woman: *or*, The Heroine of the Nineteenth Century

IN THE LATE MIDDLE AGE of the nineteenth century, no less than in its early teens, the catch-phrase of the hour was Female Education. Although Dorothea Brooke, the principal heroine of *Middlemarch,* and her sister Celia were born in the age of the bluestocking educators known to Jane Austen, they somehow escaped the more elaborate schemes and systems of mental and moral discipline available at the time to the well-placed wards of enlightened guardians. Both of the Brooke daughters, we learn, had "been educated, since they were about twelve years old and had lost their parents, on plans at once narrow and promiscuous, first in an English family and afterwards in a Swiss family at Lausanne, their bachelor uncle and guardian trying in this way to remedy the disadvantages of their orphaned condition" (CH. I). This curriculum suggests a once-over-lightly mixture of gentility with Calvinism. Nothing specific is said about the course of study except that it leaves Dorothea with a vague yearning for sainthood along with a "toy-box history of the world adapted to young ladies" (CH. X). Dorothea is ready to put aside her toy-box when we meet her, on the brink of her entrance into life at an age when Maggie Tulliver's briefer and more intense life is already over. She is ripe for Mr. Casaubon, or at least her image of him: "Her whole soul was possessed by the fact that a fuller life was opening before her," we are told as she reads over his letter of proposal; "she was a neophyte about to enter on a higher grade of initiation" (CH. V).

George Eliot concluded the first edition of *Middlemarch* with a denunciation of "modes of education which make a woman's knowledge another name for motley ignorance." Rosamond Vincy, the "flower of Mrs. Lemon's school, the chief school in the county," it is true, fares about as well as Becky Sharp and Amelia Sedley under Miss Pinkerton, picking up "all that was demanded in the accomplished female—even to extras, such as the getting in and out of a carriage" (CH. XI). Yet, with the aid of her Lindley Murray, Mrs. Garth, combatting the natural ignorance of her young charges as they trail her about her kitchen, amply demonstrates "that a woman with her sleeves tucked up above her elbows might know all about the Subjunctive Mood or the Torrid Zone—that, in short, she might possess 'education' and other good things ending in 'tion,' and worthy to be pronounced emphatically, without being a useless doll" (CH. XXIV). Her daughter Mary seems to have profited from her example. She even turns briefly to teaching, though, like Maggie Tulliver, she soon grows disillusioned with the profession, preferring, with her mind "too fond of wandering on its own way," the world to the schoolroom (CH. XIV, CH. XL).

George Eliot quite possibly was looking back over the state of education during the Regency with the hindsight of the investigators of the Schools Inquiry Commission of 1864, who had recently exposed the inadequacies of the Mrs. Lemons and Miss Pinkertons of the Victorian Age. The Commission's revelations were shocking: female teachers in girls' schools were inculcating false values; they taught too much by rote, lacked thoroughness and a systematic approach to education; their instruction was marked by "showy superficiality, inattention to rudiments, undue time given to accomplishments and those not taught intelligently."[1] There was more cause for optimism, however, in another development, the founding at Cambridge, late in 1869, of Girton College, England's first institution of higher education for women. Among the contributions received towards the launching of the new college was £50 "from the author of *Romola*." At this time, George Eliot, with characteristic tough-mindedness, wrote to a friend: "It is not likely that any perfect plan for educating women can soon be found, for we are very far from having found a perfect plan for educating men. But it will not do to wait for perfection."[2] She was suspending judgment about the benefits of university education for women, which she was born too soon to enjoy; but she tempered her scorn of private education, for the passage about "motley ignorance" appears in no edition after the first.[3]

Dorothea's education is at once a process of unlearning and relearning. The tondo-shaped engraving that decorates the mint-green wrappers in which *Middlemarch* first appeared immediately evokes the "provincial life" promised in its subtitle. Bent trees frame a peaceful hamlet with its church and manor house. The silence and solitude of the scene are disturbed only by a cart rolling down the road. Readers were prepared by this idyllic picture for another *Our Village*, perhaps, or another *Deerbrook* or *Cranford*, but, hardly for the book inside these wrappers. George Eliot's full subtitle was: "A *Study* of Provincial Life," and for her the proper study of mankind, as she indicates in her "Prelude," is "the history of man, and how that mysterious mixture behaves under the varying experiments of Time." This is the true history that replaces Dorothea Brooke's "toy-box history of the world." Because she has no Girton College open to her at the time, Dorothea makes the local village her university (with a brief period of study abroad in Rome), and her readers participate in her "higher grade of initiation."

"Her mind was theoretic," we soon learn about Dorothea, "and yearned by its nature after some lofty conception of the world which might frankly include the parish of Tipton and her own rule of conduct there" (CH. I). She is seeking, that is, to escape provinciality, to see herself in relation to mankind in general. Dorothea's mental history is a progress toward reaching a truth enunciated by the eminent theologian Frederic Denison Maurice, several years before *Middlemarch* appeared, that "the *microcosm*, the little world of man, is really not less than the *macrocosm*, the great World of Nature." Addressing the students and faculty of Cambridge in his inaugural address as Knightsbridge Professor of Moral Philosophy, Maurice set forth a conception of the universe as a series of worlds within worlds: "The grand word *Society* or *Community* really represents a number of different Societies or Communities, each of which is acting upon a certain number of individuals." Maurice offers such a "lofty conception" as Dorothea is seeking, a concentric universe radiating out from the individual to his village or town to the cosmos, interconnecting all men and women. The Community, therefore, for Maurice, is a world in miniature and is best studied not collectively but in terms of its human elements. Echoing Bentham, he declares:

> The interest of the Community is one of the most general expressions that can occur in the phraseology of Morals. . . . When it has a meaning, it is this: The Community is a fictitious body composed of the individual persons who are considered as constituting, as it were, its members. The interest of the Community then is what?—the sum of the interests of the several members who compose it. It is vain to talk of the interest of the Community without understanding what is the interest of the Individual.[4]

Dorothea's education, accordingly, leads her, along with her creator, to a "new consciousness of interdependence" (CH. XI).

The author considers her own function as historian of provincial life to be "unravelling certain human lots and seeing how they were woven and interwoven" (CH. XV) .

When she first mentioned to Blackwood the projected work that became *Middlemarch,* George Eliot referred to it not simply as a study of provincial life, but as a "Novel of English Life."[5] She was contrasting her forthcoming book with the poems she was also writing at the time, most of which had foreign locales;[6] but she meant to emphasize not its geography so much as its universality. Fundamentally, she was carrying out the conviction expressed in one of her earliest critical essays that the novelist "must watch human nature in all its phases—must acquaint himself with it both morally and physiologically—must know how to weigh the relative importance of events, and the effects of the same circumstances on different dispositions. . . ."[7] The vast aggregate of characters in *Middlemarch* are linked by the "mutual influence of dissimilar destinies," to borrow a phrase from its predecessor *Felix Holt.* George Eliot describes her interest as "little local personal history," not the national history that Scott undertook or the social history that Thackeray recorded. But so heterogeneous is the population within the more concentrated area of Lowick, Freshitt, Stone Court, and Tipton Grange, that it can be taken as an image of society itself, not merely *a* society.

George Eliot extends her local history in time as well as space. Like many other great Victorian novels, *Middlemarch* is set in pre-Victorian times, although many of its issues point forward to the later era, enabling its first readers to see their age mirrored in Dorothea Brooke's social, political, and religious world. In the late 1820's, when *Middlemarch* opens, social forces aimed at man's mental, moral, and economic progress were set into operation, the effects of which were being felt at the time when George Eliot was writing. Among these were agitation for religious liberty, extension of the franchise, improvement in farming methods (Sir James Chettham is studying Sir Humphrey Davy's *Agricultural Chemistry*) , and the transportation revolution inaugurated in 1830 with the opening of the Liverpool and Manchester Railway (which has its repercussions among the Middlemarchers). This was a period when the century was young both in years and in zeal, as George Eliot reminds her readers at the end when she informs them that Dorothea's second husband, Will Ladislaw, "became an ardent public man, working well in those times when reforms were begun with a young hopefulness of immediate good which has been much checked in our days. . . ." ("Finale").

George Eliot implies that change and advance in time do not necessarily make for amelioration. Tertius Lydgate would have recognized some improvement in medical education in Victoria's reign over that of George IV, as Dorothea would have recognized improvements in female education. Lydgate is thwarted in his work by the backwardness of some of his Hospital colleagues. Indeed, it was not until 1858 that a Medical Council was appointed, in response to a long-felt need, to set up standards for the examination of prospective physicians.[8] But Will Ladislaw, were he still in Parliament in the 1860's, would have been fighting some of his causes over again. The Catholic Emancipation Act of 1829 is under discussion in the opening chapters of *Middlemarch*. With the Newman-Kingsley pamphlet war and the *Apologia pro Vita Sua* a part of current history of George Eliot's own day, the toleration of Catholicism remained a burning—and unresolved—issue. The convert Lady Georgiana Fullerton was raising a small voice in her novels on behalf of the Church of Rome in the midst of a torrent of anti-Catholic fiction like Mrs. Henry Paul's *The Means and the End: or, The Chaplain's Secret,* Emma Worboise's *Overdale: or, The Story of a Pervert,* and Edward Massey's *Love's Strife with the Convent.* Will and Mr. Brooke campaign for the First Reform Bill of 1832. The Second Reform Bill did not come until 1867, shortly before George Eliot began writing *Middlemarch,* and it still fell short of universal suffrage. In his bumbling way, Mr. Brooke seems to speak for the author when he says to Mr. Casaubon: "I took in all the new ideas at one time—human perfectibility now. But some say, history moves in circles; and that may be very well argued; I have argued it myself" (CH. II). George Eliot maintains a healthy skepticism toward perfectibility as well as toward higher education.

Middlemarch, for this reason among others, is not a "viewy" novel concerned with issues as such, like the novels of some of George Eliot's sister novelists such as Eliza Lynn Linton, Caroline Norton, Dinah Mulock Craik, and later Mrs. Humphry Ward. Her hopes for mankind lay not with legislatures or reform movements, but in cultivation of the mind and conscience. One of her first published essays, a review of R. W. Mackay's *The Progress of the Intellect,* explores tentatively a question that was to be central to *Middlemarch*—the value of theoretical and historical learning as against practical knowledge in solving the problems of humanity. Here she sets up as the ideal scholar the man of "philosophic culture"—a kind of combination of Casaubon and Lydgate—"a nature which combines the faculty for amassing minute erudition with the largeness of view necessary to give it a practical bearing; a high appreciation of the genius of antiquity, with a profound belief in the progressive character of human development. . . ."[9]

"Largeness of view" and "philosophic culture" are what the readers of *Middlemarch,* along with Dorothea Brooke, are expected to gain from this study of provincial life, which enriches their minds while it gives them a sense of the past and extends their vision of community life. Her exhibition of "human nature in all its phases" includes a greater variety of professions and occupations than Scott depicted, showing us man thinking as well as man feeling and acting. Virtually all realms of human interest—religion, art, politics, psychology, medicine, agriculture, commerce—are represented in her fictitious community. George Eliot had Scott's passion for scholarship and recondite learning, as indicated by two surviving notebooks recording her research for *Middlemarch,*[10] but she carried it into "abstruse systems of

morals and metaphysics," realms of thought that he bypassed.
For, above all, she was seeking to give her readers what Dorothea
Brooke hoped to gain from marriage to Casaubon—"higher
initiation in ideas."

At the time when *Middlemarch* first appeared, the British
public had not seen a new novel from their greatest woman
writer for more than five years. "We gladly hail the return of
George Eliot to the domain of pure fiction where her greatest
strength lies," proclaimed a reviewer of the initial part.[11] It
might have seemed that after *Felix Holt* she was abandoning
fiction for the poetry at which she had always wanted to try her
hand and which to her had greater prestige. The poems are not
so unreadable as their present neglect suggests but are chiefly of
interest for their bearing on Dorothea Brooke's situation in
Middlemarch. A number of them involve young women moving
out of sheltered, self-centered lives to find their vocations in the
everyday world. "How Lisa Loved the King," based on a tale in
the *Decameron,* is a kind of poetic version of Dorothea's marital
career in which a heroine becomes infatuated with an elderly
king but eventually marries a young commoner. In "Agatha" a
woman renounces a life of wealth and ease to devote herself to
charity. The dramatic poem "Armgart" is centered on a prima
donna who gives up personal fame for an obscure career teaching
others.

This same critic noticed an advance in style and technique
over her early novels, observing that her new story was "after the
manner of 'Romola' rather than of 'Adam Bede.' " In a number
of respects *Romola* was an exercise for *Middlemarch.* It was the
first novel in which George Eliot demonstrated her unique gift
for domesticating cultural history and melting down scholarship
into living thought.[12] Ethics and aesthetics, Christianity and
pagan hedonism, monastic piety, and the new humanism contend
for the soul of the female neophyte Romola, torn between her
devotion to wisdom and scholarship as represented by her blind

father Bardo and the world of art and beauty as represented by
the handsome young Greek Tito Melema. Romola's story was to
be repeated, with modifications, by Dorothea Brooke several
centuries later. The father becomes a husband, not a great
scholar but a stuffy pedant—the Reverend Edward Casaubon.
The amoral aesthete becomes a moral aesthete, Will Ladislaw.
Moreover, the heroine is transformed from a chimerical fusion of
Botticelli's Venus, Cassandra Fedeles, and George Eliot to a more
ordinary and credible young woman. The Renaissance ferment
of *Romola* is transferred to early nineteenth-century England
and in the process given a texture of actuality that the earlier
book lacks.

Seeking after lofty conception and high occupation, Dorothea
Brooke was one with many another heroine of the period.
"Emancipated" women—nonconformist or discontented with the
ordinary domestic and social round—were especially conspicuous
during the 1860's. In such books as Florence Wilford's *A Maiden
of Our Own Day* (1862), Charlotte Yonge's *The Clever Woman
of the Family* (1865), and Rhoda Broughton's *Not Wisely But
Too Well* (1868) the heroines rebel against an imposed life of
leisure to take up charity work, generally to the consternation of
husband or family. In Caroline Norton's *Lost and Saved* (1863)
a sensitive young lady flouts convention as she tries to relieve the
pain of a disastrous romance through a happy marriage. Eliza
Lynn Linton proclaimed through the heroine of *Sowing the
Wind* (1867) the right of a wife to pursue an independent
intellectual life rather than subdue her mind to that of her
husband. The young bluestocking of Nina Cole's *Which Is the
Heroine?* (1870) tries to cure her spiritual malaise with a
program of independent reading (including Whateley's *Logic,*
Smith's *Moral Sentiments,* Gervinus' *Criticisms on Shakespeare,
Faust,* Schlegel's essays in the original German, and Plato's
Republic) which makes her mother fear for her chances of
marrying. The following year Jane Brookfield's novel *Influence*
was singled out by a reviewer as one more manifestation of "an

age when woman is everywhere chafing at the bonds in which unkind Nature has confined her soaring aspirations. . . ."[13] Readers were well prepared for the story of Dorothea Brooke, although George Eliot's answers to the questing soul were somewhat more complex than those offered by the more facile feminist novelists.

The characterizations of both Dorothea Brooke and Rosamond Vincy were probably conditioned more by feminine intellectualism of the 1840's and 1850's as recorded in the "Silly Novels of Lady Novelists" that George Eliot reviewed for the *Westminster Review* the year before she brought out her own first work of fiction. She looked in vain for another Jane Eyre or Lucy Snowe among the "mind and millinery" heroines, as she dubbed them, of these elegant tales. The varieties of Silly Novels—"the frothy, the prosy, the pious, or the pedantic"—are scored not so much for their display of learning as for their pretense to it. One of these novels, *Compensation,* sounds, as she describes it, like a warmed-over stew of Mrs. Radcliffe, Charlotte Dacre, and Lady Blessington, "served up with a garnish of talk of 'faith and development' and 'most original minds.' " Another uneasy mixture of manners, morality, and melodrama is *The Enigma,* "a story of quite modern drawing-room society—a society in which polkas are played and Puseyism discussed; yet with characters and incidents and traits of manner introduced which are mere shreds from the most heterogeneous romances."[14]

Through "Silly Novels," George Eliot was arguing fundamentally for the novel of ideas wrested free of romance or "storybook" conventions. In an earlier critical essay she had expressed the view that the modern novel at its best marked an advance over the Greek prose romances and the medieval tales of chivalry by mirroring the culture of its own times more fully and faithfully.[15] The authors of the novels she reviewed, in her opinion, merely toyed with topics of the day, while their characters were curious mixtures of fairy princess and bluestocking. Among the phantoms of delight that she holds up to ridicule is the inevitable beautiful heiress:

> . . . probably a peeress in her own right, with perhaps a vicious baronet, an amiable duke, and an irresistible younger son of a marquis in the foreground, a clergyman and a poet sighing for her in the middle distance, and a crowd of undefined adorers dimly indicated beyond. Her eyes and her wit are both dazzling; her nose and her morals are alike free from any tendency to irregularity; she has a superb contralto and a superb intellect; she is perfectly well dressed and perfectly religious; she dances like a sylph and reads the Bible in the original tongues.

Since George Eliot indicated in a private record that the story "Miss Brooke," the first version of the Dorothea-Casaubon-Ladislaw plot of *Middlemarch*, was considered by her as a possible theme from the time when she began the writing of fiction,[16] the character of Dorothea may appropriately be compared with the wraith described above. George Eliot's heiress is not a peeress, and in other respects as well she is scaled down from this ideal. Dorothea's admirers are all commoners also, except Sir James Chettam, who is, however, a good, not "a vicious baronet." Not all men are dazzled by her. (Lydgate, for example, thinks her "a good creature . . . but a little too earnest.") She has a religious character, along with the plain attire and scorn of frivolity that go with it. She has an inquiring mind but not "a superb intellect." It is not true that she "reads the Bible in the original tongues," though she deludes herself into hero-worship of a scholar who does. With Dorothea, George Eliot chose to take the mind without the millinery.

As for the heroine not so fortunately situated:

> . . . rank and wealth are the only things in which she is deficient; but she infallibly gets into high society, she has the triumph of refusing many matches and securing the best, and she wears some family jewels or other as a crown of righteousness at the end. . . . In her recorded conversations she is amazingly eloquent, and in her unrecorded conversations amazingly witty. . . .

Set next to this learned Cinderella, Rosamond Vincy, the beautiful parvenu of *Middlemarch,* whose wit and eloquence are derived from Mrs. Lemon's school, L. E. L., and Lady Blessington; whose great "matches" are Ned Plymdale and Caius Larcher; and who *thinks* she is getting into high society by marrying Tertius Lydgate.[17] This time we must take the millinery without the mind.

The typical fate of the "ideal woman in feelings, faculties and flounces" is also premonitory. Both heroines, the heiress and nonheiress alike, are enveloped in love complications involving a trio of men:

> . . . she as often as not marries the wrong person to begin with, and she suffers terribly from the plots and intrigues of the vicious baronet; but even death has a soft place in his heart for such a paragon, and remedies all mistakes for her just at the right moment. The vicious baronet is sure to be killed in a duel, and the tedious husband dies in his bed, requesting his wife, as a particular favour to him, to marry the man she loves best, and having already dispatched a note to the lover informing him of the comfortable arrangement.

Dorothea Brooke, as we know, "marries the wrong person to begin with." But the "vicious baronet" who sought her hand previously, far from intriguing against her, contents himself with marrying her sister. Also, Sir James' dueling is confined to verbal thrusts against Dorothea's first and second husbands. The "tedious husband" of Dorothea, to be sure, "dies in his bed" (actually in the garden house), but, far from requesting his wife "to marry the man she loves best," does all within his legal power to prevent such a union.

The sufferings of the ideal women of the Silly Novels, we gather, are not particularly trying:

> Before matters arrive at this desirable issue, our feelings are tried by seeing the noble, lovely and gifted heroine pass through many *mauvais moments;* but we have the satisfaction of knowing that her sorrows are wept into embroidered pocket-handkerchiefs, that her

fainting form rests on the very best upholstery, and that whatever
vicissitudes she may undergo, from being dashed out of her
carriage, to having her head shaved in a fever, she comes out of
them with a complexion more blooming and locks more redundant
than ever.

The *mauvais moments* of Dorothea Brooke and Rosamond Vincy
are, of course, more consequential than carriage accidents and
fevers. George Eliot sees to it that her heroines face the serious
problems of marriage, not merely the vicissitudes of romantic
love.

A sister novelist whose mind and knowledge of the feminine
heart George Eliot respected far more was George Sand. Early in
1849 she wrote to a friend: "The psychological anatomy of
Jacques and Fernande in the early days of their marriage seems
quite preternaturally true. . . .[18] [They] are merely the mascu-
line and feminine nature and their early married life an every-
day tragedy." *Jacques,* the novel to which George Eliot was
referring, is really antimarital in its drift, preaching the George
Sand-cum-Rousseau faith in the sanctity of the natural affections.
George Eliot was not in accord with the morality of *Jacques,* but
the discovery of the heroine Fernande that in marriage there is
"a great abyss" between husband and wife that cannot be
fathomed, "the past which is never effaced, and which may
poison the whole future,"[19] is precisely the painful insight that
Dorothea reaches in the course of her "everyday tragedy." Fernande, like Dorothea, is a sensitive young neophyte, freshly
emerged from a protected life and religious education, who,
though wooed by several eligible young men, chooses a suitor in
early middle age (Jacques) who appeals to her as "the noblest
man on earth." The novel traces her progressive disillusionment
with the melancholy Jacques, whose inner life she cannot share.
Jacques himself recognizes that Fernande has not been prepared
by her schooling for the chances, changes, and vexations of life.
Eventually Jacques dies (by his own hand), leaving his child-
wife free for union with a younger lover, Octave. This plot

suggests the Dorothea-Casaubon-Ladislaw triangle in essence, with sexual tensions sublimated into intellectual frustrations.[20] Dorothea, after all, was "looking forward to higher initiation in ideas, as she was looking forward to marriage, and blending her dim conceptions of both" (CH. X).

The 1860's did not lack for serious novels about marriage. Somewhat out of place in the company was Emily Eden's *The Semi-Attached Couple* (1860), a quiet, domestic chronicle of a pleasant, virtually eventless marriage looking back thirty years— when, in fact, it had been written. At the opposite extreme was Mrs. Archer Clive's *Why Paul Ferroll Killed His Wife* (1860).[21] More typical family reading, such as J. Saunders' *Abel Drake's Wife*, Emma Worboise's *Married Life* (1863), Dinah Mulock Craik's *Two Marriages* (1867), Eliza Lynn Linton's *Sowing the Wind* (1867), and William Black's *Love or Marriage* (1868) chronicle various tribulations of courtship and matrimony. With the end of the decade came Florence Wilford's *Nigel Bartram's Ideal* (1869), concerned with the plight of a wife who marries intellectually beneath her.[22] In poetry there was George Meredith's plangent, disenchanted *Modern Love* to counteract Coventry Patmore's sentimental *The Angel in the House*.

In later years when George Eliot claimed not to be much of a fiction reader, she made an exception of Anne Thackeray and Anthony Trollope as the two novelists among her immediate contemporaries with whom she was familiar.[23] Miss Thackeray's best known tales, *The Story of Elizabeth* (1863) and *The Village on the Cliff* (1867), which were widely read in their time, both center on sensitive, sheltered young ladies and their mental and spiritual coming of age. The love problem of the heroine of *The Story of Elizabeth* grows out of nothing more than a shilly-shallying cousin who finally makes up his mind, but her spiritual progress is analogous to Dorothea's as she emerges from isolation to a sense of relationship with humanity. In religion she too is converted from a Calvinistic creed to a more humane, "muscular" Christianity. Catherine George of *The Village on the Cliff*, with her idealism and frustrated sense of higher vocation, is closer to Dorothea in temperament. She too makes a precipitate marriage which proves incompatible (in this instance with a devoted but dull bourgeois) and is attracted to an aesthete who lightens up her life as Will Ladislaw does for Dorothea.[24]

References to Trollope, a close friend as well as one of her favorite novelists, turn up frequently in George Eliot's letters. In one letter she commends him for "the bracing air" of his stories and his faith in the goodness of man.[25] Nearer the time when she was writing *Middlemarch*, however, Trollope was showing his darker and generally less appreciated side—as chronicler of domestic tragedy rather than social comedy. With Louis Trevelyan of *He Knew He Was Right* (1868), in particular, he reveals a new interest in psychopathology through a study of the deranging effects of an obsessive and unfounded jealousy. As might be expected, many of Trollope's Victorian readers found the story unpalatable, but presumably not George Eliot with her well developed interest in "mental science."[26] Edward Casaubon, too, is a victim of the green-eyed monster; however, he sublimates this passion with his "sense of rectitude and an honourable pride in satisfying the requirements of honour, which compelled him to find other reasons for his conduct than those of jealousy and vindictiveness" (CH. XLII).

Trollope's better known novels set the commerce of marrying and giving in marriage and the light strife of domestic relations against the larger conflicts of Church and State in Plumstead Episcopi, Puddingdale, and Ullathorne, but *The Last Chronicle of Barset* (1867) casts a pall over the sunny greenery of his cathedral country. The paranoid Josiah Crawley is a study in the psychology of guilt and persecution, just the kind of mental anguish that Nicholas Bulstrode suffers in *Middlemarch*. Marriage is treated here in a more sober light as the center of attention shifts from youth to middle age. Not only is Josiah Crawley transformed from the comic, shabby pedant of the earlier novels to a figure in an agon, but Mrs. Proudie's voice has taken on the strident tone of a Xantippe. The Proudies (like the Lydgates in *Middlemarch*) introduce the reader to some of the painful incompatiblities of wedlock, while the Crawleys (like the Bulstrodes) show us how marriage may be strengthened by adversity. Above all, in his farewell to Barsetshire, Trollope leaves us with a harsh impression of provincial life—the "small social conditions" that exert their insidious effect in Middlemarch as in Barsetshire—such as parochial smugness, narrow-mindedness, cultural inertia, and gossip mongering.

Next to Trollope and George Eliot the most noteworthy annalist of provincial life in the 1860's was Mrs. Oliphant, whose *Chronicles of Carlingford* were inspired by both the Barsetshire novels and *Scenes of Clerical Life*. At this time, in fact, Mrs. Oliphant was considered worthy of comparison with George Eliot by some critics; and, as both authors were anonymous contributors to *Blackwood's Magazine* almost simultaneously, their works became confused with one another in readers' minds.[27] George Eliot resented comparison with Mrs. Oliphant, as she tended to do with any other author. Nevertheless, it was not farfetched at this stage of their careers. Mrs. Oliphant attempted to do for her imagined community what George Eliot did for hers—record for posterity regional social customs, Dissenting worship, speech, and ways of life. Some of the Chronicles of Carlingford look forward to *Middlemarch,* particularly in their contrast between sluggish tradition and individual aspiration. From the outset, Mrs. Oliphant's treatment of semirural life was more candid and biting than Trollope's, emphasizing the pettiness and meanness more than the homely wisdom of the provincial mind. The Reverend Arthur Vincent, the intellectual hero of *Salem Chapel* (1862), nonconformist in temperament as well as religion, hopes to awaken the minds of his congregation and do good work for Carlingford. He soon comes to realize, however, that "amid their rude luxuries and commonplace plenty, life could have no heroic circumstances," and ends in self-imposed exile. In *The Perpetual Curate* (1864), Mr. Elsworthy, dispenser of Berlin wool, newspapers, and gossip, sets the "lively imagination" of the community aflame with his wagging tongue and comes close to ruining the career of the pure-minded if indiscreet young clergyman Frank Wentworth. The heroine of *Miss Marjoribanks* (1866), a would-be do-gooder determined to create a "revolution in the taste and ideas of Carlingford," is surrounded by a cast of characters who "at one moment, thinking of nothing, were to be seen the next buffeted by the wind of Rumour and tossed about on the waves of astonishment." In the Chronicles of Carlingford, as in *Middlemarch,* strong egos clash with collective morality. Above all, Mrs. Oliphant's central characters, like the heroes and heroines of *Middlemarch,* are informed by a strong sense of vocation.

The eternal themes of love and marriage, as we have noticed, were still omnipresent in fiction while George Eliot was planning and writing *Middlemarch.* There was a growing emphasis during the 1860's on misalliances and marital troubles.[28] Inspired and aspiring young heroines make themselves increasingly felt. Panoramas of community life with its stresses and strains enabled readers to see themselves and their neighbors with the enchantment of distance in more remote villages.[29] All of these tendencies bear on *Middlemarch,* but a new trend of the times must also be taken into account—the spread of what critics called "Sensationalism." George Eliot complained to Blackwood in the middle of the decade that even the cheap editions of her novels "are not so attractive to the majority as [Miss Braddon's] 'The Trail of the Serpent.' "[30] The epidemic of murder, mystery, and sex scandal in fiction led scoffing reviewers to invent such subgenres as "bigamy novels," "enigma novels," "newspaper novels," and "passion novels."[31] Mrs. Oliphant, who herself inadvisedly succumbed to the vogue in *Salem Chapel,* attributed it to the weariness of the age with "domestic histories" and "virtuous chronicles," with the result that "we begin to feel the need of a new supply of shocks and wonders."[32]

Rosamond Vincy, we are told, read little French literature

after Racine at Mrs. Lemon's school, "and public prints had not
cast their present magnificent illumination over the scandals of
life" (CH. XLIII). As George Eliot implies, Rosamond's Victorian counterpart was not so innocent. Among those who viewed
this situation with alarm was a retired writer and clergyman, the
Reverend Francis Edward Paget, who lodged his protest in the
form of an anti-novel called *Lucretia, the Heroine of the Nineteenth Century; A Correspondence Sentimental and Sensational*
(1868). One can enjoy this delightful book today simply as a
satire on claptrap, but it was intended at the time as a moral
purgative on the order of the anti-romances known to Scott and
Jane Austen. Finding "the teaching of the sensational novels of
the day to be, on the whole, so infamous; the principles contained in them so utterly demoralizing; the conversations
retained so revolting for their looseness, wickedness and blasphemy; the scenes represented so licentious," he felt an obligation, he writes in his postscript, "to do what in him lies to
preserve the purity of the young, by putting them on their guard
against the perusal of writings, which sedulously pander to the
worse passions of our nature."[33] Paget, like some of the parodists
who preceded him, seems to have believed in homeopathic cures
for literary ills, and so Cherubina (née Cherry) de Willoughby
(née Wilkinson), the romance-reading heroine of the Regency, is
reincarnated as Lucretia (née Lucky) Beverly (née Frum-
mage), the sensation-novel-reading heroine of mid-Victorian
England.

From *Lucretia* one would never realize that this was the period
of George Eliot's rapidly rising eminence, that Trollope was now
producing some of his most powerful work, that Thackeray was
still writing (even if no longer at his best), that Mrs. Gaskell had
left behind an uncompleted masterpiece, and that a newcomer
named George Meredith was then beginning to stir critical
controversies. Among major novelists of this period only Dickens
is mentioned and he chiefly as a purveyor of thrills and chills (as
in *Bleak House*). The favorite literary fare of Lucretia reminds

us that the first best sellers of this decade were Wilkie Collins'
The Woman in White and two of the worst and most popular
novels of the Victorian age, *East Lynne* and *Lady Audley's Secret.*
These and other titles by Mrs. Wood and Miss Braddon bulk
large and lurid in the box stealthily borrowed behind her
guardian's back by Lucretia from Twaddell and Slang's Circulating Library. She envies Aurora Floyd's "grand sensational
scenes which rose higher and higher, till they culminated in her
being a suspected murderess." The trumped-up excitement of
yarns like *Trevelyn Hold* and *The Shadow of Ashlydyat* arouses
her appetite for such innocent enjoyments as blackmail, family
scandals, and bogus apparitions. She tries, like Cherubina, to
make life imitate art; with her veils and disguises, abductions,
escapes, false marriage, and inadvertent involvement in such
intrigues as false wills, theft and poisoning, she gropes her way
through a parody of the murky world of Braddon-Wood.[34] Like
Cherubina again she is eventually disillusioned with the life of
the heroine, and her last letter to her friend Miss (Evelina)
Brooke is a recantation: "Ah me! what a destiny has been mine!
No one can say that my career has not been sensational, but all
has turned out in the most vexatious, disappointing, unromantic,
vulgar way imaginable. Evelina, I hate sensation! I abominate it!
Henceforth, I abjure it utterly!"

Lucretia follows the cycle of the Fair Romance Reader—in-
flated imagination, disenchantment, adjustment to ordinary life
—although the "literature" that momentarily turns her head is
of a different order. Barrett had ridiculed Gothic fiction and
novels of sensibility for their extravagant romanticism, their
removal from the real world. Paget, on the other hand, condemns
the Sensation Novel for its excessive realism. While most of the
novels Lucretia reads would hardly strike us as mirrors of life, so
far as Paget was concerned they were all too vivid. "A tale which
contains no seduction, no adultery, no blasphemy, nor murder
. . . is weary, stale, flat and unprofitable to them [sensation
writers]," he complains. He draws up an indictment against Mrs.

Wood, Miss Braddon, Wilkie Collins, James Payn, and company
that is specific and grisly:

> They have actually exhausted all known methods of iniquity, and
> then imagined new. Through their teaching, murder has been
> made easy to the meanest capacity: the choicest and most scientific
> modes of destroying life have been revealed to us. . . . Very clever
> practical lessons in the arts of forgery and fraud are supplied . . .
> ante-nuptial connections are treated of as inevitable; adultery as a
> social necessity; and bigamy and polygamy are assumed to be the
> most natural of matrimonial arrangements, except the condition of
> divorce, which is better still!

What is worse to Paget is that so many of these writers are
women—and unmarried women at that. "Instead of taking the
opportunity to help their sex to ennoble themselves, these women
novelists degrade themselves," he exclaims. Had he set out to
destroy all novels by women that dealt with seduction, adultery,
blasphemy, and murder, he would have had to burn one of the
greatest novels of the century along with the trash. Among his
complaints about sensational novels is that "for the benefit of
students in the science of Toxicology . . . the most approved
recipes for poisoning have been set forth with medical and
surgical minuteness." Item: Raffles' death from acute alcoholism
for which Bulstrode is responsible, owing to his deliberate dis-
obedience of Lydgate's orders. "Ingenious plans are suggested for
the abstraction of wills and title-deeds," he remarks. Vid: Peter
Featherstone's attempt to persuade Mary Garth to switch his
wills in order to disinherit his family. For especially clever
"practical designs in the arts of forgery and fraud," turn to
Nicholas Bulstrode's devious means for achieving business success. Another source of Paget's uneasiness with the fiction of this
decade was the readiness of novelists to provide "all breaches of
the seventh commandment . . . with apologetic excuses." For
example, Rosamond Vincy Lydgate's flirtation with Dorothea's
admirer Will Ladislaw. It is obvious from her allusions to such
social evils as gambling (Fred Vincy), bastardy (Featherstone's

natural son Rigg), and crimes like husband murder (Madame Laure), George Eliot was no more inclined to flinch from the moral squalor of life than were her inferior rivals.[35] The titles of some of the "Books" of *Middlemarch*—"Waiting for Death," "The Dead Hand," and "Two Temptations"—would have been just as suitable to the so-called "police and passion" novels of the period, but George Eliot raised their lurid situations to the level of dramas of conscience. Spiritual, not physical, fraud, adultery, and murder were her province.

The superficial resemblances of *Middlemarch* to contemporaneous novels of female emancipation, marriage, rural society, and crime undeniably contributed to its initial appeal to the common reader of the day. A more discriminating reviewer, however, saw it as "really not so much a novel as a narrative which is made the vehicle of careful studies of characters . . . and original thought clothed in the most finished and epigrammatic language."[36] George Eliot claimed to be not much of a novel reader after she gave up literary journalism. "I daresay you will understand that for my own spiritual food I need all other sorts of reading more than I need fiction," she wrote late in life to an American friend.[37] Without holding her strictly to her word, it might be observed that the fiction reader in *Middlemarch* is Rosamond Vincy, whose taste runs to the fashionable novels lampooned by Thackeray and the "gorgeous watered silk" Keepsake proffered by her callow suitor Ned Plymdale. Mary Garth rejects even Scott's novels for Plutarch and other classics. Dorothea Brooke's favorite authors, Pascal, Jeremy Taylor, Milton, and Hooker, are drawn from George Eliot's own library, so it is not for reading such books that she is gently reproved but for seeing Edward Casaubon in their authors' image. The epigraphs that head the chapters of *Middlemarch*, drawn from religious epic, didactic drama, and poetry (including snatches of George Eliot's own), psychology, medicine, history, and moral philosophy, are intended, like Scott's erudite allusions and scholarly notes, to remove the story from "mere fiction."

For her "studies of character," in particular, George Eliot learned less from fellow novelists than from one of the most influential theologians of the 1860's, Frederic Denison Maurice, who, as an admirer of her novels, sent her a copy of the book that grew out of his first addresses on ethics at Cambridge, *The Conscience: Lectures on Casuistry* (1868). She wrote in acknowledgment: "Permit me to take up a moment of your much-occupied time by thanking you for the gift . . . which I have just read through with benefit."[38] There is strong evidence that Maurice's little moral treatise, received at the time when she was projecting *Middlemarch,* was of benefit indeed in helping her to shape her conceptions for her new novel. Maurice's principal aim, expressed in the dedication of his book, "to associate the Conscience with the acts and thoughts of our ordinary existence," is carried out by George Eliot for the inhabitants of Middlemarch. For Maurice the study of conscience is as important to man as the investigation of the physical world;[39] it embraces all human interests: "everything about which other men think most eagerly, all that occupies the mind of the historian, the poet, the tragedian, the comedian, the advocate, the statesman, the poor, the rich, the recluse, the man of the world. . . ." Remove conscience from men's affairs, he declares subsequently, "and there is no drama, no biography, no history: human existence becomes the dreariest blank; men only brutal."[40] Conscience, for Maurice, is a delicate, intangible, but powerful moral force that links human beings with their past and makes possible the bonds of friendship, marriage, and society.

Maurice found a well prepared reader in George Eliot, who as early as "Janet's Repentance," one of the *Scenes of Clerical Life,* represents a conscientious clergyman, the Reverend Mr. Tryan, coming to the spiritual rescue of the heroine. The Reverend Mr. Irwine of *Adam Bede* avoids this duty, but not Maggie Tulliver's courageous religious counsellor Dr. Kenn, whom George Eliot praises in defiance of public opinion: "The casuists have become a byword of reproach, but their perverted spirit of minute discrimination was the shadow of a truth to which eyes and ears are too often fatally sealed: the truth that moral judgments must remain false and hollow, unless they are checked and enlightened by a perpetual reference to the special circumstances that mark the individual lot" (Book Seventh, CH. II). Just this intimate and undogmatic approach to questions of conscience is urged by Maurice as the supreme virtue of the science of Casuistry. His lectures apparently rekindled her interest in this method of examination of troubled souls, and they help to account in particular for the circumspect moral tone and point of view of *Middlemarch*.

Throughout *Middlemarch* the narrator is aiding the reader toward deeper understanding of moral issues based on knowledge of "special circumstances." From the outset she displays an unusual liberality of mind toward the human condition. This author means not to lecture to the reader (as does, for example, the omniscient author of *Romola*) so much as to raise provocative questions and invite him to join in an inquiry of mutual interest.[41] She enters into the "small temptations and sordid cares" of her men and women with an attitude of tolerance rather than a disposition to judge. As she remarks of Dorothea's uncle Mr. Brooke: "it is a narrow mind which cannot look at a subject from various points of view" (CH. VII); and she endeavors to make her readers more open-minded. One means she employs is to caution them against hasty or superficial judgments of the characters in the book.

With Casaubon she first demonstrates the limitations of the ordinary individual as an assessor of character. Even after suggesting that Dorothea may have been overly dazzled by this scholar's pretensions, she defends him against the criticisms of Dorothea's family and friends: "I protest against any absolute conclusion, any prejudice derived from Mrs. Cadwallader's contempt for a neighbouring clergyman's alleged greatness of soul, or Sir James Chettam's poor opinion of his rival's legs,—from Mr. Brooke's failure to elicit a companion's ideas, or from Celia's criticism of a middle-aged scholar's personal appearance" (CH. X). Judged by such externals, she points out, even Milton would fall short. "Suppose we turn from outside estimates of a man," she suggests, "to wonder, with keener interest, what is the report of his own consciousness about his doings or capacity." She echoes here Maurice's insistence that the casuist must not allow himself to be influenced by mere appearances: "The world without, it [Casuistry] leaves to the examination of other inquirers. The Casuist's business is with him who looks into that world, who receives impressions from it, and compels it to receive impressions from him."

As arbiter of conduct, George Eliot continually exposes the inadequacies of her fictitious characters who attempt to judge their fellows. Fred Vincy, for one, "fancied that he saw to the bottom of his uncle Featherstone's soul, though in reality half of what he saw there was no more than the reflex of his own inclinations" (CH. XII). The Reverend Camden Farebrother's sermons were "not always inspiriting; he had escaped being a Pharisee, but had not escaped that low estimate of possibilities which we rather hastily arrive at as an inference from our own failure" (CH. XVIII). Will Ladislaw, with his readiness to point out Casaubon's scholarly deficiencies, "was unable to imagine the mode in which Dorothea would be wounded. Young Ladislaw was not at all deep himself in German writers; but very little achievement is required in order to pity another man's shortcomings" (CH. XXI). Lydgate, with all his vast knowledge of physical pathology, "was at present too ill acquainted with disaster to enter into the pathos of a lot where everything is below the level of tragedy except the passionate egoism of the sufferer" (CH. XLII).

These people of Middlemarch—young and old, layman and clergyman, idler and intellectual—all fall into the human habit of judging neighbors from superficial signs or seeing others in

terms of themselves. The author makes up for the deficiencies
her characters—and readers—by her display of "minute discrimination." She recognizes, as they do not, the subtle mental
sickness that eats away at Casaubon's intellectual ambition": "a
morbid consciousness that others did not give him the place
which he had not demonstrably merited . . . a melancholy absence of passion in his efforts at achievement, and a passionate
resistance to the confession that he had achieved nothing" (CH.
XLII). She thus transforms a foolish pedant into a figure of
tragedy. Similarly, by opening up the soul of Nicholas Bulstrode
on his night of reckoning she evokes compassion for a man who
outwardly is merely another Pecksniff: "Strange, piteous conflict
in the soul of this unhappy man who had longed for years to be
better than he was—who had taken his selfish passions into
discipline and clad them in severe robes, so that he had walked
with them as a devout quire, till now that a terror had risen
among them, and they could chant no longer, but threw out
their common cries for safety" (CH. LXX). The voice of the
intruding author is one of universal sympathy, seeking to understand all, if not necessarily to pardon all. By personifying and
vivifying the passions of the soul she is performing for the reader
the office of the casuist, who, as Maurice affirms, "brings us face to
face with the internal life of each one of us."

In the body of his treatise on the Conscience, Maurice gets
down to "cases" (the root, after all, of the word *casuistry*). Concerned as he was with the application of religion to everyday
affairs, he illustrates his principles with human situations, taken
both from literature and life, some of which seem to have caught
George Eliot's attention, for they are re-enacted in her fictitious
community. Maurice's case histories deal, like her "little local
personal histories," with higher vocation, reciprocal moral influences, conflicts between individuals and their society, and
dilemmas that confront men in ordinary professional or domestic
life. All of these moral problems arise out of community relations
with their crisscross of individual aims, motives, and obligations.

Basically, believing firmly that man's moral imperative lies within himself, Maurice was trying to refute theories of morality based on self-seeking or externally imposed sanctions. He was opposed in particular to Bentham's then fashionable Pleasure-Pain principle. Accordingly, he cites examples of people who deliberately court pain, a group he collectively labels Ascetics. Some of his varieties of Ascetics prefigure George Eliot's cast of characters. One type is the dedicated man "who has a work to do, and who determines that it shall be done, let the inducements to abandon it or neglect it be what they may." Maurice's chosen examples are Napoleon and Bentham himself, but Casaubon and Lydgate, in their respective spheres of scholarship and medicine, could serve as well. Maurice's second type is one who elevates pain into a good in the belief that "the best man is he who can bear pain for his fellows." Maurice has in mind here the Christian monk. Dorothea Brooke, "who knelt suddenly down on a brick floor by the side of a sick laborer and prayed fervidly as if she thought herself living in the time of the Apostles" (CH. I), obviously sees herself in this image. So does George Eliot, who describes her as "a Saint Theresa, foundress of nothing" ("Prelude").[42] A third type of Ascetic is the man who endures privations prompted by the conviction that "he may save himself from pain in a future state." Maurice apparently was thinking of the worshipers at Exeter Hall. George Eliot gives us the abstemious Evangelical banker, Bulstrode.

Maurice recognizes, however, that in life one frequently comes upon "mixed cases" where people originally committed to Pleasure or Pain as a way of life may be swerved from their path by modifying influences. "Suppose a man rich and comfortable, who never for a moment dreamed that there could be any maxim in life but that which Mr. Bentham enunciates," he writes, ". . . [but who] awakens on a certain day to the feeling that there is something which he ought to have done, or ought not to have done. . . ." Such a one is Dorothea's easygoing uncle, Mr. Brooke, in whom "the hereditary spirit of Puritan energy was somewhat in abeyance" when we first meet him, but whose awakened social consciousness leads him to buy the local newspaper and run for Parliament. Even if this burst of civic spirit proves ineffectual, it does provide the dilettante Will Ladislaw with a vocation. On the other hand, observes Maurice, no matter how impelled a man may be to live laborious days, he may be subject to inducements to forsake his work "for things, which, whether pleasant or not, are pleasant to him, which no sophistry can persuade him are not pleasant." Furthermore, "The agreeable thing accepted will make me weaker tomorrow, less capable of determining my course, more the victim of the impulses and impressions that come to me from without." He anticipates the fate of Lydgate after he is caught in the orbit of "that agreeable vision" Rosamond Vincy, with the result that "neither biology nor schemes of reform would lift him above the vulgarity of feeling that there would be an incompatibility in his furniture not being of the best" (CH. XV).

Will Ladislaw and Dorothea demonstrate a happier instance of the "mixed case," the interaction of opposite temperaments. Maurice recognized along with the nobility of Asceticism its egoistical tendency leading the monk of Christendom all too often to turn his thoughts from sacrifice for others to "how much glory his pain could bring to him." George Eliot implies that Dorothea's saintliness is morbid and streaked with spiritual pride. She means us to side with Ladislaw when he gently chides Dorothea during one of their conversations in Rome: "Would you turn all the youth of the world into a tragic chorus, wailing and moralising over misery? I suspect that you have some false belief in the virtues of misery and want to make your life a martyrdom" (CH. XXII). "We do not drop into Stoicism [e.g. Asceticism] naturally," Maurice declares. "A few may have some bias to it from education; in general when it is enforced in childhood, there is a reaction to it in later years. A few may be drawn into it by arguments or the examples of others." Will's libertinism is a reaction against the enforced privation of his

childhood, whereas Dorothea, who has enjoyed an affluent childhood, is drawn to the saintly life by her education and by "the
example of others." "More attractive arguments and other examples will probably in time break the force of these," Maurice
continues; "the Stoic may soon be turned into an Epicurean."
Ladislaw does succeed in softening Dorothea's outlook, but, at
the same time, she exerts a sobering influence on him. In
Maurice's terms their marriage represents the balance of the
Stoical and Epicurean ways of life.

For Maurice as for George Eliot, vocation, courtship, and
marriage are stages in man's moral education. So is communal
life with the tests it imposes constantly on integrity and strength
of character. Maurice insisted that "the continual protest of the
Conscience in each man" is spontaneous and innate, in opposition specifically to the theory advanced by the psychologist
Alexander Bain that men were prompted to do right primarily
by the force of social pressure. In a series of problems which he
labels "Cases of Conscience which have reference to Society,"
Maurice points out that this moral imperative, far from making
man a mere conformist, may lead the individual to oppose public
opinion:

> The cases which arise in the Conscience of a Tradesman or
> Merchant, and which often set him at variance with the customs
> and maxims of his class, are not more numerous than those which
> occur in the Conscience of the Lawyer, the Physician, the Clergy-
> man: they are of the same kind. . . . A Conscience of Duty wholly
> apart from any punishments which may be inflicted on him for the
> neglect of it is awakened; he asks whether the duty has been
> done. . . . So here again is a multitude of cases, various as the
> circumstances, and as the characters of the individuals are various,
> but all of the same kind; all beginning with the discovery in each
> man that he has responsibilities, which no class, no majority of
> men, has imposed on him, and from which no class, no majority of
> men, can release him.

Most of the important characters of *Middlemarch* are compelled to make difficult moral choices which they resolve unaided

according to their own lights. Mary Garth, alone at the bedside
of the dying miser, Peter Featherstone, is offered a bribe if she
will remove his legal will and testament from the safe so he can
burn it and substitute another (CH. XXXIII). She cannot bring
herself to accede to his wish, even though by her integrity, as it
turns out, she prevents Fred Vincy from inheriting Featherstone's
fortune. Dorothea Brooke, when she is widowed, finds herself in
an analogous situation—unable in conscience to carry out
Casaubon's last wishes. After a session of soul-searching, she
writes a note of apology on his never-to-be-published manuscript, seals it, and deposits it in her desk (CH. LIV). During
Bulstrode's one encounter with Ladislaw, the banker tries to
quell a guilty conscience, and the young man resists temptation.
Having learned that by a quirk of destiny he was indirectly
responsible for the poverty of Ladislaw's mother, Bulstrode offers
him restitution, although Will himself is unaware of the debt. In
straitened circumstances at the time, Will nevertheless cannot
bring himself to accept Bulstrode's offer because of his suspicions
of Bulstrode's past (CH. LXI). Somewhat later, Caleb Garth asks
Bulstrode to release him from his duties at Stone Court, sensing
some moral taint in his employer, although Bulstrode has not yet
been found out by the community (CH. LXIX).

All these acts confirm Maurice's theory of the self-sufficiency of
conscience. They are all done in privacy, involve personal rather
than social or legal obligations, are unwitnessed, and no penalty
is threatened. Mary Garth, thinking over her refusal of Featherstone's offer, realizes that this decision "had come imperatively
and excluded all question in a critical moment." Dorothea
Brooke, who already had obeyed her own conscience in defiance
of society by accepting Casaubon as a husband, obeys its prompt-
ings once more by refusing to continue his futile labors: "Do you
not see now that I could not submit my soul to yours, by working
hopelessly at what I have no belief in?" reads her message to the
afterworld. Bulstrode confides to Ladislaw: "You see before you
. . . a man who is deeply stricken. But for the urgency of

conscience and the knowledge that I am before the bar of One who seeth not as man seeth, I should be under no compulsion to make the disclosure which has been my object in asking you to come here tonight. So far as human laws go, you have no claim on me whatever." Will chooses to forego this intangible claim: "What I have to thank you for is that you kept the money till now, when I can refuse it," are his parting words to Bulstrode. "It ought to lie with a man's self that he is a gentleman. Good night, sir." Caleb Garth too has this instinctive sense of right and wrong. "I would injure no man if I could help it . . . even if I thought God winked at it," he declares to Bulstrode upon leaving his service. "I have that feeling inside me, that I can't go on working with you. That's all, Mr. Bulstrode. Everything else is buried, so far as my will goes. And I wish you good day." As Maurice affirms: "The Conscience will make cowards of us all, if it does not lead us to the source of courage." For him and for George Eliot it is the spiritual bond that joins together men and women, working class and professional men, uneducated and educated. Mary Garth proves herself to be truly Caleb Garth's daughter, just as Ladislaw proves himself worthy of Dorothea.

Maurice's treatise, *The Conscience,* suggests the ethical scheme of *Middlemarch,* whose characters seek moral sanctions in secular life, as well as the motivations behind some of the crucial choices made in the novel. Furthermore, two cases of temptation used by Maurice illustrating respectively the warped and the healthy conscience anticipate two entire episodes of the novel. To illustrate a category of cases "involving powers which seem to demand evil things (including perverted notions of religious sanctions)," Maurice invokes Macbeth as a moral archetype, reducing Shakespeare's supernatural beings to psychological images. Witches may or may not exist, writes Maurice. "But suggestions do come to a man now as of old which he dallies with, which mix with dreams of ambition that he has been secretly cherishing, which seem to get a wonderful encouragement from unexpected events, which are deepend by some counsellor less scrupulous than himself." Once he is tempted into crime, against his better judgment, "there rise before the imagination of the man ghastly figures which recall those whom he has put out of the way; the phantoms of superstition must be laid by fresh acts which the former have made desirable. . . ." Likewise, the converted evangelical Nicholas Bulstrode, having come to believe that "God intended him for a special instrumentality," becomes more and more steeped in subtle infamy, which he rationalizes to his conscience. The memory of those he has wronged (including Ladislaw's parents) haunts his mind, and a ghost from the past returns in the ugly form of Raffles. This lone witness to his guilty past is removed in an atmosphere of literal shadow and candle-light (evoking Macbeth's final soliloquy) when Bulstrode allows Raffles to die (CH. LXX). As Maurice remarks, this is "an ever true tale for the reign of Victoria as well as for the reign of Elizabeth or of Duncan."

The Reverend Camden Farebrother, on the other hand, repre-sents the sound religious conscience and the ideal spiritual counselor advocated by Maurice. The great need of society at this time, Maurice asserts, is for the truly conscientious man who can guide others as a result of successfully guiding himself. Such a man, Maurice argues, owes it to his fellow men to try to head them off from a wrong direction, but his aid should be offered in sympathy rather than self-righteousness: "In this instance when you speak to him, you try to arouse his conscience. . . . Many hard pharisaical censures, which lead to no result, are the consequences of our forgetting it, as well as the omission of many counsels which would benefit our neighbours because they would be the fruit of our experience of ourselves." Unlike the phari-saical Bulstrode, who adopts a superior moral tone with his neighbors, giving them gratuitous moral advice, Farebrother speaks to his charges in a tone of humility. He does his duty even at personal sacrifice when he cautions Fred Vincy against gam-bling, for his temptation is to allow Fred to pursue this evil course and consequently lose Mary Garth, whom he himself loves. His success in reforming Fred is due in part to his candor in confessing his temptation: "But I had once meant better than that, and am come back to my old intention. I thought that I could hardly *secure myself* in it better, Fred, than by telling you just what had gone on in me. And now do you understand me?" (CH. LXVI). Fred, who at first had resented censure, is moved despite himself, and the "regenerating shudder" he feels testifies that heart has reached heart.

In his last lecture, entitled "The Office of the Casuist in the Modern World," Maurice called upon novelists in particular to utilize this opportunity to enlarge the moral education of the widening reading public.[43] To Maurice the novel offered greater scope than drama for the representation of characters, through the more "careful dissection of their acts and of the influences which contributed to the formation of their acts." At least one novelist responded to his call and, in the manner of Camden Farebrother, used her knowledge of the conscience to explore the consciences of the people of Middlemarch, and at the same time invited her readers to examine their own.[44] With its first and second editions (1868, 1872) framing the inception and first publication of *Middlemarch,* Frederick Denison Maurice's *The Conscience: Lectures on Casuistry* served as one text which the novel expounds. Maurice died while the first parts of the novel were being issued, and the Reverend Camden Farebrother may be taken as a tribute to a clergyman whom Charles Kingsley called "the most beautiful soul I have ever known."

Mr. Farebrother is an enlightened as well as a dedicated clergyman. "A model clergyman," observes Lydgate, "like a model doctor, ought to think his own profession the finest in the world, and take all knowledge as mere nourishment to his moral pathology and therapeutics" (CH. XVII). Farebrother has moved beyond the old-world fundamentalist religion of his mother, sister, and aunt, and despises Bulstrode's "narrow ignorant set," who "look on the rest of mankind as a kind of doomed carcass which is to nourish them for heaven." He and Lydgate agree with George Henry Lewes that religion must become more worldly—in the best sense of the word—that, "instead of proclaiming the nothingness of this life, the worthlessness of human love, and the imbecility of the human mind, it will proclaim the supreme importance of this life, the supreme value of human love, and the grandeur of human intellect." These words appear in *Problems of Life and Mind,* Lewes' master work, which he was writing while George Eliot was conceiving *Middlemarch,* in which he sought to reconcile "the two mightiest antagonists"— Religion and Science.[45] Farebrother's collection of books on natural history and his studies in entomology, biology, and zoology indicate his interest in the world's body as well as its soul, while his friendship with Lydgate proves that a *modus vivendi* between the mighty antagonists has been achieved, at least in Middlemarch.

For Lewes, as for Maurice, man is a microcosm of the world: "Rising out of the Animal Organism there is the Social Organism, the collective life of all the individual lives," he writes, "and if we desire to decipher Human Psychology, we must study the Human Organism in its relation to the Social Medium as well as in its relation to the Cosmos."[46] Lewes, moreover, in his more systematic way, was attempting, along the lines of Auguste Comte and his English disciple Herbert Spencer, to construct a science of society by analogy with biology:

> The organism is not made, not put together, but *evolved;* its parts are not juxtaposed, but differentiated; its organs are groups of minor organisms, all sharing in a common life, i.e., all sharing in a common substance constructed through a common process of simultaneous and continuous molecular composition and decomposition; precisely as the great Social Organism is a group of societies, each of which is a group of families, all sharing in a common life—every family having at once its individual independence, and its social dependence through connection with every other. In a machine the parts are all different, and have mechanical significance only in relation to the whole. In an Organism the parts

are all identical in fundamental characters, and diverse only in their superadded differentiations; each has its independence, although all cooperate.[47]

By now Lewes himself had turned from his investigations in physiological psychology and individual differences to the more ambitious study of group man, and he and George Eliot had moved beyond the study of the physiology of common life to its sociology. *Problems of Life and Mind* provided George Eliot with a unifying organic metaphor for *Middlemarch,* with its multiplicity of individuals and families leading independent lives and yet interconnected in their destinies. The division of labor in society is appreciated also by one of its most dedicated workers:

> Caleb Garth often shook his head in meditation on the value, the indispensable might of that myriad-headed, myriad-handed labour by which the social body is fed, clothed, and housed. . . . The echoes of the great hammer where roof or keel were a-making, the signal-shouts of the workmen, the roar of the furnace, the thunder and plash of the engine, were a sublime music to him. . . . All these sights of his youth had acted on him as poetry without the aid of poets, had made a philosophy for him without the aid of philosophers, a religion without the aid of theology. (CH. XXIV)

As a primitive, Caleb's ideas about the work of the world remain elementary ones: "His classification of human employments was rather crude, and, like the categories of more celebrated men, would not be acceptable in these advanced times. He divided them into 'business, politics, preaching, learning and amusement.' He had nothing to say against the last four; but he regarded them as a reverential pagan regarded other gods than his own" (CH. XXIV). Lewes substitutes more precise categories: "By Tools and Instruments, by Creeds and Institutions, by Literature, Art, and Science, the Social Organism acquires and develops its powers."[48] These "organs" and "parts" all interact in the life of the Middlemarch community. Tools and Instruments (Caleb Garth, Mr. Hopkins, and other craftsmen and laborers) ; Creeds (Farebrother, Bulstrode, Cadwallader, and Tyke) ; Institutions (Brooke, Chettam, Featherstone, Standish, and Vincy) ; Literature (Casaubon), Art (Ladislaw), and Science (Lydgate and his less dedicated colleagues like Mr. Wrench and Mr. Peacock).

Lewes' comprehensive analysis of the Social Organism underlies the structure of *Middlemarch* just as his method of inquiry is reflected in its style. The animal and ecological imagery of *The Mill on the Floss* gives way to a new system of analogy. To Mr. Brooke, trying to advise his niece Dorothea on a choice of husband, "woman was a problem which . . . could be hardly less complicated than the revolutions of an irregular solid" (CH. IV). The community, viewed collectively, are "crass minds . . . whose reflective scales could only weigh things in the lump" (CH. XVI). Lydgate, torn between supporting Farebrother or Tyke for the chaplaincy of the hospital, "was feeling the hampering threadlike pressure of small social conditions and their frustrating complexity" (CH. XVIII). Celia Brooke regards Casaubon's learning "as a kind of damp which might in time saturate a neighbouring body" (CH. XXVIII). Casaubon's sensitivity "has not mass enough to spare for transformation into sympathy, and quivers thread-like in small currents of self-preoccupation" (CH. XXIX). Rosamond's sudden burst of weeping "was the crystallising feather-touch; it shook flirtation into love," and Lydgate finds himself an engaged man (CH. XXXI). Mr. Vincy "had no other fixity than that fixity of alternating impulses called habit" (CH. XXXVI). To prepare her readers for a shift of scene, the author writes: "In watching effects, if only of an electric battery, it is often necessary to change our place and examine a particular mixture or group at some distance from the point where the movement we are interested in was set up" (CH. XL).

"I read aloud—almost all the evening—books of German science, and other gravities," wrote George Eliot to a friend early in the summer of 1871. The following spring she informed another friend that Lewes was then "absorbed in carrying out some applications of the philosophy of mathematics to mental science."[49] As she indicates here and elsewhere, Lewes' orientation had shifted from the biological to the physical sciences. Terms like "Social Statics" and "Social Dynamics" in *Problems of Life and Mind* reveal Lewes' somewhat self-conscious efforts to apply his favorite scientist Newton's laws of motion and energy to human affairs.[50] Quick to recognize that, like natural forces, "Character . . . involves many incalculable elements organic, historic, social," Lewes conceded that behavior to an extent is fortuitous, but he believed that fundamentally it was predictable and reducible to principles. That George Eliot shared his fascination with the vectors, fields of force, and interactions of human relations is demonstrated in her letter to Blackwood in which she declared, as one indication of her forthcoming novel, to show "the gradual action of ordinary causes rather than exceptional."[51] With considerable, if at times labored, ingenuity, she tries to make the destinies of her characters appear as inevitable as the operation of natural laws.[52]

Ultimately George Eliot's more idealistic characters seek, intuitively or consciously, what Lewes set forth as the great need of the age: "a conception of the World, of Man and of Society wrought out with systematic harmonizing of principles." *Middlemarch* becomes therefore not merely a novel of ideas but of intellectual adventure. This sense of quest is symbolized in that episode in the Vatican Museum where Ladislaw, turning from a window through which he had been gazing at a magnificent mountain view, recognizes Dorothea standing next to the statue of the reclining Ariadne (CH. XIX). Though "clad in Quakerish grey," the author remarks, Dorothea showed up well against this marble beauty. Science, Lewes wrote in his introduction to *Problems of Life and Mind,* can both satisfy our intellectual curiosity and guide our actions, "not only painting a picture of the wondrous labyrinth of Nature, but placing in our hands the Ariadne-thread to lead us out of the labyrinth."[53] Behind this great novel of the "social Body," we realize, looms a novel of the

Mind, a parable of the Intellect appropriating knowledge. Dorothea and Ladislaw are central to the fable, for they are the two
characters who at once have most to learn from experience and
are most capable of development. But they are surrounded by
inquirers of all sorts—the scholar Casaubon, the medical re-
searcher Lydgate, the amateur scientist Farebrother, the gentleman farmer Sir James Chettam, whose ranks are joined later by
that "theoretical and practical farmer" Fred Vincy, to say nothing of the schoolmistress-housewife Mrs. Garth, or even Mr.
Brooke, who putters around with political documents. All of
these charge the placid air of Middlemarch with mental energy.

Part of Lewes' treatise is taken up with the methods of inquiry
itself and the criteria for validating truth. With a view of science
that was at once humanistic and pragmatic, he believed in a
proper balance of the theoretical and the practical. He assumed,
furthermore, that knowledge proceeds by abstraction, but must
be grounded in the concrete, that intuitive perception is an
approach to reality, but must eventually be conceptualized for
full insight, that analysis is insufficient without synthesis, and
that morality, beauty, and truth are equally aspects of wisdom.[54]
These principles illuminate much of the intellectual experience
we encounter in *Middlemarch.*

By these standards Edward Casaubon's "Key to All Mythol-
ogies" is doomed to failure, not because of its pretentiousness
and reconditeness, which would hardly have deterred Lewes, but
because its theories have no concrete basis. Dorothea has an
intuitive sense of the indequacy of her husband's research when
she hesitates "to devote herself to sifting those mixed heaps of
material which were to be the doubtful illustration of principles
still more doubtful" (CH. XLVIII). Mr. Brooke, whose aimless
collection of political papers parodies Casaubon's endless cumulation of notes on religious history, unwittingly exposes another
deficiency of the "Key." Seeking advice on how to arrange his
materials, Brooke learns that Casaubon stores his notes in
pigeonholes. "Ah, pigeon-holes will not do," Brooke replies. "I

have tried pigeon-holes, but everything gets mixed in pigeon-holes: I never know whether a paper is in A or Z" (CH. II) . Pigeonholes will not do for George Eliot either, any more than for Lewes, convinced as he was that "Because the significance of a phenomenon lies wholly in its relation to other phenomena, we must never isolate it from this relativity and draw conclusions respecting it *per se*." Ladislaw shows up more vividly the abstractness and irrelevancy of Casaubon's studies. While Casaubon buries himself in the manuscript vaults of the Vatican Library, his cousin enjoys "the very miscellaneousness of Rome, which made the mind flexible with constant comparison, and saved you from seeing the world's ages as a set of box-like partitions without a vital connection." Like Florence for George Eliot and Lewes, "Rome had given him [Ladislaw] quite a new sense of history as a whole: the fragments stimulated his imagination and made him constructive" (CH. XXII) . Will as yet is little more than a dabbler, but he is on his way to becoming George Eliot's man of "philosophic culture," one of whose characteristics, according to Lewes, is "carefully to discriminate between the abstract or analytical point of view, and the concrete or synthetic point of view."

Unlike Edward Casaubon, Tertius Lydgate grasps Lewes' principle that "All conceptions of Reason, however lofty, must have perception and action for their final aim." His life work, to find "the primitive tissue" out of which all life originated, bears an unlike likeness to Casaubon's ambition to discover "the elements which made the seed of all tradition," but Lydgate has the genius for synthesis that Casaubon lacks.[55] Convinced that his calling affords "the most perfect interchange between science and art; offering the most direct alliance between intellectual conquest and social good," he is prepared "to do good small work for Middlemarch, and great work for the world" (CH. XV) .

Lydgate ultimately fails, like Casaubon, to attain his goal, but out of deficiencies of perception and sensibility ("spots of commonness" as the author diagnoses them) rather than of intellect.

Early in the novel he betrays a shallowness of feeling in his initial reaction to Dorothea, whom he recognizes as a "fine girl— but a little too earnest." Lydgate feels uncomfortable around such sensitive souls who "are always wanting reasons, yet they are too ignorant to understand the merits of any question, and usually fall back on their moral sense to settle things after their own taste" (CH. X). Dorothea, "whose quick emotions gave the most abstract things the quality of a pleasure or a pain" (CH. XX), has an intuitive approach to truth that Lewes, if not Lydgate, approves. In arriving at conclusions, Lewes held, "The starting point is always Feeling, and Feeling is the final goal and test." Related to Lydgate's poverty of perception is an aesthetic blindness that makes him prey to Rosamond Vincy's siren song (a mere echo, we are told, of the soul of her music master at Mrs. Lemon's school), while Ladislaw responds to Dorothea as a true "Aeolian harp."[56] At a particularly crucial time, Lydgate's "spots of commonness" obfuscate his moral judgment when he is offered financial aid by Bulstrode, while Ladislaw's finer sensibility makes him resist being brought under obligation by the corrupt banker. Intuition serves both Ladislaw and Dorothea where unaided reason fails Lydgate. Unlike him, they are able to unite aesthetic, moral, and intellectual judgments.

As a novel essentially concerned with the process of learning, the plot of *Middlemarch* turns on mental acts and the growth of self-knowledge. Dorothea with her "theoretic" mind and "quick feelings" is on her way to acquiring the higher learning at the beginning of the novel. Before she can develop her potentialities, however, she has to pass through what Lewes describes as "the Psychological Spectrum" of Sensation, Thought, and Motion. According to Lewes, "Knowledge begins with vague conceptions and increases with increasing definiteness in the conceptions. All impressions must at first be irradiated and produce a chaos of vague sentience."[57] Such is Dorothea's state of mind at the beginning of her lonely night of soul-searching after she discovers Ladislaw alone with Rosamond in the Lydgates' drawing room

(CH. LXXX). At first tormented by a vague feeling of jealousy, "helpless within the clutch of inescapable anguish," she is in a state of shock in which "the waves of suffering shook her too thoroughly to leave any power of thought." But with the coming of daylight, she is able to take "the truer measure of things." Knowledge becomes more definite, Lewes asserts, as the mind learns to think in terms of "Extension, Duration, Likeness, Unlikeness." So Dorothea discovers, as she looks out of the window of her room: "Far off in the bending sky was the pearly light; and she felt the largeness of the world and the manifold wakings of men to labour and endurance. She was part of that involuntary, palpitating life, and could neither look out on it from her luxurious shelter as a mere spectator, nor hide her eyes in selfish complaining." Emerging literally and metaphorically into daylight out of her dark night of the soul, she recognizes an analogy between the situation of Rosamond and Lydgate and her relationship with the late Casaubon. By her unselfish act of going to see Rosamond, she saves the Lydgates' marriage and in the process discovers the true strength of Ladislaw's love for her.

The progress of Dorothea's mental activity during her night of reckoning in effect recapitulates the development of humanity as Lewes conceived it. While he derived his organic conception of society from Comte, Lewes dissented from the original Positivist view of man as merely a highly developed animal. Whereas Comte constructed his Sociology entirely out of basic biological needs, Lewes identified man's mental and moral faculties—Intellect and Conscience—as the "special products of the Social Organism." (Lydgate, significantly, does not remain satisfied with his discoveries in biology for their own sake, but tries to relate them to social needs.) According to Lewes, animals have in common with men only perceptions, emotions, and the ability to associate them ("the Logic of Feeling"), but man moves beyond the lower creatures in his ability to associate concepts and ideas ("the Logic of Signs") and out of this faculty emerge Arts,

Philosophy, Science, and Politics—all that makes human civilization possible.[58]

In the microcosmic world of Middlemarch this evolution of the Social Organism is represented in miniature. The marriage of the nonbookish and nonmathematical Caleb Garth, who identifies business with "muscular effort," to the former governess Susan is a union, on an elementary level, of the primitive with the civilized mind. For obvious reasons, the schooling of the children is left to the distaff side, and we witness in a way the beginnings of the civilizing of the human race as the savage minds of the Garth children are introduced to the Logic of Signs through the intricacies of grammar and to morality through Plutarch (CH. XXIV). If the Garth children represent the childhood of humanity, Dorothea Brooke represents its maturity as she learns to cope with the categories of thought. Some of the natives of Middlemarch never move beyond the Logic of Feeling, as Lydgate discovers to his dismay with his Rosamond when he tries "to nail down a [her] vague mind to imperative facts," to whom he can speak only the "little language of affection" (CH. LXIV); who settles arguments not with her moral sense, like Dorothea, but by caresses or tears; and who furthermore shows "a want of sensibility" during his financial and moral crisis.[59]

Mr. Brooke, Dorothea's guardian, is aware, in his usual dim way, of things of the intellect and imagination, though he admits to Casaubon that they are not for him: "Everything is symbolical, you know—the higher style of art: I like that up to a certain point, but not too far—it's rather straining to keep up with, you know" (CH. XXXIV). Not for Will Ladislaw who is engaged in a discussion of this very subject—the Logic of Signs—with his German friend Naumann when we come upon them in the Vatican Museum: "Your painting and Plastik are poor stuff after all. They perturb and dull conceptions instead of raising them," Will declares. "Language is a finer medium. . . . Language gives a fuller image, which is all the better for being vague. After all, the true seeing is within; and painting stares at you with an insistent imperfection" (CH. XIX). Will expresses this view just before he sees Dorothea in front of the reclining Ariadne. As his friend Naumann surmises, he is rationalizing his own failure as a painter at this point, but his desertion of a visual medium for an intellectual one bodes well for his future. He gives up the aimless life of the dilettante for the life of thought and political action, and with his ability to fuse feeling and thinking, abstract and concrete knowledge, it is eventually he rather than Casaubon who gives Dorothea her "higher initiation in ideas."[60]

Will Ladislaw, unfortunately, does not make as strong an impression on the reader as he does on Dorothea, but we are never to doubt that he is "right" for her, as some are inclined to do.[61] In Mrs. Cadwallader's opinion, Dorothea might as well marry "an Italian with white mice," but we do not look for transcendent wisdom from the sharp, though not particularly acute, tongue of this charming rector's wife. Sir James Chettam, Dorothea's first suitor, who has nothing but scorn for Ladislaw, is a model of the bourgeois gentry—honest, stolid, and unimaginative. The opinion of settled society—as represented by these two, along with Mr. Brooke and Dorothea's sweet and conventional sister Celia—is not to be taken as the last word toward Ladislaw any more than it was toward Casaubon.

We, who have learned a rounder view of things from the author-casuist-social psychologist, recognize that Ladislaw brings an essential element into Dorothea's life. "It is needless to insist on the great function of Art in the evolution of Humanity," Lewes wrote. Furthermore, "Beauty, if it does not take precedence of Utility, is certainly coeval with it; and when the first animal wants are satisfied, the aesthetic desires seek their gratification." In fact, as Lewes conceived the evolution of culture, despite his own passion for medical research, Ladislaw is prior to Lydgate: "Art not only precedes Science by many centuries, but by far the larger part of the early explorations of the Universe is greatly made up of data furnished by Emotion." Both Ladislaw and Dorothea, however, come to recognize, along with Lewes,

that "our first theories are predominantly emotional, and gradually become more intellectual as symbols take the place of
sensations and emotions." Lydgate and Ladislaw, then, are both
essential to the progress of civilization, but neither is self-suf-
ficient. A basic objective of Lewes' uncompleted study of society
was to show "how intimately the social and religious emotions are connected with this primary fact of the mutual dependence of two human beings, and how from it slowly emerge
all the marvels of Art and Science."[62] It follows that just as
Lydgate's ideals are thwarted by the unfeeling and unthinking
Rosamond, so Ladislaw's are furthered by his "Ariadne," the
sensitive and intellectually curious Dorothea.

Middlemarch has been misread as a study in disillusionment,
but George Eliot very clearly did not so intend it. "I need not
tell you that my book will not present my own feeling about
human life if it produces on readers whose minds are really
receptive the impression of blank melancholy and despair," she
wrote to Alexander Main early in 1872, after the first two parts
had been issued. Later, along with the last of the manuscript, she
sent Blackwood a note reassuring him "that there is no unre-
deemed tragedy in the solution of the story."[63] Dorothea does
say to her sister Celia at the end: "I never could do anything that
I liked. I have never carried out any plan yet," and "It is quite
true that I might be a wiser person . . . and that I might have
done something better, if I had been better." But Dorothea is
characteristically modest. Not too long afterward, readers learned
from Lewes that:

> The objection to ideals, on the ground of their surpassing human
> nature, is a misconception of their function. They are not the laws
> by which we live, or can live, but the types by which we measure all
> deviations from a perfect life. The mind which has once placed
> before it an ideal of life has a pole-star by which to steer, although
> his actual course will be determined by the winds and waves. . . .
> Our passion and our ignorance constantly make us swerve from the
> path to which the pole-star points; and thus the ideal of a Chris-
> tian life, or the ideal of Marriage, are never wholly to be realized,

yet who denies that such ideals are very potent influences in every soul that has clearly conceived them? . . . . Like the typical laws of physical processes, these conceptions are solid truths although they exist only as ideals; and he who imagines their validity impugned because human nature can but imperfectly realize them, is as ignorant of Life as he would be who should deny the validity of Natural Laws, because of the perturbations observable in natural events.[64]

We gather that Dorothea Brooke's spiritual energies are not destroyed, but redirected. As a moral force she resembles those physical forces whose action is slow, subtle, and cumulative: "Her finely touched spirit had still its fine issues, though they were not widely visible. . . . But the effect of her being on those around her was incalculably diffusive . . ." ("Finale").

Like Will Ladislaw, George Eliot sought the "fuller image" of mankind through language. Her novels, like the marriage of Dorothea and Will, unite Morality, Intellect, and Beauty. She carried on the tradition of her predecessors who used the novel to educate their respective generations, but, for her, fiction transcended temporal bounds to contribute to "that education of the race in which we are sharing." All of our novelists conceived their characters as archetypes of the moral ideals of their times. George Eliot saw hers in relation to "the progressive character of human development" through the ages.[65] Accordingly, her novels taken together trace man's mental growth from "the pauper imagination" of the peasant (as she phrases it in the first of her stories, "The Sad Fortunes of the Reverend Amos Barton") to his great accomplishments in arts and sciences. A motto for all her novels is supplied in a poem that heads a chapter of *Middlemarch:*

> These perfect in their little parts,
> Whose work is all their prize—
> Without them how could laws, or arts,
> Or towered cities rise?
>
> (CH. XL)

Her men range from "primitive" craftsmen like Adam Bede, Mr. Tulliver, and Silas Marner, to merchants and businessmen like Mr. Deane and Mr. Wakem, to an apprentice turned politician like Felix Holt, to aesthete-statesmen like Tito Melema and Will Ladislaw, to scholars like Casaubon, scientists like Lydgate, to mystics like Mordecai and religious idealists like Daniel Deronda. We see civilization advance from its elementary forms —the village (*Scenes of Clerical Life*) and the pastoral and farming stages (*Adam Bede, The Mill on the Floss*), through cottage industry (*Silas Marner*), the beginnings of modern urban life and humanistic learning (*Romola*), the Industrial Revolution (*Felix Holt*), through the refinement and diversification of labor, physical and mental, that characterizes contemporary civilization (*Middlemarch*).[66] With *Daniel Deronda,* her last and most cosmopolitan novel, George Eliot advances mankind into a further stage—a hypothetical future of supranationalism and universal brotherhood. Her novels in their span form a cumulative cultural epic of man's creative growth.

From *Waverley* to *Middlemarch* we have traveled in time only from the period of the stagecoach to the first railroads, but George Eliot's Study of Provincial Life places us on the threshold of the twentieth century. "George Eliot was born early enough in the last century to see an England which has almost completely passed away," wrote her friend the novelist Mark Rutherford many years after her death, "and yet her education was modern."[67] He understood her unique qualifications as interpreter of her epoch. *Middlemarch* is nostalgic, like the other novels we have been rereading, but more than any of them it looks ahead to a society that is to become increasingly secular, scientific, and specialized. Dorothea Brooke, as a representative heroine of her century, reenacts her creator's conversion from evangelicalism to Christian humanism, while she recapitulates the intellectual development of her age. By now Aestheticism is no longer an insidious influence, as with Philip Wakem, Stephen Guest, or

Tito Melema, but an awakening voice calling us to things of this world. If the marriage of Arthur Pendennis to Laura Bell represents the Regency moralized, the wedding of Dorothea Brooke and Will Ladislaw may be taken as the rescue of the Victorian age from Puritanism, or what Matthew Arnold called Hebraism, by a new Hellenism.[68] For a period when empiricism and popular education were on the rise, Dorothea's two marriages symbolize the movement of the neophyte mind from pedantry to practical wisdom. With her, the two types of heroine introduced early in the century come of age. As a spiritual Romance Reader released from outworn tradition and the ivory tower to a fresh discovery of human nature and society, she becomes the Christian Heroine secularized.

CHARACTERISTIC FICTION CONTEMPORANEOUS WITH *MIDDLEMARCH* (1871–1872)

1860 Caroline Archer Clive, *Why Paul Ferroll Killed his Wife.* (Sequel to *Paul Ferroll,* 1855)

Emily Eden, *The Semi-Attached Couple.*

Wilkie Collins, *The Woman in White.*

1861 Mrs. Henry Wood, *East Lynne.*

1862 Mary Elizabeth Braddon, *Lady Audley's Secret.*

Anthony Trollope, *Orley Farm.*

Florence Wilford, *A Maiden of Our Own Day.*

1863 Mary Elizabeth Braddon, *Aurora Floyd.*

———, *John Marchmont's Legacy.*

Caroline Norton, *Lost and Saved.*

Margaret Oliphant, *Salem Chapel.*

Anne Thackeray, *The Story of Elizabeth.*

Mrs. Henry Wood, *The Shadow of Ashlydyat.*

Emma Worboise, *Married Life.*

1864 Mary Elizabeth Braddon, *The Doctor's Wife.*

Wilkie Collins, *Armadale.*

Margaret Oliphant, *The Perpetual Curate.*

1865 Elizabeth Gaskell, *Wives and Daughters.*

Charlotte Yonge, *The Clever Woman of the Family.*

1866 Mary Elizabeth Braddon, *The Trail of the Serpent.*
  Margaret Oliphant, *Miss Marjoribanks.*
1867 Rhoda Broughton, *Not Wisely But Too Well.*
  Eliza Lynn Linton, *Sowing the Wind.*
  Anne Thackeray, *The Village on the Cliff.*
  Anthony Trollope, *The Last Chronicle of Barset.*
1868 William Black, *Love or Marriage.*
  Rhoda Broughton, *Cometh Up as a Flower.*
  Rev. Francis Edward Paget, *Lucretia; or, The Heroine of the Nineteenth Century.* A Correspondence Sentimental and Sensational.
  Anthony Trollope, *He Knew He Was Right.*
1869 Florence Wilford, *Nigel Bartram's Ideal.*
1870 Nina Cole, *Which Is the Heroine?*
1871 Jane Brookfield, *Influence.*

CHAPTER IX

CONCLUDING REMARKS

ALTHOUGH SEVEN NOVELS give us but a limited basis on which to make any really significant generalizations, it is hard to leave off discussion without venturing a few observations suggested by our backward glance. These seven novels, superior to, yet representative of, the fiction produced in their respective decades, give us some idea of the conditions which made for the prestige, together with the popularity, of the novel during the nineteenth century. This investigation has demonstrated, it is hoped, the proximity of major novelists to minor novelists in shared ideas and assumptions, and in the ambition to elevate the status of the novel. The success of the great novelists with the large public, it has been observed, was owing to this very sympathy with widespread convictions about human nature and the place of art in life. Moreover, the novel gained in intellectual maturity together with its growth as a medium of education and the extension of the instructional function of the author.

Novelists of the past century frequently combined satire with seriousness, as their criticism of fiction merged with their criticism of life. In one and the same novel they could parody fiction which distorted human nature, and provide corrective lenses to enable others to read mankind right. Beginning with an anti-

romantic attitude and in distrust of imagination as an interpreter of experience, the novelist preferred to exercise his reason
and his observation. He tried to reproduce actuality with a
density of atmosphere and a concreteness of detail that gave the
reader the illusion of life unfolding before his eyes and fixed the
reader's attention on real phenomena. Because it arose in an
ambience of educational experiment which stressed the salient
importance of reading in the moulding of character and the
cultivation of right reason, the nineteenth-century novel took a
didactic form from the very outset. This didactic conception,
however, far from constricting the scope of the novel, enlarged it,
for as the world came to be regarded as one vast schoolroom,
writers sought to represent it in all its richness, plenitude, and
diversity in an attempt to draw from experience all that it could
yield by way of moral example.

Originating in an environment of youth education, and developing in the midst of sanguine hopes for the education of the
masses through literature, the novel kept up a close relationship
with movements of thought as well as with topics of the day. It
tended to derive its subject matter and tone from prevalent
nonfiction forms—history, biography, journalism, sermon, moral
treatise, philosophy—taking on thereby the coloration of intellectual discourse. The serious novel resembled the prose of ideas
in its concern with mental stimulation and moral edification, but
the novelist prided himself on his ability, through his special
powers of evocation and imagery, to reach men's hearts and
consciences as well as their minds. His appeal therefore was not
exclusively to the "literary," but to the citizenry at large who
sought enlightenment and cultivation. Ideally, the Victorian
novelist hoped to combine the truth to life of the historian with
the exemplary power of the biographer, the moral seriousness of
the clergyman, the topical urgency of the leader writer, and the
insight of the philosopher. All of the novelists studied in the
preceding essays owed their success to their ability to convey the
collective wisdom of their times through fiction. George Eliot, as

we have seen, moved beyond the others as an original thinker. She enjoyed, of course, the advantage of union with the versatile George Henry Lewes, who as biologist, psychologist, and sociologist was a pioneer in fields that were then opening up. This age of the novel thus reaches its zenith with a unique collaboration between the scientific and the creative mind. Here is the critic serving the very function envisaged for him by Matthew Arnold, furnishing the writer with a current of fresh ideas.

Together with the enrichment of the novel as a record of human life, we have observed the enlargement of the role of the novelist. From the beginning of the century he was accepted as guide and interpreter, as against a mere narrator or *persona*, and this conversation between author and reader grew in depth and intimacy as the century moved on. He commences as tutor and chaperone with Scott and Jane Austen, acquires the fervor of the lay prophet with Dickens, the breadth of the social anthropologist with Thackeray, the candor of the confessor with Charlotte Brontë, the penetration of the casuist and the profundity of the intellectual historian with George Eliot. From one scholar-novelist, Sir Walter Scott, to another, George Eliot, the novel has attained its full development as an instrument of learning. Scott educated his readers by plunging them into active life; George Eliot educated hers by initiating them into ideas. Representation of reality for Scott meant the precise recording of environment; for George Eliot it meant the fine notation of states of mind. Starting with the phenomenal world as a demonstration of truth and a corrective of mental error, we eventually follow the operations of the mind itself in the process of absorbing that world. This movement from an external to an internal orientation also traces the course of the modern novel. The shift from the objective point of view of Scott and Jane Austen, to the idiosyncratic point of view of Dickens and Thackeray, to the subjective point of view of Charlotte Brontë and George Eliot prepares us for the consciousness-centered twentieth-century psychological novel.

The apotheosis of common life in the Victorian novel, concomitant with its closeness to home, family, church, and the
bustle of everyday existence, has led some critics to think of it as
a pageant of the humdrum. The title of Mario Praz' study of the
period, *The Hero in Eclipse in Victorian Fiction,* gives the
misleading impression that man is somehow diminished in
stature by Dickens, Thackeray, and George Eliot, whereas their
true intention was to discover potentialities for heroism among
the unsung and the uncelebrated. The domestication of the
novel begins with Scott, who recalls our barbaric past for us
mainly to make us more appreciative of settled civilization and
to adjust us to the comfort and security of the hearth. Jane
Austen at the same time shows us that charity begins at home,
and glorifies the domestic virtues. These two streams—epical and
domestic—converge in the Victorian novel, culminating with
George Eliot's "Home Epic," where the obscure lives of average
men and women are played out against the great theatre of the
world—the grand brought within the comprehension of the
ordinary mind, the ordinary elevated and assimilated into the
large scheme of things.

To trace the eventual destination of the novel into our century
is beyond the scope of the present study. Such an excursion would
have to account for the bifurcation of fiction and journalism, the
fragmentation of the reading public into reading publics, psychological circumstances that have made fiction increasingly indrawn, egocentric and solipsistic, social circumstances that have
tended to reduce the influence of the novelist. In our own times
we know that readers are more inclined to turn to the historian,
the political scientist, the sociologist, and the psychologist for the
stimulation they once sought in fiction. We have seen novelists
themselves retreating into private worlds of consciousness, obsessed more and more with the eccentric or the pathological
mind. The Victorian novelist, like Browning's Fra Lippo Lippi,
lent his mind out; it did not feed upon itself. Victorian novelists,
even at their most introspective, as with Charlotte Brontë and

George Eliot, were in touch with a solid-textured external reality and tended to view the aberrant and the abnormal against a background of the normal. Some of our better novelists themselves have admitted that they feel out of touch with the influential ideas and the vital concerns of our era, the last thing, as we have observed, that could be said of their forebears of the nineteenth century. However, it is probably futile in the long run to try to draw a moral for our century from the past one, for we can never hope to reproduce that conflux of conditions— economic, literary, and social—that once made for a wide readership for the best that was known and thought as distilled in fiction. Meanwhile we have seen some representative novelists from one of the richest periods of fiction the world has ever known carrying out an aim announced as early as 1835 in the preliminary announcement of a literary collection called *The American Popular Library:* "the union of polite literature, sound learning, and Christian morals."

NOTES

II. *Waverley:* Edward Waverley and the Fair Romance Reader

1. *Letters of Sir Walter Scott,* ed. H. J. C. Grierson (London, 1932), III, 456–57 (hereafter referred to as *Letters*).

2. Lord Cockburn, *Memorials of His Time* (New York, 1856), p. 266; Archibald Alison in *Blackwood's Magazine,* LVIII (September, 1845), 341. Quoted in James T. Hillhouse, *The Waverley Novels and Their Critics* (Minneapolis, 1936), p. 8. Lord Jeffrey, in the *Edinburgh Review,* described *Waverley* as a "sudden glory" bursting upon the public.

3. Scott relates the circumstances of the writing and publication of *Waverley* briefly in the final chapter ("Postscript") and in more detail in the General Preface written for the 1829 edition of the Waverley Novels. These accounts are supplemented in Lockhart's *Memoirs of the Life of Sir Walter Scott,* Cambridge ed. (Boston, 1901), CH. XXVII. A fragment of the original manuscript was rediscovered as late as 1943 in the attic of the house in Ashiestiel where Scott wrote the opening chapters. See Gillian Dyson, "The Manuscripts and Proof Sheets of Scott's Waverley Novels," *Edinburgh Bibliographical Society Transactions,* IV, Part 1 (1960), 36–37.

4. *Scots Magazine and Edinburgh Literary Miscellany,* LXXVI (July, 1814), 524.

5. "A Health to Lord Melville" [n. p. 1806]. In Berg Collection, New York Public Library; reprinted in Lockhart, *Life,* CH. XV. Lord Melville had been accused of misappropriating funds intended for the use of the navy, while he served as First Lord of the Admiralty. His case was a national event because for nearly thirty years he was the most

powerful man in Scotland, and, as the election agent for the government, controlled the elections of the Scotch representative peers, as well as of the Scotch members of the House of Commons.

6. December 8, 1806. Part of this letter is quoted in *Letters,* I, 341, note, and another part in *Familiar Letters of Sir Walter Scott* (Boston, 1894) , I, 66, note 2, where the date also is supplied.

7. See letter to Lady Abercorn, April 23, 1814, *Letters,* III, 257.

8. To Moritt, [March, 1814?] *Letters,* III, 420.

9. See in particular the review in the *Scots Magazine* cited above (note 4) . The critic for the *Edinburgh Review* observed that *Waverley* belonged "rather with the most popular of our modern poems, than with the rubbish of provincial romances" (XXIV [November, 1814], 208) . At the conclusion of his review he wrote: "There has been much speculation, at least in this quarter of the island, about the author of this singular performance—and certainly it is not easy to conjecture why it is still anonymous . . . and this at least we will venture to say, that if it be indeed the work of an author hitherto unknown, Mr. Scott would do well to look to his laurels, and to rescue himself from a sturdier competition than any he has yet to encounter" (p. 243) .

10. Letter from Margaret Maclean Clephane, afterwards Marchioness of Northampton, quoted by Lockhart in *Life,* ch. xxxiii, p. 532.

11. *Critical Review,* 5th series, I (1814) , 288, quoted by Hillhouse, p. 76.

12. *Monthly Review,* LXXV (November, 1814) ; *Edinburgh Review,* pp. 208–9. Scott's own journal, the *Quarterly Review,* went so far as to express the regret that *Waverley* was not written as straightforward history (XI [July, 1814], 377) . This reviewer thought that the mixture of real and fictitious personages and of actual with "fabulous" events could only confuse a reader.

13. Although he makes fun of *The Wild Irish Girl* in a veiled way, Scott seems to have modeled his characterization of Flora Mac-Ivor on Lady Morgan's popular heroine. Glorvina is the daughter of a chieftain and, like Flora, incongruously combines elegant manners and continental culture with a warlike disposition and an atavistic, savage spirit. *The Wild Irish Girl* was published in 1806, after Scott had allegedly composed the first chapters of *Waverley,* but before Flora was introduced into the story. Donald Davie, in *The Heyday of Sir Walter Scott* (New York, 1961) , p. 27, notices the resemblance of Flora to the "heroine with a profusion of auburn hair," but does not refer to Scott's possible sources.

14. He pays tribute to *The Cottagers of Glenburnie* in his Postscript, the only contemporary work of fiction he mentions throughout *Waverley*, besides "the admirable Irish portraits drawn by Miss Edgeworth," but indicates that it came out after he began his own novel, and unlike his work is "confined to the rural habits of Scotland."

15. Quoted in Lockhart's *Life*, CH. XXXIII, p. 531.

16. Review of *Fleetwood; or, The New Man of Feeling*, *Edinburgh Review*, VI (April, 1805), 182. In this same review he condemned Godwin's *St. Leon* on the ground that "the marvellous is employed too often to excite wonder, and the terrible is introduced till we have become familiar with terror." The hero of *Fleetwood* bears a slight resemblance to Waverley as a sheltered romantic, but Scott detested him as self-indulgent and egocentric.

17. "Robert Bage," *Lives of the Novelists* (Everyman ed.), p. 290.

18. *The Journal of Sir Walter Scott* (Edinburgh, 1890) I, 164 (March 28, 1826).

19. In his *Journal*, March 14, 1826, Scott praised the talent of the author of *Pride and Prejudice* "for describing the involvements and feelings and characters of ordinary life, which to me is the most wonderful I have ever met with."

20. "Henry Fielding," *Lives of the Novelists*, especially pp. 99, 107; "Tobias Smollett," ibid., especially p. 165.

21. Prince Hussein will be recognized from the *Arabian Nights*. Malek the Weaver had figured in the more recent *Tales of the East* (1812), edited by Scott's amanuensis Henry Weber.

22. *A Series of Popular Essays, Illustrative of Principles Essentially Connected with the Understanding, the Imagination and the Heart* (Edinburgh, 1813), Essay III, pp. 176–77. These essays are a refashioning of her earlier *Letters on the Elementary Principles of Education* (Bath, 1801). I am drawing upon the later version here because I also make use of it in the chapter on *Mansfield Park*. Mrs. Hamilton was the author of the novel *The Cottagers of Glenburnie* (see above, note 14).

23. Letter XIV, pp. 125–32; pp. 135–36. Mrs. West's *Letters to a Young Man* was first published in 1801 and went into six editions by 1818. It was followed by the equally popular *Letters to a Young Woman* (1806). Under the pseudonym of Prudentia Homespun, Mrs. West also wrote an education tract sugarcoated as a tale, *Advantages of Education; or, The History of Maria Williams* (1796, 1803). Among her other works of fiction are: *The Gossip's Story* (1797), *A Tale of the Times*

(1799), *The Infidel Father* (1802), *The Refusal* (1810), and two historical romances, *The Loyalists* (1812) and *Alicia de Lacy* (1814).

24. From his preface to his daughter's *Moral Tales.*

25. In most editions of *Waverley,* Flora is compared to "one of those lovely forms which decorate the landscapes of Poussin. . . ." The first two editions read "landscapes of Claud." Scott made the change in the third edition on the advice of his friend Morritt, in whose opinion "to compare young ladies to figures in Claud Lorraine's pictures is not happy, as *his* figures are notoriously poor . . . substitute Pussin [sic]." (See *Letters,* III, 495, note.)

26. Mrs. Lennox was influenced by Marivaux's *Pharsamon; ou, les Folies Romanesques; ou, le Don Quichotte Moderne,* a parody of Mme. de Scudéry.

27. Mrs. Lennox was among the literary lionesses admired by Dr. Johnson, who is supposed to have collaborated on *The Female Quixote.* He is known to have written the dedication to the Earl of Middlessex, and tradition credits him besides with the next to the last chapter (Book IX, CH. XI) entitled "In the Author's Opinion the Best Chapter in This History." This chapter consists of a logical disputation between the heroine and a learned divine in which she is convinced of the falseness of the romances she has been reading and is persuaded to be guided by reason and experience, not imagination, in judging character and actions. Johnson reviewed *The Female Quixote* favorably (*Gentleman's Magazine,* XXIX [March, 1752], 146), quoting in turn a eulogy by Fielding. He later cited its author under the definition of "Talent" in his Dictionary.

28. The critic for the *Anti-Jacobin Review* felt that "the very touches of satire tickle rather than wound the feelings of those writers who have deviated beyond nature and propriety," and predicted that even "the mere novel-reading Miss" who missed the point could be engaged by the excitement of the story. (Quoted by Dorothy Blakey, *The Minerva Press, 1790–1820* [London, 1939], p. 62.) Among Miss Charlton's more "straightforward" works were: *Andronica* (1797), *Ammorvin and Zallida* (1798), *Phedora; or, The Forest of Minski* (1798), *The Pirate of Naples* (1801), *The Reprobate* (1802), *The Philosophic Kidnapper* (1803), and *The Rake and the Misanthrope* (1804). (See Index of Authors in Blakey, *The Minerva Press,* and Montague Summers' *A Gothic Bibliography.*)

29. The last two characters at least can be pinned down from Mrs. Gunning's *The Gipsy Countess* and Mrs. Bennett's *The Beggar Girl and Her Benefactors.*

30. "The Knapsack," for example, is meant to exemplify the virtues of the soldier; "The Prussian Vase" is intended for prospective lawyers; "The Good French Governess" is a "lesson to teach the art of giving lessons"; "The Good Aunt" is concerned with the proper education of a young man intended for the clergy.

31. Mrs. Green's own prolific and miscellaneous output shows a certain feeling after the market. Her writing ranges from the *chronique scandaleuse* (*The Private History of the Court of England*, 1808), to edifying tales for parents (*Gretna Green Marriages; or, The Nieces*, 1823; *Parents and Wives; or, Inconsistency and Mistakes*, 1825). She also tried her hand at the society novel (*Deception*, 1813) and tales "from the German" (*Raphael; or, A Peaceful Life*, 1812). Earlier she had written an educational treatise, *Mental Improvement for a Young Lady, on Her Entrance into the World; Addressed to a Favourite Niece* (1793).

32. Its popularity is indicated by the fact that Colburn published a second edition in 1814 (with "considerable additions and alterations" by the author, and with the subtitle changed to *Adventures of Cherubina*), followed by a third in 1815. In this century it has been reprinted with an introduction by Walter Raleigh (London, 1909) and more recently with the valuable notes of Michael Sadleir (London, 1927). Sadleir identifies the works satirized and restores the delightful parody-within-a-parody *Il Castello di Grimgothico* by Lady Hysterica Belamour, mysteriously dropped by Barrett in later editions. According to Sadleir, *The Heroine* is related to early nineteenth-century romanticism as Gilbert and Sullivan's *Patience* is related to Victorian aestheticism.

Barrett was celebrated in his day as a political satirist. He also gained fame for a much reprinted didactic poem, *Woman*, a eulogy on feminine virtue, written in imitation of Pope. He died in 1820, at the age of thirty-four, with a vast amount of miscellaneous writing to his credit. By the middle of the century a correspondent in *Notes and Queries* refers to him as "now almost forgotten" (July 12, 1856). However, Anthony Trollope refers to *The Heroine* in his lecture "On English Prose Fiction as a Rational Amusement," delivered in 1870.

33. Edith Birkhead has suggested that here Barrett may have been parodying specifically Catherine Smith's *The Misanthropic Parent; or, The Guarded Secret* (1807). See her *The Tale of Terror: A Study of Gothic Romance* (London, 1921), p. 135.

34. "It is evening; we have drunk tea, and I have torn through the third vol. of the 'Heroine.' I do not think it falls off. It is a delightful

burlesque, particularly on the Radcliffe style" (March 2, 1814, to Cassandra, *Jane Austen's Letters to Her Sister Cassandra and Others*, ed. R. W. Chapman [London, 1952], p. 377).

35. See Ernest Baker, *History of the English Novel*, VI, 95, note.

36. In the General Preface prepared for the first collected edition of the Waverley Novels in 1829 he recalls the freedom with which he was allowed in his early years to indulge his appetite for reading during a period of illness: "The vague and wild use which I made of this advantage I cannot describe better than by referring my reader to the desultory studies of Waverley in a similar situation; the passages concerning whose course of reading were imitated from recollections of my own.—It must be understood that the resemblance extends no further."

37. Despite Scott's own apology in his General Preface that his first novel "was put together with so little care that I cannot boast of having sketched any distinct plan of the work," *Waverley* has been widely praised for its construction. Among modern critics the novelist John Buchan, echoing Stevenson, has observed: "With the evolution of the narrative inside the main theme [Scott] has obviously taken pains, for the actual plot of *Waverley* . . . is better wrought than that of any of the other novels" (*Sir Walter Scott* [London, 1932], p. 132). For a systematic and detailed critical analysis, see Stanley Stewart Gordon, "*Waverley* and the Unified Design," *ELH*, XVIII (June, 1951), 107–22.

The best general estimate of Scott as novelist and social historian is David Daiches' two-part article "Scott's Achievement as a Novelist," *Nineteenth-Century Fiction*, VI (September, December, 1951), 81–95; 153–57; reprinted in his *Literary Essays* (New York, 1957), pp. 88–121. Alexander Welsh discusses Edward as the first of a long line of so-called "passive" young men who grow into representative modern civilized gentlemen in his stimulating *The Hero of the Waverley Novels* (New Haven, 1963).

38. Preface to *Peveril of the Peak* (1822).

39. Scott describes this project, undertaken at the end of 1807 at the request of John Murray, in the General Preface. The two chapters that Scott wrote to complete "Queenhoo-Hall" are included among the fragments that make up the Appendix to the General Preface. In general they resemble *Ivanhoe* more than the Scottish novels of the Waverley canon.

40. The popular Lady Morgan was moving in a similar direction. In the preface to her *O'Donnell: A National Tale,* published in the same month as *Waverley,* she confides to her readers that "I have for the first

time ventured on that style of novel which simply bears upon the 'flat
realities of life.' " Bowing to the taste of the times, she has decided "to
abandon pure abstractions, and 'thick-coming fancies' to philosophers
and poets; to adapt, rather than create; to combine, rather than invent;
and to take nature and manners for the grounds and groupings of
works, which are professedly addressed to popular feelings and ideas."
Furthermore, in shifting to modern times, she has "exchanged the rude
chief of the days of old, for his polished descendant in a more refined
age. . . ." Scott wrote in a letter to a friend at this time: "I agree with
you that Lady Morgan has fairly hit upon her forte—for O'Donnell is
incomparably superior to the Wild Irish Girl—having nature and reality
for it's [sic] foundation" (to Matthew Weld Hartsonge, July 18, 1814,
Letters, III, 465).

41. Mrs. Green has a character affirm that "the author of Waverley" is
not so deplorable as his inferior imitators, among whom are included
Galt and Hogg.

42. Review of *The Abbot, Monthly Review,* XCIII (September,
1820), 68.

43. Review of *Waverley, Edinburgh Review,* p. 242.

44. *Miscellaneous Criticism,* ed. Thomas Raysor (Cambridge, Mass.,
1936), p. 341.

45. "Henry Fielding," *Lives of the Novelists,* p. 79.

46. In his essay on Fielding he speaks of the novelist's power to place
before the reader's eye "landscapes fairer than those of Claude, and
wilder than those of Salvator"; Smollett is compared to Rubens *(Lives
of the Novelists,* p. 165); in *Caleb Williams* "several scenes are painted
with the savage force of Salvator Rosa" (review of *Fleetwood, Edinburgh Review,* p. 182); in Crabbe's *Tales of the Village,* "it is scarcely
possible to look at his portraits without recognizing them as painted
from nature, though one may never have met with the originals whom
they resemble" (letter to Lady Abercorn, *Letters,* III, 255). Unoriginal
characters to Scott are "the finished and filled-up portraits of which the
sketches are to be found elsewhere," whereas originality is "the illustration of some particular class of characters, or department of life [not
previously drawn]" *(Journal,* II, 347 [January 27, 1827]). Later he
likened the world of fiction to an island opened up by explorers: "If
they [the pioneers] can make anything of their first discovery the better
luck theirs, if not, let others come, penetrate farther into the country,
write descriptions, make drawings, or settlements as they please" (Ibid.).

47. "Henry Fielding," p. 80.

48. Letter to Lady Abercorn, April 22, 1813, *Letters,* III, 256–57.

49. "The Waverley Novels," *Literary Studies,* ed. Richard Holt Hutton (London, 1895), II, 123.

50. John Henry Raleigh, "What Scott Meant to the Victorians," *Victorian Studies,* VII (September, 1963), 10. Raleigh brings out in this extensive and well documented survey of Scott's reputation that much of his prestige grew out of the rich concreteness and solidity of detail in his novels that gave the impression of a real world. He is mistaken, I believe, in asserting that Scott was not didactic in intention.

III. *Mansfield Park:* Fanny Price and the Christian Heroine

1. September 9, 1814. To Anna Austen. *Letters to Her Sister Cassandra and Others,* ed. R. W. Chapman (Oxford, 1952), p. 404. Hereafter referred to as *Letters. Mansfield Park* was published in May 1814; *Waverley* in July.

2. February 4, 1813. *Letters,* p. 299.

3. December 11, 1815. *Letters,* p. 443.

4. November 16, 1815. *Letters,* p. 430. Also reprinted in *Plan of a Novel,* ed. R. W. Chapman (Oxford, 1926).

5. From "Opinions of Mansfield Park" (Collected by the Author), appended to *Plan of a Novel,* pp. 14–17.

6. *The Opposing Self* (New York, 1955), pp. 213–14. In a much quoted letter to Cassandra, Jane Austen wrote: "Now I will try and write of something else, & it shall be a complete change of subject—ordination" (January 29, 1813, *Letters,* p. 298). This passage has traditionally been taken to refer to the subject of *Mansfield Park,* but this interpretation is disputed in a recent article by Charles E. Edge, who contends that Jane Austen refers not to the novel she was then writing, but announces rather that she was shifting her topic in the letter. (See his *"Mansfield Park* and Ordination," *Nineteenth-Century Fiction,* XVI [December, 1961], 269–74.)

7. Among recent studies, Henrietta Ten Harmsel in *Jane Austen: A Study in Fictional Conventions* (The Hague, 1964) explores Miss Austen's roots in later eighteenth-century didactic novels, particularly *Sir Charles Grandison* and *Camilla;* and A. Walton Litz, in *Jane Austen: A Study of Her Artistic Development* (New York, 1965), makes excellent use of her juvenilia. Neither treats Miss Austen's early nineteenth-century contemporaries.

8. Annette B. Hopkins, "Jane Austen the Critic," *PMLA,* XL (June, 1925), 425.

9. *Passages of a Working Life* (London, 1864), pp. 226–27.

10. *The Northanger Novels: A Footnote to Jane Austen.* English Association Pamphlet No. 68 (London, 1927).

11. *Monthly Review,* LX (October, 1809), 212.

12. Charlotte Brontë recreates two model products of the age in the Sympson sisters, who "knew by heart a certain young-ladies'-schoolroom code of laws on language, demeanour, etc.; themselves never deviated from its curious little pragmatical provisions; and they regarded with secret, whispered horror, all deviations in others" (*Shirley*, CH. XXVI).

13. November 6, 1813, *Letters,* p. 372. In this letter she indicates her pleasure at learning that Mrs. Hamilton was given a copy of *Sense and Sensibility,* which had just come out in a second edition.

14. *A Series of Popular Essays Illustrative of Principles Essentially Connected with the Improvement of the Understanding, the Imagination and the Heart* (Edinburgh and London, 1813), Introduction, p. xlii.

15. Essay II ("On the Agency of Attention in the Development and Cultivation of Intellectual Powers"), ibid., pp. 88–90.

16. Fanny's name has been traced to Crabbe:

> Sir Edward Archer is an amorous knight,
> And maidens chaste and lovely shun his sight;
> His bailiff's daughter suited much his taste,
> For Fanny Price was lovely and was chaste.
>
> *(Parish Register,* Part II)

Quoted in Ten Harmsel, *Jane Austen,* p. 104.

17. Introduction, p. xlii; Essay III ("On the Effects Resulting from a Peculiar Direction of Attention on the Power of Imagination and in Producing the Emotion of Taste"), p. 250. Mrs. Hamilton's aesthetic ideas were influenced by the Scottish philosopher Archibald Alison, to whom her book was dedicated.

18. Essay III, p. 231.

19. In advising her niece Fanny Knight on marriage, late in the year when *Mansfield Park* was published, Jane Austen wrote. "There *are* such beings in the World perhaps, one in a Thousand, as the Creature You and I should think perfection, Where Grace & Spirit are united to Worth, where the Manners are equal to the Heart & Understanding, but such a person may not come in your way, or if he does he may not be the eldest son of a Man of Fortune, the Brother of your particular friend, & belonging to your own County" (November 18, 1814, *Letters,* pp. 410–11).

20. Although *Coelebs in Search of a Wife* is strangely missing from the catalogues of Mudie's Select Library, it is evident that its reputation survived well into the Victorian period—even if largely as the object of lampoon. Miss More's Collected Works were issued by Bohn in 1856. In 1860 appeared another parody, *Coelebs in Search of a Cook*. Mrs. Oliphant, naming the Emma-like heroine of her *Miss Marjoribanks* (1866) Lucilla, seems to have been sharing a sly joke with her readers. Two years after the 1879 reprint of Miss More's Regency best-seller appeared *Young Coelebs* by Percy Fitzgerald. The hero's last name is Sillop, but to his consternation it is taken for "Coelebs" by an older officer when he joins the army:

> "Sillop," I corrected him good-naturedly, "not Coelebs."
> "Ha! ha ha!" laughed the colonel loudly. "Very good indeed! 'Coelebs in Search of a Wife.' That was a book we all read when I was a lad, written by some tabby of an old maid. Very good indeed." (I, 64).

To his continued embarrassment, the mistaken name sticks to the hero.

21. XIV (April, 1809), 145. The reviewer has since been identified as Sydney Smith. (See *DNB* sketch of Hannah More.)

22. LXXIX (February, 1809), 151.

23. January 24, 1809. *Letters*, p. 256. In a subsequent letter to Cassandra she scoffs at the name of the hero: "The only merit it could have, was in the name of Caleb, which has an honest, unpretending sound; but in Coelebs, there is pedantry & affectation.—Is it written only to Classical Scholars?" (January 30, 1809, *Letters*, p. 259). In a late revision of one of her juvenilia, "Catherine; or, The Bower" (*Volume the Third*) she substituted a reference to *Coelebs* for a reference to Bishop Secker on the Catechism. (See Litz, *Jane Austen*, p. 174.)

24. November 18, 1814. *Letters*, p. 410. A facsimile of the original appears in *Five Letters from Jane Austen to Her Niece Fanny Knight* (Oxford, 1924).

25. There is a striking resemblance between the idealized Lucilla and a contemporaneous real-life portrait. Coelebs writes:

Lucilla Stanley is rather perfectly elegant than perfectly beautiful. I have seen women as striking, but I never saw one so interesting. Her beauty is countenance; it is the stamp of mind intelligibly printed on the face. It is not so much the symmetry of features as the joint triumph of intellect and sweet temper. A fine old poet has well described her:

Her pure and eloquent blood
Spoke in her cheeks, and so distinctly wrought
That one could almost say her body thought.

Her conversation, like her countenance, is composed of liveliness, sensibility and delicacy. She does not say things to be quoted, but the effect of her conversation is that it leaves an impression of pleasure on the mind, and a love of goodness on the heart. . . . Though she has a correct ear, she neither sings nor plays; and her taste is so exact in drawing, that she really seems to have le compas dans l'oeil; yet I never see a pencil in her fingers except to sketch a seat or bower for the pleasure ground. Her notions are too just to allow her to be satisfied with mediocrity in anything, and for perfection in many things, she thinks that life is too short, and its duties too various and important. (CH. XIV)

Cf. this encomium from an article in the Gentleman's Magazine, LXVIII (July, 1818), 53:

Of personal attractions she possessed a considerable share. Her stature was that of true elegance . . . Her features were separately good. Their assemblage produced an unrivalled expression of that cheerfulness, sensibility and benevolence which were her real characteristics. Her complexion was of the finest texture. It might with truth be said, that her eloquent blood spoke through her modest cheek. Her voice was extremely sweet. She delivered herself with fluency and precision. Indeed she was formed for elegant and rational society, excelling in conversation as much as in composition. In the present age it is hazardous to mention accomplishments. [She] would, probably, have been inferior to few in such acquirements, had she not been so superior to most in higher things. She had not only an excellent taste for drawing, but, in her earlier days, evinced great power of hand in management of the pencil. Her own musical attainments she held very cheap. Twenty years ago they would have been thought more of, and twenty years hence many a parent will expect their daughters to be applauded for meaner performances. She was fond of dancing, and excelled in it.

This passage appears in the review of the posthumously published volume containing Northanger Abbey and Persuasion as a quotation from the prefatory Biographical Notice of the Author written by her brother, the Reverend Henry Austen. Not only is Miss Austen praised for the very virtues and graces that are supposed to have adorned

Lucilla, but the lines that Coelebs quotes from Donne's "Of the Progress of the Soul" are paraphrased by Henry Austen.

26. One reviewer, at least, approved: "Coelebs attempted too much by endeavouring to make our fine people as religious as nuns and friars; and perhaps the efforts of Celia to infuse in them a little common sense may equally be thrown away. Can a luxurious capital be reformed by sermons, poems or novels?" (*Monthly Review*, LX [October, 1809], 212).

27. One should not make too much of the name of Celia's pious governess—Mrs. Mansfield—inasmuch as her worldly sister is named Fanny. However, there is a plot detail that Jane Austen may have taken over and modified. The Bertons' dissolute son succeeds in seducing an innocent country girl by obtaining a post in the army for her brother. (Cf. Henry Crawford and William Price.)

28. October 11, 1813, *Letters*, p. 344.

29. A contemporary reviewer for an Edinburgh journal commented upon its first publication: "We do not recollect even among the most popular productions of the present day any one, the appearance of which excited a more immediate and general interest throughout this metropolis" (*Scots Magazine*, LXXIII [March, 1811], 203). Because of the high moral tone of this novel the reviewer indicated that this journal was making an exception to its usual practice of ignoring works of fiction. *Self-Control* was subsequently translated into French and much later reprinted in Bentley's Standard Novels (No. 15, 1832). Its popularity appears to have been sustained well into the Victorian period, to judge from its continuous appearance on Mudie's lists through 1884.

30. Laura flees to the New World to escape the unwelcome attentions of Hargrave. In the wilds of Canada she falls among savages, but not noble ones. Even this unnerving experience confirms her faith in a wise Providence, for, as the pious farmer who rescues her observes, had she not been strapped to the canoe by the Indians, the force of the rapids would have hurled her to her death. "I declare I do not know whether Laura's passage down the American River is not the most natural, possible everyday thing she does," wrote Miss Austen to Cassandra (see note 28 above). More than a year later she wrote peevishly to her friend Anna Lefroy, taking umbrage at an unidentified friend's adverse criticism of *Mansfield Park:* "I will redeem my credit with him, by writing a close imitation of Self Control as soon as I can; I will improve upon it;—my Heroine shall not merely be wafted down an American river in a boat by herself, she shall cross the Atlantic in the same way &

never stop until she reaches Gravesend" (November or December, 1814, *Letters*, p. 423) . She seems to have kept the promise when drawing up her *Plan of a Novel*, in which the harassed heroine and her father, "hunted out of civilized Society, denied the poor shelter of the humblest cottage," are transported to Kamschatka. Eventually the heroine "crawls back towards her former Country—having at least 20 narrow escapes of falling into the hands of the Anti-hero." (The MS of *Plan of a Novel* is in the Pierpont Morgan Library, New York City; it was first printed in William Austen-Leigh and Richard Arthur Austen-Leigh, *Jane Austen: Her Life and Letters. A Family Record* [New York, 1913], pp. 337–40.)

31. According to her record, Miss Austen began *Mansfield Park* "somewhere about February, 1811," and finished it "soon after June 1813." (See notes appended to *Plan of a Novel*.) Its inception coincides with the first publication of *Self-Control*.

32. Among her cherished memories of childhood was a visit by Johnson when he unwittingly used her shoulder as a wig block. She is best remembered for her two volumes of *Memoirs, Anecdotes, Facts and Opinions* (1822, 1824) , in which are preserved conversations and impressions of many of the numerous celebrities of the eighteenth century entertained by Sir John Hawkins in the family home at Twickenham. She offered them to posterity as "experience that can be useful, or true occurrences which may inform the unwary, or teach those who may be smarting under the injustice of the world, to despise its corrections, as long as they stand firm in the acquittal of their own consciences" (Preface, Vol. I) . Her fiction was intended to serve a similar exemplary purpose.

33. December, 1814, *Letters*, p. 422. In *Rosanne,* a young lady is won away from the corrupting influences of a worldly father, libertine society, and French sentimentalism by the example of two daughters of a country gentleman who have been brought up on Christian principles.

34. She contrasts the ideal Lady Startwell with the miserly Lady Pennywise. The later novel *Rosanne* was dedicated to a noble patroness, the Countess of Waldegrave, who had pointed out by her example "the inestimable advantages attendant on the practice of pure Christianity." A Minerva Press publication of the same year as *Rosanne* and *Mansfield Park* was *The Prison House; or, The World We Live In* by Bridget Bluemantle (pseudonym of a minister's wife, Elizabeth Thomas) . In this novel a young orphan becomes a domestic in the house of a family of quality—the Modishes—and is disillusioned to

discover that aristocratic men and women do not live in accordance with the precepts of the Bible.

35. *Popular Essays,* Introduction, p. xxxvi. Essays IV and V are devoted respectively to "The Idea of Self" and "The Benevolent Affections."

36. This was one of the opinions recorded in *Plan of a Novel.* The reader is identified as Lady Gordon.

37. Ibid., Lady Rab.

38. March 23, 1817, to Fanny Knight, *Letters,* p. 486.

39. Here Edmund is making a fine eighteenth-century distinction between the permanent disposition of the mind or soul and a character trait that is subject to change or influence. In the *OED* the following lines from Pope's *Essay on Man* are cited to illustrate the meaning of *principle:*

> Two principles in human nature reign:
> Self-love to urge, and Reason to restrain.

Temper is illustrated by this passage from Blair's *Sermons:* "Temper is the disposition which remains after these emotions are past; and which forms the habitual propensity of the soul."

40. I disagree with A. Walton Litz, who contends that in *Mansfield Park* Jane Austen made a heroine of a girl who is "essentially passive and uninteresting, and in doing so she deliberately rejected the principle of growth and change which animates most English fiction" (*Jane Austen,* p. 129). Fanny undergoes a process of what we call today directed change. Actually, she is the only one of Jane Austen's heroines whom we watch grow from childhood into maturity.

41. Cf. Litz: "The form of *Mansfield Park* expresses all too clearly that the values of art are not the ultimate ones" (*Jane Austen,* p. 130).

42. November 6, 1813, *Letters,* p. 370.

43. November 18, 1814, *Letters,* p. 410.

44. Henrietta Ten Harmsel conjectures that with *Mansfield Park* Jane Austen "sensed the ill effects of overt didacticism and decided to present the theme and the conventional elements of *Emma* in a much subtler and more effective way" (*Jane Austen,* p. 129). I think *Emma* is as didactic as *Mansfield Park,* with the heroine coming under the guidance of a secular mentor (Mr. Knightley) rather than a religious one.

45. Review of *Emma, Quarterly Review,* XIV (October, 1815), 188–201.

46. Review of *The Abbot, Monthly Review,* XCIII (September, 1820), 81–82.

47. "The Novels of Jane Austen," *Blackwood's Magazine,* LXXXVI (July, 1859), 112–13. Carrying on the analogy with painting, habitual with Victorian as well as Romantic critics, Lewes thought of Miss Austen's novels as "miniatures" compared with Scott's "frescoes." "Her place is among the Immortals," he concludes his essay, "but the pedestal is erected in a quiet niche of the great temple."

48. *Northanger Abbey,* Ch. II, summing up Catherine Morland's attributes.

49. Barbara Bail Collins calls *Mansfield Park* "the earliest of the great Victorian novels" in her article "Jane Austen's Victorian Novel," *Nineteenth-Century Fiction,* IV (December, 1949), 175–85. Curiously, she considers its didacticism and praise of "the advantages of early hardship and discipline" a "foreign note" in Jane Austen's writing, which makes it "a new novel, a novel with a message." To Miss Collins, *Mansfield Park* is "a forerunner of the dowdy propriety and piety which blossomed in the fifties." Are *The Daisy Chain, The Newcomes,* and *The Mill on the Floss* "dowdy"? More recently, Thomas R. Edwards, Jr., in "The Difficult Beauty of Mansfield Park," *Nineteenth-Century Fiction,* XX (June, 1965), 51–67, praises its fusion of morality and art. He concludes that here Miss Austen gives conscience and moral influence "a fullness of treatment not to be equalled with the triumphs of George Eliot and James" (p. 55). Along with some other modern critics, he believes, without offering evidence, that Miss Austen praises Fanny and Edmund with tongue in cheek.

IV. *Oliver Twist:* The Fortunate Foundling

1. The background information supplied by Humphry House in *The Dickens World* (London, 1960) is supplemented by Edgar Johnson, *Charles Dickens: His Tragedy and Triumph* (New York, 1952), I, 275.

2. Summarized by John Manning in *Dickens on Education* (Toronto, 1959), pp. 17–18; p. 150.

3. Ibid., p. 18.

4. "The Political Young Gentleman," *Sketches of Young Gentlemen,* Standard Library Edition (Boston, 1894), XXVIII, 243. *Sketches of Young Gentlemen* was first published by Chapman and Hall in 1838.

5. Preface to *Elizabeth and Her Three Beggar Boys* (1830).

6. The Foundling Hospital owns an unpublished letter dated

February 26, 1840 from Dickens to Brownlow apologizing for not having given notice of change of residence and relinquishing his pew in the chapel. By now the prosperous author had moved from Doughty Street to Regent's Park.

7. In connection with Oliver's famous asking for more, it might be noted that after 1840 the allowance of meat, potatoes, bread and butter was increased, and oatmeal was discontinued altogether (R. H. Nichols and F. A. Wray, *The History of the Foundling Hospital* [London, 1935], pp. 277–78).

8. Although the serialization of *Oliver Twist* in *Bentley's Miscellany*, which began in February, 1837, extended to April, 1839, its first edition in book form appeared on November 9, 1838. This burletta by George Almar, staged just ten days later at the Royal Surrey Theatre, has the dubious distinction of being the first to be based on the entire novel. At least three earlier dramatizations were on the boards during the previous spring, before Dickens had even completed the writing of the story. (For the stage record, see Forster's *Life of Dickens*, ed. J. W. T. Ley [London, 1928], p. 129.) According to Kathleen Tillotson ("Oliver Twist," *Essays and Studies*, 1959, pp. 87–88), Dickens had finished only two-thirds of the novel by mid-July, 1838. Almar's version, which had a revival as late as 1893, is reprinted in Lacy's *Acting Edition of Plays*, Vol. 33, No. 494 (1858).

9. The name given in the serial version to the village where Oliver was born—Mudfog—suggested a continuation of *The Mudfog Papers*, another set of pieces that Dickens contributed to *Bentley's Miscellany*. In subsequent editions the place is referred to merely as "a certain town, which for many reasons it will be prudent to refrain from mentioning and to which I will assign no fictitious name."

Apart from his sketch writing, Dickens had some theatrical reputation at this time as collaborator with John Hullah of a musical farce, *The Village Coquettes,* and sole author of a burletta, *The Strange Gentleman*. Many years later he requested that the composer leave his name off a republication of *The Village Coquettes*. (See *Dickens' Correspondence with John Hullah* [Printed by Walter Dexter for His Friends, September, 1933], p. 19.)

10. The critic for the *London and Westminster Review* admired the *Sketches by Boz* for their wit, humor, and keen observation, but thought they tended toward monotony because of their slightness and repetitiousness. He observed of the *Pickwick Papers* that while their author hits off "little traits of conduct" and describes "the more obvious peculiarities of mind and person" nicely, "he does not appear to

appreciate the minute shades of characters; and, above all, he shows no particular skill in developing character in action" (July, 1837, pp. 198–99) . However, this reviewer detected signs of maturity in *Oliver Twist,* which he found "indeed remarkable, as a specimen of a style rather more serious and pathetic than any other of the author's longer works" (p. 213) . The critic for the *Quarterly Review,* having feared on the basis of a "decline visible in the later number of Pickwick" that Boz' talent was in danger of running into the ground, was pleased to find that in the first numbers of *Oliver Twist* "there is a sustained power, a range of observation, and a continuity of interest in this series, which we seek in vain in any other of his works" (October, 1837, p. 518) .

11. So called by the critic for the *London and Westminster Review* (cited in note 10 above) .

12. According to Forster, he lay on the floor of his box practically throughout the performance that he attended. (See *The Life of Charles Dickens,* ed. Ley, p. 125.)

13. Dickens defends himself here against periodical reviewers who, unlike the writer of the playbill quoted above, had denounced *Oliver Twist* as vicious and obscene. See particularly *Atlas,* November 17, 1838; *Spectator,* November 24, 1838; and *Quarterly Review,* June, 1839.

14. Elizabeth Longford, *Queen Victoria: Born to Succeed* (New York, 1964) , p. 90.

15. Oxford Thackeray, ed. George Saintsbury (London, 1908) , III, 185.

16. For the best account to date, admittedly tentative, of its tangled textual history, see Kathleen Tillotson, *"Oliver Twist* in Three Volumes," *The Library,* 5th Series, XVIII (1963) , 113–32.

17. October 6, 1859, from Gad's Hill Place. *Letters of Charles Dickens to Wilkie Collins, 1851–1870,* ed. Laurence Hutton (London, 1892), p. 104.

18. *Athenaeum,* October 26, 1839, p. 804.

19. J. Hain Friswell, "Mr. Charles Dickens," *Modern Men of Letters Honestly Criticised* (London, 1870) , pp. 133–34.

20. *Quarterly Review,* p. 484. This reviewer affirms that "the portrait of the author of 'Pelham' or 'Crichton' was scraped down or pasted over to make room for that of the new popular favourite in the omnibuses." However, the advent of Dickens hardly ended the vogue of Ainsworth and Bulwer.

21. CH. IV begins: "In great families, when an advantageous place cannot be obtained, either in possession, reversion, remainder, or

expectancy, for the young man who is growing up, it is a very general custom to send him to sea. The board, in imitation of so wise and salutary an example, took counsel together on the expediency of shipping off Oliver Twist in some small trading vessel bound to a good unhealthy port. . . .'' Advertisements of such novels as Captain Glascock's *Land Sharks and Sea Gulls,* Cooper's *Homeward Bound,* and Captain Chamier's *Life of a Sailor* and *Ben Brace* formed a fitting backdrop to this passage.

22. Quite possibly an allusion to Mrs. Gore's *Pin Money* (1831).

23. He progressively combed out "damns" and other oaths, even references to profanity, from his manuscript and the serial version as he revised it for subsequent editions. (See Tillotson, "Oliver Twist," *Essays and Studies,* p. 100.)

24. *Cecil the Peer,* I, CH. II.

25. Book II, CH. I ("Society and Manners"), pp. 97–98.

26. W. Massie, *Sydenham; or, Memoirs of a Man of the World,* CH. VI.

27. *Athenaeum,* October 26, 1839, p. 804. Thackeray, ridiculing *Oliver Twist* among other "Newgate novels" in his mock-novel *Catherine,* seems not to have recognized that Dickens' book was related in genre to his own. Both authors were making an analogy between society and criminal life, in imitation of *The Beggar's Opera.*

Early in his career the writer with whom Dickens was most frequently associated was Theodore Hook. Hook preceded Dickens as a chronicler of town life, and his popularity as a humorist grew out of various devices that we now associate with Dickens, such as the clumping of quaint detail, whimsical "humours" characters, and the exposure of fraud and humbug. A typical butt of ridicule for Hook was the middle-class parvenu, such as Gervase Skinner, Peregrine Bunce, Jack Brag, and young Danvers. Dickens extended this line of satire down to the lower depths. For detailed parallels between Hook and Dickens, see Myron F. Brightfield, *Theodore Hook and His Novels* (Cambridge, Mass., 1928), pp. 313–31.

28. *The Beggar Girl,* Mrs. Bennett's fifth novel, first published in 1797 by the Minerva Press, reached a third edition in 1813, five years after the author's death. Although it does not appear on Mudie's lists, it is reported late in the century that it was at that time "still a popular 'number' book and shares the pantry shelf with *Pamela, Fatherless Fanny,* and a host of similar rubbish" (*Notes and Queries,* 4th Series, VIII [December 9, 1871], 348).

29. Written on the flyleaf of his copy of *Conciones ad Populum* (1795) . (See Blakey, *The Minerva Press,* p. 54.) In a letter of April 8, 1820 to his friend Thomas Allsop, Coleridge placed her in distinguished company by affirming that he never found in all of Scott "a character that approaches Parson Adams, Blifil, Strap, Lieutenant Bowling, Mr. Shandy, Uncle Toby, Trim, Lovelace, Miss Byron, Clementina, Emily or Betty in Mrs. Bennett's Beggar Girl" *(Letters, Conversations and Recollections,* ed. Thomas Allsop [New York, 1836], p. 40) . In *Table Talk* he spoke in similar glowing terms of Rosa's benefactor Colonel Buhanun, and, according to his nephew, "the character was frequently a subject of pleasant description and enlargement with Mr. Coleridge and he generally passed from it to a high commendation of Miss Austen's novels" (Coleridge, *Complete Works,* ed. Shedd [New York, 1854], VI, 305) .

30. Some years later, Miss Mitford, author of *Our Village,* wrote to her friend Barbara Hofland: "The prodigious quantity of invention, the identity of the characters, particularly a certain Mrs. Feversham and Betty Brown, and above all a total absence of moral maxims of the do-me-good air which one expects to find in Miss Edgeworth gives a certain freshness and truth to the *Beggar Girl,* which I never found in any fiction except that of Miss Austen" *(Letters,* ed. Henry Chorley [London, 1872], I, 68) .

31. In its first appearance the story was entitled "Elizabeth and Her Boys; or, The Beggar's Story."

32. In the longer version that appears in *Tales of the Priory* are two comic characters who prefigure Mr. Bumble and Mrs. Corney—the mean and avaricious parish beadle Mr. Gunner and his shrewish wife. Like Dickens' officious beadle, Gunner suffers so from the nagging of his Xantippe that he takes it out on the poor boys under his supervision.

33. The only copy of *Hans Sloane* that I have been able to locate is, appropriately, in the British Museum. The sketch of Brownlow in Nichols and Wray's *The History of the Foundling Hospital* (pp. 277–78) refers to this book mistakenly as a biography of Sir Hans Sloane. Brownlow subsequently expanded the historical sections of his book in *Memoranda; or, Chronicles of the Foundling Hospital, Including Memoirs of Captain Coram* (London, 1847) , and *The History and Design of the Foundling Hospital* (1858; four editions by 1881) , but the fictitious interlude concerned with the orphan Hans was dropped.

34. Although Dickens left the neighborhood of the Foundling Hospital after *Oliver Twist* made him rich (see note 6 above), his

interest in the institution did not cease. As late as *Little Dorrit* (1855) he has the Meagles change the name of Harriet Beadle to Tattycoram after the "blessed creature" who founded the home they took her from. Among the documents preserved at the hospital is a copy of a Christmas number of *All the Year Round* (December, 1868) inscribed by the editor. Brownlow rose to the position of Secretary of the Foundling Hospital in 1849, retaining this office until his retirement in 1872. On this occasion, the Governors, granting him a superannuation allowance, wished him "that full measure of ease and comfort which he has so well earned by a course of life singularly disinterested, benevolent and charitable" (Nichols and Wray, p. 278). He lived a year and a half beyond his retirement, surviving Dickens by three years.

35. *National Magazine*, December, 1837, pp. 445–46. This was the most enthusiastic of the early reviews. It is assigned to Lewes in *The Letters of Charles Dickens* (Pilgrim Edition), I, 403, n. 5.

36. Among critics who have traced Carlylean ideas and imagery in Dickens' novels are: Arthur A. Adrian, "Dickens on American Slavery: A Carlylean Slant," *PMLA*, LXVII (June, 1952), 315–29; Kathleen Tillotson, *"Barnaby Rudge," Dickens at Work* (London, 1958), p. 84; John Butt, "The Topicality of *Bleak House*," *Dickens at Work*, p. 178.

37. Carlyle describes the very section of London in which CH. XXVI of *Oliver Twist* takes place, even anticipating Dickens' detail about the goods on display: "Field Lane, with its long fluttering rows of yellow handkerchiefs . . . where, in stifled jarring hubbub, we hear the Indictment which Poverty and Vice bring against lazy Wealth, that it has left them there cast-out and trodden under foot of Want, Darkness and the Devil. . . ." ("Old Clothes"). Cf. Dickens' description, quoted above, where Carlyle's "rag-fair" is depicted literally.

Thackeray's *Catherine* and *Oliver Twist* also have in common the influence of *Sartor Resartus*. Thackeray illustrates the idea that "Society is founded upon Cloth" through the ease with which his criminals are able to simulate class by simply disguising themselves. He goes so far as to introduce as a character in his mock-novel a tailor named Bein-kleider, "a German . . . skilful in his trade (after the manner of his nation, which in breeches and metaphysics—in inexpressibles and incomprehensibles—may instruct all Europe) ."

38. February 4, 1846. Reprinted in *Works,* Gadshill Edition (London, 1908), XXXV, 25–29.

39. J. Hain Friswell wrote of *Oliver Twist* that "amidst vice, depravity, cunning, theft, and murder, the author treads firmly and

cleanly, and teaches us that best of lessons—to pity the guilty while we hate the guilt. . . ." (*Modern Men of Letters Honestly Criticised*, p. 14).

40. It is now generally assumed that through Rose Maylie, Dickens was in part releasing his sorrow over the untimely death of Mary Hogarth, which occurred while he was writing *Oliver Twist*.

V. *Pendennis*: Arthur Pendennis and the Reformed Coxcomb

1. Edgar Johnson, *Charles Dickens*, I, 220.

2. "A Box of Books," *Fraser's Magazine*, February, 1844, pp. 153–69.

3. Letter to his mother, Mrs. Carmichael-Smyth, January 7, 1848, *Letters and Private Papers of William Makepeace Thackeray*, ed. Gordon N. Ray (Cambridge, Mass., 1944), II, 333 (hereafter referred to *Letters*).

4. "Thackeray and Dickens, Dickens and Thackeray—the two names now almost necessarily go together," begins one of the early reviews ("Arthur Pendennis and David Copperfield," *North British Review*, XV [May, 1851], 57). This reviewer observes that "the public has learned to think of them in indissoluble connection as friendly competitors for the prize of light literature." *David Copperfield* and *Pendennis* were both published by the same firm, Bradbury and Evans, and were frequently reviewed together.

5. Letter to Lady Holland, March 28, 1848, quoted in Gordon N. Ray, *Thackeray: The Uses of Wisdom* (New York, 1958), p. 40. The change was figurative rather than literal, for *Pendennis* was first issued in the same "jaundiced" covers as *Vanity Fair*. The "rose colour" refers to the covers of his Christmas books, such as *Our Street* and *Mrs. Perkins' Ball*.

6. Review of *The Book of Snobs, Morning Chronicle*, March 6, 1848.

7. *The Leader*, December 21, 1850, pp. 929–30.

8. These phrases appear in one of Thackeray's first articles, "Hints for a History of Highwaymen," *Fraser's Magazine*, IX (1834), 279–87, in which he reviewed Charles Whitehead's *Lives and Exploits of English Highwaymen, Pirates and Robbers* and indirectly set forth his program as a writer. See Robert A. Colby, "*Catherine*: Thackeray's Credo," *Review of English Studies*, XV (November, 1964), 391–96.

9. The original publication points up this scheme more emphatically than the present editions, each monthly part ending with some moral crisis or other in Pen's career.

10. *North British Review*, XIII (August, 1850), 335–36.

11. Lewes thought *Pendennis* an advance over *Vanity Fair* in its substance, as well as balance of tone, "a great, a masterly work, weighty with knowledge, luminous with beautiful thoughts, caustic, subtle, pathetic. . . ." (*The Leader*, p. 930).

12. In a letter written to his friend Mrs. Sartoris late in 1850, Thackeray comments on the recent conversion of a friend of theirs: "And have you heard how Miss Adelaide Procter has been received into the one true and indivisible Church Catholic Apostolic and Roman? That is the chief news about our friends and I don't care for it, do you?" This passage does not appear in the portion of this letter printed in *Letters*, II, 701–4. The original is in the Fales Collection, New York University.

13. Thackeray intrudes here his own memory of French politics, with which he gained some familiarity as Paris correspondent for the short-lived newspaper *The Constitutional*. Among other things, he commented on the attempts of Thiers to regain popular favor after his ousting as premier, and the longwindedness of his rival Guizot. See Harold Strong Gulliver, *Thackeray's Literary Apprenticeship* (Valdosta, Georgia, 1937), CH. V.

14. Thackeray, disturbed by similarities between *Pendennis* and *David Copperfield* as the two novels were being issued in monthly parts (e.g. analogous characters like Agnes Wickfield and Laura Bell; Dora Spenlow and Warrington's unnamed child wife; Traddles and Warrington; as well as analogous episodes like the school scenes), introduced the Fleet Street episodes in an effort to outdistance his rival.

15. Thackeray betrays his own youthful conflict over romantic poetry in a letter to his mother in the middle of 1829, when he was a student at Cambridge: "I think I said I should bring home Shellys [sic] Revolt of Islam with me, but I have rather altered my opinion, for it is an odd kind of book, containing poetry which would induce one to read it through, and sentiments which would strongly incline one to throw it in the fire" (*Letters*, I, 74).

16. Her stepfather Colonel Altamont (whom Thackeray claims in his preface to have saved from hanging at the last minute) is best appreciated as a parody of one of these "high souled convicts" combined with the Sue-Dumas hero. See Thackeray's article "Thieves' Literature of France," *Foreign Quarterly Review*, April, 1843, pp. 231–49, in which he reviewed Sue's *Les Mystères de Paris* and glanced at other French writers of the galley-and-gallows school.

17. Thackeray undoubtedly was rationalizing his own failure at law study. One of the more literal-minded reviewers took him to task for his belittling of Paley: "There may be too great engrossment in any one pursuit, but Mr. Paley might have been supporting his mother, while Mr. Pendennis was impoverishing his" ("*David Copperfield* and *Pendennis*," *Prospective Review*, VII [1851], 173).

18. On the basis of a conjecture by Thackeray's daughter Lady Ritchie, the prototype of Warrington has been thought to be Edward Fitzgerald, with whom Thackeray was friendly at Cambridge and afterward (see *Works*, Centenary Biographical ed., II, xxx). Contemporary reviewers, however, like Lewes and the critic for the *North British Review* (May, 1851), detected character traits of Thackeray in Warrington. This binary relationship is suggested by John W. Dodds in *Thackeray: A Critical Portrait* (New York, 1941), pp. 152–53. Pen enjoys Thackeray's literary success, but Warrington has the unfortunate marriage.

19. *Times,* January 11, 1838.

20. *Character Sketches, Works* (Oxford ed.), I, 565–66; *Works* (Biographical ed.), VIII, 353.

21. *Fraser's Magazine,* March, 1838; reprinted: *Comic Tales and Sketches* (1841); *Miscellanies,* II (1856); *Works* (Oxford ed.), I, 207–18. Nevertheless, as Matthew Whiting Rosa points out, Thackeray used Lady Charlotte's *Diary* as a source for *The Four Georges* (see his *The Silver Fork Novel* [New York, 1936], p. 156).

22. On February 12, 1828 he wrote to his mother from Charterhouse: "I have not read any novel this term except one by the Author of *Granby* [*Herbert Lacy,* published in 1828, seems to be the novel referred to], not so good as *Granby*" (*Letters,* I, 22). According to Matthew Rosa, "The fashionable novel, as opposed to the novel which for didactic or romantic reasons uses fashionable people, was firmly established by *Granby*" (*The Silver Fork Novel,* p. 70). *Granby* maintained its vogue into midcentury, as indicated by its appearance on Mudie's lists for 1848 and 1858. A minor character in *Pendennis* is named Granby Tiptoff (CH. XXIX).

23. He pays Miss Austen a lateral compliment through the feather-brained Lady Harriet Duncan, who engages in literary chatter with the dandy Trebeck (modeled after Beau Brummell): "But tell me your favourite novels. I hope you like nothing of Miss Edgeworth's or Miss Austen's. They are full of commonplace people that one recognises at once. You cannot think how I was disappointed in Northanger Abbey and Castle Rack-rent, for the titles did really promise something. Have

you a taste for romance? You have? I am glad of it" (I, 149–50) . Lady Harriet prefers *Melmoth the Wanderer,* Mary Shelley's *Valperga,* and De la Motte Fouqué's *Peter Schlemihl.*

24. It concludes Rosa's study of the genre.

25. *Pendennis* is not "the first true Bildungsroman in English fiction," as Gordon Ray asserts (*The Uses of Wisdom,* p. 110) , but it is one of the best of them. *Waverley* is really the earliest forerunner that has survived.

26. This passage, which echoes one about George Osborne in *Vanity Fair* (CH. XXIX) , does not appear in all editions of *Pendennis,* being part of the matter describing "the disreputable Mr. Bloundell" that Thackeray dropped from the edition published in 1864, the last that he revised. See *Works* (Oxford ed.) , XII, Appendix, note 6 to p. 228.

27. Ravenna, February 16, 1821, *Works of Lord Byron,* ed. Rowland E. Prothero (London, 1922) , XII, 242.

28. The name alludes to Hook's reputation as a practical joker and punster. In connection with his youthful prank known as the Berners-Street Hoax, the *Times* of October 31, 1809 referred to the then unknown perpetrator as "some wag." The hero of *Gilbert Gurney,* modeled after his creator, writes a farce called "Wag in the Windmill."

29. For evidence of Hook's popularity from 1825 until his death in 1841, see Myron F. Brightfield, *Theodore Hook and His Novels* (Cambridge, Mass., 1928) , especially the Introduction and CH. VIII. In an article in *Fraser's Magazine,* April, 1834, Thackeray praised Hook as a humorist, but deplored his hackneyed plots and weakly drawn characters. Brightfield summarizes Thackeray's critical opinion of Hook (pp. 331–33) .

30. Brightfield notes the analogue (p. 336) . Thackeray intrudes a sly reference to Hook's story in CH. XIII of *Pendennis,* where he mentions a "Mr. Skinner of this city, a most respectable Grocer and Wine and Spirit Merchant and a Member of the Society of Friends" whom some actors in Captain Costigan's company have fleeced out of payment. At one point in Hook's story, Gervase Skinner, priding himself on his benevolence, despite his stinginess, throws open his wine cellar to his friends, who respond by draining him of his store and walking off also with the "comestibles of the commissariat" which he had laid by like a squirrel. In most other respects the story of Gervase Skinner diverges from that of Pendennis. Gervase is not a fledgling, but a somewhat overgrown gull of forty-three, and it takes an elopement with the actress (who is already married) and desertion by her to bring him to his senses.

Harold Strong Gulliver has attributed to Thackeray, on the basis of a close prefiguring of the Fotheringay episode, a piece called "Early Life and Early Loves of a College Graduate Narrated by Himself," which appeared in the *Torch*, November 11, 1837, a publication for which Thackeray is known to have written. In this humorous essay the narrator recollects his naive infatuation for an actress performing at Cambridge on tour, who seemed to him at the time the personification of innocence, natural grace, and beauty. (See *Thackeray's Literary Apprenticeship*, pp. 131–32.)

31. In the *Fraser's* review cited above (note 29), Thackeray wrote: "Would that he would at some time or other seriously sit down to write what he knows! A novel from Hook, with Sheridan, for instance, as a hero . . . and with Hook's own compotators and companions for characters, and the adventures of Hook himself and friends for incidents, would be a work that would bring us back to the days of *Tom Jones* and *Humphry Clinker*." (Quoted by Brightfield, p. 333.) To a limited degree, Hook complied with *Gilbert Gurney*, substituting Colman (who is introduced in CH. II) for Sheridan.

32. Brightfield points out a similarity in tone and material between *Gilbert Gurney* and *Mon Voisin Raymond* by Paul de Kock (p. 290). Thackeray also seems to have drawn on this popular vulgarian. An escapade of de Kock's Raymond anticipates Pen's embarrassment with Fanny Bolton. De Kock's young boulevardier takes up with a flower girl, brings her to his room to seduce her, fails to accomplish his goal but is accused by his sister of having an affair with her—on the evidence of compromising appearances. Also, there is a roughhouse scene in the Tivoli Gardens of Paris that resembles the Vauxhall episode of *Pendennis*. De Kock is mentioned several times in *Pendennis*. He translated *The Great Hoggarty Diamond* into French.

33. "Lords and Liveries" first appeared in *Punch* on June 12, 26, 1847. It is reprinted: *Miscellanies* II (1856); *Works* (Biographical ed.), VIII, 66–78; *Works* (Oxford ed.), VIII, 114–25.

34. Ray, *The Uses of Wisdom*, p. 53.

35. *Letters*, II, 724–25. Thackeray remained in correspondence with Mrs. Gore at least through 1860, when he wrote to her to deny that Colonel Newcome was based on a character in her *The Banker's Wife* (*Letters*, IV, 196). On July 11, 1860, Thackeray wrote to his friend Henry Wadsworth Longfellow to introduce Mrs. Gore's son, Captain Augustus Gore, who was then making a trip to America (unpublished letter, Fales Collection, New York University).

NOTES FOR PAGES 163 TO 165

36. Letter to Mrs. Procter, from Paris, March 19, 1841, *Letters*, II, 13.
The error is easily explained. In her preface to the first edition of *Cecil*,
Mrs. Gore lampoons critics by quoting a pompous discourse on
Flippancy from a *Times* review. The article quoted was actually a
review of Thackeray's *Comic Tales and Sketches,* a series which he had
published under the pseudonym Michael Angelo Titmarsh. (See review
of *Cecil* in the *Athenaeum*, March 6, 1841, p. 186.)

37. May 24, 1832, *Letters*, I, 203.

38. One of these tales, "Hearts and Diamonds," is cited by Thackeray
among the previous works of the authoress of "Lords and Liveries." In
this tale, by the way, is introduced a Lady Clendennis, a religious
woman from Devonshire, who feels out of place in London society.

39. The reviewer of *The Fair of Mayfair* in the *Westminster Review*,
a journal generally indifferent to fiction, impressed by "the ultimate
triumph of sincerity and integrity" in her work, concluded, "If we are
to have fashionable novels at all, let them be by Mrs. Gore" (October,
1833, p. 478). Mrs. Gore came to the Silver Fork novel after Bulwer,
Disraeli, and Lady Charlotte Bury had made it popular. Before that she
had tried her hand at historical romance with *Theresa Marchmont*
(1824) and *The Lettre de Cachet* (1827) and had some success also as a
playwright and song writer. Her later career parallels Thackeray's, both
moving from the fashion novel into the *familienroman*. Mrs. Gore
averaged some six books a year during her three and a half decades of
literary activity, with a total output of close to two hundred volumes.

40. Now in middle age he recalls vividly the literary fashions of the
turn of the century. The exotic French dinners of those lavish times
linger in his memory, "black, spicy, opaque and mysterious as one of
Radcliffe's romances." Among versifiers, "The severest poetry tolerated
by May Fair was that of Hayley, William Spencer and Samuel Rogers.
In short, people had supped full of horrors during the Revolution, and
were now devoted to elegiac measures." As for drama, "the sentimental
school was in the ascendant. People cried at 'The Stranger' or 'Pen-
ruddock' on the stage." Tastes apparently had not changed much by the
1820's, for young Pen also weeps while watching Miss Fotheringay
perform as Mrs. Haller.

41. Another passage in *Cecil* describes the siren figure pictured by
Thackeray. Cecil thinks of his false love as a wicked enchantress:

She was a *feu follet,* a will-o'-the-wisp—'Earth has its bubbles and
she was one of them.' I thought of Melusina the sorceress, beloved
by the Comte de Poitiers, whose face was that of an angel, whose

body was that of a serpent. I thought—but why recapitulate the foolish fancies of a lover or madman?—after all, if I had fallen into the snare of an enchantress, there was some pride in having retained, after a college education, the generous weakness which admits of being a dupe. (II, CH. I)

42. In a letter to Lady Blessington, August 20, 1848, announcing that he was about to begin *Pendennis,* he promised her a story for the Annual the following year. This story, "An Interesting Event," is reprinted in *Stray Papers,* ed. Lewis Melville (London, 1901), pp. 259–65.

43. Marmaduke's "fatal error" is hardly any less venial than young Pen's with Fanny Bolton, but it leads to far more dire consequences. Young Herbert kisses a young lady while she is asleep in a wood, causing her to run off and dash herself to death by a fall from a cliff. The hero subsequently marries the ill-fated maiden's sister, keeping his guilty secret to himself, but feels impelled to reveal it to his young daughter—the occasion for his memoirs. Thackeray simultaneously exploits and parodies Lady Blessington's plot devices involving obscure parentage and the return of lost fathers (cf. the Amory-Altamont business in *Pendennis*). Not infrequently, a threat of incest hovers over the young lovers. In *Meredith,* for example, the hero has reason to suspect that his beloved Selina is the daughter of Lady Mellingcourt by his own father, but all ends well when it develops that she is really the stolen child of an Italian duke and duchess. Thackeray, in an ingenious inversion of this hackneyed theme, plays with the reader by referring to Laura intermittently as Pen's "sister" because she has been adopted by Helen, but does not trick us into believing that she really is.

44. There is a transition to *Pendennis* in Thackeray's *Punch* sketches "Mr. Brown's Letters to His Nephew" (March 24–August 18, 1849) which ran concurrently with the first numbers of *Pendennis,* in which the title character advises his young relative, who has just completed his academic studies and is about to commence his career in London, "in respect of your pleasures, amusements, acquaintances, and general conduct as a young man of the world." At a club to which the elder Mr. Brown takes the younger, a member is snoring over Number 7 of *Pendennis. David Copperfield* is also lying on a reading table. These letters are reprinted: *Miscellanies,* II (1856) ; *Works* (Oxford ed.) , VIII, 259–345; *Works* (Biographical ed.) , IX, 229–78.

45. *"David Copperfield* and *Pendennis," Prospective Review,* p. 177.

46. *The Leader,* December 21, 1850, p. 929. "Disraeli sees society—not

very clearly, but he sees it," wrote Lewes; "Thackeray sees it, and sees through it, sees all the human feelings, all the motives, high and low, simple and complicated, which make it what it is . . . he seizes *characters,* where other writers seize only *characteristics;* he does not give you a peculiarity for the man, he places the man himself, that 'bundle of motives' before you."

47. Thackeray was probably indirectly criticizing his own mother's possessiveness and prudery here. Some months before the Fanny Bolton section was written, Mrs. Carmichael-Smyth had readily believed a rumor that her son was having an affair with the children's governess. (See Gordon N. Ray, "The Love of Thackeray for Mrs. Brookfield," *Listener,* August 4, 1949, p. 197.)

48. Thackeray frequently took advantage of the picaresque form of his narrative to intrude his own emotional preoccupations. The publication of the Fanny Bolton episode coincided with a hiatus in his relationship with Mrs. Brookfield, and Pen's flirtation with Fanny was presumably the author's way of suggesting to his ideal lady that he might take up with a trull on the rebound. Mrs. Brookfield commented on this portion of the story, in a tone that echoes Laura's reaction: "I liked a *great deal* of this June [1850] number, but cannot help being sorry you dignify the F. B. fancy with the name of 'love'—it seems degrading to apply it to the dear little girl who drops her H's" (Ray, *Listener,* pp. 196–98) .

49. In a generally patronizing recent article, Thackeray is praised for his manipulation of "a perpetual, deliberate and ironic ambiguity," and his ability to show us characters under shifting lights and from varied points of view. (See Martin Fido, *"The History of Pendennis:* A Reconsideration," *Essays in Criticism,* XIV [October, 1964], 363–79.

50. It has been suggested that Miss Bunion is a composite of Felicia Hemans and Laetitia Elizabeth Landon ("L.E.L.") . (See *Cambridge History of English Literature,* XII, 138.) Miss Landon is the more likely prototype, having lived in Brompton, as does Miss Bunion, been linked with Maginn, and written for Colburn. Besides, one of her most famous poems, "Violets," was parodied by Thackeray in a projected but never published magazine, "The Carthusian." (See Ray, *The Uses of Adversity,* pp. 90–91.) This parody, entitled "Cabbages," is reprinted in *Works* (Centenary Biographical ed., VIII, xxi) .

51. "Vanitas Vanitatum," *Works* (Centenary Biographical ed.) , XV, 127–29.

52. *Novels and Novelists from Elizabeth to Victoria* (London, 1858) , II, 28.

VI. *Villette:* Lucy Snowe and the Good Governess

1. Letter to W. S. Williams, December 11, 1847. The Shakespeare Head Brontë, ed. Thomas J. Wise and John Alexander Symington (London, 1931–38), *Life and Letters,* II, 160. Hereafter referred to as SHB, *Life and Letters.*

2. Letter to W. S. Williams, August 14, 1848, SHB, *Life and Letters,* II, 244; letter to W. S. Williams, March 29, 1848, SHB, *Life and Letters,* II, 201; letter to W. S. Williams, December 11, 1847, SHB, *Life and Letters,* II, 160.

3. Mrs. Humphry Ward, in her introduction to the Haworth Edition of *Villette* (London, 1899), points out the similarity between Lucy Snowe's reactions to Monsieur Paul's lectures at the Hôtel Crécy (CH. XXVII) and Miss Brontë's reactions to Thackeray's second lecture on the English Humorists, which she heard in Willis's Rooms in London. The publication of Thackeray's lectures is announced at the end of Volume I of the first edition of *Villette.* Mrs. Gaskell cites an eyewitness account by an unnamed friend who accompanied Charlotte to this lecture: "When the lecture was ended, Mr. Thackeray came down from the platform, and making his way towards her asked her for her opinion. This she mentioned to me not many days afterwards, adding remarks almost identical with those I subsequently read in 'Villette' where a similar action on the part of M. Paul Emanuel is related" (*Life of Charlotte Brontë,* Haworth Edition, p. 532).

4. In a letter Miss Brontë commented that *Rebecca and Rowena* is "like [Thackeray] himself, and all he says and writes; harsh and kindly, wayward and wise, benignant and bitter; its pages are overshadowed with cynicism; and yet they sparkle with feeling" (January 9, 1850, SHB, *Life and Letters,* III, 65). See also letter to W. S. Williams, December 11, 1847, SHB, *Life and Letters,* II, 160.

5. Because of the central position of the child Polly in the opening chapters, May Sinclair believed that she was originally intended to be the heroine of the novel, but that Miss Brontë changed her mind part of the way through and allowed Lucy to usurp the role. (See Miss Sinclair's introduction to the first Everyman edition of *Villette,* which in part has influenced Margaret Lane's introduction to the second Everyman edition.) This argument, in my opinion, misses the essential idea of the story. Janet Spens is acute on this point: "The personality of the author is divided between Lucy Snowe and Paulina, which accounts for the introduction of the latter at the very beginning.

Paulina's misery on parting from her father, and again at the indiffer-
ences of Graham, gives out the theme of heart-sickness that is to be the
subject of the book" ("Charlotte Brontë," *Essays and Studies,* XIV
[1929], 66).

6. January 27, 1853, SHB, *Life and Letters,* IV, 39.

7. For a brief account of the founding of Queens College for Women
in 1848, see Patricia Thomson, *The Victorian Heroine* (London, 1956),
CH. II ("That Noble Body of Governesses"). Harriet Martineau's "The
Old Governess," which originally appeared in *The Leader,* November
9, 1850, portrays a superannuated governess, left behind by her
employers when they emigrate to Canada. The lady is not only without
means, but her methods of teaching are too outmoded for her to secure
a new position, so she considers ending her days teaching her "fellow
paupers" in a workhouse. This is the story which, Lewes told Miss
Brontë, had "touched him and made him cry." (See letter to Lewes,
November 23, 1850, SHB, *Life and Letters,* III, 183–84.)

8. This book was commented upon in *The Leader* of August 3, 17,
and 31, 1850. For details on Miss Brontë's friendship with Sir James
and Lady Kay-Shuttleworth, see Mrs. Gaskell, *Life of Charlotte Brontë,*
CH. XXI and passim.

9. January 27, 1853, SHB, *Life and Letters,* IV, 39.

10. July 3, 1849, SHB, *Life and Letters,* III, 4–6.

11. October 30, 1852, SHB, *Life and Letters,* IV, 13–14.

12. Letter to W. S. Williams, October 28, 1847, SHB, *Life and
Letters,* II, 151.

13. Letter to W. S. Williams, September 13, 1849, SHB, *Life and
Letters,* III, 20. Williams had compared *Jane Eyre* with *David
Copperfield.*

14. Letter to Lewes, November 6, 1847, SHB, *Life and Letters,* II,
152–53.

15. Review of *Shirley, Edinburgh Review,* XCI (January, 1850), 153.

16. February 14, 1852, SHB, *Life and Letters,* III, 314–15.

17. In the next paragraph she writes: "The present successors of the
apostles, disciples of Dr. Pusey and tools of the Propaganda, were at
that time being hatched under cradle-blankets, or undergoing regeneration by nursery baptism in wash-hand basins." Pusey's Church of St.
Saviour, which several priests had left for Rome, was located in nearby
Leeds.

18. November 9, 1850, p. 780. In the same issue reference is made in
the "Books on Our Table" department to Ambrose Lisle Phillips' *A
Letter to the Right Honourable Earl of Shrewsbury on the Reestablish-*

ment of the English Catholic Church, and the Present Posture of Catholic Affairs in Great Britain. Phillips' pamphlet, it is explained, defends the appointment of Cardinal Wiseman as an administrative change abolishing the office of Vicars Apostolic and placing the English Catholic Church under the government of ordinary Bishops.

19. November 23, 1850, SHB, *Life and Letters,* III, 183–84.

20. Miss Brontë was recalling her own experience in the Cathedral of St. Gudule during her attendance at the Pensionnat Heger. Auricular confession was one of the sacraments revived by the Ritualists that was opposed by more conservative Anglicans.

21. She interrupted the writing of another story, *Laneton Parsonage,* to write *Margaret Percival,* at the request of her brother, the Reverend William Sewell, who was disturbed by the number of conversions resulting from the fervor induced by the Oxford Movement. This novel proved popular enough to elicit a spurious sequel by an anonymous New England writer—*Margaret Percival in America* (1850).

22. Other novels had tried to put readers on their guard. Geraldine Jewsbury's *Zoe: The History of Two Lives* (1845), for example, although set back in the period immediately following the French Revolution, carried ominous overtones for the 1840's and 1850's. At the beginning, the hero's father returns to England from a sojourn on the continent, with the avowed intention to "raise up the persecuted church in this Apostate country." This issue is treated with typical irreverence by Frank Smedley in his satirical novel *Lewis Arundel; or, The Railroad of Life* (1852). In one episode a wily publisher, Mr. Non-pareil, offers to pay for religious novels according to "the exact height of the principles." The principles of the heroine, a prospective authoress, measure up: "Ah! the *via media:* yes, I see—very good—nothing could be better. Just at the present time, the *via media* is, if I may be allowed the expression, the way that leads to fortune; nothing sells like it—it's quite safe you see; the heads of families buy it in preference to any more questionable teaching . . ." (CH. XXXII).

23. April 13, 1853, SHB, *Life and Letters,* IV, 58.

24. Miss Martineau's review, alluded to in Charlotte's letter to Miss Wooler, appeared in the *Daily News,* February 3, 1853. It is reprinted in Vera Wheatley, *The Life and Work of Harriet Martineau* (London, 1957), pp. 399–401. Other reviews objecting to the anti-Catholicism of *Villette* appeared in the *Guardian,* the *English Churchman,* and the *Christian Remembrancer.*

25. *The Atlas,* February 12, 1853, p. 106. In an unpublished letter of March 7, 1853 (probably to W. S. Williams), Miss Brontë notes this

among reviews called to her attention that she was especially eager to see. (Yale University, Beinecke Library, MS Vault File.)

26. "Puseyite Novels," *Prospective Review*, VI (1850), 512–34. This is an omnibus review of several of Miss Sewell's novels, including *Margaret Percival*.

27. November 16, 1850, p. 808.

28. February 17, 1852, SHB, *Life and Letters*, III, 318.

29. "This growing revolt of sixty against one" was an afterthought. In the manuscript of *Villette* (BM MS 43480 [May, 1949]), Miss Brontë first wrote merely, "This Case," which is crossed out and the more belligerent words substituted. There are other places in this chapter where she intensified her language.

30. In *Henry Esmond,* published several months before *Villette* and advertised in the first edition, Thackeray had bolstered the national sense of security by recalling earlier victories over the French.

31. *Atlas*, p. 106.

32. "*Ruth* and *Villette*," *Westminster Review*, LIX (April, 1853), 490.

33. November 6, 1852, SHB, *Life and Letters*, IV, 18.

34. The manuscript of this letter in the Fitzwilliam Museum, Cambridge University, has a penciled notation "? 1846," and appears among the letters for this year in SHB, *Life and Letters*, II, 116–17. However, Mildred Christian, who is at work on a new edition of the Brontë correspondence, has since tentatively redated it late 1852.

35. April 12, 1850, to W. S. Williams, SHB, *Life and Letters*, III, 99. The letter concludes: "Jane Austen was a complete and most sensible lady, but a very incomplete, and rather insensible (not *senseless*) woman, if this is heresy—I cannot help it. If I said it to some people (Lewes for instance) they would directly accuse me of advocating exaggerated heroics, but I am not afraid of your falling into any such vulgar error." Previously she had confided to Lewes her preference for George Sand, whose "grasp of mind . . . if I cannot fully comprehend, I can very deeply respect: she is sagacious and profound; Miss Austen is only shrewd and observant" (January 12, 1848, SHB, *Life and Letters*, II, 180). Lewes also thought Jane Austen lacked profundity (see above, CH. III, p. 102), but he put Miss Brontë to school to her because he thought the author of *Jane Eyre* needed to restrain her fancy and exuberance of language and to learn how to describe more clearly.

36. A late eighteenth-century edition (Berwick, 1791) bearing Miss Brontë's autograph is listed in an inventory of her books in the Brontë Society *Catalogue of the Museum and Library* (Haworth, 1927).

37. "The Good French Governess" is followed in the *Moral Tales* by "Mademoiselle Panache," a kind of pendant to its predecessor, illustrating "the necessary consequence of imprudently trusting the happiness of a daughter to the care of those who can teach nothing but accomplishments." In CH. XXX of *Villette* there is introduced briefly a Mademoiselle Panache, a brash young apprentice instructress at the Pensionnat Beck, who incurs Monsieur Paul's particular displeasure. The *Moral Tales* were republished in a cheap edition in 1850.

38. The publication of *Agnes Grey* and *Wuthering Heights* together in one volume was not so incongruous in 1847 as it appears today, for they are both, their profound differences aside, memoirs of educated servants.

39. Looking back from the end of the century, Mrs. Oliphant wrote:

> I remember well the extraordinary thrill of interest which in the midst of all the Mrs. Gores, Mrs. Marshs, &c . . . came upon the reader who, in the calm of ignorance, took up the first volume of 'Jane Eyre.' The period of the heroine in white muslin, the immaculate creature who was of sweetness and goodness all compact, had lasted in the common lines of fiction up to that time. Miss Austen indeed might well have put an end to that abstract and empty fiction, yet it continued, as it does continue more or less the primitive ideal. But 'Jane Eyre' gave her, for the moment, the *coup de grace.* That the book should be the story of a governess was perhaps necessary to the circumstances of the writer: and the governess was already a favorite figure of fiction. But generally she was of the beautiful, universally fascinating, all-enduring kind, the amiable blameless creature whose secret merits were never so well hidden but that they might be perceived by a keen sighted hero. I am not sure, indeed, that anybody believed Miss Brontë when she said her heroine was plain . . . ("The Sisters Brontë," *Women Novelists of Queen Victoria's Reign* [London, 1897], pp. 17–18) .

40. Cf. for example the conclusion of Lady Blessington's *Memoirs of a Femme de Chambre,* in which the waif heroine Selina falls into afluence through the kindness of a former benefactress who wills her a fortune.

41. George Smith identified himself and his mother as the prototypes of the Brettons in his reminiscent article "Charlotte Brontë," *Cornhill,* n.s. IX (July-December, 1900) , 778–95; Ginevra Fanshawe has been identified with a fellow student of Miss Brontë's at the Pension Heger, Maria Miller, and Polly Home is said to have been based upon Fanny

Whipp, the young niece of a friend (SHB, *Life and Letters*, I, 190, 255).
Mrs. Humphry Ward makes other identifications—such as the galvanic
acting of Vashti (CH. XXIII) with a performance of Madame Rachel in
Phèdre that Charlotte attended with the Smiths, and the fire that ends
that episode with a similar catastrophe at Devonshire House, where she
watched Dickens perform. (See Mrs. Ward's introduction to the
Haworth Edition of *Villette*.) A visit Charlotte made to a London art
gallery seems to have been utilized in the "Cleopatra" (CH. XIX), and
her admiration for Turner may be reflected in the sea descriptions
dispersed throughout the story.

42. A letter to Miss Wooler of February 14, 1850, describing her first
visit to London late in the previous year, anticipates the mixture of
fascination and bewilderment that Lucy feels on her first experiences in
the metropolis. (SHB, *Life and Letters*, III, 76–77.)

43. In June, 1851, during her third visit to London, Miss Brontë
went to consult a prominent phrenologist of the day, along with her
publisher George Smith. Under the assumed names of Mr. and Miss
Fraser they submitted to character analyses. The character reading of
"Miss Fraser" gave Miss Brontë a rare opportunity to view herself with
detachment and in the round. It is interesting, therefore, to see some of
the traits noted by the phrenologist—nervous temperament, melancholic
disposition, circumspection, religious devotion without superstition,
poetic feeling, eloquence, and strong intellect—repeated in the characterization of Lucy Snowe. This incident is recalled by George Smith in
his *Cornhill* article (see above, note 41), which includes the character
sketch of "Miss Fraser." ("A Phrenological Estimate of the Talents and
Dispositions of a Lady," by T. P. Browne, M.D.) Dr. Browne's "Estimate" has since been reprinted in SHB, *Life and Letters*, III, 256–58.

44. Shortly after *Shirley* was published, Miss Brontë sent a copy to
Harriet Martineau with the following note: "When C.B. first read
Deerbrook he [Currer Bell] tasted a new and keen pleasure, and
experienced a genuine benefit. In his mind *Deerbrook* ranks with the
writings that have really done him good, added to his stock of ideas and
rectified his view of life." (SHB, *Life and Letters*, III, 56; quoted from
Miss Martineau's *Autobiography*.) When *Villette* was published,
Charlotte very eagerly awaited Miss Martineau's review, placing great
value on her judgment. The review was generally favorable, but Miss
Martineau objected not only to the religious prejudices reflected in the
novel (see above, p. 186), but also to what she considered its undue
obsession with love. The latter criticism offended Miss Brontë, and as a

result relations between the two writers became strained to the point where the friendship ceased.

45. The two authors became acquainted when Miss Kavanagh wrote to Miss Brontë to express her admiration of *Jane Eyre*. They corresponded for a number of years. Smith and Elder also published several of Miss Kavanagh's books, and the editor, W. S. Williams, arranged a meeting between the two during Charlotte's 1850 visit to London. (See SHB, *Life and Letters*, II, 182, 185; III, 118.) Their relationship is an interesting example of literary cross-fertilization, *Nathalie* having been influenced by *Jane Eyre* and in turn influencing *Villette*.

46. January 21, 1851, SHB, *Life and Letters*, III, 203. Miss Brontë was not alone in her admiration for *Nathalie*, for it was both a critical and a popular success in its time. It was reprinted in Tauchnitz's Collection of British Authors in 1851, and Hurst and Blackett reissued it as late as 1898. Miss Kavanagh's *Women of Christianity Exemplary for Piety and Charity* and *Women in France during the Eighteenth Century* were advertised in the first edition of *Villette*.

47. Another possible prototype of Monsieur Paul is a minor character in *Nathalie*, a middle-aged professor of dancing at the school, who befriends Nathalie, and whom the heroine admires for his warmth and tenderness, as well as his "old-fashioned courtesy of bygone times, with his reverence for love, passion and women" (CH. III).

48. *Atlas*, p. 106.

49. *The Bachelor of the Albany*, CH. I.

50. Posthumously published in *The Orphan of Pimlico and Other Sketches, Fragments and Drawings*, edited by his daughters (London, 1876). Reprinted in *Works*, Centenary Biographical edition (London, 1911), XXVI, 26–39.

51. Miss Brontë reported to W. S. Williams that Mrs. Ellis had made a "morning call" at Haworth and praised *Jane Eyre* and *Shirley*. (January 10, 1850, SHB, *Life and Letters*, III, 66) Mrs. Ellis continued *The Daughters of England* (1842) with *The Wives of England* (1843) and *The Mothers of England* (1843). Mrs. Martin, governess to the Spread children in Marmion Savage's *The Bachelor of the Albany*, is author of *Godmothers of England*.

52. Charlotte wrote to her friend Ellen Nussey: " 'Margaret Maitland' is a good book, I doubt not, and will just suit your mother" (December, 1851, SHB, *Life and Letters*, III, 299).

53. Mrs. Burbury and Miss Brontë had the same publisher. Charlotte praised *Florence Sackville* in two letters to George Smith, who seems to have had a particular regard for it (November 20, 28, 1851, SHB, *Life*

and Letters, III, 293–94) . Its much-tried heroine—love-starved, imaginative, introspective, and strongly religious—has some temperamental affinities with Lucy Snowe, though her tribulations end more conventionally with a belated inheritance and a prosperous marriage.

54. Miss Sewell, like Charlotte Yonge, who had been influenced by her, drew for her fiction upon her experience in teaching religion to children. Her first work of fiction, *Stories on the Lord's Prayer*, was an attempt to improve on the tracts she disseminated for the Christian Knowledge Society, which struck her as "intensely dull." *Amy Herbert,* her first success, was prompted, according to her testimony, by her displeasure with a story by Mrs. Sherwood, whose children seemed to her unnaturally pious and priggish (*The Autobiography of Elizabeth M. Sewell,* ed. by her Niece Eleanor L. Sewell [London, 1907]) . For a brief and generally favorable estimate of Miss Sewell's abilities as a novelist and psychologist, see Margaret M. Maison, *The Victorian Vision* (New York, 1961) , pp. 41–47.

55. George Smith's editor, W. S. Williams, expressed concern over the slow pace and lack of narrative suspense in letters to Miss Brontë while *Villette* was in progress. In her reply she anticipated more excitement in the "third volume," and indeed most of the "story" of the book is concentrated in the chapters from "Monsieur's Fête" on, which seem to have been written in a blaze of white heat. (See in particular her letter of November 6, 1852, SHB, *Life and Letters,* IV, 17–18.)

56. November 6, 1847, SHB, *Life and Letters,* II, 152–53.

57. Miss Brontë was well acquainted with *The Italian,* as is obvious from CH. XXIII of *Shirley,* where Caroline Helstone reads it over the shoulder of Rose Yorke.

58. Actually this motif of the novel is prefigured in a sonnet written in a German exercise book used by Miss Brontë at the Pension Heger in 1843:

> The Autumn day its course has run,
>   The Autumn evening falls,
> Already risen the Autumn moon
>   Gleams quiet on these walls;
>
> And twilight to my lonely house
>   A silent guest is come:
> In mask of gloom, through every room
>   She passes dusk and dumb
>
> Her veil is spread, her shadows shed
>   O'er stair and chamber void,

But now I feel her presence steal
Even to my lone fireside.

Sit, silent Nun—sit here and be
Comrade and confidante to me.

(SHB, VIII, 235–36)

59. This book is reviewed in *The Leader,* November 9, 1850, p. 784. This issue contains the article by Lewes that Miss Brontë commented on (see note 18 above). Mrs. Crowe herself was an occasional contributor to *The Leader.* Miss Brontë met her at a dinner party at Thackeray's home during a London visit (see SHB, *Life and Letters,* III, 124).

60. The publication of an abridged translation of Diderot's *La Religieuse* (*The Nun, A Recital of the Convent*) during the previous year may have revived this stereotype in some readers' minds. For other possible sources, see Robert A. Colby, " 'Villette' and the Life of the Mind," *PMLA,* LXXV (September, 1960), 419.

61. For her remarks on *Consuelo,* see her letter to Lewes, January 12, 1848, SHB, *Life and Letters,* II, 180. The comment on *Illusions Perdues* appears in her letter to Lewes, October 17, 1850, SHB, *Life and Letters,* III, 172–73. Lewes had sent her this along with another Balzac novel, *Modeste Mignon,* whose heroine, like Lucy Snowe, is given to literary daydreams inspired by *The Arabian Nights* and other exotic tales, which are shattered by experience.

62. See *The Love Letters of Charlotte Brontë to Constantin Heger,* ed. Thomas James Wise (London, 1914). They are reprinted, without Wise's introduction, in SHB, *Life and Letters,* II, 9–11, 17–19, 21–24, 67–71.

63. This episode appears to be a domestication of the myth of "the bridal hour of Genius and Humanity," part of the *devoir* from Saint-Pierre's *Fragments de l'Amazone* that Louis Moore reads to Shirley Keeldar (*Shirley,* CH. XXVII).

64. For specific parallels with Saint-Pierre's style in the storm scene and elsewhere in Miss Brontë's writing, see John M. Ware, "Bernardin de Saint-Pierre and Charlotte Brontë," *Modern Language Notes,* XL (June, 1925), 381–82.

65. "Currer Bell's New Novel," *The Leader,* February 12, 1853, p. 164. "More adroit 'construction,' more breathless suspense, more thrilling incidents, and a more moving story, might easily have been manufactured by a far less active, inventive, passionate writer," Lewes declared, "but not such a book."

66. November 16, 1847, SHB, *Life and Letters*, II, 152–53.

67. November 6, 1852, SHB, *Life and Letters*, IV, 17.

68. *The Professor*, Author's Preface. This was printed, with an explanatory note by the author's husband, the Reverend Arthur Bell Nicholls, in the first edition of 1857, published two years after her death.

69. July 22, 1854, to Catherine Winkworth, from Cork, SHB, *Life and Letters*, IV, 137–38. She was married to Nicholls on June 29, 1854. Her death occurred on March 31 of the following year.

70. Hearing the wind that forebodes Miss Marchmont's death, Lucy sighs: "Three times in the course of my life events had taught me that these strange accents in the storm—this restless, hopeless cry—denote a coming state of the atmosphere unpropitious to life" (CH. IV). During a period of delirium, "Methought the well-loved dead, who had loved *me* well in life, met me elsewhere, alienated" (CH. XV). The manuscript contains a few other pointed references that do not appear in the novel as published. In CH. XII, between "Oh my childhood!" and "I had feelings," the phrase "Oh lost affections" is lined out. In CH. XV the sentence reading, "My heart almost died within me; miserable longings strained its chords," originally included the phrase, "for society, for a home" after "longings." In CH. XVI, an entire sentence, "Many a solitary struggle have I had in life, and this was one," is excised. Miss Brontë's still fresh griefs over the deaths of Branwell, Emily, and Anne could not help showing through despite attempts to prune the manuscript of personal allusions.

71. Introduction to "Emma," I (April, 1860). The fragment consists of a narrative by a middle-aged widow, set in a genteel ladies' school, with no hint as to how it was to develop.

72. *Fraser's Magazine*, December 1847, p. 693; *The Leader*, February 12, 1853, p. 163.

73. February 15, 1853, to Mrs. Charles Bray, *The George Eliot Letters*, ed. Gordon S. Haight (New Haven, 1954), II, 87.

VII. *The Mill on the Floss:* Maggie Tulliver and the Child of Nature

1. Maggie is confident that "everything would be quite charming when she had taught the gypsies to use a washing basin, and to feel an interest in books" (Book First, CH. XI). Unfortunately, unlike the garrulous young "Word-Master" of George Borrow's *Lavengro* (1851) and *The Romany Rye* (1857), who edifies his semicivilized neighbors with

lectures on folklore and linguistics, Maggie soon concludes that "it was impossible she should ever be queen of these people, or even communicate to them amusing and useful knowledge." Norwich gypsies appear to have been more colorful and educable than their Dorsetshire kinfolk.

2. *Saturday Review,* IX (April 14, 1860), 470. The reviewer compared her with Jane Austen for her "minuteness of painting and a certain archness of style," and with Charlotte Brontë and George Sand as novelists who "like to dwell on love as a strange overmastering force which, through the senses, captivates and enthrals the soul" (p. 471).

3. *The Leader,* February 13, 1858.

4. Quoted in *The Leader,* March 13, 1858, p. 257.

5. From *The Examiner,* as quoted in *The Leader,* January 2, 1858. A second edition of *A Woman's Thoughts about Women* appeared in 1859. During the next year it was published in Tauchnitz's Collection of British Authors. One sign of its popularity was that shortly afterward it was translated into Swedish. It was still in vogue in the 1870's, as indicated by its inclusion in the catalogue of W. H. Smith and Son's Railway Library. One of Miss Mulock's early novels, *Olive* (1850), concerns the struggles of a gifted young woman for success in an artistic career.

6. For parallels between CH. XI ("Lost Women") of *A Woman's Thoughts about Women* and *Adam Bede,* see Robert A. Colby, "Miss Evans, Miss Mulock and Hetty Sorrel," *English Language Notes,* II (March, 1965), 206–11.

7. June 7, 1860, to François D'Albert-Durade, *The George Eliot Letters,* III, 302 (hereafter referred to as *Letters*). D'Albert-Durade had called her attention to an article in *La Revue Britannique,* April, 1860, in which the critic Amédée Pichaud referred to Miss Mulock and "sa rivale, Miss Evans."

8. Bob Jakin is guileless like John Halifax, but speaks in dialect rather than in young John's cultivated voice and is semiliterate. George Eliot's older men of commerce in turn have managed quite well without the Bible and the classics that feed the soul of the self-taught John Halifax. Mr. Deane assures Tom that "Your Latin and rigmarole may soon dry off you, but you'll be but a bare stick after that. Besides, it's whitened your hands and taken the rough work out of you" (Book Third, CH. v) ; Mr. Wakem is "one of those men who can be prompt without being rash, because their motives run in fixed tracks, and they have no need to reconcile conflicting aims" (Book Third, CH. VII).

9. Review of *A Noble Life* in *The Nation*, March 1, 1866. Reprinted in *Notes and Reviews* (Cambridge, Mass., 1921), pp. 167–72.

10. June 23, 1860, to John Blackwood, *Letters*, III, 307.

11. Miss Mulock was deeply impressed by *The Mill on the Floss* as a work of art, but was dissatisfied with the tragic fate that George Eliot chose for her heroine:

> Yet what—we cannot help asking—what is to become of the hundreds of clever girls, born of uncongenial parents, hemmed in with unsympathising kindred of the Dodson sort, blest with no lover on whom to bestow their strong satisfaction, no friend to whom to cling for guidance and support? They must fight their way, heaven help them! alone and unaided, through cloud and darkness, to the light. And, thank heaven, hundreds of them do, and live to hold out a helping hand afterwards to thousands more. . . . Will it influence for good any other lives—this passionately drawn picture of temptation never conquered, or conquered just so far that we see its worst struggle is just beginning; of sorrows which teach nothing, or teach only bitterness; of love in its most delicious, most deadly phase; love—blind, selfish, paramount, seeing no future but possession, and, that hope gone, no alternative but death— death, welcomed as the solution of all difficulties, the escape from all pain? ("To Novelists—and a Novelist," *The Unkind Word* [Leipzig, 1869], I, 305–307)

12. January 12, 1861, *Letters*, III, 371.

13. George Eliot suggested "The Tullivers; or, Life on the Floss" as a possible title for her novel, but it was eventually rejected because of possible confusion with the numerous other family novels in circulation at the time. See *Letters*, III, 240–41, 243, 244, 245.

14. Richard Holt Hutton, "George Eliot as Author," *Essays on Some of the Modern English Guides to Thought in Matters of Faith* (London, 1891), p. 159.

15. She quotes from this novel in a letter to her friend Sara Hennell (February 4, 1849, *Letters*, I, 275).

16. She was referring to a dramatization, prepared by the author, that she saw on a continental trip. (See letter to Mr. and Mrs. Bray from Geneva, February 15, 1850, *Letters*, I, 330.)

17. Julia Kavanagh, author of *Rachel Grey*, reviewed by George Eliot (*The Leader*, January 5, 1856), announced as her intention in that novel "to show the intellectual, the educated, the fortunate that minds which they are apt to slight as narrow . . . are often blessed and graced

beyond the usual lot." In one chapter she anticipates George Eliot's famous analogy with Dutch painting that opens Book Second of *Adam Bede*. George Eliot approved of Miss Kavanagh's intention but felt that she failed to carry it out because of her lack of knowledge of the speech and ways of life of ordinary folk.

18. One of the first reviewers of *Adam Bede* remarked:

> Those who draw the materials of fiction from the romance of the workshop, for the amusement of the educated classes, labour under much the same difficulties as the writers who purvey the Mysteries of the Court for the penny journal. They are writing about things with which they can have but a very imperfect acquaintance. Even the very best of such stories, in spite of their cleverness and popularity, give us but a stage view, after all, of the life and feeling of the lower classes. And as to most attempts of the kind, the characters are about as real as the shepherds and milkmaids of the Trianon. But in the volumes before us we think we have the genuine article; the village lion is here, the real animal, and not the 'gentle beast of good conscience' made up for the ladies . . . He [the author of *Adam Bede*, elsewhere referred to as "Mr. Eliot"] does not conceal or palliate the weaknesses of humanity; there is no attempt to paint rural life as an Arcadia of innocence. . . . (*Blackwood's Magazine*, LXXXV [April, 1859], 490–504) .

19. In the opening chapters of *Eric; or, Little by Little* the young hero and his brother, as they lie asleep, are described in words that might fittingly accompany a genre piece by Morland or Vigée-Lebrun: "The small, shining, flower-like faces with their fair hair—the trustful, loving arms folded round each brother's neck—the closed eyes and parted lips—made an exquisite picture, and one never to be forgotten." However, this Eden is lost, for Eric's story, unlike Tom Brown's, is one of corrupted innocence.

20. From preface to the Third Edition. Hughes was replying to criticism that his boys were too solemn and priggish.

21. *The Heir of Redclyffe*, CH. v. Philip Morville, speaking to Amy, is referring to the peculiarity of their cousin Guy who has been privately tutored.

22. December 12, 1859, *Letters*, III, 234.

23. George Eliot is questioning here the traditional assumption of Tom's master, presumably shared by his Victorian successors, "that all boys with any capacity could learn what it was the only regular thing to teach: if they were slow, the thumb-screw must be tightened." Her

criticisms of children's education are more specific and more firmly grounded than those of Dickens. Among the books that Lewes studied while she was composing *The Mill on the Floss* was J. Moreau de Tours' *La Psychologie Morbide* (Paris, 1859). (See Lewes' Journal for September 5–16, 1859, *Letters,* III, 148–50.) In the preface to this work, Moreau advanced the doctrine, revolutionary at the time, that children differ in their aptitudes for learning, and that education can only bring their innate abilities to fruition, not increase their mental capacity. Lewes reviewed *La Psychologie Morbide* in *Blackwood's Magazine* the following year (September, 1860, pp. 302–11).

24. Yvonne ffrench calls attention to *The Moorland Cottage* as a source for *The Mill on the Floss* in her essay on Mrs. Gaskell in *From Jane Austen to Joseph Conrad,* eds. Robert C. Rathburn and Martin Steinmann, Jr. (Minneapolis, 1958), p. 136.

25. For the background of this series, see Christabel Coleridge, *Charlotte Mary Yonge: Her Life and Letters* (London, 1903), pp. 164–65. Miss Yonge's preeminence and popularity as a religious novelist are affirmed by the heroine of Mrs. Oliphant's *Phoebe, Junior* (1876): "One reads Scott for Scotland and Miss Yonge for the Church." Phoebe meets a family also named May and mentions the coincidence, to the annoyance of the youngest daughter: " 'Oh! I know,' cried Janey, 'the Daisy Chain. We are not a set of prigs like those people. We are not goody, whatever we are. . . .' " (CH. XIX). Janey may be taken as representative of the rebellious new generation, but Miss Yonge's popularity continued well into our century.

26. Contrasted to the tribute paid by George Eliot in epigraphs and mottoes are reactions expressed by some of the characters in the novels. In *Adam Bede* Arthur Donnithorne, presumably representing gentlemanly opinion of the late eighteenth century, scoffs at the *Lyrical Ballads,* which have just come off the press: "Most of them seem to be twaddling stuff; but the first is in a different style—'The Ancient Mariner' is the title." Mrs. Transome, who was a young girl at the time, remembers having "laughed at the *Lyrical Ballads*" (*Felix Holt,* CH. I). George Eliot seems to have regarded insensitivity to Wordsworth as one sign of moral shallowness.

27. See in particular the letters to Frederic Harrison, April 19, 1880 and to Mrs. Elma Stuart, December 11, 1880, *Letters,* VII, 261, 346. Herbert Lindenberger, in "The Reception of *The Prelude,*" *Bulletin of the New York Public Library* LXIV (April, 1960), 202, notes that George Eliot was one of the few mid-Victorian writers to refer to it.

28. There are explicit parallels between the poems and the novel, such as the appearance of the gypsies in Sonnet VI and the accidental catching of the fish in Sonnets VII and VIII. (Cf. Maggie's experience in Book First, CH. v of *The Mill*.) The origin and date of composition of these neglected poems are obscure. The MS in the British Museum is dated 31 July 1869 (BM Add. MS. 34, 038, ff 80–90), which accounts for the imprint of Thomas J. Wise's spurious "first edition." They were first published in the collection *The Legend of Jubal, and Other Poems* (1874). The year before their publication, George Eliot wrote to John Blackwood: "A good while ago I made a poem, in the form of eleven sonnets after the Shakspeare type, on the childhood of a brother and sister—little descriptive bits on the mutual influences in their small lives. This was always one of my best loved subjects" (April 21, 1873, *Letters*, V, 403).

29. *Examiner*, June 16, 1860.

30. The first critic to treat the influence of Lewes, among others, was P. Bourl'honne in *George Eliot: Essai de Biographie Intellectuelle et Morale, 1819–1854* (Paris, 1933), which is marred by the author's attempts at amateur psychoanalysis. Among recent articles, the most substantial is Alice R. Kaminsky, "George Eliot, George Henry Lewes, and the Novel," *PMLA*, LXX (September, 1955), 997–1013. Mrs. Kaminsky confines herself for the most part to Lewes' literary criticism, but she points out that his studies in biology and physiological psychology gave him an insight into human behavior beyond what was available to most of his contemporaries. Some studies of George Eliot's ideas in relation to Lewes' metaphysics and ethics are cited in the next chapter.

31. See *Letters*, III, 33 (note 8), 145.

32. See George Henry Lewes' Journal, September 5–16, 1859; November 9–10, 1859, *Letters*, III, 148–50, 196.

33. Lewes' former private library is now deposited in Dr. Williams' Library in London. Among numerous works on physiology and psychology listed in the inventory of the Lewes Collection are: Cuvier's *Leçons d'Anatomie Comparée*, Grainger's *Observations on the Spinal Cord*, Lister and Turner's *Observations on Nerve Fibers*, Owen's *On the Classification of Mammalia*, Bernard's *Leçons de Physiologie*, Münter's *Anatomische Grundlagen zur Seelenlehre*, Carus' *Geschichte der Psychologie* and *Vergleichende Psychologie*, Robin's *Programme du Cours Comparée*, Inman's *Phenomena of Spinal Irritation*, Michea's *De Delire des Sensations*, Klencke's *Organische Seelenkunde*, and Dumont's

La Sensibilité. These titles suggest the range of his curiosity, but only begin to indicate the enormous extent of his reading.

34. The cheap format of its first edition (1859) —monthly parts bound in flimsy paper wrappers—its careless printing, as well as its distribution in railway bookstalls, all indicate that it was aimed for the popular market. It is listed in the 1876 Catalogue of W. H. Smith and Sons, the only list that has survived from the firm's records. Incidentally, it is among the books read by Sonya in *Crime and Punishment* in her efforts at self-education—a further indication of its wide audience.

35. The interrupted reverie that opens the novel illustrates the phenomena of unconscious perception and involuntary mental association produced by nerve stimuli. The narrator is suddenly called back to herself from a semiconscious state in which past and present coalesced, and she had imagined herself amidst the sights and sounds of her girlhood: "Ah, my arms are really benumbed. I have been pressing my elbows on the arms of my chair, and dreaming that I was standing on the bridge in front of Dorlcote Mill, as it looked one February afternoon many years ago."

36. In her Journal of November 23, 1859, George Eliot wrote: "We began Darwin's work on 'The Origin of Species' tonight. It seems not to be well written: though full of interesting matter, it is not impressive, from want of luminous and orderly presentation" (*Letters*, III, 214, n. 9). Both Darwin and Lyell were impressed by Lewes' breadth of knowledge in their fields. (See *Letters*, V, 8.)

37. In a recent article, George Levine has written: "Quite deliberately, she was creating a society which has not yet moved beyond the egoism of man's animal beginnings to the sympathy and benevolence which Feuerbach and Comte believed would grow out of egoism" ("Intelligence as Deception: *The Mill on the Floss*," *PMLA*, LXXX [September, 1965], 403). I think he misconstrues the essential purpose of the animal analogies.

38. In CH. II of *The Daisy Chain,* Charlotte Yonge distinguishes the various combinations of family traits in the May children, but confines herself to physical features: "Ethel was almost an exaggeration of the doctor's [her father] peculiarities . . . Norman had his long nose, sallow complexion, and tall figure, but was much improved by his mother's fine blue eyes. . . . Little Tom was a thin, white, delicate edition of his father; and Blanche contrived to combine great likeness to him with a great deal of prettiness."

39. George Eliot's friend and French translator François D'Albert-Durade, who was also humpbacked, has been suggested as the prototype of Philip. However, Philip may also have been derived from the

deformed aesthete Julius St. John in Lewes' novel *Rose, Blanche and Violet.*

40. A whole essay could be written on the shift from the scenic and pictorial view of nature in *Adam Bede,* which evokes a placid eighteenth-century idyll ("High up against the horizon were the huge conical masses of hill . . . not distant enough to be clothed in purple mystery, but with sombre greenish sides visibly specked with sheep, whose motion was only revealed by memory, not detected by sight") to the dynamism of *The Mill on the Floss,* which plunges us in the midst of emergent life.

41. Richard Holt Hutton, "George Eliot as Author," pp. 194–95.

42. Joan Bennett, *George Eliot: Her Mind and Art* (Cambridge, 1948), p. 130. This should be supplemented by the balanced evaluation of Gordon S. Haight in his introduction to the Riverside Edition of *The Mill on the Floss* (Boston, 1961).

43. See note 11, above.

44. "George Eliot as Author," p. 195.

45. April 14, 1860, pp. 470–71. For a useful summary of the immediate reception in periodicals of *The Mill on the Floss,* see Mathilde Partlett, "The Influence of Contemporary Criticism on George Eliot," *Studies in Philology,* XXX (January, 1933), 103–32.

46. April 11, 1860 (?), in National Library of Scotland. Quoted by Gordon S. Haight in his introduction to the Riverside Edition of *The Mill on the Floss,* p. xv.

47. July 9, 1860, to John Blackwood, *Letters,* III, 317–18. Italics mine.

48. December 12, 1859; March 7, 1860, *Letters,* III, 233, 272.

49. Frank, it develops, is not engaged to Erminia, as Maggie had mistakenly supposed. Maggie, however, out of supervening family loyalty chooses to accompany her brother Edward to America, the brother being in disgrace in England for criminal acts. This remaining obstacle to her happy marriage is removed when Edward is drowned in a shipwreck, from which Maggie is rescued.

50. Late in this decade a rather iconoclastic reviewer, William Rathbone Greg, pointed out in several women's novels that came to his attention a tendency toward "false notions of honour," "egotistical notions of self-sacrifice," "sinful notions of compassion," and "distorted notions of the relative enormity of various failings and offenses" ("The False Morality of Lady Novelists," *National Review,* VIII [January, 1859], 144–67; reprinted in his *Literary and Social Judgments* [London, 1868]). The best known of the novels discussed by Greg is Mrs. Gaskell's *Ruth,* in which a pure-minded young woman who has suffered social stigma because of her one lapse from virtue sacrifices her life in

saving her seducer. The other novels represent acts of self-denial that are equally masochistic but less tragic. In *Leonie Vermont* (by Hamilton Murray) the heroine renounces a nobleman she loves when she learns that her brother is a political criminal, because she thinks her blood unworthy to be mingled with that of her lover. In *Kathie Brande* (by Holme Lee) the heroine postpones marriage to a worthy young curate because of her obligation to support her unworthy brother, and then, freed of the obligation, subsequently refuses to marry him because the marriage would make her mother dependent on the curate. In *Framleigh Hall* (by Julia Wedgwood) the beautiful, vivacious heroine loves a refined aesthete, but is persuaded to marry an unprincipled coxcomb in the hope of reclaiming him.

51. Eventually he defers to Maggie's moral judgment. His final letter to her refers to "that partial divided action of our nature which makes half the tragedy of the human lot" (Book Seventh, CH. III) .

52. See letter to Dr. Joseph Frank Payne, January 25, 1876, *Letters*, VI, 216. This phrase gives the title to the most recent and fullest study of George Eliot's ideas in relation to her novels, Bernard J. Paris, *Experiments in Life: George Eliot's Quest for Values* (Detroit, 1965) .

53. George Levine relates the conclusion of *The Mill* to Feuerbach's symbolic interpretation of water as the sacrament which "asserts man's dependence on nature" and through which man is enabled to see and think more clearly ("Intelligence as Deception: *The Mill on the Floss*," p. 408) .

54. Isaac Evans did not break his long silence toward his sister until her marriage to John Walter Cross seven months before her death. (See letter of May 17, 1880, *Letters*, VII, 280.)

55. Her accuracy in psychology is verified with Teutonic thoroughness in a four-part article by Max Isenbarth, "Die Psychologie der Charaktere in George Eliot's *The Mill on the Floss*," *Neuren Sprachen*, XXI (1913) , 296–312 ff. To prove the soundness of her characterization, he sets her observations alongside the findings of such psychologists as Wundt and Fechner, but ignores the source closest at hand.

VIII. *Middlemarch:* Dorothea Brooke and the Emancipated Woman

1. Education Commission, 1864, *Parliamentary Papers*, XX, XXI (1864) , I, 548–61. Quoted in Manning, *Dickens on Education*, p. 122.

2. October 4, 1869, to Mrs. Nassau John Senior, *Letters*, V, 58. George Eliot was friendly with Emily Davies, who was active in the founding of

Girton College and became its first secretary. (See *Letters,* IV, 399, 401, 425; V, 58; VI, 285–87.) Miss Davies' *Higher Education of Women* (1866) is among the books listed in the catalogue of the Lewes Collection in Doctor Williams' Library.

3. The canceled passage is reprinted in the Riverside Edition of *Middlemarch,* ed. Gordon S. Haight (Boston, 1956), p. 612.

4. *The Conscience: Lectures on Casuistry* (London and Cambridge, 1868), Lecture I, p. 27; Lecture II, pp. 46–47. These lectures, originally delivered in 1866, attracted great attention. This appointment to the chair vacated by John Grote amounted to a rehabilitation for Maurice, who had been in the academic shade since 1853, when his *Theological Essays* were deemed heretical, and he was forced to resign from his professorship of Ecclesiastical History at King's College, London. His influence on George Eliot is discussed in greater detail later in this chapter.

5. See letter of February 18, 1869, from John Blackwood, *Letters,* V, 15.

6. In her Journal for January 1, 1869 appears this entry: "I have set myself many tasks for the year—I wonder how many will be accomplished?—A Novel called Middlemarch, a long poem on Timoleon, and several minor poems" (*Letters,* V, 3). The poem on Timoleon, the ancient Corinthian liberator of Syracuse, appears never to have been written, although one of her notebooks of the period records some research she did in Greek history. Among the "minor poems," "How Lisa Loved the King" is set in Renaissance Italy and "Agatha" in modern Germany. Her more ambitious poetic tragedy *The Spanish Gypsy* was completed in 1867.

7. "The Progress of Fiction as an Art," *Westminster Review,* LX (October, 1853), 374.

8. A detailed account of the Medical Council appears in an unpublished notebook kept by George Eliot called "Miscellaneous Quotations," now in the Folger Shakespeare Library, Washington, D.C.

9. Review of *The Progress of the Intellect, as Exemplified in the Religious Development of the Greeks and Hebrews,* by R. W. Mackay, *Westminster Review,* LIV (January, 1851), 353–68. This review is reprinted in *Writings of George Eliot,* Large Paper Edition (Boston, 1908), XXII, 275–301. More recently it has been reprinted, with explanatory notes, in *Essays of George Eliot,* ed. Thomas Pinney (New York, 1963), pp. 27–45.

10. One of these, known as the "Quarry for Middlemarch," once owned by the poet Amy Lowell, has been edited by Anna Theresa

Kitchel (Los Angeles, 1950; issued as a supplement to *Nineteenth-Century Fiction*, Vol. IV) . It contains notes on medicine and hospitals, the political history of the Reform Bill, and numerous outlines and diagrams which show the architectonic planning that went into the novel. Jerome Beaty has made good use of the "Quarry" in his *Middlemarch, from Notebook to Novel* (Urbana, Ill., 1960) , a thorough study of the stages of composition.

Not so well known is another notebook, begun in August, 1868, labeled "Miscellaneous Quotations" (see note 8 above) , which has other items bearing on *Middlemarch,* including more medical history and *materia medica,* as well as excerpts from studies in Comparative Mythology and Religion, Language, Plutarch's Moral Works, and quotations from Robert Burton and Sir Thomas Browne that appear as epigraphs to chapters in the novel.

11. *British Quarterly Review,* January 1, 1872, p. 267. The first part ("Miss Brooke") was published December 1, 1871. The rest was published at two-month and one-month intervals through December, 1872. For the sequence of publication, see *Letters,* V, 221.

12. A notebook known as the "Quarry for Romola," recently acquired by the British Museum (BM Add. MS. 40, 768) , contains a list of "Books on Florentine Subjects" extending to two and a half pages, apparently the basis of the list compiled by Cross in his account of the research done for *Romola* in the Magliabecchian Library. (*George Eliot's Life as Related in Her Journals,* II, 325–26.) The rest of the notebook is replete with detail on government, transportation, family life, religious observances, costume, the lives of Savonarola, and numerous statesmen, scholars, and humanists. There is also a list of typical names (including Romola, Tessa, Baldassare, Brigida, and Luca) , titles of books published during this period, and a long chronology of Florentine history. This is the earliest complete record extant of George Eliot's research for a single work, affording us insight into her documentary technique.

13. *Athenaeum,* January 21, 1871, p. 77.

14. *Westminster Review,* LXVI (October 1856) , 442. Reprinted in *Writings of George Eliot,* Large Paper Edition, XXII, 186–200; *Essays of George Eliot,* ed. Pinney, pp. 300–24.

15. "The Progress of Fiction as an Art," pp. 342–74.

16. Journal, December 2, 1870, *Letters,* V, 124.

17. On the other hand, Gwendolen Harleth, the heroine of *Daniel Deronda,* gets into high society, but in winning Grandcourt is far from "securing the best." Also, the family jewels cause her grief.

18. February 9, 1849, to Sara Sophia Hennell, *Letters*, I, 278. *Jacques* was first published in 1834, but was not translated into English until 1846 (by Anna Blackwell) .

19. The story is related in a series of letters by the three principal characters to their confidantes. The passage quoted is from Letter XXI, from Fernande to a school friend.

20. This parallel is also pointed out by Patricia Thomson in her article "The Three Georges," *Nineteenth-Century Fiction*, XVIII (September, 1963) , 137–50.

21. This was a sequel to her powerful *Paul Ferroll* (1855) , in which the hero, unhappily married and in love with another woman, murders his wife and eventually confesses to the deed when an innocent man is suspected. The later novel was intended as a "key" to the first, explaining the husband's motivations and the circumstances that led up to his crime in greater detail. *Paul Ferroll* was praised in its day for its psychological insight and realistic treatment of its sordid subject matter.

22. In her popular novel of the previous decade, *Agnes Waring* (1856) , Annie French Hector decried in her preface "the fatal errors into which women, through weakness, tenderness, mistaken self-devotion, and virtues grown beyond rational bounds, have been led to commit on the all-momentuous question of marriage—the long domestic martyrdoms—the obscure tragedies, that have risen from stifling nature's instinct. . . ." Her heroine takes an extreme step to free herself from an incompatible marriage—making it appear that she has been killed in an avalanche while on holiday in Switzerland, then fleeing to London, where she takes up a new life under an assumed name.

23. See letter to Elizabeth Stuart Phelps, November 10, 1877, *Letters*, VI, 418.

24. George Eliot indicates that she enjoyed *The Story of Elizabeth* in her letter of December 4, 1865 to Mrs. Richard Congreve (*Letters*, IV, 209) . She records having read *The Village on the Cliff* in a diary entry of April 19, 1878 (*Letters*, VII, 22) .

25. October 23, 1863, *Letters*, IV, 110. Many other letters refer to his friendship with both George Eliot and Lewes, as well as to her reading of his books.

26. For a discussion of the critical reception of this novel, see Bradford A. Booth, *Anthony Trollope: Aspects of His Life and Art* (Bloomington, Ind., 1958) , p. 187. George Eliot interested herself in the courtship stage as much as in marriage, whereas Trollope plunges Louis Trevelyan and Emily Rowley into marriage almost immediately and introduces the jealousy intrigue early. Trollope also treats the theme

more melodramatically, bringing the jealous husband almost to the point of madness.

27. False attribution operated in both directions. "Amos Barton" was mistaken by Joseph Langford, Blackwood's London manager, for a story by Mrs. Oliphant on its first appearance in *Maga,* and George Eliot subsequently was credited with the earliest of The Chronicles of Carlingford—*The Rector, The Doctor,* and *Salem Chapel* (see *Letters,* II, 435, n. 5; IV, 25).

28. The reviewer of *Middlemarch* for the *British Quarterly Review* (see note 11 above) indicates that George Eliot was falling in with another contemporary trend. "What has come to the novelists of the season that they all marry charming young girls of eighteen to old men of fifty?" he asks. "Perhaps our novel writers are combining to ban such marriages, if so we wish them God speed, otherwise they need a statute of limitation." He commends George Eliot for making Casaubon a "dusty and priggish pedant" instead of idealizing the June-January relationship as other novelists tended to do. The two contemporaneous novels cited by this reviewer, *Half a Dozen Daughters* by J. Masterman (Victoria Baker Rybot) and *Cruel as the Grave* by the Countess von Bothmer, were advertised in the first part of *Middlemarch.*

29. While writing *Middlemarch,* George Eliot praised Harriet Beecher Stowe for her portrait of early nineteenth-century Massachusetts village life in *Old Town Folks* (1869). "I think few of your many readers can have felt more interest than I have felt in that picture of an elder generation, for my interest in it has a double root," she wrote; "one is my love for old-fashioned provincial life which had its affinities with contemporary life even all across the Atlantic. . . . The other is, my experimental acquaintance with some shades of Calvinistic orthodoxy. . . . A thorough comprehension of the mixed moral influence shed on society by dogmatic systems is rare even among writers, and one misses it altogether in English drawing-room talk" (July 11, 1869, *Letters,* V, 48).

30. September 11, 1866, *Letters,* IV, 309–10.

31. Twenty-four popular shockers were surveyed with wit and urbanity in the article "Sensation Novels," *Quarterly Review,* CXIII (January, 1863), 418–54. The reviewer has been identified as Henry Mansel. The *Spectator* waged a campaign throughout the decade against thrillers; e.g., the reviews of *The Castleford Case* (December 28, 1861); *Rosedale; or, The Deserted Manor House* (February 1, 1862); *Carr of Carlyon* by Hamilton Aidé (March 15, 1862); *The Trail of the Serpent* by Mary Elizabeth Braddon (August 11, 1866), and *The*

Moonstone by Wilkie Collins (July 25, 1869) ; and an omnibus review, "Tigresses in Literature" (March 10, 1866) tries to account for the hold on readers of the degenerate Becky Sharps who dominate such scabrous fiction as *Bella Donna* by Gilbert Dyce, *Lady Audley's Secret* by Miss Braddon, *Jenny Bell* by Percy Fitzgerald, and *Land at Last* by Edmund Yates.

32. "Sensation Novels," *Blackwood's Magazine*, XCII (May, 1862), 564–84.

33. Paget is dimly remembered as the author of the once popular didactic fairy tale *The Hope of the Katzekopfs* (an analogue to Thackeray's *The Rose and the Ring*) , which furnished Kipling with the title for his *Rewards and Fairies*. In his earlier years he also wrote several religious novels and a satire on Gothic romance called *The Owlet of Owlstone Edge*. *Lucretia* set off a subleader in the *Spectator* on "Sensational Novels" in which their authors were denounced as inferior artists who "heap together startling and exceptional incidents in defiance of all probability" (August 8, 1868, pp. 931–32) .

34. Both ladies went on to write better novels of the domestic type, but it was their fate to be associated ever after with their first melodramatic hits.

35. At least one current scandal found its way into *Middlemarch* in a veiled way. The sudden appearance of Joshua Rigg, the ugly illegitimate son of Peter Featherstone, to claim his natural father's estate (CH. XXXV) was undoubtedly suggested by the notorious case of the Tichborne Claimant, whose trial George Eliot and Lewes attended early in 1872. (See letters to John Blackwood and Sara Sophia Hennell, *Letters*, V, 237, 243.) The shrewd John Blackwood noted the resemblance while reading this portion in manuscript. (See *Letters*, V, 255.) Some years before, George Eliot and Lewes had also followed with interest one of the most sensational sex scandals of mid-Victorian England, the trial of the notorious Madeleine Smith for the arsenic poisoning of her former lover, Emile l'Angelier. The charge was dismissed as "not proven," "a moral condemnation though a legal acquittal," as Lewes put it. (See *Letters*, II, 360, 362, 363, 366.)

36. *Blackwood's Magazine*, CXII (December, 1872) , 727.

37. Letter to Elizabeth Stuart Phelps, *Letters*, VI, 418. After she ceased regular reviewing of current fiction, her preferences in literature, to judge from her letters, seem to have been the classics and old favorites like Scott and Jane Austen.

38. August 30, 1868, *Letters*, IV, 471. Her first mention of *Middlemarch* occurs in a Journal entry for January 1, 1869. Maurice is best

remembered today as the founder of the Christian Socialist Party and for his establishment, along with Charles Kingsley and Thomas Hughes, of the Working Men's College. His name has been coupled with the latitudinarian position known as the Broad Church—but he did not coin the name and is supposed to have detested it. At the time when Maurice's controversial *Theological Essays* was published, George Eliot considered them "muddy" (*Letters*, II, 125), but she gained respect for him when she went to hear him preach at the behest of her friend Sara Sophia Hennell (*Letters*, IV, 102, V, 284). A friendly correspondence grew up between them after Maurice wrote to congratulate her on *Romola*.

39. Maurice's lectures were published very close upon Huxley's famous lecture "On a Piece of Chalk," a coincidence made much of by the reviewer of *The Conscience* in the *Spectator*. This reviewer (probably Thomas Hughes) spoke of Maurice as "the most practical of living English metaphysicians," compared his effect on young Victorian minds with that of Socrates on Athenian youth, and thought that with his open, inquiring mind, he "fills the place in moral, analogous to that of Professor Huxley, in physical science" (September 26, 1868, p. 1135).

40. Lecture I ("On the Word 'I' "), p. 27; Lecture II ("The Word 'Conscience' ") pp. 30–31.

41. Tito Melema, the most vividly realized character in *Romola*, is a study in the progressive deterioration of "a guilty consciousness." For George Eliot he is representative of the civilized pagan with a highly developed mind and feelings but an atrophied moral sense. Maurice cited him in one of these lectures as an example of "the refined man who lacks the words 'I ought' and 'I ought not' in his vocabulary," by contrast with Tennyson's Northern Farmer, a peasant with an innate sense of right and wrong.

42. There was a revival of interest in Saint Theresa at this time. David Lewis' translation of her autobiography was published in 1870, followed the next year by his translation of *The Book of the Foundations of Saint Theresa*. A few years earlier an author named Miss Lockhart had brought out *The Life of Saint Theresa*, edited by the Bishop of Winchester (1865) and *The Spirit of Saint Theresa* (1866).

43. He specifically cites Thackeray as an example of a novelist who addresses his readers as a casuist. Thackeray, says Maurice, "understands the command 'Judge not lest ye be judged' " (Lecture IX, "The Office of the Casuist in the Modern World").

44. The reviewer for the *Spectator*, commenting on Part II of *Middlemarch* when it first appeared, found George Eliot's technique of

analysis disturbing without, apparently, understanding the basis of it. He described the novel as it had progressed so far as "a tolerably even and placid, but morbidly intellectual tale." "She crowds her book as full of eyes as some of the lower insects are said to be," he continues; "she dissects her characters till she spoils the charm of some of them" (March 30, 1872, pp. 404–6).

45. While he was writing the book, Lewes feared that his claims for the power of science to explain man and the mysteries of the universe would disturb the orthodox. He was right. Blackwood was so disconcerted by his reading of the first sections in manuscript that he asked Lewes to find another publisher. Lewes arranged for publication with Trübner, who specialized in controversial works, on the day after Blackwood's rejection. The amicable parting of ways can be traced in *Letters*, V, 371, 400, 410, and 413–14. The first two volumes of *Problems of Life and Mind* came out in the fall of 1873, and a new edition was called for by the beginning of the following year.

46. *Problems of Life and Mind*. First Series. The Foundations of a Creed (London, 1874), I, 140.

47. Ibid., p. 105. In an unpublished doctoral dissertation, "A Study of *Middlemarch*" (Princeton, 1960), Richard Smilie Lyons points out the basic importance of this passage, but does not explore further the influence of *Problems of Life and Mind*. He has done some excellent work on the earlier intellectual background of the novel, particularly in George Eliot's critical essays. Two recent books discuss Lewes in relation to other formative influences on George Eliot's thought. U. C. Knoepflmacher's *Religious Humanism and the Victorian Novel: George Eliot, Walter Pater and Samuel Butler* (Princeton, 1965) points out that the "Philosophy of Necessity" she learned from Bray was modified by Lewes' more complex theories of causation. Bernard Paris in *Experiments in Life: George Eliot's Quest for Values* (Detroit, 1965) traces the cumulative effect of Strauss, Hennell, Feuerbach, and Comte on her intellectual development. In my treatment I confine myself to what I believe were the most specific and immediate influences on *Middlemarch*.

48. *Problems of Life and Mind*, p. 115.

49. June 6, 1871, to Mrs. Peter Alfred Taylor; March 29, 1872, to Alexander Main, *Letters*, V, 150, 261.

50. He pays tribute to Newton in *Problems of Life and Mind* as a model scientist who steered a course between the extremes of the "metaphysical" and "mechanical" interpretations of the universe (Introduction, pp. 2–5; CH. II, p. 44, pp. 52–53). Among contemporary

books cited by Lewes in his Journal for 1871 are Herschel's *Outlines of Astronomy*, Bayma's *Elements of Astronomy*, and studies by the German physicists Häckel, Hirn, Reis, and Wundt (*Letters*, V, 150, Note 5). The catalogue of the Lewes Collection in Doctor Williams' Library indicates that his reading in the field was both omnivorous and polyglot. This inventory consists of numerous titles of books in English, French, German, and Italian on astronomy, mechanics, atomic physics, electricity, optics, and mathematics.

51. July 24, 1871, *Letters*, V, 168.

52. She showed a speculative interest in this kind of investigation as early as her review of Mackay's *Progress of the Intellect*, where she wrote: "The master-key to this [divine] revelation is the recognition of the presence of undeviating law in the material and moral world—of that invariability of sequence which is acknowledged to be the basis of physical science, but which is still perversely ignored in our social organization, our ethics and our religion" (*Writings of George Eliot*, XXII, 279). Some years later, in criticizing Lecky's treatment of religion in his *History of Rationalism*, she wrote:

> The supremely important fact that the gradual reduction of all phenomena within the sphere of established law, which carries as a consequence the rejection of the miraculous, has its determining current in the development of physical science, seems to have engaged comparatively little of his attention. . . . The great conception of universal regular sequence, without partiality and without captrice—the conception which is the most potent force at work in the modification of our faith, and of the practical form given to our sentiments,—could only grow out of that patient watching of external fact and that silencing of preconceived notions which are urged on the mind by the problems of physical science.

("The Influence of Rationalism," ibid., X, 323–24; this review appeared originally in the *Fortnightly Review*, I [May 15, 1865], 43–55.) It is reprinted in *Essays of George Eliot*, ed. Pinney, pp. 397–414.

53. Cf. Rosamond, momentarily grieving over Lydgate's neglect during the early stages of their courtship: "Poor Rosamond lost her appetite and felt as forlorn as Ariadne—as a charming stage Ariadne left behind with all her boxes full of costumes and no hope of a coach" (CH. XXXI).

54. *Problems of Life and Mind*, Introduction, Part II ("The Rules of Philosophising"), pp. 82–92. For a brief interpretation of Lewes'

theories of knowledge, see Jack Kaminsky, "The Empirical Metaphysics of George Henry Lewes," *Journal of the History of Ideas,* XIII (June, 1952), 314–42.

55. Bichat's theory of homology that inspires Lydgate is reduced by George Eliot to a domestic image in her comment on the mixture of romantic and materialistic impulses in Rosamond: "Our passions do not live apart in locked chambers, but dressed in their small wardrobe of notions, bring their provisions to a common table and mess together, feeding out of the common store according to their appetite."

56. Lewes uses this image to illustrate his belief, in agreement with Aristotle, that the soul is indissolubly bound up with the body. He was opposed both to mechanists who denied its existence and to dualists who thought of the soul as "a spiritual Agent acting *upon,* not acting *by* its own processes, a musician playing on a musical instrument, not an aeolian harp thrilling to the accordant tremors of the surrounding air" (*Problems of Life and Mind,* II, Problem III, p. 129). When Ladislaw first hears Dorothea speak, he is reminded of "the voice of a soul that had once lived in an Aeolian harp" (CH. IX). Rosamond, on the other hand, is literally and figuratively a musician playing on an instrument as she beguiles Lydgate (CH. XXVII).

57. *Problems of Life and Mind,* pp. 132 ff ("Psychodynamics"). Lewes calls these principles the Laws of Irradiation and Restriction.

58. During the time he was formulating these ideas, Lewes wrote in a now famous essay summing up Dickens' achievement shortly after his death that he was a writer who "sees and feels, but the logic of feeling seems the only logic he can manage. Thought is strangely absent from his works. . . . Compared with that of Fielding or Thackeray, his was merely an *animal* intelligence, i. e. restricted to perceptions" ("Dickens in Relation to Criticism," *Fortnightly Review,* XV [February 1, 1872], 151). Lewes obviously had some second thoughts about a writer he had started out by praising for "a deep and subtle philosophy" (see Ch. IV above, p. 128), but by now he had a far more impressive writer to measure him against than Theodore Hook or Harrison Ainsworth.

59. It is on this elemental level that Dorothea reaches Rosamond during their one meeting in CH. LXXXI. ("The cordial, pleading tones which seemed to flow with generous heedlessness above all the facts . . . came as soothingly as a warm stream over her [Rosamond's] shrinking fears"; "The emotion had wrought itself more and more into her [Dorothea's] utterance, till the tones might have gone to one's very marrow, like a low cry from some suffering creature in the darkness"; "Rosamand, taken hold of by an emotion stronger than her own . . .

could find no words, but involuntarily she put her lips to Dorothea's forehead which was very near her, and then for a minute the two women clasped each other as if they had been in a shipwreck.")

60. Ladislaw's choice of career would, incidentally, have met with the approval of Maurice, who believed that "the soundest Moral Science will be that which is demanded by the necessities of Practical Politics. . . . The Moralist never maintains his own position so well as when he asserts the highest dignity for the Politician" (Lecture IX, "The Office of the Casuist in the Modern World," p. 194).

61. Will Ladislaw is generally considered the one weakly realized character of the book. The deficiencies in his characterization, however, are not faults of conception, as with Stephen Guest, but of execution. He is the one major character of the novel who is seen mainly through the eyes of others, particularly from the point of view of Dorothea, which is excusably idealized. We never precisely grasp the texture of his mind, for his vocation of artist is the one that least lends itself to verbal articulation. Nor do we ever really learn what he *does,* since he is never totally integrated into Middlemarch society, as are the other important newcomers Lydgate and Bulstrode, and his parliamentary career is outside the novel. As U. C. Knoepflmacher observes: "If Ladislaw's unsatisfactoriness persists, this is so, not because of his unsuitability as Dorothea's husband, but because as a character, he serves too many different roles in the novel's ideological scheme" (*Religious Humanism and the Victorian Novel,* p. 106).

62. *Problems of Life and Mind,* II, Problem IV ("Matter and Force"), CH. II ("The Range of Emotion"), pp. 219–20; I ("The Socio-logical Data"), p. 162.

63. March 29, 1872, *Letters,* V, 261; August 4, 1872, *Letters,* V, 296. By this time George Eliot was disturbed by R. H. Hutton's articles in the *Spectator* that referred to her as "the most melancholy of authors." His essay "George Eliot as Author" reflects this attitude toward *Middlemarch.*

64. *Problems of Life and Mind,* I, Problem I, CH. v ("Moral Types"), pp. 280–81. Lewes wrote to Blackwood in the summer of 1872 to complain that his health was hampering him in his work: "It is all the more provoking as I am 'bursting' with ideas—and want to give them birth. The shadow of old Casaubon hangs over me and I fear my 'Key to all Psychologies' will have to be left to Dorothea! . . . (July 13, 1872, *Letters,* V, 291). His grim premonition was borne out. The final volume was completed and published by George Eliot after his death.

65. See above, p. 262.

66. "The Legend of Jubal," a poetic fable George Eliot composed in 1869, based on the account in the Book of Genesis of the children of Lamech, who sprang from the seed of Cain, is a mythic history of civilization. Of the three sons of Lamech, Jabal is the archetypal shepherd and farmer; Tubal-Cain is the primitive industrial man; and Jubal is the progenitor of the arts.

67. "George Eliot as I Knew Her," *The Bookman,* XXII (August, 1902), 160.

68. U. C. Knoepflmacher considers the three most important aspects of her thought that entered into her novels, "her scientific positivism, her humanization of Christianity, and her Arnold-like belief in the force of tradition" (*Religious Humanism and the Victorian Novel,* p. 27).

INDEX